The Day the Presses Stopped

The Day the Presses Stopped

A History of the Pentagon Papers Case

David Rudenstine

UNIVERSITY OF CALIFORNIA PRESS
Berkeley · Los Angeles · London

Contents

Acknowledgments

At last I have the opportunity to thank publicly the many individuals who graciously assisted me and the institutions that generously supported me in the writing of this book.

The Jacob Burns Institute for Advanced Legal Studies at Cardozo Law School and the Reed Foundation provided financial support that permitted me to concentrate on the research and writing of this book in a way that would otherwise have been very difficult. Dean Frank Macchiarola and former Dean Monroe Price of Cardozo Law School each assured needed institutional support for the project.

Former Solicitor General Charles Fried, former United States Attorney Rudolph W. Giuliani, and Steven R. Shapiro, Legal Director of the American Civil Liberties Union, assisted me in getting many relevant documents declassified. Geri Thoma, my literary agent, was a source of tremendous encouragement and advice throughout the writing of this book. Tom Engelhardt used his wealth of experience as an editor to give me sound counsel on many different matters. My editor at the University of California Press, Naomi Schneider, has helped on numerous issues. I would also like to extend my special thanks to David Severtson for the care and intelligence he exercised in copy editing the manuscript.

I am also very grateful to the students who have aided me in a variety of ways. They are Paul Brusiloff, Dierdre Burke, Sandy Cobden, Jaime Dursht, Robin Flicker, Jason Goldstein, Jonathan Gross, Elizabeth Holland, Gary Holtzer, Edward Lubin, Todd Schwartz, Michael Schwenk, Diane Venezia, Hope Weiner, Marla Whitman, and June Wolfman.

I wish to thank the participants in the faculty workshops at Miami Law School and Brooklyn Law School for their thoughtful comments.

Steve Diamond provided lively encouragement and valuable advice during the research and early writing phases of my book. Betsy Clark, David Rosner, and Elliott Weiss read portions of the manuscript and gave me useful suggestions. Jim Weill and Paul Wachtel commented upon the entire manuscript; their observations greatly strengthened the manuscript. My brother, Neil, provided the kind of editorial review a writer usually only dreams of.

Lastly, Zina Steinberg, my wife, gave important editorial assistance, and together with Aaron and Sasha, my children, made sacrifices and provided support that made the difference.

Introduction: A Reconsideration

The presses began to roll at 6:13 P.M. on Saturday, June 12, 1971. Three minutes later the first newspapers arrived in the city room at the *New York Times*. In 24-point type over columns 4–7 on page 1 the understated headline for the Sunday paper of June 13, 1971, read as follows:[1]

VIETNAM ARCHIVE: PENTAGON STUDY TRACES
3 DECADES OF GROWING U.S. INVOLVEMENT

The opening paragraph of the news article written by Neil Sheehan stated that a "massive" Pentagon study commissioned by former Secretary of Defense Robert S. McNamara on "how the United States went to war in Indochina" demonstrated that four administrations "progressively developed a sense of commitment to a non-Communist Vietnam, a readiness to fight the North to protect the South, and an ultimate frustration with this effort—to a much greater extent than their public statements acknowledged at the time."[2]

The next day, Monday, the *Times* ran a second article by Sheehan under a headline that stated: "VIETNAM ARCHIVE: A CONSENSUS TO BOMB DEVELOPED BEFORE '64 ELECTION, STUDY SAYS." The lead paragraph of this second report stated that the "Johnson Administration reached a 'general consensus' at a White House strategy meeting on September 7, 1964, that air attacks against North Vietnam would probably have to be launched" in early 1965. The report claimed that this consensus on bombing "came at the height" of the presidential election contest between President Lyndon B. Johnson and Senator Barry Goldwater, "whose advocacy of full-scale air attacks on North Vietnam had become a major issue."[3] The *Times* promised additional reports with supporting government documents in the succeeding days.

The *Times* series was based on a secret Pentagon study prepared between June 1967 and January 1969. It was officially entitled "History of U.S. Decision Making Process on Vietnam Policy." Only fifteen copies of the completed study were made, and they were classified "top secret—sensitive." The study was bound into forty-seven volumes, consisted of two-and-a-half million words, and weighed sixty pounds. The *Times*'s disclosure of the top secret study was probably the single largest unauthorized disclosure of classified documents in the history of the United States.

The *Times* reports caught President Richard Nixon and his top White House aides completely off guard, and, with few exceptions, neither Nixon nor his aides seemed to know of the existence of the Pentagon study. Nixon's initial reaction was not to interfere with the *Times* series.[4] But by early Monday evening he had changed his mind and decided that his administration would ask the courts to enjoin the *Times* from publishing further reports, which it did on Tuesday in federal court in Manhattan. It was the first time since the adoption of the U.S. Constitution that the federal government had sued the press to stop it from disclosing information because of national security.

The government's request for an injunction went before U.S. district judge Murray I. Gurfein, a Nixon appointee who questioned the *Times*'s patriotism for publishing classified material that pertained to the war. Gurfein granted the government a temporary restraining order and scheduled an evidentiary hearing for Friday of that week.[5] His order was the first ever to enjoin publication because of national security. Suddenly, the Pentagon documents became the most sought-after set of papers in the nation, and the government's success in blocking publication, at least temporarily, attracted national and international attention: the case pitted Nixon's administration against the nation's premier newspaper, would determine whether the Pentagon study would be published, and held out the promise of defining press freedoms during wartime.

By Friday, June 18, the *Washington Post* had gained possession of some of the Pentagon Papers and had begun to publish parts of the classified history. This action forced the government to begin a second lawsuit, which it filed in U.S. district court in Washington, D.C.

Meanwhile, Judge Gurfein's courtroom Friday morning was electric with excitement and anxiety as the crowd awaited the morning's hearing, which began with a number of preliminary motions. Professor Alexander M. Bickel, a Yale Law School professor and the *Times*'s lead attorney, told

Gurfein the government contended that the nation's security would be gravely harmed if the *Times* published one more installment of what the press had already labeled the Pentagon Papers. Bickel then announced that the *Washington Post* had published its own Pentagon story in that morning's newspaper using some of the same classified documents the *Times* possessed and that as far as he could ascertain the Republic still stood.[6] The crowd cheered; Gurfein banged his gavel, demanding quiet. Eventually, Judge Gurfein announced that the public would be excluded from that part of the hearing during which the government would present its evidence as to why further disclosures would injure the nation's security.

The Friday hearing lasted well into the night, ending shortly after eleven o'clock. During most of the proceedings Gurfein was obviously sympathetic toward the government and agitated, if not hostile, toward the *Times*. Gurfein's disposition was so undisguised that by the time the public was excluded and the courtroom doors were locked and guarded to prepare for the national security witnesses, the government's lawyers must have felt confident they would win the day. But as it turned out, the closed hearing was a disaster for the government. Because of a variety of factors, including the refusal of the government witnesses to anchor their general assertions that further disclosures would injure the national security in the details of the classified study, Gurfein emerged from the closed hearing deeply annoyed and exasperated.

On Saturday Judge Gurfein denied the government's request for a preliminary injunction. In his opinion he wrote that the government had failed to offer any "cogent reasons" to support its request for an injunction. He claimed that the case did not present a "sharp clash" between the *Times*'s right to publish and the government's legitimate interest in keeping some national defense information confidential. He also reminded his readers that security is not "at the ramparts alone." A secure nation requires a free press, even one that is "cantankerous," "obstinate," and "ubiquitous."[7]

On Monday U.S. district judge Gerhard A. Gesell, who presided over the government's action against the *Washington Post*, reached the same result. By Wednesday, June 23, two U.S. courts of appeals had reviewed the two cases but had reached different conclusions: the Second Circuit sitting in New York ordered Judge Gurfein to hold additional hearings in the *Times* case; the D.C. Circuit affirmed Judge Gesell's order denying the government a prior restraint.

Both the *Times* and the government requested the Supreme Court to review the cases immediately: the *Times* because it considered every moment under restraint an unwarranted intrusion into its editorial discretion in deciding what to publish, the government because it considered further disclosures of the top secret study as potentially endangering the national security. On Friday, June 25, the U.S. Supreme Court announced it would immediately review both cases. Because of this development, the *Times* case never returned to Judge Gurfein. The Court ordered the parties to file their legal briefs and participate in oral argument the very next morning. On Wednesday, June 30, a mere fifteen days after the government first went to court against the *Times*, the Supreme Court denied the government the injunctive relief it sought, thereby freeing the newspapers to continue publishing their reports. The nine justices divided six to three and wrote ten opinions—an unsigned majority opinion plus nine individual opinions.[8]

The sole fact that the government lost its first effort to restrain the press made the Supreme Court's decision in the Pentagon Papers case unusually important, even when assessed against the background of American legal history—a history studded with significant judicial decisions. But the significance of the Pentagon Papers case is far greater and more compelling than that. Because no previous administration had tried to enjoin the press from publishing information it possessed, there were no controlling judicial decisions. Many Supreme Court decisions bore some relationship to the constitutional issues raised by the government's lawsuits, but the similarities were not sufficiently close to be strongly binding. As a result the court was left with substantial discretion as to how to decide these two cases. Moreover, it was extremely likely that the Court took very seriously the government's forceful representation, including the dozens of specific citations to the classified documents that it declared would injure national security if disclosed. The government also appealed to the Court's sense of fundamental fairness by contending it needed more time to prepare its evidence, given the voluminous nature of the documents and their importance. Finally, the Court had ordinarily deferred to the government in cases involving national security. Given the fact that the disputed classified documents in this case pertained to the Vietnam War, which was still in progress—and in which large numbers of American soldiers were directly involved in combat—one might well have expected the Court to accede to the government's request for an injunction.

Yet instead of deferring to the government's judgment on military, intelligence, and diplomatic matters, the Court concluded that the government's evidence fell short of what was legally required. It reached its conclusion even though it could simply have remanded the two cases to the district courts for additional hearings, thus avoiding—at least temporarily—a final resolution on the issue of the injunction. It reached this conclusion in spite of the fact that more than a majority of the justices concluded (whether rightly or wrongly) that the newspapers had already—or were likely—to disclose information harmful to the nation's security.

Although the *Times* and the *Post* resumed publication of the Pentagon Papers immediately following the Supreme Court decision, these disclosures did not directly or immediately alter the course of the Vietnam War. The disclosures did disturb President Nixon, and they became the occasion for a major congressional debate over the war. But there is no evidence that the actual publication of the Pentagon Papers reports caused Nixon to change his war policies.

Nor did the publication revitalize the somewhat moribund antiwar movement. President Johnson's decision not to seek reelection in 1968 and President Nixon's reduction of the number of U.S. troops in Vietnam from 1969 to 1971 cooled the antiwar fires. Although Nixon's decision to invade Cambodia in 1970 caused opposition to the war to flare up once again, the episode was short-lived. Thus, the antiwar movement lacked a sharp focus or strong impetus when the *Times* first published its initial extracts from the Pentagon Papers, and the Supreme Court's decision allowing publication to continue did not change this situation.

Nor is there any evidence that the *Times* or the *Post* actually published any of the information that injured national security. As former Solicitor General Erwin N. Griswold, who represented the government before the Supreme Court, concluded years after the case was over: "none of the material which was 'objectionable' from my point of view was ever published by anyone, including the newspapers, until several years later."[9]

But the sheer disclosure of the Pentagon Papers did wreak political havoc within the United States. The publication sparked a huge controversy about whether the government—and the Johnson administration in particular—had intentionally misled the American public about the war. This had a powerful impact on the political prospects of many Democratic party leaders, some of whom were considering running for the party's presidential nomination in 1972. It intensified dissension within the Democratic party, and that in turn weakened the party's capacity to elect a president from its own ranks. It increased the public's distrust of the national government, especially the executive branch. This public distrust has deepened over the years and must now be seriously taken into account by any president who wishes to govern effectively.[10]

The Pentagon Papers episode ultimately had a devastating impact on Nixon and his administration. During the sixteen days of litigation, Nixon decided to use the entire dispute as a means to strike at those he considered to be his political enemies; to intimidate the press; to strengthen his reelection bid in 1972; and to divide the Democrats. The Supreme Court's ruling only intensified his feelings that his administration needed to do more to protect itself from those he believed were conspiring to undermine his capacity to govern. The result was that Nixon and his top aides, especially Henry Kissinger, created an atmosphere of crisis, making possible a number of decisions and actions that ultimately proved disastrous. It was in this atmosphere that the so-called Plumbers Unit was created, leading eventually to the Watergate break-in and all the events that John Mitchell termed the "White House horrors." The cover-up following the Watergate burglary was an outgrowth of this sequence. When the burglary and cover-up became public, they were central factors in undermining Nixon's political support, thus forcing him to resign the presidency in August 1974.[11] The Pentagon Papers affair, in short, led directly to the unraveling and final disintegration of the Nixon presidency.

But there is more to the significance of the Pentagon Papers affair than even these important considerations. The Pentagon Papers case was a crucible for testing the strength and resilience of many elements that are critical to the democratic order, and the entire history of the case discloses the subtle and complex workings of institutions that are vital to a democratic process. Ironically, it reveals that much of the strength or weakness of a democracy can depend upon two institutions that are not in any strict sense accountable from a political perspective: the press and the courts. These institutions, depending on how they function, clearly have enormous power either to strengthen or to weaken the power of the executive branch. This balance and counterbalance of different kinds of power is of course inherent in our Constitution and its underlying theory. The Pentagon Papers case provides an unusual opportunity to examine the interaction among the separate but independent powers and to assess how effectively—and how scrupulously—they perform.

A history of the Pentagon Papers affair also chronicles the activities of the press, the courts, and the executive branch as they struggled with one of the most important challenges facing any modern-day democracy—the balance between the legitimate needs of government to keep some information secret and of the people to be informed about their government and matters of vital importance. How, for example, should the press approach the question of its responsibilities when its reports bear on important national security matters? What responsibilities should courts assume—and what principles should they follow—in resolving disputes between the press and the government when national security issues are involved? A detailed history of this case cannot possibly offer definitive answers to these questions. It can go far to explain, however, how the Supreme Court addressed these questions, and how it arrived at its conclusions, in one of the most dramatic and important legal conflicts in American history. It also lays bare the multitude of considerations at stake for different individuals and groups at major turning points in the turbulence of events. One can, in other words, watch democracy in action, at a time of crisis, and attempt to evaluate how it resolved issues that were laden with immediate practical consequences and profound theoretical implications.

▪ ▪ ▪ ▪ ▪

At the time it was my belief that the government was merely trying to suppress information that would be politically embarrassing and might undermine support for its war policies. I also had the impression from news reports that the government was trying to steamroll its way to a legal victory by having national security officials make dire warnings of what might happen if the government lost. Indeed, I accepted as true what many said at this time—the government did not offer any specific references to the Pentagon Papers to support its allegations that publication of the top secret study would seriously harm national security.

There were several reasons for my skepticism. The Pentagon Papers seemed no more than a history (which was what the government entitled the study) of America's involvement in Vietnam from 1945 to 1968.[12] In addition that is what the *Times* said the documents were: "The documents in question belong to history. They refer to the development of American interest and participation in Indochina from the post–World War II period up to mid-1968, which is now almost three years ago. Their publication could not conceivably damage American security interests, much less the lives of Americans or Indochinese."[13] At the time and under the circumstances of the case I placed more trust in the *Times* than I did in the Nixon administration. Judge Gurfein's ultimate ruling against the government seemed to confirm my initial disbelief that continued publication of the remaining Pentagon Papers would injure current military, diplomatic, or intelligence interests. Once the Supreme Court ruled against the government and the newspapers published their reports with no apparent harm to the national security, the evidence seemed overwhelming that the government's lawsuits against the *Times* and the *Post* were nothing more than an effort at brazen and unwarranted censorship.

That remained my view until I decided to obtain some of the basic legal documents in the case in the late 1980s. One of the first I obtained was labeled "Special Appendix," a government document submitted to a federal appeals court in the *Times* case that was sealed during the litigation. It alleged that further publication of the classified material would injure current troop movements, disclose current and important intelligence matters, and harm current diplomatic efforts aimed at ending the war and gaining the release of American prisoners. In support of these allegations it provided numerous specific page references to the Pentagon Papers. This document, along with others, eventually caused me to begin rethinking the meaning of the litigation over the Pentagon Papers, just as many had claimed that the disclosures of the Pentagon Papers themselves had caused them to reconsider the U.S. military intervention in Vietnam.

Reconsidering the Pentagon Papers case was an incremental, uncertain, and complex process. My first expectations were quite limited, but the more I inquired, the more I expanded the scope of my inquiry. Before long I began to focus on why McNamara had originally decided to commission the study, why Daniel Ellsberg had decided to make the papers available to the *Times*, why the *Times* and the *Post* had determined they would publish the papers, and why the Nixon administration sued the newspapers. Suddenly, every aspect of the litigation seemed open to careful review and analysis and less clear-cut than I had originally thought.[14]

This book is a consequence of that reconsideration. It is based in large part on fresh material not previously available, as well as information that may have been available but was not generally considered in full detail by those who have already written—and very helpfully—about this important episode in American history.

The conclusions I eventually reached differed substantially from the conception of the case I once held and from what I think was (and remains) the dominant view of the case.[15] Although I strongly approve—as I did in 1971—of the Supreme Court's decision, I no longer regard the legal dispute as an effort by the Nixon administration merely to withhold deeply embarrassing information. Nor do I understand the legal attack on the *Times* simply as part of the administration's general campaign to intimidate the press or view the case as one in which the ultimate outcome was relatively predictable because it was based on the application of well-settled, concrete, and definite legal principles applied to a situation in which the government's evidence was unequivocally insufficient.

Instead, I think that the Justice Department lawyers, who first determined whether the government should respond to the *Times* series, and the national security officials with whom they consulted accepted that the *Times*'s Pentagon Papers series potentially threatened important national security interests. They urged the administration to sue the *Times* for a prior restraint because it was the only way to gain time to assess the full implications of this massive leak of classified documents and because it was the only effective legal remedy against the *Times*. Moreover, by the time the litigation was reviewed by the Supreme Court, the government had significantly marshaled its evidence and sharpened its allegations. Indeed, it now appears that the Pentagon Papers did contain some information that could have inflicted some injury—at least to a degree that makes the concerns of national security officials understandable—if disclosed, which it was not.

For example, the government's sealed brief in the Supreme Court, which contained many references to the Pentagon Papers, claimed that the disclosure of this information would cause "immediate and irreparable harm to the security of the United States." It stressed that making public the recent diplomatic history of the war would likely "close up channels of communication which otherwise would have some opportunity of facilitating the closing of the Vietnam war." It claimed that further disclosures might reduce the rate of American troop withdrawal from Vietnam. It asserted that the top secret documents identified some CIA agents and activities as well as other intelligence operations and assessments. It also alleged that the classified material contained current military plans.[16]

Although the government's references to the Pentagon Papers did not in the end convince the justices on the high court that additional publication would cause immediate and irreparable harm to the national security, that did not mean that further publications would necessarily be totally harmless. There is an enormous difference between concluding that the Pentagon Papers contained absolutely no information that could injure the national security in one respect or another and concluding that it contained information that would result in immediate and irreparable harm. Thus, concluding that the government's evidence fell short of the legal requirements for a prior restraint did not mean the government's overall case was so weak that further disclosures did not threaten national security.

I also think that prior judicial decisions did not compel the outcome in the case. There was, of course, a wealth of prior cases construing the First Amendment and delineating numerous aspects of freedom of the press. But the Pentagon Papers litigation was the federal government's first effort to enjoin the press because of national security considerations. As a result this was a case of first impression, a lawyer's term meaning that there was no prior judicial decision in a similar case that was directly applicable. This gave the judges substantial discretion in defining the pertinent legal standard. In fact the judges had such discretion that they could have enjoined the newspapers from publishing the Pentagon reports without overruling even one prior decision.

Thus, prior case law left unresolved several highly important questions as to what the government had to prove to win a prior restraint. For example, precisely what kind of injury to the national security did the government have to prove to win? Would it be sufficient for the government merely to prove that additional disclosures of classified information would possibly injure diplomatic efforts aimed at securing a peace settlement? Or would the government have to prove that additional reports might reveal information that would endanger the lives of one, ten, or one hundred soldiers? Or would the government have to prove that public disclosure would inflict some irreparable and profound blow to the overall security of the nation?

Prior judicial decisions also left undefined what the government had to prove with regard to the quickness and directness with which a disclosure would cause the feared injury. Thus, would it be enough for the government merely to prove that the disclosure would cause the threatened injury at some indefinite time in the future? Or would the government have to prove that the harm to the nation's security would follow almost immediately and directly after publication? Furthermore, how likely must it be that the publication would cause injury? Would it be sufficient if the government only proved it was possible that publication would injure national security? Or would the government have to prove it was highly likely, if not a virtual certainty, that disclosure would inflict injury? Or were the relevant considerations so complicated that no simple formulation of a legal standard was possible?

Because prior decisions did not answer these questions, the outcome in the Pentagon Papers case was hardly a foregone conclusion. Indeed, the Supreme Court could have decided the Pentagon Papers case either way—for the press or for the government—without straying beyond the parameters defined by prior case law.

Moreover, the difficulty of the case—and ultimately its full significance—cannot be fully appreciated without recognizing that the nation was at war when the government tried to suppress these documents marked top secret. Another day's installment of the Pentagon Papers would endanger military, diplomatic, and intelligence matters, the government claimed; it asserted that in cases involving national security the courts had an obligation to defer to the executive branch; and it maintained that the judges lacked the training, information, and experience to make sound judgments when national security matters were in dispute.

Nonetheless, the newspapers prevailed. The fact that they did in the midst of all these circumstances makes their triumph a matter of exceptional importance not only for the freedom of the American press but for American democracy as a whole.

I surprised myself as I came to these conclusions. But I was also taken aback by how difficult it was to persuade others to reconsider their own views, not about the ultimate legal outcome, but about the strength of the government's overall claim, the indeterminacy of legal precedent, and the complexity of the issues presented. Once, when I gave a paper on my evolving reassessment of the case at a Benjamin N. Cardozo School of Law conference, Leonard B. Boudin, a prominent lawyer who represented many leaders of the antiwar movement (including Daniel Ellsberg), asked to make a comment when I finished speaking. Although I have long forgotten his precise words, the gist of his statement was a sense of disbelief that anyone could think the government lost the Pentagon Papers case for any reason other than that its allegations concerning the threat to national security were fabricated. Boudin was certainly not alone in his reaction. I was often struck by a particular irony: individuals deeply committed to a strong free press consistently arguing that the Pentagon Papers case was in fact not so significant, essentially because the final outcome was all but inevitable.

The writing of this book involved another surprising turn. When I began my research I was only partially aware of the unusually close links between the Pentagon Papers episode and Nixon's Watergate scandal. Some writers had of course already identified these links and had characterized the Pentagon Papers case as an important turning point in the evolution of Nixon's presidency.[17] My own study confirmed this linkage and its significance to Nixon's presidency. Previous studies, however, have tended to focus on Nixon's presidency as a whole. They have inevitably treated the Pentagon Papers case as a relatively minor episode within a larger and more complex whole, without focusing intensely on the complicated dynamics that led the Nixon administration to sue the *Times* or on how the struggle over the Pentagon Papers so embroiled the Nixon administration that it became a watershed experience for Nixon and his top aides. This book addresses these important matters, explaining why the Nixon administration sued the *Times* and why and how the administration's efforts to keep the Pentagon Papers confidential transformed it so as to set the stage for decisions and actions that made its ultimate demise possible.

PART ONE

The Pentagon Papers Become Public

CHAPTER ONE

McNamara's Study

On a wintry February day in 1968 Washington officials packed the ceremonial East Room of the White House to bid farewell to Robert S. McNamara, who was resigning as secretary of defense after seven years. Chief Justice Earl Warren, Senators Robert F. and Edward M. Kennedy, cabinet members, the White House staff, as well as scores of others listened to President Lyndon B. Johnson praise McNamara as a "brilliant and good man" and award him the Medal of Freedom, the highest award a president may give to a civilian. Johnson told the overflowing crowd that McNamara would be an outstanding president of the World Bank, and he predicted that "20 years from today some other President will stand here and say: 'A revolution in the developing nations began'" once McNamara became the bank's leader. The audience stood and broke into a "ringing applause."[1]

McNamara was overwhelmed. Tears came to his eyes, and he was "choked with emotion" as he stood before so many whom he had known for so long. When the time came for him to speak, he couldn't. All he could do was tell those assembled: "I cannot find the words to express what lies in my heart and I guess I better respond on another occasion."[2] As Johnson watched his former defense secretary become uncharacteristically speechless, he must have felt confident that McNamara would remain loyally quiet and not publicly criticize the administration's Vietnam War policies once he left the government. As it turned out, Johnson's confidence was justified; McNamara did not speak up, at least not before 1995.[3]

Johnson was unaware, however, that McNamara had left behind at the Defense Department three dozen analysts who were writing a secret history of America's involvement in Vietnam. The study was not even half completed the day Johnson paid tribute to McNamara, and it was not obvious to those writing the history that it would ever be finished. But the massive 7,000-page project was completed within a year.

Johnson may have first learned about the Pentagon Papers study when he read the first reports of it in the *New York Times* in June 1971, nearly three years after he left the presidency. He was outraged by the disclosures and convinced that the *Times*'s decision to publish the secret history meant the newspaper was out to destroy his reputation and the legacy of his presidency.[4]

■ ■ ■ ■ ■

To understand the sharp juxtaposition of feelings and attitudes just described, the disclosures of the Pentagon Papers study, as well as the Nixon administration's effort to suppress the study, we must begin at a much earlier point in time.

Five weeks after McNamara became president of the Ford Motor Company, where he had spent the previous fifteen years working his way up the corporate ladder, President-elect John F. Kennedy asked McNamara to become his secretary of defense. McNamara did not think he was qualified for the office, but he agreed to do it if Kennedy would agree that "he be left to run the department as he thought best and to appoint whomever he wanted," and that he be free of any obligation "to go to parties or be 'a social secretary.' "[5] Kennedy agreed.

By early 1962 McNamara had emerged as the dominant policy strategist for Vietnam within the Kennedy administration.[6] Many factors combined to make this so. Because he regretted his "me-too role [that he played] in the Bay of Pigs debacle," McNamara was determined not to allow a similar mistake to happen to him again on any defense matter. And if Vietnam was becoming an international testing ground for the U.S. military, as it appeared to be, McNamara decided that he would not permit others to do his thinking for him. He was convinced that the survival of a noncommunist government in South Vietnam was vital to U.S. economic, political, and military interests. He believed that the entire Indochina peninsula would be at risk if South Vietnam fell to the communists. He also believed that the United States had to meet the communist challenge in Vietnam in order to deter the Soviet Union's premier, Nikita Khrushchev, who had stated bluntly his determination to challenge the United States at vital points throughout the world. With these concerns

McNamara was determined to exercise an influential hand in shaping Vietnam policy. In the end he was so influential that the war in Vietnam eventually became known as "McNamara's war," which McNamara said he did not mind: "I'm proud to be associated with it."[7]

Throughout 1962 and 1963 McNamara was optimistic about the progress made in defeating communist forces in Vietnam. "Every qualitative measurement we have shows we're winning this war," he publicly reported after his first visit to Vietnam in 1962. During this period he favored increasing the number of U.S. military advisers in South Vietnam while continuing support for Ngo Dinh Diem's government. Following a trip to South Vietnam in March 1964 McNamara and General Maxwell D. Taylor, chairman of the Joint Chiefs of Staff, urged enlarging the U.S. commitment of aid to South Vietnam so that the South Vietnamese armed forces could be increased by 50,000. They also wanted the United States to provide greater budgetary and political support to the South Vietnamese government. About the same time, McNamara ordered Pentagon aides to identify bombing targets in North Vietnam. In late summer of 1964 McNamara was instrumental in persuading Congress to approve the Tonkin Gulf Resolution, which Presidents Johnson and Nixon both cited as legal authority for the use of U.S. military forces in the Vietnam War, absent a formal congressional declaration of war.[8]

In January 1965 McNamara urged Johnson to use American military forces in Vietnam to prevent the communists from taking over the south. After the Viet Cong assaulted American forces at the Pleiku air field in the Central Highlands in February McNamara urged immediate retaliatory air raids on North Vietnam targets. Under McNamara's supervision these sporadic raids gave way to systematic air attacks by the end of the month. In July 1965 McNamara supported Johnson's decision to send U.S. combat troops to South Vietnam. Throughout the fall the defense secretary orchestrated the buildup of American forces, which surpassed 200,000 by the end of the year. In November McNamara recommended a pause in the bombing, ostensibly to induce North Vietnam to accept political terms it had previously rejected. Johnson accepted the recommendation, but the pause failed to bring about any change of attitude in North Vietnam, and the war continued. During the next ten months McNamara pursued a strategy of gradually increasing U.S. military pressure on North Vietnam, on the assumption that the North would eventually capitulate and accept a political settlement.[9]

By the fall of 1966 McNamara's study of the data persuaded him that the North Vietnamese had increased their forces roughly in proportion to the increase in American forces. That meant that the United States would be unable to achieve decisive attrition by introducing more troops and that a standoff with larger forces on each side was in the making. Reports revealed that the extensive air war was ineffective in preventing North Vietnam from sending supplies and troops to the South. Evidence from the field indicated that the pacification programs in the southern countryside had not been a success. McNamara concluded that U.S. policy had failed and that it would continue to fail.[10]

As fall turned into winter, McNamara's understanding of his miscalculations deepened. He had underestimated the determination, tenacity, and resourcefulness of North Vietnam. He had misjudged the effectiveness of American military power in a rural society criss-crossed with tropical and treacherous terrain. He had overestimated popular support for the South Vietnamese government, exaggerated the capacity of programs to strengthen the government's popular base, and undervalued the degree to which the conflict in Vietnam resisted a military solution because it was caused primarily by political and economic considerations.

As McNamara came to accept that the war was unwinnable, other factors also began to affect him. He worried that the powerful political dissent the war had ignited within the United States was tearing the country apart. He was troubled that intellectuals and academics he respected opposed the war and that a few of his most trusted civilian aides—men like John T. McNaughton and Adam Yarmolinsky—were questioning the efficacy of the war's policy and aims. He was increasingly upset because some of his closest friends—such as Senator Robert Kennedy—were becoming some of the war's most public critics.[11]

As 1966 came to an end McNamara wanted Johnson to change his war policies. McNamara wanted to stabilize the U.S. air offensive at its existing level, because increasing the air raids would have little impact on the North Vietnamese and might lead to an open war with China. He wanted to limit American combat troops to about 500,000—well under the 700,000 fighting force General William Westmoreland was planning. He wanted to strengthen the pacification program and coerce political reforms within the South Vietnam government. He wanted the administration to encourage a political settlement through another bombing halt and by giving the Viet Cong a voice in governing the South.[12]

As important as these proposed changes were, they were nonetheless limited. McNamara did not press for a unilateral military withdrawal, an unconditional cease fire, or even a substantial military pullout. Nor did he turn his back on the basic tenet that had guided him for years: that the primary aim of American foreign policy and military power was the containment of communism. Nevertheless, McNamara's shift was perceived as out of step with the administration, and President Johnson, Secretary of State Dean Rusk, national security adviser Walt W. Rostow, and the Joint Chiefs of Staff increasingly isolated him.[13]

It was while McNamara was concluding that the administration's policies had failed in the fall of 1966 that he first considered commissioning a study that would trace the history of U.S. involvement in Vietnam. It is likely that the idea for such a study occurred to him during a visit to the Kennedy Institute of Politics at Harvard University in November 1966. At a meeting with faculty—who were generally opposed to the administration's policies—the discussion focused on how and why the United States had become involved in Vietnam, what the United States had accomplished in Vietnam, and what opportunities the United States had missed and what mistakes it had made in Vietnam. Someone apparently suggested that McNamara try to obtain answers to those and other questions and that he might use as a model the kind of analysis (dealing with a totally different subject) prepared a few years earlier by Richard E. Neustadt. Neustadt had studied the dispute between the United States and Britain in 1961–1962—a dispute that arose when the Kennedy administration canceled the Skybolt missile, which the British had expected to use as a nuclear deterrent.[14]

McNamara was attracted to the idea of a study that explained why the United States was engaged in an Indochina war. It might help explain why the administration's Vietnam policy had failed, and it might help justify a change in the administration's policies. But McNamara delayed in taking any action to get the study off the ground. It was not until the spring of 1967 that McNamara told John McNaughton, his assistant secretary for international security affairs, to ask Neustadt if he would undertake such a study. Neustadt told McNaughton that he might be willing; but within a few weeks Neustadt was notified that there would be no study.[15]

By April 1967 McNamara was distraught. He had been pressing Johnson to move away from a policy aimed at winning the war in favor of trying to convince North Vietnam that it was in no better position to achieve victory than the United States. But McNamara made no headway. Johnson, with the support of others within the administration, was unwilling to change his policy midstream. As a result McNamara found himself increasingly marginalized and was tempted to quit. But he feared his resignation would leave unopposed those within the administration who would "unleash the war" with terrible consequences. He felt trapped. The strain was intense and visible. Rumors spread throughout Washington that McNamara was "deeply troubled," "coming apart," or "close to an emotional breakdown."[16]

In June 1967 McNamara finally commissioned the historical study that he had been considering for over a half year. Morton H. Halperin, one of McNamara's top aides, first learned about this decision when he met with McNaughton and Colonel Robert Guard, a military aide to McNamara. Guard told Halperin that McNamara wanted an "encyclopedic history of the Vietnam War" written within the department, and he wanted Halperin to consider how the project should be carried out. Halperin prepared a memorandum that proposed that McNamara establish a task force attached to the secretary's office, identified the kinds of documents that should be collected and how they might be organized, and urged that he, Halperin, direct the enterprise.[17]

McNamara approved Halperin's plan. He also agreed that Halperin should have general supervisory responsibilities for the study, but he did not want Halperin to devote all his time on it, because he needed Halperin for other matters. Someone else should direct the study on a daily basis. McNamara suggested that the Harvard University historian Ernest R. May be asked, but May turned it down (although he did eventually participate in the venture).[18] Halperin then suggested Leslie H. Gelb. Gelb was working with Halperin on the policy planning staff and had been a senate aide before he joined the Pentagon's Office of International Security Affairs in 1966.[19] McNamara gave his approval, and Gelb accepted the position.

▪ ▪ ▪ ▪ ▪

The precise reasons McNamara commissioned the Pentagon Papers remain uncertain and continue to be a subject of controversy. This is in large part true because McNamara did not commit his own thoughts to paper, and none of his aides—McNaughton, Halperin, Gelb, and Paul C. Warnke—have made public any notes, diaries, or memoranda commenting on McNamara's motives. McNamara did not discuss the project with Gelb or with any members of the staff. The one person at the Defense Department with whom he did plan and discuss the matter was John McNaughton, who died in a plane crash a month after McNamara commissioned the project.

McNamara has insisted that he authorized the study to preserve for scholars the government documents that chronicled the key decisions resulting in the United States's involvement in an Asian land war. He has said that he became convinced that the written record would eventually be lost or destroyed.[20] There is no reason to doubt McNamara's basic contention. Government documents do get "lost" in government files, are selectively destroyed, and are sometimes removed by officials who consider them their personal property. In fact the project staff for the Pentagon Papers encountered exactly such problems: they were far less successful in locating key documents prepared during the Truman and Eisenhower administrations than in collecting documents from later periods.[21]

McNamara's own conduct at the time supported his claim that he wanted to preserve the record for scholars. He told McNaughton that he wanted nothing more to do with the study once it was begun, because he did not want to taint the effort in any way or provide any basis for the suspicion that he had influenced the selection of materials. More important, McNamara complied with his own directions. Once he authorized the study, the staff was unable to receive any guidance from him or any description of what he wanted.[22] McNamara even refused to meet or discuss the project with the staff, including Gelb. Nor is there any evidence that McNamara reviewed the contents of the study as it was prepared. He kept his hands completely off the project and limited his comments to informal remarks such as "let the chips fall as they may."[23]

Neither President Johnson nor Secretary of State Rusk accepted McNamara's claims that he commissioned the study merely to preserve the historical record. When Johnson first learned of the massive study in June 1971 *Newsweek* reported that Johnson told friends he believed the "ghostly hand of Robert Kennedy is on the Pentagon study. Bobby indeed may well have inspired the report."[24] Johnson believed that Kennedy "needed an issue for his intended [presidential] challenge" in 1968. Johnson did not think Kennedy could find any weakness in his "record on civil rights, race, health, education, environment or anything else. He pinned his hopes on Vietnam, and McNamara was a Kennedy man."[25] *Business Week* had a similar report: "Johnson has passed on to newsmen—not for quotation or even indirect attribution to him—his suspicion that McNamara ordered the Vietnam study to help elect Robert Kennedy president in 1968."[26]

Dean Rusk shared Johnson's view. According to his authorized biographer, Thomas J. Schoenbaum, Rusk "became convinced the study was intended to help Robert Kennedy in his political campaign against the President."[27] Rusk has pointed to several factors to support his suspicions not only that McNamara was hiding the study from him and the president but that he commissioned the study to help Kennedy. McNamara did not have the study prepared by the historians at the Defense Department who normally were responsible for historical studies. The analysts who did the study were promised anonymity. The study was considered complete and final without it being circulated for review, comment, or approval to top echelon Pentagon officials or high ranking officials within the State

Department, the CIA, the National Security Agency, the National Security Council, or the White House. Two analysts who worked on the study confided to Rusk that they had the impression they were writing campaign documents for Kennedy's use in the 1968 Democratic party presidential nomination.[28]

Rusk has conceded that McNamara asked him for State Department cooperation in a document collection project. But Rusk considered McNamara's description of the project to be so different from the completed study that, as he stated in his autobiography, "I never knew about the project." Indeed, Rusk felt betrayed not only by McNamara but by his own State Department colleagues: "this forty-four-volume study was prepared under my very nose by, among others, colleagues working twenty yards down the hall from me," and they never disclosed it. When the study was completed a copy was delivered to Under Secretary of State Nicholas de B. Katzenbach just before Rusk left office, and still no one mentioned the study's existence to him.[29]

Johnson's and Rusk's suspicions were not unreasonable. McNamara did not ask Johnson for permission to do the study, and he did not inform the president or Walt Rostow, the president's national security adviser.[30] McNamara did tell Rusk, but Rusk felt that McNamara seriously misled him as to its scope.[31] McNamara had directed the project's staff to keep it a secret. Moreover, as David Halberstam has written, McNamara and Robert Kennedy "had remained close friends and in 1966 they began to feed each other's dissent, McNamara confirming to Kennedy that the war was not going well, Kennedy confirming McNamara's impressions of what the war was doing to this country."[32] In fact nine days after the *New York Times* began publishing excerpts from the Pentagon Papers in June 1971, the reporter Tom Braden wrote a news column based on a conversation with McNamara. Braden stated in part: "It was Robert Kennedy who encouraged McNamara to leave behind him an objective record of the decision-making process which led his country from a game of bluff against a lot of little men in black pajamas to a devastating and terrible war."[33]

Johnson's and Rusk's charges deeply angered McNamara, and he has refused to accept the idea that either Johnson or Rusk could have believed him to have been so devious and disloyal.[34] Several of McNamara's former government associates—Halperin, Warnke, and Katzenbach—supported McNamara's view that there was no basis for Johnson's and Rusk's suspicions, Katzenbach going so far as to characterize them as "nuts."[35] In addition to pointing out that the suspicions were based entirely on unconvincing evidence these former McNamara associates have also offered other plausible reasons for Johnson's and Rusk's suspiciousness. Johnson, for example, was haunted by the Kennedys, and when Robert Kennedy criticized the administration's war policies, McNamara's friendship with Kennedy caused Johnson to distrust McNamara's loyalty. Rusk also had a complicated relationship with the Kennedys. Although he had served as President Kennedy's Secretary of State, he was not (in contrast to McNamara) part of Kennedy's inner circle. Rusk's situation changed significantly when Johnson took office, and Rusk became a Johnson confidant, especially as opposition to the war mounted. Once Kennedy emerged as a threat to Johnson's presidency, Rusk viewed McNamara as a Kennedy supporter and distrusted him.

Although Johnson's and Rusk's suspicions are understandable, it is highly unlikely that McNamara commissioned the Pentagon Papers study to help Kennedy challenge Johnson for the presidency. Kennedy had ample information to criticize Johnson's Vietnam policies without needing the secretary of defense to authorize an exhaustive documentary history. McNamara extended the deadline for the study three times, and it was completed after McNamara had left the administration, after Kennedy had been assassinated, and just a few days before Richard Nixon was sworn in as president. If McNamara had intended the study to further Kennedy's presidential ambitions, he would have insisted that it be completed before the presidential primaries began. Finally, everything we know of how the study was actually conducted—including McNamara's initial choice of two Harvard scholars to direct the project and his total lack of day-to-day involvement—fails to support Johnson's and Rusk's suspicions.

McNamara's reasons for commissioning the study almost certainly changed over time. At first, McNamara probably viewed the project as a means of changing the administration's war policy. By the time he told McNaughton to assemble a staff for the project, however, he was already giving serious thought to leaving the administration. He had even had a conversation with the president during which Johnson asked him what he wanted to do once he left government. McNamara responded that he would like to head the World Bank, and Johnson said he would help him become the bank's president. Thus, by the time McNamara had commissioned the study, he knew that he had lost influence with Johnson, that he was not going to be able to change the administration's course in Vietnam, and that it was only a matter of time before he would be out of the government.[36]

Although there is no reason to doubt that McNamara wanted to preserve the historical record for scholars, as he has insisted, it is likely that McNamara's reasons for having the study done were more complex than that. McNamara was the war minister who "may have done more than any other individual to mold U.S. policy in Vietnam," and who many considered the "principal architect of the American intervention."[37] And yet McNamara commissioned a study that he must have known would treat him harshly. Beyond his desire to preserve the historical record, his decision to commission the Pentagon Papers study must have been pushed by something deeper, more profound, and inevitably obscure. One can only speculate about what those deeper, unexpressed feelings might have been. But they have a character that resembles an act of confession—an indictment as a means of absolution. After all, McNamara not only fashioned the policies that resulted in an intractable war that caused the death of tens of thousands but he continued to implement those policies—resulting in many more deaths—long after he had concluded that the administration's course of action in Vietnam had failed and would continue to fail.

As a result it is difficult to believe that McNamara's decision to commission the study was solely a scholarly one. Rather, it would seem that McNamara's decision was also balanced with feelings of responsibility, regret, guilt, and sorrow. At least that is what Nicholas de B. Katzenbach thought: "I think what happened was that the Vietnam War was one of the worst experiences that McNamara ever had. He saw everything he had done in the Pentagon going down the drain. He spent money on Vietnam and had no way of getting out of Vietnam. . . . He really did not know how this terrible mistake had been made. Where did he go wrong? I think he was assuaging a guilt feeling that he had about Vietnam when he directed the study done. If you know Bob McNamara that is a perfectly good reason."[38]

▪ ▪ ▪ ▪ ▪

McNamara had originally conceived of the Pentagon Papers as resulting in a collection of documents that would require a professional staff of six and take approximately three months to complete. He emphasized that he merely wanted the "record assembled" and indexed so that information would be readily retrievable.[39] About a month after the project began, however, Halperin and Gelb recommended that McNamara's modest conception of the study be substantially transformed. After they had reviewed some documents they concluded that the materials "shed interesting light on the current" situation, which could best be understood if placed in a historical context. They recommended not only collecting documents but also writing narrative histories on selected topics based solely on the documentary materials. They proposed about thirty studies; the final report followed this proposal quite closely.[40]

McNamara has refused to take responsibility for approving the historical studies and has insisted he does not recall authorizing them. He has claimed that he was surprised the final report contained these studies, that he never intended such studies, and that the project's staff never notified him they were preparing them.[41] "Total baloney," says Gelb, who has claimed that he and Halperin submitted written memoranda that outlined the historical essays they intended to prepare. "Literally everything that happened, every decision that I had to make, I would do a memo and send it up to McNamara and get an answer back."[42] McNamara has maintained that he never read Gelb's memoranda, that he never knew the staff was preparing historical studies, and that if he gave his approval to the studies, he gave it without knowing what he was approving. McNamara has contended that he was far too busy with other, more important matters to give his attention to the study once he commissioned it.[43] Halperin has supported McNamara's position: "I don't think he looked at" the memoranda.[44]

Halperin and Gelb probably would not have had interpretative essays prepared unless they believed McNamara had authorized them. It is also unlikely that McNamara gave only his nominal approval to the essays—that is, that he did not know what he was actually approving. He paid too much attention to detail to have allowed that to happen. Also, McNamara probably would not have approved additional staff or extensions for the project without being told that both were required to write the historical essays. What is a puzzle is why McNamara has continued to insist he was unaware of the interpretative essays. Perhaps Gelb put his finger on the reason when he speculated that including the essays in the study ultimately made McNamara feel he had in some sense betrayed Johnson and Rusk.[45]

▪ ▪ ▪ ▪ ▪

Gelb and his staff, who had a suite of offices within the secretary of defense's office, had exceptional access to material. As Gelb has stated, the staff had "total access" to McNamara's and McNaughton's files, and this also gave them access to memoranda from the Joint Chiefs of Staff, to a "vast array of tightly held memos" by White House and State Department principals, and to "routine and special CIA studies." The staff also gained "full access" to the State Department historical files and to "what seemed to be a thorough collection of [State Department] staff papers and studies." Gelb made a personal "arrangement with the CIA" that permitted him to get material upon request. Disregarding McNamara's direction, Gelb also obtained material from "several members of the White House staff." Altogether, the volume of material obtained was enormous, filling thirty to forty cabinets.[46]

As bountiful as this material was, there were gaps. The staff did not have access to records of White House meetings, White House "'cover memos' (the memos which McGeorge Bundy and Walt Rostow, etc. put on top of external memos, informing the President what the external memorandum meant, giving opinions and recommendations)," and telephone conversations. Nor did the task force have a full set of the positions taken by the different military services prior to the formal position taken by the Joint Chiefs of Staff, or to the "back channel" cables sent to and from the Joint Chiefs and General Westmoreland in Vietnam.[47]

The professional staff was composed of young, bright, well-educated individuals "with significant experience of Vietnam or of the foreign-policy-making process." They were drawn from the mid-level ranks of the Pentagon, State Department, and military services; from "think tanks" such as RAND and the Institute for Defense Analysis; and from universities, some of whose faculty acted as consultants.[48] In looking back on the thirty-six so-called Pentagon historians who wrote the studies former Deputy Secretary of State Katzenbach has observed that the group did in fact fulfill McNamara's hopes: he wanted "to put together a team of knowledgeable people, knowledgeable enough to write about it, but not people who had had a lot of responsibilities with respect to Vietnam."[49] Staff members were promised anonymity when recruited so they would feel free to make candid judgments in writing the case studies.

Gelb has conceded that he and the other writers of the histories had their "prejudices and axes to grind, and these shine through clearly at times [even though the group] tried . . . to suppress and compensate for them."[50] But he has taken strong exception to the criticism that the study was the work of doves: "We were not a flock of doves working our vengeance on the Vietnam War."[51]

Gelb had a frustrating time getting the project completed. The staff was "borrowed" or "loaned" from other parts of the government; consequently, few members stayed long enough to complete a particular study. Frequent staff rotation meant that Gelb had to devote much of his own time recruiting new people.[52] It also meant, as Gelb has written, that "almost all the studies had several authors, each heir dutifully trying to pick up the threads of his predecessor."[53] The result was, as one student thoroughly familiar with the study has noted, that the "process gave the history a fragmented character and it does not reflect consistent themes throughout, as would a history written by one author or a group of authors who shared a similar overview of events."[54]

The only exception to this were the four volumes that traced the diplomatic history of the war from 1964 to 1968. These volumes—which totaled over eight hundred pages of analysis and documents—were compiled by Gelb and Richard Moorsteen. Because these volumes were prepared on the assumption that they might be used as background papers should negotiations develop, and because they concerned unresolved and controversial issues, they were treated "as especially sensitive, with only three or four people having access to them."[55] In fact Gelb considered the four volumes so sensitive that he failed to mention them in his transmittal letter that accompanied the completed study, which he sent to Defense Secretary Clark Clifford: he stated that the total number of volumes was forty-three instead of forty-seven.[56]

The staff feared the project would be terminated and its work destroyed if news of its existence spread too far within the government. McNamara had contributed to this atmosphere when he enjoined the task force to keep the project's existence secret.[57] But the staff's reasons for keeping the study secret differed from McNamara's. McNamara was worried about his relationships with Johnson, Rusk, and Rostow. In contrast the staff thought the substance of the study posed a political threat to the administration and its policies. Thus, staff members worried whether they would be allowed to finish the study and whether any copies of it would survive if it were completed. Halperin felt confident that if Rostow or Johnson learned about the project, they would terminate it.[58]

▪ ▪ ▪ ▪ ▪

When completed in early 1969 the study's 7,000 pages were bound into forty-seven volumes; 3,000 pages were devoted to historical studies, which Gelb described as "stick[ing], by and large, to the documents and do not tend to be analytical,"[59] and 4,000 pages contained government documents. Each of these studies, which Gelb thought varied considerably in "quality [and] style," contained a "summary and analysis" written by Gelb and attempting to "capture the main themes and facts of the monographs—and to make some judgments and speculations which may or may not appear in the text itself."[60] Each study also contained a chronology that highlighted "each important event or action in the monograph by means of date, description, and documentary source."[61]

The first several volumes of the study focused on the years between 1940 and 1960, which in Gelb's view contained "many interesting tidbits" but which were mainly "nonstartling."[62] These volumes reviewed U.S. policy toward Indochina during and immediately following World War II. They covered the refusal by the United States to extend assistance to Ho Chi Minh despite his requests. They also make clear the fact that Ho was acknowledged to be a genuine nationalist, as well as a communist, who was intent on maintaining his independence from the Soviet Union and China. These volumes also examined the United States's involvement in the Franco-Viet Minh War between 1950 and 1954, the Geneva Conference of 1954, and the origins of insurgency from 1954 to 1960.

Most of the study was devoted to the years following the election of President Kennedy in 1960. Thus, there were detailed reviews of the overthrow of Ngo Dinh Diem; the Tonkin Gulf episode; the decision to begin and expand the air war against North Vietnam; the decision to deploy U.S. ground forces in Vietnam; the buildup of those forces; the strategy for the use of those troops; and the history of the war's diplomacy from 1964 to 1968.

The four volumes tracing the war's diplomacy were organized around thirteen separate initiatives or contacts that occurred during the period in question. For each episode a brief summary and analysis was followed by a lengthy chronology that recounted the events of each episode on an almost day-to-day basis.[63] The volumes described the evolution of American policies toward a negotiated settlement, the episodic diplomatic contacts between the United States and North Vietnam, and the unsuccessful efforts of numerous third parties to bring the embattled antagonists to the peace table. They candidly assessed the Johnson administration's response to domestic and international pressures for negotiations, the level of the administration's commitment to a negotiated settlement, and the reasons the various peace initiatives failed.

The Pentagon Papers had its obvious shortcomings. It had important gaps because of McNamara's direction that the staff not attempt to collect White House documents or conduct interviews, and because the CIA as well as other branches of the government withheld documents. The historical studies, meanwhile, were clearly not a complete history of U.S. involvement in Vietnam. They were based only on the documents, and as Gelb has written, they did not create "so much a documentary history, as a history based solely on documents."[64] In addition the authors largely neglected the war's political consequences within the United States. Thus, the range of topics was limited, and even those topics addressed were dealt with in a relatively limited way, without the kind of thorough, exhaustive assessment that an independent historian might provide.

The four volumes chronicling the diplomatic history of the war from 1964 to 1968 also contained deficiencies. They were based almost exclusively on cable traffic drawn from State Department files and therefore represented only a fraction of the overall record. Moreover, cable traffic tended to be concerned mainly with operations and rarely included historical and political background pertinent to an issue or an analysis of the reasons behind major policy decisions.[65] The absence of White House files meant that the study shed little light on the thinking of President Johnson and his top advisers. The study generally presented the peace moves in a vacuum; only infrequently were they discussed in the larger context of simultaneous strategic decisions or military and political developments. The so-called negotiating volumes also focused heavily on the United States, providing only glimpses into the policies and methods of operation of the many other actors.[66]

More important, for those who had followed the war closely the papers revealed "relatively few new facts" and served "primarily to confirm private suspicions and publicly expressed doubts."[67] This was also true for the negotiating volumes, which contained "no real bombshells." A careful review of these materials reveals that most of the events described in them had been previously covered in newspaper reports and books.[68]

■ ■ ■ ■ ■

In spite of all these shortcomings the Pentagon Papers study remains an impressive work. It contains thousands of pages of complete government documents, as opposed to selective quotations, which give it the kind of undeniable authenticity and reliability that only primary sources can provide. If it is in many respects incomplete, it is nonetheless a formidable compilation—especially if we take into account the extraordinary circumstances under which the project was carried out. The war was still raging; the political situation was highly volatile; and while the study was intended to be a "historical" record, it chronicles events that had contemporary significance, were highly charged, and were still in a state of rapid, unpredictable movement.

As one researcher at the time summarized it:

> The Pentagon's study, United States-Vietnam Relations 1945–1967, provided such a mass of significant data as to ensure its enduring usefulness to anyone with a serious interest in the United States' long involvement in Indochina. This enormous collection of documents and commentary undoubtedly deepens

> our understanding of the political premises and strategic objectives that have underlain the Indochina, and especially the Vietnam, policies of four American administrations. And, on the military level, these papers marshal a large body of important documentation and analysis bearing on discussions and decisions within several administrations concerning U.S. efforts to achieve these objectives.[69]

Given all these factors, Gelb and Halperin believed they were obligated to classify the study "top secret—sensitive."[70] This was hardly surprising, given that the executive order establishing the classification system broadly defined the term "top secret" as appropriate for information that "could result in exceptionally grave damage to the Nation" if improperly disclosed. As examples of "grave damage," the order included information "leading to a definite break in diplomatic relations affecting the defense of the United States, an armed attack against the United States or its allies, a war, or the compromise of military or defense plans, or intelligence operations, or scientific or technological developments vital to the national defense."[71] The order did not state that injury had to occur within a specified amount of time after disclosure of top secret information. Nor did it require that the disclosure of information result with some degree of certainty in a specific form of harm. In other words the executive order did not restrict the top secret designation to information that would definitely result in an immediate or near-certain break in diplomatic relations of the United States or irreparably harm the defense of the United States or result in an immediate armed attack on the United States or compromise military, defense, intelligence, or scientific matters affecting the national defense. In short the order was broad in scope and imposed very little in the way of defined standards with respect to possible or probable effects.

Furthermore, under the classification rules that existed at the time, Gelb and Halperin were required to classify the *entire* study top secret, even if some of the material within it was classified at a lower level—such as secret or confidential—or not classified at all.[72] This rule often led to results that were anomalous and that could well appear to be the product of sheer mindlessness or obsessive secrecy. The Pentagon Papers were no exception. Thus, articles from the *New York Times* and public presidential addresses, included in the study, were classified top secret along with diplomatic cables, military plans, and intelligence information. That was the rule, and Gelb and Halperin followed it.

Halperin and Gelb used the term "sensitive" in the classification designation because they wanted to keep the very existence of the study as confidential as possible. The term "sensitive" was not authorized by statute or executive order, but it was often used within the Pentagon. It signaled that the information contained in the document might cause bureaucratic and political embarrassment, apart from any effect that its disclosure might have on national security. Halperin and Gelb feared that Johnson or Rostow would destroy the study if they learned of it, and they did not want that to happen.

▪ ▪ ▪ ▪ ▪

Gelb declared the project completed on January 15, 1969, only five days before Richard Nixon took the presidential oath. But the study still needed to be typed and reproduced. Because Gelb, Halperin, and Warnke were concerned about the actual survival of the study, they shipped twenty-eight completed volumes to a government-approved classified storage safe at the RAND Corporation in Washington, D.C.[73] Also, Gelb decided to stay at the Defense Department through the change of administrations in order to shepherd the study through to conclusion. By late April Gelb felt sufficiently comfortable that the final phase of the work would go smoothly; he resigned from the government and joined the Brookings Institute.

Shortly thereafter, and after consulting with McNamara, Gelb made a list for the distribution of the report. Although it is not known for certain, Melvin R. Laird, Nixon's defense secretary, likely approved the list. Only fifteen copies of the report were made, and, of that, five copies were placed in Laird's safe at the Pentagon. Of the ten distributed copies, only one went to an official of the Nixon administration—Henry Kissinger, Nixon's national security adviser. The remaining nine went to the Kennedy and Johnson libraries and seven former Johnson officials. McNamara, Clifford, and Paul H. Nitze, former deputy secretary of defense, each received one. A copy was placed with the private papers of Katzenbach and former Assistant Secretary of State William P. Bundy, both of whose papers were stored at the State Department. Warnke claimed a copy, and Gelb and Halperin jointly claimed the last copy. Not surprisingly, no copy of the report was sent to Walt Rostow, Dean Rusk, or Johnson himself. No announcement describing the study was circulated within the government.

Warnke, Gelb, and Halperin so feared that the study might be destroyed that they deposited their own two copies in the Washington offices of the RAND Corporation. These copies were marked as under the collective control of Gelb, Halperin, and Warnke, who wished to have it appear as if the report belonged to them personally. Under a special arrangement made with Henry Rowen, RAND's president, the top secret study was not "logged into the Rand 'Top Secret Control' system."[74] Although the trio probably had no legal basis for claiming any kind of personal ownership of the classified study, what they did was not unusual among former government officials, who frequently took classified documents with them when they left office.

Gelb, Halperin, and Warnke were determined to do what they could to protect the report; as Gelb later remembered, "I think Paul, Mort, and I were all concerned that the papers survived."[75] Indeed, Gelb was so worried that the study might be destroyed that he went so far as to ask his friend, Richard Ullman, a Princeton professor, to inquire about the possibility of storing a set of the volumes in a secure safe at the university. Ullman made some inquiries and reported to Gelb that it was not possible.[76]

In addition to worrying about the survival of the study, Gelb, Halperin, and Warnke worried about a possible leak. In their view the Papers contained an extraordinary amount of information that was properly classified top secret, that could seriously harm the national security if prematurely disclosed, and that was politically sensitive. They therefore agreed that they would not permit anyone to have access to the study they stored at RAND unless two out of the three of them so agreed.[77]

CHAPTER TWO

Daniel Ellsberg

There would have been no Pentagon Papers but for Robert McNamara, and there would have been no leak of the papers but for Daniel Ellsberg. What is peculiar about McNamara and Ellsberg is not their obvious differences but their less visible yet nonetheless striking similarities. As the decade of the 1960s wore on, it was apparent that the lives of each of these two men would be tied inextricably with the Vietnam War.

Both men began the decade as strong advocates of American policy and with a deep conviction that American goals were worthy and attainable. Both advocated and supported the war. Both were involved in the historical study that became known as the Pentagon Papers. Both gradually became persuaded that the war was misguided and wrong, and both sought ways to change the course of American policy. Each experienced a crisis in confidence during these years, crises that led to actions that, in one way or another, affected the balance of their lives. Together, their tales—so dramatically different, yet oddly parallel—trace the creation of the fateful secret study and its explosive release. Together, they dramatize how significant political history emerges from the complex interaction of personalities and motives, especially when the times are highly charged, as they were.

▪ ▪ ▪ ▪ ▪

Daniel Ellsberg was born in 1931 in Chicago. His parents were middle-class Jews who converted to Christian Science and eventually moved to Detroit, where Ellsberg grew up.[1] In 1948 Ellsberg entered Harvard on a scholarship, studied economics, became president of the *Advocate*, an undergraduate literary magazine, and was elected to the editorial board of the *Crimson*, the college daily newspaper. By his junior year he was married to Carol Cummings, a Radcliffe sophomore and the daughter of a Marine colonel.

He graduated summa cum laude and third in his class in 1952.[2] After another year of study as a Woodrow Wilson Fellow at King's College, Cambridge University, Ellsberg entered the Marines in 1954, where he excelled and obtained the distinction of Marksman. He served as a rifle platoon leader, rifle company commander, and operations officer. Whereas other lieutenants usually had to surrender their command within a few weeks to captains, Lieutenant Ellsberg was not replaced because his company "won more awards than any other in the battalion and was foremost in inspections and on maneuvers." After Egyptian leader Gamal Abdel Nasser seized the Suez Canal in 1956 Ellsberg extended his enlistment for eight months, so that he could accompany his battalion to the Sixth Fleet in the Mediterranean.[3]

In 1957 Ellsberg returned to Harvard as a junior member of its Society of Fellows, "the most illustrious assemblage of young scholars in American academia," to work on his doctorate, which he earned in 1962.[4] In March 1959 Ellsberg delivered the Lowell Institute Lectures at the Boston Public Library on "The Art of Coercion: A Study of Threats in Economic Conflicts and War," an outgrowth of his academic interest in the theory of bargaining, a popular interest among academics during the 1950s.[5] About the same time Henry Kissinger, a Harvard professor, invited Ellsberg to give two lectures at his seminar on "the conscious political use of irrational military threats."[6]

Ellsberg's lectures were called "The Political Uses of Madness," and they explored how an otherwise sane and modest political leader might contrive to appear capable of using an immensely destructive weapon as a threat in negotiations. They pointed out that, precisely because the weapon was so extreme, its use did not have to seem very likely for the threat to be effective, especially if the threat was made on behalf of only moderate negotiating demands. Ellsberg noted one particular way to make the threat credible. The leader should not appear to be completely rational. Ellsberg illustrated his point with references to Hitler's tactics and behavior. Ellsberg's lectures impressed Kissinger and contributed to the professor's praise of Ellsberg years later when he declared: "I've learned more from Dan Ellsberg about bargaining than [from] anyone else."[7]

Following his honorable discharge from the Marines, Ellsberg worked as a strategic analyst in the Santa Monica office of the RAND Corporation, a civilian research institute as well as "the brain trust" of the Air Force. He helped to perfect plans for nuclear war against the Soviet Union, China, and other communist states. While there he was given clearances beyond top secret—clearances designated by codes so secret that even members of Congress were unaware of them. Ellsberg then gained potential access to the "nation's most highly classified secrets."[8]

On the first day of the Kennedy administration, Ellsberg became a consultant with the Pentagon because of his relationship with Paul Nitze, whom he had met at RAND and again during the presidential campaign. Because of his "special knowledge and presumed expertise, the coin of influence for a government intellectual," Ellsberg's career flourished, and top Pentagon officials wanted his services.[9] In the fall of 1961 Ellsberg made an intense, one-week visit to South Vietnam as a member of a research team examining problems of nonnuclear, limited warfare.[10] Ellsberg also wrote memoranda for McGeorge Bundy and McNamara "recommending changes in the Joint Strategic Capabilities Plan." In addition he worked on the crisis-management team that Paul Nitze formed at the Pentagon and Walt Rostow organized at the State Department during the Cuban missile crisis in October 1962.[11] Ellsberg continued as a consultant with the Defense Department through 1963, spending as much as half of each year in Washington at the Pentagon, working with Henry Rowen and other former RAND colleagues.

Ellsberg left RAND in August 1964, immediately after the United States retaliated for alleged North Vietnamese attacks on U.S. vessels in the Gulf of Tonkin. He joined the Defense Department at the highest possible civil service level, the "super-grade" rank of a GS-18.[12] He became an assistant to John T. McNaughton, McNamara's assistant secretary of defense for international security affairs, whom Ellsberg had known for a couple years. McNaughton headed the Pentagon's foreign-policy office and played a key role within the Pentagon on Vietnam issues.[13] McNaughton told Ellsberg that he was spending 70 percent of his time on Vietnam and that he wanted Ellsberg to spend 100 percent of his time on it. Ellsberg knew little about Vietnam, but he was eager to learn and anxious to observe the government's decision-making process from the inside.[14] During the spring of 1965 he helped plan for the dispatch in June of U.S. ground troops to Vietnam. He also defended Rolling Thunder, the code name for U.S. air attacks against North Vietnam, to members of Congress and to audiences on college campuses.[15]

The following year Ellsberg's personal life disintegrated when his wife insisted on a divorce. Ellsberg had two children and became despondent.

That, combined with a sense of romanticism, a need to prove himself, and a sense of duty that he should be with the soldiers in Vietnam since he helped develop the plans that put them there, led Ellsberg to want to return to Vietnam. McNaughton had become "skittish" about Ellsberg because he boasted about what he knew—a characteristic that became heightened by his divorce. As a result McNaughton let Ellsberg leave the Pentagon without a struggle. Ellsberg volunteered to fight in Vietnam as a Marine company commander but was informed that he ranked too high in the civilian bureaucracy for such "mundane" military duty. He then managed to find another way to return to Vietnam—by becoming a special liaison officer under retired Major General Edward G. Lansdale, "a free-wheeling expert on counterinsurgency." Lansdale was returning to South Vietnam as a member of the State Department, attached to the U.S. embassy in Saigon. Officially, Lansdale and his team were assigned to act as a liaison between the embassy and Saigon's Rural Reconstruction Council, a group that theoretically coordinated the government's pacification programs. In fact Lansdale's operation was trying to reform the Saigon regime and develop an effective pacification program.[16]

During his Vietnam tour as a civilian, Ellsberg studied the pacification program and went out on patrol with Marine units in central Vietnam and accompanied Army units in the Mekong Delta. During these military operations he carried a carbine, was repeatedly caught in combat, and risked his life on several occasions.[17] Years later, Ellsberg vividly recalled these patrols: "a couple of times when I was with the lead squad going through a paddy, Vietcong rose from the paddy we had just walked through and fired at the people behind us."[18]

While in Vietnam, Ellsberg became friendly with John Paul Vann, whose military and civilian service in Vietnam spanned a decade. He also met Kissinger once again when Kissinger visited South Vietnam at the request of Ambassador Henry Cabot Lodge. Ellsberg was impressed by Kissinger; he gave him a list of knowledgeable Americans and Vietnamese and urged him to speak with them informally so they would talk openly. Ellsberg met Richard Nixon when the former vice president traveled through South Vietnam and had lunch at Lansdale's home.[19] Ellsberg also became friendly with Neil Sheehan, a news reporter stationed in Vietnam, and with Anthony Russo, a young engineer and political scientist from the RAND Corporation who was studying the motivation of the Viet Cong by interviewing prisoners and converts to the South Vietnamese side.[20]

Ellsberg's Vietnam experiences profoundly affected him. When he arrived in Vietnam in 1965, Ellsberg thought of "the war's tactics . . . [as] morally justified on the assumption that the war itself was necessary."[21] A few years later he himself summed up his views to a *Look* reporter: "I had accepted the official answer, . . . namely that there was a civil war going on, that we had a right to intervene and pick one side or the other if our interests were involved, and our interests were involved. That if the wrong side should win this war, it would be worse for the Vietnamese people, worse for the United States and for world peace. It would mean victory for the people who wished us ill and who would behave more aggressively in other parts of the world, which we would also have to counter."[22] However, by the spring of 1967, when a severe case of hepatitis caused Ellsberg to return to the United States, he had become discouraged by the continuing violence of the war and by the unwillingness of the United States to change its approach.[23] Overwhelmed by the war's futility, he felt a growing sense that "the programs we were pursuing had no chance of succeeding."[24] He was convinced that the programs in Vietnam "were not in any way proceeding as people thought they were back in Washington," and he had essentially concluded that the United States "should get out of the war."[25]

▪ ▪ ▪ ▪ ▪

This was Ellsberg's frame of mind when, in the late summer of 1967, Halperin and Gelb asked him to join the staff of the Pentagon Papers project. Ellsberg has stated that Halperin and Gelb "were very anxious to get" him to become one of the so-called Pentagon historians and that he was one of the first people they approached. From a personal point of view Ellsberg thought it was "crucial" for him to become part of the staff, since he viewed the study as a way of rethinking U.S. policy and discussing what had gone wrong. Ellsberg has said that he insisted as "the price . . . [of] participating as a researcher" that he be permitted to read "the whole study," but neither Halperin nor Gelb recall such an understanding.[26]

Ellsberg chose the Kennedy administration's 1961 policy in Vietnam for his assignment, largely because he felt more familiar with this period.[27] He spent roughly four months locating documents and assembling research material. Then, in December 1967, he wrote approximately 350 pages of a draft report.[28] He wanted to return to the West Coast to finish the draft, but Gelb objected because he worried that Ellsberg would not complete the work if he left Washington. Ellsberg left anyway and has claimed that his essay remained largely intact when the full study was eventually concluded. Leslie Gelb has stated, however, that "very few of Ellsberg's words finally appeared."[29]

Ellsberg's attitudes, perspective, and values continued to shift during 1968. In early April he attended a conference on "America in a Revolutionary World" at Princeton University. For the first time in his life he met "activists" from the antinuclear movement of the 1950s and the civil rights and antiwar movements of the 1960s. At his luncheon table he sat across from a young woman from India who was dressed in a sari and who had a dot of red dust on her forehead. Her name was Janaki. At one point during the conversation Janaki said: "I come from a culture in which there is no concept of 'enemy.' " Ellsberg was confused by the statement and captivated by the woman. He felt that he came from a culture "in which the concept of 'enemy' was central, seemingly indispensable: the culture of RAND, the Marines, the Defense and State Departments, international and domestic politics, game theory and bargaining theory."[30]

Identifying and understanding the enemy had been part of Ellsberg's "daily bread and butter, part of the air I breathed." Now he was "intrigued" by this Indian woman and what he considered her "Gandhian algebra." He talked with her throughout the day and into the evening. He learned about her life and her commitment to nonviolence. He asked what books she thought he should read if he wanted to learn more about Gandhi and his way of thinking. At the end of the day they learned that Martin Luther King had just been killed and that "Washington was burning."[31]

Clearly, Ellsberg was deeply disoriented and in the process of major shifts in thought and belief. Indeed, his deepening rejection of his prior support of the war; his sudden fascination with nonviolence; his apparent willingness to accept that there are cultures with no concept of enemy; and his later recollection that this was the day "when my life started to change": all of these, as well as other factors, suggest a set of beliefs and attitudes that were in the midst of intense and radical change.[32]

Tumultuous public events of the late winter and spring of 1968 fueled Ellsberg's evolution. The Tet offensive, which had occurred shortly before Ellsberg met Janaki, seemed to intensify his conviction that the violence in Vietnam was senseless and immoral. The assassination of Senator Robert F. Kennedy—only a couple months after King's—caused Ellsberg to lose confidence in the efficacy of traditional political processes. After the Democratic party rejected a peace plank at its Chicago national convention Ellsberg felt even less confidence in the political system. Increasingly unanchored and without a political compass, Ellsberg got little work done, dated many women, and began psychoanalysis with Doctor Lewis Fielding in Beverly Hills.[33]

▪ ▪ ▪ ▪ ▪

Soon after his election in 1968, Nixon appointed Henry Kissinger as his national security adviser. One of Kissinger's first moves was to telephone

Henry Rowen, president of RAND and a former Pentagon official, to ask him to prepare a paper that listed the administration's possible options for the Vietnam War. Rowen asked Ellsberg to take on the assignment and he accepted. On Christmas Day Rowen, Ellsberg, and another RAND official flew to New York and met with Kissinger at Nixon's transition headquarters in the Pierre Hotel. Ellsberg's paper did not include a "win" or a "threat" option, but it did list an option of unilateral withdrawal by the United States. Thomas C. Schelling, a Kissinger colleague from Harvard, commented on the absence of the "win" and "threat" alternatives. Ellsberg told the group that he did not think "there is a win option in Vietnam" but that he would include a "threat" option even though he did not understand "how threatening bombing is going to influence the enemy because they have experienced four years of bombing." Before the paper was completed Kissinger arranged for the elimination of the "withdrawal" alternative.[34] Shortly thereafter, Kissinger asked Ellsberg to prepare an exhaustive list of questions about Vietnam that could be presented to various parts of the government, including the Defense and State Departments, the CIA, and the American Embassy in Saigon. In February 1969 Kissinger again asked Ellsberg to return to Washington, this time to summarize the answers to the questionnaire. Ellsberg worked on the project through most of March.[35]

It was around this time (and for reasons that are not clear) that Ellsberg decided he wanted to read the entire Pentagon Papers. He was working on a Defense Department project at the RAND Corporation, but he did not need access to the classified study to complete his research. Nor did he seem to have any larger political purpose for reading the report. What seems likely is that, given his own deep involvement with Vietnam and his complete change of viewpoint, he was beginning his own search into the historical records to understand what had happened in Vietnam; to trace his own relation to the war as it had evolved; and perhaps to find a far greater clarification or revelation of the entire experience than had so far been fully grasped by anyone.

Ellsberg asked Henry Rowen to help him gain access to the top secret Pentagon study. Since Morton Halperin and Paul Warnke had stored a copy of the report at RAND, Rowen contacted Halperin, who telephoned Gelb. But Gelb did not trust Ellsberg to protect the confidentiality of the study and would not consent to the request. Shortly afterward, Halperin contacted Gelb again, this time pressing harder, arguing that Ellsberg had worked on the project, that he was doing an assignment for the Pentagon, that access to the classified report would be useful, and that Ellsberg had all the requisite security clearances. He added he did not believe they had any reasonable basis for turning Ellsberg down. All these reasons made it awkward for Gelb to continue his objections. Halperin passed the word along to Rowen, so Ellsberg gained access to the secret history.[36]

Ellsberg's six-month study of the Pentagon history greatly affected his thinking. It was not any one document or any one incident or series of incidents that had such an impact on him. What was most striking was the fact that American policy in 1969 appeared to be a direct descendant of the policy pursued by the Truman administration immediately following World War II. As Ellsberg explained to a reporter in 1971: "The startling thing that came out of them was how the same sets of alternatives began to appear to each President, and ultimately the choice was neither to go for broke and adopt military recommendations, nor negotiate a settlement to get out. The decisions year after year were to continue the war, although all predictions pointed to a continued stalemate with this kind of approach and thus to prolong the war indefinitely." As a consequence of his analysis, Ellsberg came to see the war not as "Kennedy's war or Johnson's war" but as the result of a "pattern of behavior that went far beyond any one" president. "It was a war," Ellsberg concluded, "no American President had . . . the courage to turn down or to stay out of." When Ellsberg applied these insights to the Nixon administration, he concluded that "Nixon was the fifth President in succession to be subjected to the same pressures that had led four other Presidents to maintain involvement; that his assurances that he had no intention of staying in Indochina were no more to be believed than other Presidents' assurances; . . . that whatever his feelings were as of '69, the more he got involved, the more sure it was that he would stay involved."[37]

Even before he studied the Pentagon Papers, Ellsberg had already begun to change his view of what Nixon was prepared to do in Vietnam. He wanted to believe Kissinger's representations that the Nixon administration intended to extricate the United States from the war, and he had initially hoped that the conflict would soon begin to wind down. By September 1969, however, Ellsberg had concluded that Nixon and Kissinger intended to escalate hostilities in hopes of coercing North Vietnam to accept a political settlement acceptable to the United States. Specifically, Ellsberg thought Nixon would not go into the 1972 elections without having mined Haiphong harbor. Ellsberg believed this because of information that Halperin, who had by now resigned from the national security staff, had passed on to him.[38]

About the same time Ellsberg attended a conference at Haverford College organized by the War Resisters International. Ellsberg did not think of himself as a pacifist, and indeed he mentioned once that he particularly admired the character played by John Wayne in the *The Sands of Iwo Jima*. Now, however, he noticed that those whom he admired were often women and nonwhite, and he now "wanted to meet people who did see themselves" as pacifist.[39]

Ellsberg was impressed by the draft resisters he met at Haverford. He found them "conscientious, reasonable, and not fanatics. . . . They just seemed to feel that they could not collaborate in the war and were prepared to go to jail."[40] But it was a young man named Randy Kehler who most affected Ellsberg. Kehler had been impressive earlier at the conference. He was one of the organizers of the entire session, and Ellsberg noted that Kehler "listened carefully, responded thoughtfully and with good sense. Of the many younger American activists I had met at the conference, he was the one I most wanted to see more of." Kehler struck Ellsberg as having a "simple and direct manner," as well as "warmth and humor." When Kehler finally spoke on a panel on the last day of the conference, Ellsberg was "surprised" to learn that, like himself, Kehler had gone to Harvard—"a credit to Harvard!" he thought at the time. Kehler spoke of friends who had recently gone to prison and of his own impending imprisonment because of draft resistance. He spoke with fervor. Some in the audience stood silently; others applauded.[41]

While listening to Kehler, Ellsberg began to cry. His friend Janaki was to speak next, but he was too upset to stay. He left the amphitheater and made his way down the back corridor to a men's room. Once inside he began "to sob convulsively, uncontrollably." He remained there alone, for over an hour, without getting up, his head sometimes tilted back against the wall, sometimes in his hands.[42]

It was at this moment that Ellsberg began to consider seriously what he might do to change American war policy in Vietnam. He also felt that, if he were going to take a major risk, he wanted to be certain he could have a major impact. Because Ellsberg had been close to power and to people in power, it is most unlikely that he could imagine being an unsung imprisoned war resister or another anonymous body in a protest crowd. What is more likely is that Ellsberg imagined he would be in the center of events, with a central role in whatever drama was to be enacted.

Before long Ellsberg found himself thinking of the 7,000-page top secret report that was in the RAND safe. Reading the report had convinced him that U.S. efforts to maintain or to escalate the war would fail to bring North Vietnam to the bargaining table, and he began to believe that others might be similarly affected if they could see the documents. He also thought he might be able to change the political calculus, so that Nixon would begin to be more fearful of political attacks from the antiwar constituency than from those who would attack him if North Vietnam were to win the war—or at least to hold its own indefinitely.[43] Ellsberg brooded over whether he could actually leak the classified study. He had been a RAND employee, a Pentagon employee, a White House consultant, and a confidant of high-ranking Pentagon and State Department officials. Could he actually betray his friends, his colleagues, and the trust that had been placed in him by making the top secret report public?

Ellsberg's indecision ended on September 29, when he learned that Secretary of the Army Stanley R. Resor had decided not to file charges against six Special Forces men accused of assassinating an alleged South Vietnamese double agent. Ellsberg thought that in its most immediate sense the army's decision to drop charges meant that military officials could not be trusted to hold soldiers responsible for their conduct. But, more generally, what was left of Ellsberg's faith in the military's willingness to enforce its own rules was undermined by Resor's announcement.[44]

Ellsberg telephoned Anthony Russo, his friend from Vietnam and RAND who was also strongly opposed to the war. Ellsberg asked Russo if he knew of a photocopy machine that could be used to duplicate the Pentagon Papers. Lynda Sinay, Russo's girlfriend, ran her own advertising agency, and she agreed to let the two men use the agency's machine. Ellsberg had no trouble bringing the top secret documents out of RAND or returning them. He would fill his briefcase with parts of the study about 11:30 P.M., carry the briefcase past the security guard, who did not examine his bags, presumably because he knew Ellsberg. Ellsberg would photocopy the documents for several hours, have breakfast at a local restaurant, and return the documents to his RAND safe early in the morning. He followed this pattern for several weeks, sometimes making as many as forty or fifty copies of a particular document. On occasion Russo would help Ellsberg, and at least once Ellsberg's two children helped out.[45]

■ ■ ■ ■ ■

Ellsberg consulted a few lawyers, whom he has refused to identify, about whether his disclosure of the report would subject him to any criminal liability.[46] Ellsberg's memory of what he was advised is vague and incomplete. But it seems likely, given that Ellsberg came to believe that he ran the risk of long-term imprisonment if he made the Pentagon Papers public, that the lawyers told him he would be liable under existing espionage laws if he gave the documents to anyone not authorized to receive them. Consequently, the best way for Ellsberg to avoid criminal liability was to give the papers to someone who had the proper security clearance. One option that Ellsberg aggressively pursued, for example, was to give the documents to a member of Congress who had the requisite clearances and would be willing to make the papers public in Congress or at a congressional committee hearing so they might be published in the *Congressional Record*. Members of Congress are protected from criminal prosecution by the Constitution in accordance with the speech and debate clause for actions they undertake consistent with official duties and responsibilities. Ellsberg did remember that the lawyers advised him that "the surest way to get myself in prison for a long time" was to give the Pentagon Papers to the press.[47]

In early October Ellsberg met with Senator J. William Fulbright, chairman of the Foreign Relations Committee and the senate's leading dove; he also had the necessary security clearances. Ellsberg told him about the Pentagon Papers, gave him some documents from the study, plus a summary of the entire study and what he thought it revealed. Fulbright had previously scheduled public hearings before the Foreign Relations Committee on Vietnam, with the aim of considering legislation to stop funding for the war. Fulbright invited Ellsberg to be a witness and to make public whatever he wanted. But shortly thereafter, Fulbright backed away from his intention to hold public hearings. He told Ellsberg he had changed his mind, because "I believe the President's own statement that he is trying to wind down the war in Vietnam." Ellsberg tried to persuade Fulbright to change his mind by convincing him that Johnson had deceived him over the Tonkin Gulf Resolution. But Ellsberg could not budge Fulbright, and eventually Fulbright informed Ellsberg that there was no support in his committee for testimony critical of the war.[48] Fulbright, however, did tell Ellsberg that he would write Secretary of Defense Melvin Laird and request that the classified history be declassified and released to his committee.[49]

Laird denied Fulbright's request and ignored his subsequent ones.[50] By this time Laird had learned that Fulbright had a partial set of the papers. Laird also believed that Fulbright knew he suspected Fulbright of already having some of the papers. Laird has not disclosed how he learned that Fulbright had a portion of the Pentagon Papers, but it is possible that Kissinger, who was close to Fulbright at the time, was the source.

Ellsberg eventually concluded that Fulbright was not going to make the documents public. He was frustrated and unsure of what to do next. He spoke with more lawyers about the possibility of a war crimes investigation in which he might appear as a witness and disclose the documents. In this way, particularly if the documents were subpoenaed, he [illegible] criminal liability would be minimized. But the lawyers ap- [illegible] not think the proposal was practical and did not follow up [illegible].[51]

[illegible] Ellsberg began to explore several alternatives. He became [illegible] Senator Charles Goodell and helped to prepare testimony the senator gave before the Senate Foreign Relations Committee in February 1970. Goodell was testifying in support of a bill that would require the withdrawal of U.S. troops from Vietnam.[52] In the process Ellsberg gave Fulbright more pages from the classified history, including the Joint Chiefs of Staff study of the Tonkin Gulf incident, hoping the senator would make the documents public.[53] He also gave a substantial portion of the study to Marcus G. Raskin and Richard J. Barnet, who were based at the Institute for Policy Studies and were writing a book on the Vietnam War.[54] But as active as Ellsberg was in trying to find an outlet for the Pentagon Papers, he was still unable to do so.

▪ ▪ ▪ ▪ ▪

In March 1970 FBI agents visited Patricia Marx, whom Ellsberg would marry that summer. The agents wanted to interview Ellsberg about his photocopying of the Pentagon Papers study. Ellsberg has claimed that the agents learned of his involvement from his former wife.[55] When Patricia Marx told Ellsberg of the visit, he decided that the agents would soon find him at RAND and that they would seize the documents. Ellsberg has said he wanted to minimize embarrassing RAND and his RAND colleagues, so he resigned his position and accepted a research post at the MIT Center for International Studies.[56] He flew east on April 15, carrying copies of the Pentagon Papers with him.[57]

Twelve days later FBI agents did visit RAND inquiring about whether Ellsberg had photocopied the Pentagon Papers. Henry Rowen informed them that the study was historical in nature and did not contain information threatening to the national security. The agents asked whether Ellsberg had given the study to Senator Fulbright, and Rowen replied that Fulbright was authorized to receive the study. Rowen was asked not to inform Ellsberg of this visit and its purpose.[58]

The FBI investigation apparently stopped at this point. The agents may have been satisfied that the possible disclosure of the Pentagon Papers was a minor matter, although that seems unlikely. What may be more probable is that the FBI decided to forgo further investigation because it might implicate Senator Fulbright and embarrass the bureau.[59]

Whatever the reason, Ellsberg was not contacted or questioned at that time, and he returned to RAND shortly thereafter. No one at RAND told him about the FBI inquiry, and he simply continued his work with full access to classified documents as before. Ellsberg took advantage of this opportunity to complete photocopying the final section of the Pentagon Papers. He also duplicated many other documents, including drafts of the papers that became part of the Pentagon Papers, a study prepared by the Joint Chiefs of Staff on the Tonkin Gulf incident, and a memorandum for the National Security Counsel (NSSM #1) that he had prepared for Kissinger and that summarized answers submitted by government officials to dozens of questions relating to the Vietnam War.[60]

By late summer of 1970 Ellsberg was convinced that the Nixon administration was approaching a serious escalation of the war even while it continued to reduce the overall number of U.S. fighting forces in South Vietnam. He took advantage of a meeting with Henry Kissinger—set up by Lloyd Shearer, an editor of *Parade* magazine—to discuss the Pentagon Papers and what they might mean for U.S. policy in Vietnam.[61] Ellsberg urged Kissinger to read the study, and Kissinger is reported to have expressed strong doubt that there was really much to be learned from the documents.

In January 1971 Ellsberg turned to Senator George McGovern for possible help. McGovern was a sponsor of a major end-the-war amendment and the first announced candidate for the 1972 Democratic party presidential nomination. Ellsberg told McGovern that he was in possession of classified documents that would expose the misguided nature of U.S. policy in Vietnam and, if revealed, could hasten the end of the war. McGovern was initially interested in discussing the study with Ellsberg but then abruptly decided against any involvement in an effort to place classified documents in the public domain. He terminated further conversations with Ellsberg, stating he did not trust him. McGovern counseled Ellsberg to turn the papers over to the *Times* or the *Post*.[62] But that makes little sense if McGovern was convinced the documents were authentic, and he seems to have accepted their authenticity. Distrust may well have played some role in McGovern's decision. But McGovern also must have realized that disclosure of the top secret history might strike a large portion of the public as irresponsible and thus undermine his effort to convince the public that he had the stature to be president.

By late January 1971 Ellsberg was so frustrated that he took a step that essentially ended his relationship with Kissinger. At a conference sponsored by MIT Ellsberg took advantage of the question period to ask Kissinger, who had made a presentation, about the administration's estimate of the Asian casualties that would result from Vietnamization. Kissinger hesitated and then characterized Ellsberg's question as "cleverly worded" and stated that "I answer even if I don't answer." Kissinger then tried to avoid the question, but Ellsberg interrupted, repeated the question, and stated: "can't you just give us an answer or tell us that you don't have such estimates?" Kissinger did not answer the question, and the student moderator, sensing the sudden tension in the room, abruptly ended the panel discussion.[63]

▪ ▪ ▪ ▪ ▪

In February Ellsberg began to give more serious consideration to the advice that several political leaders, including McGovern, had given him: to give the classified study to the *New York Times*.[64] Ellsberg had been reluctant to do this, because he feared the possibility of criminal prosecution. But he no longer had any other apparent option. He had asked many prominent members of Congress, including Senator Fulbright, Senator McGovern, Senator Charles Mathias, and Representative Paul N. (Pete) McCloskey, to release the documents, but all had refused. His efforts with Kissinger had also come to naught. The issue Ellsberg had to decide now was which reporter to contact. His most likely prospect was Neil Sheehan of the *New York Times*.

Sheehan first began reporting on Vietnam when he was twenty-five and was working for the UPI. He quickly established himself as a gifted reporter and, according to David Halberstam, just missed a Pulitzer Prize in 1964. By 1965 he was writing for the *Times*, and his stories gave a vivid sense of the war's impact on Vietnam. They often reflected a pessimistic view of the war—a view that angered American officials. In 1967 Sheehan returned to the United States and was assigned to the *Times*'s Washington bureau.[65]

Ellsberg and Sheehan had met in Vietnam and again in Washington. Ellsberg has claimed that he even leaked information to Sheehan during the late 1960s and that he was favorably impressed with how Sheehan had dealt with the information and had protected him.[66] In December 1970 Ellsberg became convinced that Sheehan might be the right reporter to get the Pentagon Papers to the public when he read Sheehan's highly critical book review of Mark Lane's *Conversations with Americans* in the *Times*. In the course of the review Sheehan called for an inquiry into "war crimes and atrocities" committed by the U.S. military in Vietnam, an idea Ellsberg supported. Sheehan wrote that the "country desperately needs a sane and honest inquiry into the question of war crimes and atrocities in Vietnam by a body of knowledgeable and responsible men not beholden to the current military establishment." Sheehan thought the "men who now run the military establishment cannot conduct a credible investigation." Sheehan claimed that the "need" for such an inquiry was "self-evident," since "too large a segment of the citizenry" believed such acts had occurred.[67]

Nevertheless, Ellsberg did not contact Sheehan until mid-February.[68] When they met, Sheehan showed Ellsberg a draft of a long essay, eventually published in the *New York Times* book review section, reviewing thirty-three antiwar books and addressing the question of whether the United States had committed war crimes in Vietnam. Ellsberg was impressed, but he did not give Sheehan the Pentagon Papers.[69] Ellsberg returned to Washington during the last weekend in February. He was scheduled to participate in a panel discussion at the National War College on Vietnam on Monday.[70] He met with Raskin and discussed his frustration with making the Pentagon Papers public. Raskin urged Ellsberg to discuss with Sheehan the possibility of having the *Times* publish the papers. Ellsberg was persuaded. He telephoned Sheehan on the last Sunday in February. They met at Sheehan's Washington home and spent the night discussing the war.[71]

Ellsberg told Sheehan of the study and what it contained. Sheehan already knew of the study; he had probably even discussed it with Raskin, Barnet, and Ralph Stavins, all of the Institute for Policy Studies, when they contacted him after Sheehan's December book review was published.[72] Ellsberg asked Sheehan's advice on what he should do with the history. From the start Sheehan took the position that he could not help Ellsberg unless he read the study.[73] He also told Ellsberg that he could not make any commitments on behalf of the *Times* and that the *Times* would not make any commitments until its editors had read the study.

Ellsberg told Sheehan that he had two conditions that had to be met before he could give the study to the *Times*. One, he wanted the *Times* to devote substantial space so that a great portion of the 7,000 pages was published. Two, he wanted the newspaper to print documents. It would not be enough to print a report based on the documents. Ellsberg wanted readers to read the documents themselves.[74] Sheehan made it clear to Ellsberg that he and the *Times* editors had to see the documents first. The meeting ended without either man making a commitment of any kind.

CHAPTER THREE

The *New York Times* Publishes

Throughout the litigation and thereafter the *Times* publicly took the position that the Pentagon Papers study was nothing but a history with absolutely no relevance to current military, diplomatic, and intelligence interests. It expressed outrage that the Nixon administration had the temerity to sue it for a prior restraint on the preposterous grounds that the top secret material implicated national security. It pretended it was shaken with surprise by the lawsuit and portrayed itself as flabbergasted that anyone could maintain in good conscience that grounds existed for what it termed "an unprecedented example of censorship."[1]

The position the *Times* took in court belied the turmoil within the paper's ranks over whether it should publish the papers at all. *Times* officials argued vehemently over whether the newspaper should publish the top secret reports. Those opposing publication worried it might inadvertently injure one aspect or another of national security interests or undermine government officials' confidence that their communications would be kept confidential. Moreover, the *Times*'s lawyers had warned that publication would violate federal espionage laws and that the administration might even seek an injunction barring the *Times* from publishing the classified reports. These warnings affected the *Times*'s publisher, Arthur Ochs Sulzberger, who seriously thought he might be criminally prosecuted for violating the espionage laws. Indeed, the possibility of publishing the Pentagon Papers created such a furor within the *Times* and ignited such dire warnings of criminal and civil liability that Sulzberger took the highly unusual step of retaining for himself the final authority to publish the reports. Thus, the *Times*'s publication of the Pentagon Papers only followed acrimonious debate over the serious potential risks inherent in the enterprise. The fact that the *Times* went forward under these circumstances is evidence of how important it considered the planned news reports. It reflected its belief that it had a constitutional right to publish the information even if publication gave rise to a legal confrontation. It also indicated that the *Times*, similar to the government, considered the publication of the Pentagon Papers to be an extraordinary event in the history of the press, an event raising profound questions concerning the press's obligations and legal rights.

■ ■ ■ ■ ■

Neil Sheehan was uncertain whether the *New York Times* would publish the top secret Pentagon Papers, assuming he could get his hands on them. He did not know how the newspaper's managing editor, A. M. (Abe) Rosenthal, would react, given that he supported the American war effort in Vietnam. He worried that the *Times*'s renowned columnist James Reston might oppose publication, because he was friendly with many former government officials, especially former Defense Secretary Robert S. McNamara, who would be embarrassed, if not discredited and shamed, by the disclosures. He knew that reporters and editors doubted whether Sulzberger would ever permit the newspaper to publish information that might lead to a head-on collision with the government.[2]

A relative newcomer to the *Times*, Sheehan was also unsure how to determine whether the *Times* would publish the Pentagon history. He turned first for advice from Robert Phelps, a news editor, in early March 1971. Phelps told him to speak to Max Frankel, the Washington bureau chief, or Reston.[3]

Sheehan next spoke to *Times* columnist Tom Wicker. Wicker had met Ellsberg in Vietnam in 1966, when Wicker accompanied Vice President Hubert H. Humphrey on a tour of Asian capitals.[4] They had kept up with each other over the years, and Ellsberg had mentioned the Pentagon Papers to Wicker a few weeks before during a telephone conversation. So when Sheehan asked Wicker what his reaction was to the idea of a secret Pentagon history of the war, Wicker quipped: "Oh, you're getting this from Dan." Sheehan's response was noncommittal. Wicker advised Sheehan to speak to Reston: if Reston favored publication, it would probably be published; if he opposed it, probably not.[5]

Reston's career "had been magic from the start," and by the end of World War II he was considered by Arthur Hays Sulzberger, then the publisher of the *Times* (and father of Arthur Ochs Sulzberger), as the "single most important asset on the newspaper."[6] During the 1950s Reston was, in the view of journalist and author David Halberstam, "the dominant Washington journalist . . . and owned that town as no print reporter would ever own it again."[7] In his study on the press Wicker concurred: "by anyone's measure [Reston was] the most prestigious and respected reporter in Washington."[8]

Sheehan met with Reston and told him he had a chance of obtaining a classified, multivolume, secret history of the Vietnam War prepared at the Pentagon while McNamara was defense secretary. He explained it would put Reston's friend McNamara in a critical light. He asked whether the *Times* would publish the classified material. Reston said he would try to find out. Although Reston seems to have consulted only with Ivan Veit, a close adviser to the publisher, Reston told Sheehan a few days later that he could proceed with the endeavor.[9]

Within a few days Frankel returned to the Washington office and learned of these developments. He then told Sheehan he could not support the project or discuss it with Rosenthal until he saw some of the classified material.[10]

A few days later Sheehan gave Frankel documents concerning the Tonkin Gulf incident. Sheehan did not get these documents from Ellsberg. The two were having conversations about the documents during these first few weeks in March, but Ellsberg had not allowed Sheehan to read any of them. It is uncertain who gave these documents to Sheehan, and he has not identified his source. He might have obtained them from someone in Senator Fulbright's office or from some other public official to whom Ellsberg may have given them. What is more likely is that he obtained the documents from Marcus G. Raskin and Richard J. Barnet of the Institute for Policy Studies.[11]

Frankel and Sheehan examined the Tonkin Gulf documents in Frankel's office. It did not take Frankel long to be convinced of their authenticity and importance. He then went to New York, taking the documents with him for a discussion with Rosenthal, James Greenfield, the foreign affairs editor, and Seymour Topping, the assistant managing editor. They agreed that the documents seemed genuine and that the secret Pentagon study might constitute a major story. But until Sheehan obtained the study, there was nothing more to be done.[12]

▪ ▪ ▪ ▪ ▪

On March 13, 1971, thirty-eight-year-old James C. Goodale, a vice president and general counsel of the *Times*, attended the annual Gridiron Club dinner in Washington as Max Frankel's guest. Goodale had previously worked at the New York law firm of Lord Day & Lord but began working for the *Times* when its legal work increased to a point that it needed an inside attorney.

The membership of the Gridiron Club was limited to leading members of the print and electronic press. The annual dinner was attended by politicians and press figures and featured a show that spoofed politicians, especially presidents. During the evening Frankel confided to Goodale that his bureau had obtained some highly classified documents concerning the Vietnam War. Frankel said nothing more and sought no advice. When Goodale returned to New York, however, he looked into the *Times*'s legal liability if it published classified material.[13]

Goodale focused on two provisions of the federal espionage laws. Section 794(a) criminalized the disclosure of information "relating to the national defense" to a foreign government, when the disclosure was done with the intent of injuring the United States or giving an advantage to a foreign government.[14] Goodale thought this statute punished "old-fashioned espionage"—the unauthorized disclosure of defense information to a foreign enemy—and thus irrelevant to the *Times*'s possible publication of classified material.[15]

Goodale was less certain about the *Times*'s legal liability under Section 793(e). That provision prohibited a person who had "unauthorized possession" of information "relating to the national defense" from communicating it to a person unauthorized to receive it, provided that the person believed the disclosure could injure the United States.[16] Since the *Times* was not authorized to possess top secret government documents, at least as that term was used in the regulations, the *Times* might be liable under that particular espionage provision.

Goodale thought the phrase "relating to national defense" might provide an out for the *Times*. Because the phrase was vague, a court might construe it narrowly so that it did not encompass the documents possessed by the *Times*. Goodale was unable to assess this issue, however, since he had neither seen the documents nor received a detailed description of them.

Goodale had a second reaction to Section 793(e). Judicial decisions had established that fundamental due process required that criminal statutes be written with clarity and precision so that a person could determine what conduct was legal and what was proscribed. Goodale thought the phrase "relating to national defense" was perhaps so vague that it did not satisfy constitutional requirements. Although a court may avoid declaring a statute unconstitutional by giving it a definite meaning, Goodale did not think a court would give Section 793(e) a definite meaning by construing it to refer only to government documents classified confidential, secret, or top secret. Too much government information that bore little or no relationship to the national defense was classified to permit such a construction. Thus, Goodale thought that a court might declare the statute void and unenforceable because it was impermissibly vague rather than give it an unpersuasively narrow interpretation.[17]

▪ ▪ ▪ ▪ ▪

After several discussions Ellsberg agreed to make the papers available to Sheehan. On Friday March 19 Sheehan and his wife, Susan, a writer, traveled to Cambridge, Massachusetts, and checked into the Treadway Motor Inn as Mr. and Mrs. Thompson. As previously arranged, Sheehan met with Ellsberg, who took him to an apartment in Cambridge. Ellsberg allowed Sheehan to read the Pentagon Papers, the Joint Chiefs of Staff report on the Tonkin Gulf incident, and early drafts of some historical studies that ultimately became part of the Pentagon Papers. He withheld from Sheehan the four volumes that traced the diplomatic history of the war from 1964 to 1968, so as to minimize any criticism that he had jeopardized peace discussions, and the footnotes, out of fear they might compromise U.S. intelligence interests.[18]

The understanding between Ellsberg and Sheehan remains unclear to this day. What seems likely is that Ellsberg gave Sheehan permission to read the classified material and to make notes on what he read. He did not give Sheehan permission to copy or to duplicate the documents in any way.[19] Sheehan accepted these terms, and Ellsberg gave Sheehan a key to the apartment so he could come and go as he pleased over the weekend.

Ellsberg must have realized he was taking a risk by leaving Sheehan unmonitored with thousands of pages of newsworthy, top secret documents. Sheehan was an able news reporter who had already publicly called for a war crimes investigation. Sheehan might well look upon the secret history not only as evidence of war crimes but as the spark that might prompt an official war crimes inquiry. Indeed, the whole situation suggested that Ellsberg wanted and expected Sheehan to do precisely what he told him not to do: photocopy the documents.

Ellsberg wanted the documents out and the *Times* was the best option he had for making them public. But Ellsberg did not want to give Sheehan the documents, because lawyers had told him he ran the risk of going to prison if he gave the documents to the press. Thus, Ellsberg may have decided that the best way to reduce his risk of criminal prosecution was not to give Sheehan the documents but to place him in a situation in which he could do precisely what Ellsberg told him not to do.

Once alone with the documents, Sheehan apparently swiftly proceeded to photocopy the documents. From a pay phone Sheehan called William Kovach, the *Times*'s Boston correspondent. Sheehan told Kovach he wanted to copy some important documents he had obtained from MIT and that he had to return them by Monday morning. He also told Kovach he needed money to pay for the photocopying. Kovach called the owner of a photocopy shop in Bedford who agreed to hire additional help for the weekend so the job could be completed by Monday morning. Sheehan and his wife loaded the documents into several shopping bags and took a taxi to Bedford. Kovach telephoned the *Times*'s New York office and asked that $1,500 be wired to him, which it was. Although the photocopying machines in Bedford broke before the job was completed, a second shop was located, and the job was completed by the end of the weekend.[20] It is not known if Sheehan or Ellsberg saw or spoke to each other at the conclusion of the weekend.

Although Sheehan has not offered a public explanation for his actions, he was likely motivated by several considerations.[21] As did Ellsberg, Sheehan believed that the disclosure of the secret Pentagon history might well shorten the war and force a war crimes investigation. Sheehan was unsatisfied with his reporting assignments, and his prospects at the *Times* seemed limited. Getting his hands on McNamara's secret Vietnam history may have been a way of resuscitating his reporting career and his chances of becoming a *Times* editor. It would also give him a crack at winning a Pulitzer Prize.

Sheehan and Ellsberg stayed in touch with each other during the next several weeks. Apparently Sheehan never told Ellsberg he had photocopied the documents, and Ellsberg never told Sheehan—at least in so many words—that he could do so. What they said to each other is not known, but the conversations served to keep each somewhat informed of the other's actions. Ellsberg, who was still hoping to orchestrate the disclosure of the Pentagon Papers, wanted to stay abreast of Sheehan's activities. Sheehan, worried that Ellsberg might give the papers to another reporter, wanted to stay informed of Ellsberg's movements.[22]

▪ ▪ ▪ ▪ ▪

Upon his return to Washington Sheehan immediately set to work trying to make sense of the disorganized and voluminous documents. After a few weeks it was clear he needed assistance. Greenfield sent Gerald Gold, one of his assistants, to help Sheehan digest the documents and plan the news reports. Gold arrived in Washington on April 5 and registered at the Jefferson Hotel on Sixteenth Street in Washington, just a few blocks from the White House. For the next two weeks he and Sheehan pored over the unorganized material. They tried to identify information that seemed new and to make judgments about the comparative importance of the information contained in the history. It was a demanding task, given the array of documents: military reports, texts of cables, historical analyses, and memoranda. After two intensive weeks the reporters told Frankel they were ready to make a report.[23]

While Gold and Sheehan worked their way through the documents in Washington managing editor Rosenthal was wrestling with the idea of publishing the Pentagon's secret history. Rosenthal was the most politically conservative editor at the newspaper by the spring of 1971. He was not against the war, and he hated the idea of publishing top secret information that would bolster opponents of the war whom he did not respect. But the more he learned about the secret history, the more convinced he became that it was not only newsworthy but of great significance, because he thought it proved—through government documents themselves—that successive administrations had misled the public and the Congress on Vietnam policy.[24]

Rosenthal, however, had two initial worries. First, was the material genuine? Did it really come from the government? He often inquired how Frankel, Sheehan, and Gold could be certain the documents were not fabricated. They reassured him they were familiar with the events covered and were acquainted with many of the government figures who participated in the key decisions and wrote some of the documents. They told Rosenthal that the documents had the unmistakable ring of authenticity about them.[25]

Second, Rosenthal worried that publication of the material might gravely weaken privacy in the government. To answer the question of whether government officials would write candid reports if the *Times* published such a massive leak, Rosenthal and Greenfield, one of Rosenthal's closest allies, canvased nearly four dozen books written by former government officials during the Kennedy and Johnson years. The *Times* editors posed one question: To what degree did these former officials disclose classified information in their books? They concluded that former government officials often disclosed classified information, and that the proposed *Times* publication would not measurably aggravate the problem of governmental confidentiality.[26]

■ ■ ■ ■ ■

The fact that Sheehan had obtained the top secret documents and that he and Gold were studying them in Washington was itself a guarded secret within the *Times*. Indeed, it is uncertain whether anyone apart from Rosenthal, Frankel, Greenfield, Reston, and Wicker was aware of these developments until mid-afternoon of April 20. At that time a dozen *Times* reporters, editors, and executives crowded into James Reston's cluttered office to hear Sheehan's report on the project. Sheehan described the origins of the study, its scope, the nature of the documents that composed it, the topics covered, and what the study revealed about these events. He told those assembled that he had not obtained four volumes detailing the diplomatic history of the war. He expressed the conviction that the documents were authentic. He stated that many people knew of the existence of the study and that some individuals had a copy and might leak it to the press, thus scooping the *Times*.[27]

A general discussion ensued, most of it centering on two issues. The first was whether the study was significant enough to warrant publication. Although only Sheehan and Gold had studied the documents carefully, those gathered agreed, based on Sheehan's report, that the papers established that the U.S. government had systematically deceived the American people during several administrations about the purpose of American involvement in South Vietnam, the risks of involvement, and the likely duration, destruction, and costs of the war. They agreed that, to the extent the documents proved these points, they warranted publication.

The second issue was how the *Times* should present this secret history. A distinction was made between the *Times* writing a history of the war using the secret study as a source and the *Times* featuring as its report the government's history of U.S. involvement in South Vietnam. It was agreed that what was significant and special about the study was that it constituted the thinking of government officials about why and how the United States was involved in Vietnam and that the focus of the *Times* report should be presentation of the government's documenting history.[28]

At Frankel's request James Goodale attended the meeting. Goodale explained that it was possible the Nixon administration would sue the *Times* for a prior restraint. He expressed the view that he felt "instinctively" that "a judge would sign a temporary restraining order . . . simply because he would be afraid, as would any normal person, of the unknown," having had an enormous amount of material "dumped in his lap with 'top secret' marked on it."[29] He stated that the chances of a prior restraint action would be significantly increased if the *Times* published the material over several days or if word of the planned reports leaked out prior to publication. He urged those present to keep the project's existence confidential even within the *Times*.[30]

■ ■ ■ ■ ■

Arthur Ochs Sulzberger had unexpectedly become the *Times* publisher at the age of thirty-seven—the youngest chief executive the paper had ever had—when his brother-in-law, Orvil Dryfoos, suddenly died after being publisher for a brief two years.[31] Because it was not expected that Sulzberger would occupy the powerful publisher's post, "he had been in no way prepared for the job."[32] As he candidly confessed to Harrison Salisbury, "My career did not look promising. I'd go up to Orv occasionally and ask him to give me something to do. I was in charge of the cafeteria and purchasing. Nobody wanted to give me anything to do—no honest-to-God-job. But then all the proverbial shit hit the fan and overnight there was the change."[33]

Sulzberger, as described by Gay Talese, "was a friendly, unostentatious, young man who had curly, dark hair, smoked a pipe, wore Paul Stuart suits, and always said hello to whoever was in the elevator."[34] But as friendly and approachable as he was, Sulzberger did not inspire confidence or trust in the news department. As Salisbury, the memoirist of the Sulzberger family, has written: by 1971 Sulzberger "had been running the *New York Times* for eight years but he was still thought of by his associates as young, relatively untested, something of an uncertain factor."[35] David Halberstam reached a similar conclusion in his study *The Powers That Be*: "There was a general feeling in the newsroom . . . that he was a pleasant well-meaning young man whose main preoccupation was with the business side and making money."[36] Sulzberger was liked but not seen as a source of strength and leadership within the newspaper.

It was only after the meeting in Reston's office that Sulzberger learned the newspaper had the Pentagon Papers and was preparing them for publication. Reston himself may have been the one who informed Sulzberger of the project, and then by telephone.[37] It is also not known what the publisher's very first reaction was to the project.

What is certain, however, is that once Sulzberger's advisers—Harding F. Bancroft, an executive vice president, Ivan Veit, a senior vice president, and Sydney Gruson, the publisher's assistant—learned of the project, they warned Sulzberger that publication of the classified material might create serious legal problems.[38] Bancroft also telephoned Louis M. Loeb, a senior partner at Lord Day & Lord who had been giving the *Times* legal advice since 1929, and told him of the development. Loeb was furious that the *Times* would even consider publishing the top secret report. He thought it out of character—perhaps irresponsible—for the *Times* to publish classified material that might endanger national security. Bancroft almost certainly informed Sulzberger of Loeb's reaction.[39]

A few days later, at Sulzberger's request, Loeb and two assistants met with Sulzberger, Reston, Bancroft, Goodale, Rosenthal, Greenfield, and Topping at the *Times*.[40] Loeb made clear that he strenuously opposed the *Times* disclosing top secret information. He advised that publication would violate the criminal espionage statutes as well as the executive order creating the classification system. He warned that the government would criminally charge the *Times* and its officials, that it would gain a conviction, and that some *Times* personnel would be imprisoned. Loeb also said that he considered the proposed publication unpatriotic and outside the *Times*'s tradition. He urged the newspaper officials to return the documents to the government. If they were unwilling to return them immediately, Loeb said they must inform the government that the newspaper possessed the material and then comply with the government's directives.[41]

Goodale disagreed with Loeb. He did not share Loeb's view that the *Times* would betray its own tradition if it published the classified history. Rather, Goodale thought the *Times* would betray itself if it refused to publish the material. Goodale also claimed that he thought it was far from certain whether the proposed publication of the classified information would violate any aspect of the federal espionage law. Under these circumstances, and because he generally believed that obstacles to publication could usually be circumvented, Goodale urged publication. In doing so Goodale conceded that the administration might sue the *Times* for an injunction but stated he did not think this possibility should bar the *Times* from going ahead with plans.[42]

Although it may have been apparent only to Goodale, Loeb's analysis of the *Times*'s potential legal liability had its shortcomings. Whether publication of the classified material would violate the espionage laws was an unsettled legal question. Even if a court concluded that publication of classified material violated one aspect or another of the espionage laws, it would be a serious legal question whether the espionage laws violated the constitutional guarantees for a free press. As for Loeb's point that publication would violate the executive order that established the classification system—that was totally irrelevant to the *Times*, since the executive order did not impose penalties on persons outside the executive branch.

▪ ▪ ▪ ▪ ▪

Sulzberger had serious doubts about the project. He thought the classified material was less significant than his editors did. He disliked the idea of publishing the text of top secret government documents. He was scared by Loeb's advice that he might go to prison if the *Times* published the Pentagon history.[43] Accordingly, he told Rosenthal that he was withholding approval to publish the material, that he was retaining that authority for himself in this project, and that he wanted to see all the material slated for publication before he would consider granting final approval.[44]

Rosenthal remained committed to the project. He thought that the point made by the Pentagon Papers—that successive administrations had misled the Congress and the public about American involvement in Vietnam and the war—was of overwhelming significance and that the *Times* had to publish. Rosenthal also saw the disclosure of the study as an extraordinary opportunity for the *Times* and himself. Rosenthal did take seriously Loeb's warning that he might go to prison for violating the espionage laws, but he was confident that the editors and reporters would edit the documents so no information damaging to the national security was disclosed. Under all the circumstances Rosenthal was determined to go forward and risk imprisonment.[45]

Rosenthal worried about Sulzberger's reaction to the project. To assure that the project went along smoothly and to minimize the possibility that Sulzberger would ultimately withhold his approval, Rosenthal decided to supervise the project more directly than he might have otherwise, and he placed Greenfield in direct charge. He ordered the reporters to prepare the material for publication in New York.[46]

Loeb's dire warnings also heightened Rosenthal's eagerness to keep the project confidential. He worried that the FBI might learn that the *Times* had the documents and that it might try to seize them. He also was concerned that if other news organizations learned of the project, they might manage to obtain their own copy of the Pentagon history and somehow publish before the *Times* did, and Rosenthal did not want to get scooped. To protect the project's confidentiality, Rosenthal first located it in out-of-the-way offices within the *Times*'s Forty-third Street headquarters in the hope it would go unnoticed. But he quickly concluded that tighter security was required. He directed an assistant, Peter Millones, to identify adequate hotel space in which to hide the project. Millones rented some rooms in the Hilton Hotel. Rosenthal gave the project a code name—Project X—and ordered everyone associated with the project to keep its existence confidential. He directed the reporters not to contact any of the authors of the Pentagon Papers study or any of the participants in the government decisions that led to the U.S. military involvement in Vietnam. He ordered the reporters he had brought from out of town to assist on the project to report only to the Hilton, to keep their presence in New York a secret, and not to appear at the *Times*'s offices on Forty-third Street. He hired security guards to watch the hotel rooms twenty-four hours a day and routinely had the telephones and hotel rooms checked for listening devices.

The meeting with Loeb triggered a series of debates within the *Times* that lasted several weeks. Top officials who had been informed about the project argued over whether the newspaper should publish the material at all. Rosenthal, who was supported by Reston, Frankel, Wicker, Greenfield, and Goodale, strongly favored publication. They believed the classified history constituted groundbreaking news.

The major opponent to publication within the *Times* was Executive Vice-President Harding Bancroft. Bancroft had served with the Office of Price Administration, then as counsel to the Lend-Lease Mission in North Africa, and finally as a lieutenant in the Navy during World War II. Following the war he served in the State Department, assigned to the Bureau of United Nations Affairs and then as deputy United States representative to the United Nations Collective Measures Committee, a panel concerned with peace and security. In 1953 he left the foreign service to work as legal counsel for the International Labor Office, a UN affiliate with its headquarters in Geneva. Bancroft joined the *Times* in 1956 as assistant secretary and associate counsel. He was promoted as secretary the next year and then became executive vice president in 1963.[47]

Bancroft shared Loeb's perspective that it was out of character for the *Times* to publish this classified material. What that meant to Bancroft—or to Loeb for that matter—was not at all clear. The *Times* certainly published classified material on a regular basis. Indeed, as the *Times* was to claim during the subsequent litigation over the Pentagon Papers, the publication of classified material was the lifeblood of meaningful reporting, at least with regard to diplomatic and military affairs. Perhaps Bancroft was disturbed by the dimension of the security leak or that the leaked material was relevant to a war that still engaged over 150,000 American soldiers. Like Loeb, Bancroft also worried about the economic and political consequences that might befall the newspaper if it published the material, especially since the government had substantial power over the newspaper's television stations.[48] He accepted Loeb's legal advice that publication would constitute a felony and that the government would prosecute the newspaper and those individuals responsible. He urged that the newspaper terminate the project.[49]

Apart from the threshold issue of whether the *Times* should publish the information at all, *Times* officials had to contend with three other significant matters affecting publication. First, they were concerned that the

Times not publish material that would injure current military plans or undermine intelligence interests. Rosenthal had several individuals read through the material time and again with an eye toward identifying such information. As they studied the documents, they concluded that the classified material contained little information that would threaten current military or intelligence interests if disclosed. As a result *Times* officials withheld very little information from the public, and no one can remember precisely what this information was, precisely why it was withheld, or how much there was of it, but it is unlikely that it was much.[50]

Second, *Times* officials had to decide whether to publish the material in one installment or several. Goodale wanted all the material published in one day, an approach that would eliminate the possibility that the administration would seek a prior restraint against the *Times*. Rosenthal, Reston, and Frankel strongly opposed Goodale's proposal. They viewed Goodale's suggestion as tantamount to running from the sheriff, and they would have nothing to do with it. They wanted to publish the material over several days: a single, massive issue would be too much for the average *Times* reader to read and digest.[51]

Last, *Times* officials quarreled over whether to publish the text of government documents that formed the basis of the historical narratives written by government analysts and that constituted about one half of the overall study or, rather, to quote selected portions or to paraphrase them. Again Rosenthal took a strong position. Rosenthal believed that publication of the documents was essential to the success and integrity of the project. If the *Times* was going to disclose a secret government history of a war that was tearing the nation apart, Rosenthal thought it had better anticipate sharp and demanding questions about the accuracy of its report. In his mind the *Times*'s best and most persuasive response to the inevitable and expected challenge was the government documents themselves. Thus, Rosenthal wanted them published so readers could decide for themselves whether the *Times* fairly presented the government's history.[52]

Bancroft, John Oakes, the editor of the editorial page, and Lester Markel, former editor of the Sunday edition disagreed with Rosenthal.[53] They made several arguments: publication of the documents themselves would undermine government confidentiality; the *Times* could gain whatever support it needed to guard against charges of distortion by selectively quoting from the documents; and publication of the documents would cause the administration to sue for a prior restraint.

Sulzberger had a second meeting with the Lord Day & Lord attorneys on May 12. This time Loeb was joined by Herbert Brownell, Eisenhower's former attorney general, an influential member of the Republican party, and the senior partner at the firm. Sulzberger asked Gruson, Bancroft, and Goodale to join him; he invited no one from the news department to the meeting.[54]

The substance of the attorneys' advice had not changed. Brownell repeated Loeb's warning that *Times* officials would violate the espionage laws if they published the classified material. Loeb emphasized, as he had in the April meeting, that publication would violate the executive order establishing the classification system. He claimed that the publisher's father, Arthur Hays Sulzberger, would not have published the material.[55] Neither Loeb nor Brownell raised the possibility that the administration might seek a prior restraint against the *Times*, and the issue was not discussed.

Goodale answered Loeb and Brownell's arguments. He contended that the *Times*'s publication plans would not violate the espionage laws or the classification rules. He recited the arguments that had persuaded him in March when he first researched the question of legal liability. Goodale also urged Loeb and Brownell to examine the classified material themselves so that they too could become convinced that this was historical material that did not threaten current national security interests. But they refused. Brownell insisted that reading the papers might itself be a crime and impose upon them an obligation to inform the government that the *Times* had the papers.[56]

After hearing all the arguments, Sulzberger adjourned the meeting without disclosing what he thought.

▪ ▪ ▪ ▪ ▪

Tension at the *Times* increased toward the end of May. It was nerve racking enough that basic questions—whether to publish the story or not and whether to publish the documents or not—remained unresolved. But the slow pace at which the *Times* was readying the material for publication convinced many that another news organization would scoop it. This was certainly a worry for Rosenthal and Frankel: "'We were just tormented by the notion that somebody else would dribble this stuff,'" Sanford Ungar has quoted Frankel as confessing.[57] Sheehan was also anxious. He knew that Ellsberg was driven to make the papers public and that he was still trying to persuade prominent public officials to release them.[58]

As much as Rosenthal remained staunchly in favor of publication, he became increasingly worried that publication might gravely harm the *Times*. As he reflected years later, the material in question was "not just history. . . . The government didn't consider this just history. The government consider[ed] it confidential secrets. They were marked 'secret,' 'top secret' . . . and [it was] kind of terrifying in a sense to look at it in a middle of a war." Rosenthal had the terrifying vision of President Nixon gathering former Presidents Truman, Eisenhower, and Johnson together on television to denounce the *Times* for jeopardizing the national security. He had images of the *Times* readership rebelling against the newspaper because it put the nation at risk during wartime. Rosenthal brought these concerns to Sulzberger's attention.[59]

Rosenthal was also upset because he was uncertain that Sulzberger would ultimately permit publication. Rosenthal felt so strongly that the *Times* should publish the material that he decided he would resign if the publisher terminated the project. He even went so far as to ask a colleague at the *Times* to calculate his benefits if he quit.[60]

Goodale was also distraught over the turmoil. Although he thought the threat of criminal liability was minimal, he was agitated that he had failed to persuade the editors to publish the material all at once and thus avoid a prior restraint action. He was also upset that Loeb, Brownell, and Bancroft might have persuaded Sulzberger to end the project. Indeed, the fact that Sulzberger had not as yet closed the door on this horrendous possibility made Goodale feel that the publisher undervalued his legal advice. By the time Goodale took a week off following the birth of his daughter he believed that Brownell and Loeb had finally persuaded Sulzberger to cancel the project. If this happened he decided that he would quit.[61]

The struggle over the project also affected the reporters working on it—and by now they included Hedrick Smith, E. W. Kenworthy, and Fox Butterfield, in addition to Sheehan. They had heard that Brownell and Loeb vigorously opposed publication and had warned that publication would violate the espionage laws. They lacked confidence in Sulzberger's willingness to risk a confrontation with the Nixon administration. As they logged long hours, day after day, polishing the copy, they feared that Sulzberger would decide against publication.

In late May Rosenthal wheeled a large shopping cart into Sulzberger's office. The cart was filled with Sheehan's latest copy and a set of documents that had been edited for publication. This was the first time Sulzberger saw the classified documents or the draft news articles. After he read Sheehan's copy and discussed it with Bancroft and Gruson his serious doubts about the project became firmer. As Salisbury has recounted, Sulzberger thought Sheehan's copy was confusing and "hardly sensational," and he could not see allocating as much space to the project as Rosenthal wanted. Sulzberger even began to think that perhaps "it didn't have to be published after all."[62]

During the next few days Sulzberger changed his mind. Several considerations apparently made the difference. Although Sulzberger did not share Rosenthal's enthusiasm, he decided it was important for the public to have access to the classified study. Sulzberger was influenced by Reston, who urged publication. He was also concerned by the morale problems he expected he would face in the news department if he terminated the project after letting it proceed so far.[63]

When Sulzberger returned the material to Rosenthal some days later he gave his approval. He told Rosenthal that he supported a ten-part series to run on ten consecutive days. He also set June 13 as the publication date for the first installment, the day just before he was to leave for London. Sulzberger also told Rosenthal that he was imposing a six-page daily limit for the series because he was disappointed with the strength of the story and the quality of the copy. He emphasized to his editor that he was still exerting ultimate control over the project: "I want to remind you that I haven't yet given permission for this story. I must see every word of the copy."[64] Sulzberger also told Rosenthal that he remained undecided about the publication of the text of government documents.

Why Sulzberger so resisted publishing the text of government documents was unclear. Publishing the documents did not pose any more of a threat to national security than publishing the information they contained. But Sulzberger may have been concerned that publishing the actual text of government cables might annoy foreign governments, result in substantial criticism of the *Times*, and alienate a portion of the *Times*'s readership. Sulzberger may also have feared that publishing the documents would goad the Nixon administration into seeking a prior restraint or initiating a criminal prosecution, and he was hoping to avoid a legal confrontation with the government. Whatever the reason, Sulzberger remained troubled at the idea of publishing the documents.

▪ ▪ ▪ ▪ ▪

On Thursday afternoon, June 10, Sulzberger read a new lead and a summary of Sheehan's story that was slated for the Sunday paper. It had been worked and reworked by Sheehan and Frankel, and it was better than the earlier version that the publisher had read, and he knew it would be improved upon by Sunday. He was also confident that the news copy did not contain information injurious to the national security, because he had some *Times* officials, most notably Bancroft and Gruson, who did not normally play a role in preparing copy for publication, comb through it.[65] But when Sulzberger met Rosenthal that afternoon, he told his editor that he did not think the story lived up to the editors' promises and hopes for it.

He said he remained unwilling to publish the documents but would agree to their publication if Rosenthal insisted. Sulzberger indicated that they would meet the next morning to decide the issue once and for all.[66]

Once the meeting ended, Sulzberger repeated his reservations about publishing the text of government documents to Gruson, who offered to pursue the question with Rosenthal. He telephoned Rosenthal, told him he wanted to talk with him, and offered to drive him uptown once he was ready to leave the office. As they drove through rush-hour traffic, Gruson pressed Rosenthal on why he was so determined to publish the government documents. As Rosenthal got out of the car, he promised Gruson that he would consider the publisher's preferences and discuss them with Frankel.[67]

Rosenthal and Frankel met at Greenfield's home late that evening. Rosenthal pressed his two colleagues to justify the publication of the documents. He pressed the publisher's point of view as if it were his own. Publishing the documents would increase the cost of the project because of the extra newsprint, would enhance the likelihood that the government would seek a prior restraint, would bore the readers, and would disproportionately dramatize the importance of the story. Frankel and Greenfield gave the answers that they had found persuasive all along: the charge of deliberate, long-term deception by the government—by presidents and cabinet members—was so central to the story that the *Times* had to publish the supporting evidence so readers could judge for themselves whether the reports were reliable. The discussion went on for hours, and the three colleagues did not part until about 3:30 in the morning.[68]

At 9:30 the next morning Rosenthal and Frankel met with Gruson at the *Times*. Gruson wanted to know what they had decided before they met with Sulzberger. Rosenthal recounted the night's discussion and reported, "[I] had come out more firm than when I went in. I'm absolutely sure. No documents, I say, no story." Gruson met with Sulzberger and told him that his top editors were strongly united in favor of publishing the documents and that he would "face a wholesale revolt" unless he supported their decision. He had "to do it their way."[69]

An hour later Rosenthal and Frankel went to Sulzberger's office. They were nervous, ready to argue for their position, and worried that the publisher would make a decision that placed their professional lives in turmoil. After greeting his editors and commenting on the long hours they had been working, Sulzberger said quietly, "I've decided you can use the documents—but not the story." The editors were silent. They were totally confused by what they had heard. It took them a moment to realize that Sulzberger was agreeing to go ahead with the project as they wanted and that he was joking with them. Sulzberger told his editors that he was continuing to impose a six-page daily limit and that, while he was out of the country, Bancroft and Gruson would examine the documents and the text "to make sure there were no military secrets."[70]

▪ ▪ ▪ ▪ ▪

Rosenthal was eating lunch with Greenfield at a delicatessen on Forty-seventh Street on Saturday about half past one when the cashier told Rosenthal that his office had called and asked that he return immediately. The two men rushed to the *Times*. They did not know what could be so urgent. Perhaps the Nixon administration had learned of their publication plans and had telephoned the *Times* seeking information about the publication or, worse, threatening legal action. Or perhaps the publisher had changed his mind, even though the presses would begin to roll into action within four and a half hours. When Rosenthal arrived at the news department, he was handed a copy of Reston's column that was to appear in Sunday's paper. The column's headline was "THE MCNAMARA PAPERS," and the first few sentences informed the reader that the Pentagon's secret history was being published that day. Rosenthal was told that Reston had dictated the column from his mountain retreat at Fiery Run, Virginia, over the telephone to the *Times*'s dictation bank twenty minutes earlier.[71]

Rosenthal was aghast. Reston knew of the security precautions the *Times* had taken to keep the publication project a secret. He knew of the broad concern that the Nixon administration might learn of the project prior to publication and that it was not out of the question that the FBI might raid the *Times*'s offices. And yet Reston had used the ordinary telephone to dictate a column. Rosenthal was beside himself with frustration and confusion. But what Rosenthal did not then know would likely have shocked him even more. Reston apparently thought so little of the need to keep the project confidential that he had told McNamara that the *Times* had the papers and that it was about to publish them.[72]

Rosenthal's anxiety increased. He wanted the afternoon to pass, the presses to roll, and the first installment of the Pentagon Papers to hit the street. The minutes ticked by. He waited. Nothing else happened. Finally, the presses began. At 6:16 P.M. the first papers came up to the city room. The story was out.

CHAPTER FOUR

Nixon's Turnabout

Richard Nixon hated the press. It was his enemy. It attacked his policies without warrant, treated him unfairly, and impeded his efforts to govern. He also hated people who leaked information to the press. He imagined them as thousands of civil servants, appointed during successive Democratic administrations, hidden within the bureaucracy, scheming to undermine his efforts to make good on the mandate the American people gave him when they elected him president.[1]

Considering these attitudes, one would have expected Nixon to become furious as he read the Sunday *Times* of June 13 and learned that the newspaper was embarking on a multipart report based on the Pentagon Papers. After all, the documents were obviously leaked, and the leak was one of the most massive in the nation's history. Although the Pentagon's secret study was nominally entitled a "history," it was certain to have immediate political consequences, and it was likely to have an impact on the war effort, one way or another. Moreover, Nixon believed that the *Times* publication would make it more difficult for his administration to execute his war policies. It would stimulate distrust in South Vietnam, politically embarrass foreign leaders who had secretly acted as intermediaries with the North Vietnamese at the behest of the United States, and give new impetus to the antiwar movement at home.[2]

Surprisingly enough, however, Nixon was not immediately enraged by the *Times* disclosures. He probably was troubled and concerned, but he did not order retaliatory action against the *Times* or demand to know who leaked the classified study. Instead, Nixon decided that his administration should do nothing to interfere with the *Times*'s publication plans and take no action to identify the source of the leak.[3]

This initial reaction, however, proved to be highly transient. By early Monday evening, a mere thirty-six hours later, Nixon's attitude toward the *Times* reports had completely changed. By then Nixon had authorized the Justice Department to sue the *Times* and to seek a prior restraint barring it from publishing further excerpts from the Pentagon Papers. Furthermore, Attorney General John Mitchell had sent the *Times* a telegram requesting it to cease its publication of the classified documents, a preliminary step to suing the *Times*.

What happened between Sunday morning and Monday afternoon to cause Nixon and others in his administration to decide to seek to enjoin the nation's most prestigious newspaper? Who was responsible for this dramatic shift in position? Was the legal action simply part of the administration's offensive against the liberal press? Or did the legal offensive result from more complex personal motivations and understandable national security concerns?

▪ ▪ ▪ ▪ ▪

For about three months the *Times* succeeded in keeping secret the fact that it had a copy of the Pentagon Papers and that its staff, hidden in the Hilton Hotel, was preparing a multipart report based on the papers. Only shortly before June 13—the actual publication date—did news of the impending release seep out from the narrow circle of *Times* personnel who knew of the project.

About ten days before the *Times* began to publish its series, Hedrick Smith, a member of the team helping Neil Sheehan prepare the publication, telephoned Leslie Gelb to get the names of other people who had worked on the secret history. Smith tried to pursue his inquiry without raising any suspicions that the *Times* actually had a copy of the study or was about to publish excerpts from it. Gelb considered Smith's call "strange," but he did not immediately conclude that the *Times* had the classified report. About a week later, however, Smith called Gelb for a second time to ask more questions. Gelb's doubt now vanished. He concluded that the *Times* had the secret history and was about to publish a story based on it.[4]

Gelb had worried all along that the decision he and Halperin had made to permit Ellsberg access to their study would come back to haunt them. Gelb had feared that Ellsberg might make an unauthorized copy of it and bring it to the public's attention. Smith's call convinced Gelb that Ellsberg had done just that and that the *Times* would break the story of the study on Sunday.[5]

Gelb was distraught at the thought of the *Times* report. He felt partially responsible for the security breach, which he could not countenance. He did not think the disclosure of the secret history would help end the conflict in South Vietnam. Although he was working then at the Brookings Institute, a liberal Washington think tank closely associated with the Democratic party, he wanted to return to government and perhaps make a career out of government service. He worried that the *Times* publication would be "so sordid a business" that it really would "ruin" his chances for important government work in the future.[6]

After Smith's second call Gelb telephoned both Halperin and Paul Warnke and told them of Smith's calls and of his surmise. Warnke telephoned Robert McNamara and Clark Clifford, both former secretaries of defense, and told them about Smith's inquiries and Gelb's conviction that the *Times* would break the story of the Pentagon Papers on Sunday.[7] McNamara already knew from James Reston that the *Times* had the study and was going to publish it.[8] For reasons that neither can recall, neither of these two former secretaries of defense alerted anyone within the Nixon administration of this extraordinary security breach.[9]

On Saturday, June 12, word of the *Times*'s imminent publication circulated among a few journalists. Indeed, Reston again breached the newspaper's effort to keep its publication plans secret during his son's wedding in Virginia by telling Donald Graham, son of the publisher of the *Washington Post*, that the *Times* would be publishing a report in Sunday's paper based on classified documents about the origins of the Vietnam War. Graham later telephoned the *Post* and passed along Reston's comment.[10] The same day, David Kraslow of the *Los Angeles Times* said to Tom Wicker, a *New York Times* columnist, on a tennis court: "I hear you guys are going to drop a blockbuster on us tomorrow." Wicker only grinned.[11]

▪ ▪ ▪ ▪ ▪

This seepage did not reach the Nixon administration. Its attention, especially Saturday afternoon, was on the wedding of Nixon's daughter, Tricia, to Edward Finch Cox. After a ceremony in the White House Rose Garden Nixon danced with the bride and his wife (it was the first and only time Nixon danced in the White House) and chatted and laughed with old and new friends.[12]

It was only during the wedding reception that aides to Secretary of Defense Laird learned of the *Times* Pentagon Papers report, when they read the first installment on the *Times* news wire.[13] They informed Laird of the development, and also Alexander Haig, assistant to Henry Kissinger, Nixon's national security adviser.[14]

Laird learned of the "McNamara papers," as he referred to the secret history, when he took office. He claimed he often consulted it to develop policy and to evaluate Senator Fulbright's requests to have it declassified.[15] In spite of his familiarity with the content of the study Laird's concern about the *Times* report on Saturday evening was narrowly focused. He was scheduled to appear Sunday morning on CBS's news program *Face the Nation* and was uncertain about what to say if asked by any of the correspondents about the administration's reaction to the *Times* report. Late Saturday night or early Sunday morning, Laird spoke with Attorney General John Mitchell about what he should say. Mitchell knew nothing about the study apart from what Laird had told him and what he had read in the *Times*. They agreed that Laird would state that the *Times* disclosure endangered national security and that he had asked the Justice Department to review the matter.[16] As it turned out, Laird was asked twenty-seven questions during the thirty-minute news program, and not one of them concerned the Pentagon Papers, even though one of the correspondents questioning Laird was John Finney, a senior *New York Times* Washington correspondent.[17]

Haig had a different reaction to the *Times* report. He had been asked by Gelb and Halperin to participate in the study, so he knew who had authorized it and worked on it and had some impression of the study's scope. Haig telephoned Walt Rostow, who had been Lyndon Johnson's national security adviser while the study was being prepared and was now a University of Texas professor. Haig was in frequent contact with Rostow at the time and called to ask him what he knew of the study and who might have leaked it.[18] Rostow knew little about the history, since the study's staff had tried to keep its existence a secret, at least from him.[19] Harrison Salisbury's *Without Fear or Favor* offers the following account of their telephone conversation:

> "What is this Vietnam study which is going to be in the *New York Times* tomorrow?" Haig asked Rostow.
>
> "Who leaked it?" Rostow replied.
>
> "We think it is a guy named Ellsberg," Haig said.
>
> "The son of a bitch!" Rostow said. "He still owes me a term paper."[20]

Haig surely informed Kissinger of the *Times* report on Saturday evening. Given what he knew of who prepared the report, who might have had access to it, and who might have been motivated to leak the report, Kissinger almost certainly concluded that Ellsberg likely leaked the report.

Kissinger had known of the Pentagon Papers study almost from the time the project began. Kissinger and Gelb had met at Harvard while Gelb was a doctoral student in the government department in the early 1960s. Gelb became Kissinger's assistant and colleague and helped Kissinger teach his defense policy seminar. When McNamara handed Gelb the Pentagon Papers project, Gelb "instinctively" reached out to Kissinger for assistance. As Gelb later explained to Seymour Hersh: "It was utterly natural to think of him. . . . He was my professor at Harvard and I wanted somebody outside the system to get involved." Kissinger even spent a day in Gelb's office discussing the project with Gelb and Halperin (another former Kissinger student), and although he decided not to join Gelb's staff, he maintained a "special status" with the study.[21]

Kissinger not only knew of the study but was familiar with its contents and had used it on at least two occasions to develop negotiating strategies. When Kissinger participated in Johnson's secret effort to end the war by negotiating with Hanoi through two Frenchmen in Paris (an episode described in the Pentagon Papers), Gelb permitted Kissinger access to the drafts of the study's four most sensitive volumes, those detailing prior negotiations with the North Vietnamese. Kissinger also consulted the four diplomatic volumes a second time after he assumed office as Nixon's national security adviser in January 1969, this time as a basis for developing policy.[22] Moreover, Kissinger and Haig may have been the only people in the administration apart from Laird with regular access to it, since they had a copy of the study in Kissinger's White House safe.[23]

Kissinger also knew Ellsberg. From the time he heard Ellsberg lecture in the late 1950s he knew Ellsberg was intense and at times driven. He knew Ellsberg had done a complete about-face over the war and had gone from being a fervent supporter to strenuous opponent of the war. He also knew from Ellsberg himself that the Pentagon Papers had had a tremendous impact on his thinking about the war and America's involvement in Vietnam and that Ellsberg held out hope that others would be similarly affected if they only had an opportunity to read the secret history. Because the Pentagon Papers were massive, the leaker had to be one of the few people who had easy access to the study and who was daring and motivated enough to try to pull off the largest leak of classified documents in the nation's history. In short, all the signs that Kissinger knew of pointed toward Ellsberg.

Although one might think these circumstances would have prompted Kissinger to inform Nixon about the leak before he departed for California Sunday morning, they did not. He left Washington without discussing the *Times* publication with Nixon, even though he thought the disclosures would affect the war and he considered the leak to be a "massive hemorrhage of state secrets."[24]

■ ■ ■ ■ ■

Nixon learned of the *Times* report only on Sunday morning. He was completely surprised and had not known of the study until he read about it in the *Times*.[25] And that was true even though the study's existence had been reported in the press several times by then.[26]

Nixon met with H. R. Haldeman at ten o'clock Sunday morning in the Oval Office. Haldeman made copious notes of Nixon's remarks, as he routinely did whenever he met with the president. For five minutes Nixon discussed his daughter's wedding, the tensions between Pakistan and India, Laird's recent effective support of the president, and the *Times* publications. Nixon told Haldeman that the *Times* report was "really tough" on Kennedy; it made "victims" of Kennedy, McNamara, and Johnson; it made Walt Rostow the "key villain"; it "hurt the war" and "will cause terrible problems with SVN [South Viet Nam]"; and it was "criminally traitorous" for someone to turn the documents over to the *Times* and for the *Times* to publish them. But Nixon emphasized to Haldeman that the *Times* publication "doesn't hurt us," that "we need to keep clear of the *Times*' series," and that the "key is for us to *keep out of it*."[27]

Unlike his strong emotional reaction to so many prime news reports, Nixon's initial reaction to the *Times* Pentagon Papers report was calm. Nixon believed it would make it more difficult for his administration to execute his war policies, and he thought that the report would damage the reputations of the Kennedy and Johnson administrations as well as the Democratic party in general. But he did not believe that the *Times* publication hurt his own administration. Nixon seems to have calculated that his potential political gain from the report far outweighed the injuries the disclosures would cause U.S. military and diplomatic interests.

Like Nixon, White House aides were undisturbed by the *Times* publication of the Pentagon Papers. Neither Haldeman nor John Ehrlichman took any steps to discover anything more about the study than what they read in the *Times*. They did not ask aides to investigate the matter, request White House counsel to evaluate the legal implications of the publication, or call anyone at Justice, State, Defense, the CIA, or the National Security Agency to inquire about the national security consequences resulting from the report.

The Justice Department officials were similarly calm. John Mitchell was not concerned by the report when he read the Sunday *Times*, having heard about it from Melvin Laird the previous day. He took no steps to find out anything about the study on Sunday—who prepared it and when, what it contained, and what impact publication might have on the course of the war. Nor did he have attorneys within the Justice Department review the legal remedies the government might have against the *Times* for publishing the top secret material.[28] William Rehnquist, the assistant attorney general who headed the Office of Legal Counsel and whose office regularly spearheaded legal research projects for the administration, paid no special attention to the *Times* publication on Sunday and can recall taking no action in response to the Sunday *Times* report.[29] Robert Mardian, the assistant attorney general in charge of the Internal Security Division, whose office might investigate such a leak, did not learn of the *Times* story until he returned from California to the Justice Department Monday morning.[30]

▪ ▪ ▪ ▪ ▪

During a thirteen-minute, long-distance telephone conversation mid-Sunday afternoon, Kissinger challenged Nixon's decision to let the *Times* go forward with its publication plans without interference.[31] Neither Nixon nor Kissinger has publicly disclosed the details of this call, but Kissinger has admitted that he "encouraged" Nixon to oppose "this wholesale theft and unauthorized disclosure."[32] In addition Haldeman has maintained that Kissinger, who "really knew how to get to Nixon," told Nixon that his decision to do nothing "shows you're a weakling, Mr. President." According to Haldeman, Kissinger argued that Nixon's decision to "keep out of it" indicated that the president "didn't understand how dangerous the release of the Pentagon Papers was." Kissinger claimed that "the fact that some idiot can publish all of the diplomatic secrets of this country on his own is damaging to your image, as far as the Soviets are concerned, and it could destroy our ability to conduct foreign policy. If other powers feel that we cannot control internal leaks, they will never agree to secret negotiations."[33]

Ehrlichman and Charles Colson, a Nixon aide, shared Haldeman's view that Kissinger pushed Nixon into retaliating against the *Times*. Ehrlichman has written that Kissinger "fanned Richard Nixon's flame white-hot" and claimed that "without Henry's stimulus during the June 13-to-July 6 period, the President and the rest of us might have concluded that the Papers were Lyndon Johnson's problem, not ours. After all there was not a word about Richard Nixon in any of the forty-three volumes."[34] Colson has quoted Kissinger as charging that there "can be no foreign policy in this government," because these "leaks are slowly and systematically destroying us," and insisting that "the President must act—today."[35]

In his memoir Kissinger offered several reasons for pushing Nixon into acting against the *Times*. He claimed that because the documents "in no way" damaged the Nixon presidency, "there was some sentiment among White House political operatives to exploit them as an illustration of the machinations of our predecessors and the difficulties we inherited." But Kissinger asserted that this attitude was "against the public interest." As a general matter, Kissinger contended that our "foreign policy could never achieve the continuity on which other nations must depend, and our system of government would surely lose all trust if each President used his control of the process of declassification to smear his predecessors or if his discretion in defending the classification system became a partisan matter." More particularly, Kissinger claimed that the *Times* disclosures threatened the ongoing secret negotiations with China and North Vietnam, the Strategic Arms Limitation Talks (SALT) and the delicate Berlin negotiations.[36]

Haldeman and Seymour Hersh, Kissinger's biographer, however, take issue with Kissinger's claim that he prodded Nixon to retaliate against the *Times* for disinterested reasons of state. They claim that Kissinger acted out of purely personal motives. Haldeman summarized his view this way: "What really bothered Kissinger . . . was a personal factor. . . . Henry had a problem because Ellsberg had been one of his 'boys.'"[37] Hersh's words were slightly different, but the idea was the same: "Ellsberg was a personal security threat" to Kissinger.[38]

As complicated as Kissinger's reasons and motivations may have been, there seems to be something undeniably persuasive about Haldeman's and Hersh's judgment that self-interest was a major factor guiding Kissinger. Nixon had long blamed Kissinger's staff for the leaks that Nixon believed bedeviled his administration. As early as the spring of 1969, Nixon decided that Halperin, who had left the Pentagon to join Kissinger's staff, was undermining his administration by leaking information to the press that was harmful to his policies. Since then, Nixon was "convinced . . . that most of the serious leaks" came from one or another of Kissinger's national security staff. He thought that Kissinger's staff was "disloyal and overpopulated with liberal democrats."[39] As a result it did not require much imagination on Kissinger's part to anticipate that Nixon would consider the *Times* publication of the Pentagon Papers yet one more example of Kissinger's poor judgment in staffing his office. Kissinger also must have gauged that his rivalry with Haldeman and Ehrlichman would lead them to use Nixon's irritation over this episode to strengthen their own influence within the White House.

Kissinger had several reasons to fear that his close ties to Ellsberg were already known to Nixon, Haldeman, or Ehrlichman or that they would be revealed once Ellsberg was publicly suspected of having given the study to the *Times*. As already indicated, Kissinger had used Ellsberg to prepare an exhaustive Vietnam study after he became Nixon's national security adviser in 1968. During late summer of 1970 Kissinger met Ellsberg twice at Nixon's San Clemente retreat. Kissinger knew that Ellsberg was friendly with Halperin, who Nixon believed had leaked damaging information to the press. Kissinger also knew that the FBI had placed a wiretap on Halperin's telephone in an effort to secure evidence against him, and he feared that the logs of the monitored telephone conversations, which included fifteen conversations between Halperin and Ellsberg, went to the Oval Office.[40]

Kissinger likely realized that the leak to the *Times* threatened his position in the administration. When he spoke with Nixon on the telephone Sunday afternoon from California he probably calculated that he had to take a position that would shore up his standing with the president. By urging Nixon to be tough and to retaliate against the *Times* and whoever leaked the study, Kissinger was probably trying to do what he could to guard against predictable recriminations that he was indirectly to blame for this latest, most serious leak.

▪ ▪ ▪ ▪ ▪

Kissinger's prodding had an impact. By early Monday morning Nixon's reaction to the publication had changed dramatically. He was now seething, furious at the *Times* and at whoever was responsible for the leak. And he wanted something done about it.

Nixon told Haldeman to assess the *Times*'s criminal liability. He had not decided that criminal charges should be brought against the *Times*—that decision would have to wait for a legal analysis to be completed—he only wanted the possibility evaluated.[41]

Nixon also instructed Haldeman—on the second day of the *Times* reports—to have the administration take the offensive against those who were likely suspects for leaking the study. Nixon ordered Haldeman to focus on Gelb, the former Pentagon Paper's staff director; on others who had worked on the project; and on the Brookings Institute, which he considered a center for antiadministration activity. Nixon told his aide he was impatient with those White House staff members who hesitated to criticize Gelb absent some evidence, and he ordered him to "get the story out on Gelb right away." He also suggested that Thomas C. Huston or Patrick Buchanan, two members of the White House staff, "get [the] facts," presumably about Gelb and other Democrats who were responsible for preparing the report, and that Haldeman get Victor Lasky (a reporter Nixon had long admired) to write it in one of his columns. Nixon also told Haldeman to get a senator to make a speech to "smoke Brookings out," to imply that Gelb and others had leaked the report, and to "demand charges against him," presumably meaning Gelb. But for reasons that he either did not offer or went unrecorded in Haldeman's notes, Nixon did not want the senator who made the speech to be Robert Dole, Barry Goldwater, or Strom Thurmond.[42]

At the same meeting Nixon directed Haldeman to be "tougher" with the *Times* and told him it was now time to "really cut them off." Though he cautioned Haldeman that no one should do anything obvious, he emphasized that he wanted the *Times*'s access to the White House strictly limited.[43]

Nixon's instruction to Haldeman was typical. He had frequently sought to intimidate journalists by curtailing their access to White House news sources. After a September 1969 column by Rowland Evans and Robert Novak contained what Nixon considered extremely negative comments on his administration he sent a note to Herb Klein, his communications director: "1. Get some tough letters to these guys from subscribers. 2. Be sure they are cut off."[44] During one four-week period in the fall of 1969 Jeb Stuart Magruder counted twenty-one occasions on which Nixon ordered his aides to "retaliate against what he believed were inaccurate or unfair press reports."[45] When Nixon became dissatisfied with Hugh Sidey of *Time* magazine, he wrote Haldeman: "No contact with him for 30 days will shake him—order this to all hands."[46]

Nonetheless, Nixon's reaction to the *Times* Pentagon Paper series took on an intensity and bitterness that was distinctive even for him. He told Haldeman he wanted everyone within the White House to know that ostracizing the *Times* "must be done." He did not want anyone to return any of the *Times*'s calls, and he did not want any *Times* reporters to be part of any reporter pools that interviewed him or other White House officials or traveled on any of the administration's airplanes.[47]

Not satisfied with mere oral directives, Nixon inscribed his instructions to Haldeman in a five-paragraph, typed memorandum that he initialed and had at the top in bold letters the words "EYES ONLY." Nixon wrote that the *Times*'s "irresponsibility and recklessness in deliberately printing classified documents without regard to the national interest" had convinced him that some action must be taken within the White House. Nixon then ordered: "Until further notice under *no circumstances* is anyone connected with the White House to give any interview to a member of the staff of the *New York Times* without my express permission. . . . Under absolutely no circumstances is anyone on the White House Staff on *any subject* to respond to an inquiry from the *New York Times* unless I give express permission (and I do not expect to give such permission in the foreseeable future)." Nixon informed Haldeman that he considered this a "delicate matter," that Haldeman should give his orders "orally," and that he did not want Haldeman to show this memorandum to anyone. He instructed Haldeman that he should "particularly . . . bring this to the attention of Kissinger, Peterson, Rumsfeld, Finch, Safire, Ehrlichman, Ziegler, Klein and anyone else on the White House staff who might be approached by the *New York Times* for information or for a special story." Nixon insisted that there be "absolutely no deviations within the White House staff because if there is the message will not get through" to the *Times*.[48]

In his memorandum Nixon anticipated that some White House staffers would raise objections to this policy and argue that "we are only hurting ourselves by" it. But Nixon wrote that the matter was closed and was not open to further discussion unless he himself raised it: "I have made the decision because of the national interest and the decision is not subject to appeal or further discussion unless I bring it up myself."[49]

CHAPTER FIVE

The Justice Department's Recommendation

On Monday morning Nixon wanted the *Times*'s criminal liability evaluated, but he did not give Haldeman the sense that he wanted the evaluation done immediately. Taking his cue from the president, Haldeman routinely passed the matter to Ehrlichman, who asked John Dean, White House Counsel, to provide the answer.[1] If no one else within the administration had urged legal action against the newspaper, Nixon's interest in criminally prosecuting the *Times* might have faded away, and his order to freeze the *Times* out of routine White House news channels might have quelled his anger.

But pressure to take some action came from the Justice Department. Despite Mitchell's initial lack of interest in the *Times*'s scoop, one of his subordinates was not so complacent. Robert Mardian was a politically conservative Californian whose family owned a successful contracting business in Phoenix, Arizona, and was active in Republican party politics. In 1964 Mardian had been recruited by his close friend, Richard Kleindienst, to help out in Senator Barry Goldwater's presidential campaign. When John Mitchell turned to the upper echelon of the Goldwater campaign staff to help Nixon win the nomination and the election in 1968, Mitchell became friendly with Kleindienst, who was now his deputy at the Justice Department, as well as Mardian, with whom he played golf regularly.[2]

When the Nixon administration began to make appointments to top government jobs, Kleindienst insisted that Mardian become general counsel to the Department of Health, Education, and Welfare. While there,

Mardian often battled with liberals over the administration's school desegregation policies.[3] When college campuses exploded in May 1970 over the administration's invasion of Cambodia, and the Weathermen and the Black Panthers became increasingly prominent in the news, Mitchell decided that the administration had to respond to what he considered a threat to public order—a threat he believed included bombings, attacks on police, and campus violence. Mitchell asked Congress to pass new antisubversive legislation and shifted some investigative and prosecutorial functions within the Justice Department to the Internal Security Division. In November 1970 Mitchell and Kleindienst brought Mardian to the Justice Department as an assistant attorney general charged with pumping new life into the moribund Internal Security Division, which had dwindled in size and activity over the years.

By June 1971 Mardian had become a controversial figure inside and outside the administration. He was excitable and coarse (even Bob Haldeman, whose abrasiveness was legendary, found Mardian difficult) to the point that he was tagged with the nickname "crazy Bob." His aggressive investigation and prosecution of left-wing political activists and antiwar demonstrators earned him a reputation for disregarding civil liberties and civil rights.

Mardian knew nothing about the *Times*'s Pentagon Papers series until he reached his office Monday morning, June 14, having just arrived in Washington from Los Angeles on the red eye. When he read the Monday Pentagon Papers report, he was alarmed by its national security ramifications. He sent for the Sunday *Times* and consulted with Mitchell and officials from the Departments of State and Defense to determine the publication's effect on national security and diplomatic relations.[4]

Mardian had no trouble persuading Mitchell that the *Times* publication required Justice Department review. Mitchell liked Mardian and shared his political predilections and had great confidence in him.[5] They decided to establish several task forces, drawing lawyers from different parts of the Justice Department to staff them. Each task force was assigned a specific problem or question to research: these issues included the potential criminal liability of the *Times* and its source for publishing the Pentagon Papers; the scope and character of the Pentagon Papers study itself; the national security consequences of the *Times* publication; and the drafting of various legal documents in the event that the administration decided to initiate legal proceedings against the *Times*.[6] Mitchell by-passed both the Justice Department's Civil and Criminal Divisions when he told Mardian to direct and coordinate the review of the *Times* publication.

As of Monday morning neither Mitchell, Nixon, nor Mardian had a clear idea whether the administration would initiate legal proceedings against the *Times* and if it did whether the proceeding would be civil or criminal.[7]

▪ ▪ ▪ ▪ ▪

Mitchell and Mardian asked William Rehnquist to evaluate the government's chances of securing an injunction that would stop the *Times* from publishing future installments of its Pentagon Papers series.[8] Rehnquist had graduated first in his class at Stanford Law School and clerked for Supreme Court Justice Robert Jackson. After settling in Phoenix he developed a successful legal practice, became active on behalf of conservative political causes, and met Richard Kleindienst. In 1969 Kleindienst, now the number two man at the Justice Department, persuaded Rehnquist to become the assistant attorney general in charge of the Office of Legal Counsel within the department.[9] Monday, June 14, was Rehnquist's first day in the office following back surgery, and he worked only half a day.[10] Nevertheless, the fact that Mardian asked him to evaluate the law of prior restraint meant that he would play an important role as the administration decided how to react to the *Times* publication.

Although he almost certainly read a number of relevant Supreme Court opinions, Rehnquist's legal assessment of the hurdles facing the government if it sued the *Times* was guided mainly by *Near v. Minnesota*, the leading Supreme Court case on prior restraint decided forty years earlier.[11] In *Near* a county attorney in Minneapolis sued a local newspaper, *The Saturday Press*, its editors, and its publisher for publishing "malicious, scandalous and defamatory articles" that in substance stated that "a Jewish gangster was in control of gambling, bootlegging, and racketeering in Minneapolis, and that law enforcement officers and agencies were not energetically performing their duties." The state supreme court affirmed the lower court order permanently enjoining the newspaper from further publication and the individual defendants from editing, publishing, circulating, or selling any publication that was malicious, scandalous, or defamatory. By a 5-to-4 vote the United States Supreme Court reversed the judgment of the Minnesota court.[12]

Rehnquist was interested in that portion of Chief Justice Hughes's majority opinion that discussed the circumstances in which a court might grant a prior restraint. Although Hughes wrote that the "chief purpose" of the First Amendment was to guard against prior restraints, he conceded that courts may grant them "in exceptional cases." He quoted Justice

Oliver Wendell Holmes's familiar statement that "when a nation is at war many things that might be said in time of peace are such a hindrance to its effort that their utterance will not be endured so long as men fight." Hughes also stated that he thought that a prior restraint could be secured to stop "obscene publications"; secure community life against "incitements to acts of violence and the overthrow by force of orderly government"; bar " 'words that may have the effect of force' "; and "prevent actual obstruction [of governmental] recruiting service or the publication of the sailing dates of transports or the number and location of troops."[13]

Apart from these suggestions Hughes did not detail the circumstances as to when a court might prohibit the press from publishing a report. But what he wrote allowed Rehnquist to emphasize that the ongoing war in Vietnam enhanced the administration's chances of securing one. It also permitted him to advise that if the *Times* publication threatened national security in a way comparable to the examples offered by Hughes in *Near*, the administration might succeed in stopping the *Times* from further publishing the classified history. In writing his memorandum Rehnquist made no evaluation of the harm to national security resulting from the *Times* publication, and he never reviewed the Pentagon Papers study itself.[14]

The importance of Rehnquist's role that Monday did not depend upon his exceptional legal ability. There was nothing insightful about his conclusion that Hughes's opinion did not completely close the door on prior restraint; Hughes had stated that much. Rather, the significance of Rehnquist's role resulted from his influence within the administration. That influence certainly reflected the general perception that he was a lawyer of superior ability. But it was also based on his conservative political credentials. Rehnquist had been a strong supporter of Barry Goldwater in 1964. He was also considered politically loyal within the Nixon administration, having vigorously defended the invasion of Cambodia and supported Nixon's law-and-order measures, including the right to wiretap citizens when national security was involved.[15] Although Nixon called him a "clown" because of his pink shirts and sideburns and pronounced his name as if it were spelled "Renchburg," he respected Rehnquist's judgment on legal questions, as did others at the Justice Department and the White House.[16] As Kleindienst wrote in explaining why Nixon nominated Rehnquist to the Supreme Court: "For over two and a half years he discharged the difficult requirements of his position with such distinction that he was indeed regarded by all as *the* lawyer for the Department of Justice, as well as the executive branch."[17] Ehrlichman's memoirs contained a similar view: "In 1969, when I was [White House] counsel, I sent him more than a few tough questions, mixed issues of law and policy, and he handled them well, with a sensitivity to the President's objectives and to the practicalities of our situation."[18]

■ ■ ■ ■ ■

While Rehnquist evaluated the law of prior restraint Mardian and his aides encountered many obstacles as they assessed the national security consequences of the *Times* publication. The State Department was of little to no help to Mardian. As the department's spokesman, Charles W. Bray III, told news reporters early Monday morning, it was "difficult" for the department to comment on the classified history because it was unable to determine even if it had a copy of it. Only later in the day, after the study was found in the personal files of William P. Bundy, who had been assistant secretary of state for East Asian and Pacific affairs in the Johnson administration, were department analysts in a position to begin reviewing the enormous document.[19] But whatever efforts these analysts might have made, Mardian does not remember ever receiving an evaluation of the defense and diplomatic consequences of the *Times* publication from the State Department.[20]

The inability of the State Department to locate a copy of the classified history did not prevent Secretary of State William P. Rogers from commenting on the situation. Apparently because foreign leaders complained to the State Department about the *Times*'s disclosures, Rogers told Mitchell, as Mitchell remembered many years later, that further publication of the Pentagon Papers by the *Times* was "inimical to the national interest."[21] Rogers also told Mardian that he was "outraged" by the *Times* publication, and he advised the assistant attorney general to sue the newspaper in an "action in replevin"—a legal action to regain possession of stolen property. Rogers took this tough line against the *Times* even though he had been on the board of directors of the *Washington Post* and had served as its chief counsel before becoming Nixon's first secretary of state. As for Roger's legal advice, Mardian dismissed it, since he considered Rogers a "dummy."[22]

The White House was no more help to Mardian than the State Department as he tried to assess the national security consequences of the *Times*'s disclosures. Only Kissinger and Haig had any firsthand knowledge of the study. But Kissinger spent Monday flying from California to Washington, and Haig seems not to have told anyone that he was familiar with the study. Indeed, Haig may not even have volunteered to his White House colleagues that a copy of the classified history was in the National Security

Council safe. As for Nixon's other White House aides, the existence of the study was a "mystery," as Herb Klein characterized it. It was Klein's impression that when White House staff members tried to determine what the administration should do in response to the *Times* report, there was "more confusion within the White House than at any other time" during his tenure.[23]

In contrast to the White House and State Department, the Defense Department was in a strong position to help Mardian evaluate the risks to national security posed by the *Times* report. The study was prepared at the Pentagon, and although no one who had worked on the study was still employed there, the department had several copies of the study; in addition, Laird and some of his aides were familiar with its contents. As a result Mardian did receive some assistance from the Defense Department, but not as much as he believed he should have.[24]

Laird met with his top aides early Monday morning, as he routinely did. At the meeting Fred J. Buzhardt, the department's general counsel and former aide to Senator Strom Thurmond, reported on a review he had made of the Pentagon Papers on Sunday. Buzhardt had been alerted to the study's existence a few months before by General Robert Pursely, chief military aide to Laird and a former aide to McNamara at the time the Pentagon Papers project was begun. Buzhardt told the group that the *Times* could injure the national security if it published portions from the study's last four volumes, which traced the diplomatic history of the war.[25]

After the meeting Buzhardt telephoned Deputy Attorney General Kleindienst. Kleindienst told him that Mardian was coordinating the review of the *Times* report and that he should call him. Buzhardt, who spoke by telephone with Mardian in the morning and met with him in the afternoon, outlined his concerns over the four diplomatic volumes and perhaps some other passages within the study that some Defense Department officials believed compromised intelligence matters. Buzhardt also gave Mardian a brief memorandum that he and Pursely prepared that outlined the scope of the study and stated who authorized and prepared it.

Laird's position fluctuated that Monday as the administration decided what to do. Mitchell remembered that Laird telephoned him to report that further publication by the *Times* would harm national defense.[26] But Laird has denied that he ever offered that assessment to Mitchell or anyone else in the administration. Laird contended that he was glad the papers were in the public domain, for he felt they strengthened his policy recommendations that the United States should pull its troops out of South Vietnam far more quickly than it was doing.[27]

In different ways Mardian and Kissinger have supported Laird's contention. Mardian has accused Laird of "foot-dragging" on that critical Monday. He has claimed that he asked Laird to have the Pentagon review the national security threat posed by the *Times* publication but that he never received this report.[28] Kissinger has also indirectly supported Laird's claim. When the *Times* broke its story Kissinger thought that Laird had leaked the classified study to promote his own views.[29] Kissinger was probably being facetious, but his suspicion makes credible Laird's contention that he viewed the disclosure of the Pentagon Papers as aiding him in his opposition to Nixon's and Kissinger's war policies.

As pleased as Laird might have been that the papers were out, he was sufficiently loyal to the Nixon administration to make a public statement in which he asserted that the Pentagon Papers contained "highly sensitive information . . . [that] should not have been made public." Laird also criticized the paper's release on the ground that national energy should be directed toward extricating the United States from Vietnam, not raking past policies "over the coals."[30]

What seems plausible is that Laird was genuinely upset about the national security threat posed by the possible publication of excerpts from the four diplomatic volumes or from some of the few passages he believed contained important intelligence matters. But he was also pleased that the newspaper had published the classified material. As a result, when Laird talked to Mitchell he probably stopped far short of urging Mitchell to sue the newspaper. Given the haste with which these conversations were conducted, Mitchell probably understood Laird's qualified concerns as meaning that further publication by the *Times* would jeopardize national security and passed that judgment along to Mardian as further evidence that the administration must act.

▪ ▪ ▪ ▪ ▪

Mardian met still other difficulties as he tried to assess the national security risks presented by the *Times* publication. No one in the Justice Department was familiar with the Pentagon Papers study; indeed, neither Mardian, nor Mitchell, nor any of their aides even knew of the study before the *Times* broke the story. Moreover, they experienced some delay in trying to secure one of the small number of copies of the study then in existence. But when they did receive it, they were nothing short of overwhelmed by the study's size. Surely no lawyer at the Justice Department was going to be able to quickly read the study from cover to cover and identify passages that were injurious to the national security. As a result Mitchell and Mardian never even attempted to review the study once it arrived at Justice.[31] Mardian would have to rely upon the judgments of others in trying to assess the risks to national security presented by the *Times* publication.[32]

Government officials advising Mardian and his aides were themselves handicapped, since they were not able to determine precisely which documents the *Times* had.[33] In its news reports on Sunday and Monday the *Times* announced it had "most" of the Pentagon Papers study, described as consisting of 3,000 pages of analysis and 4,000 pages of official documents. As a result the government officials assumed for the purpose of advising Mardian that the *Times* had the entire study.

Moreover, as government officials reviewed the *Times* report, they concluded that the *Times* had documents in addition to the Pentagon Papers. They identified some of the documents as early drafts of what became the final version of the Pentagon Papers. They knew that other documents were part of a classified study on the Tonkin Gulf incident—a document prepared by the Defense Department's Weapons System Evaluation Group in 1965. But there were still other papers that they could not identify at all.[34] It was difficult enough for Mardian, his aides, and defense officials to assess the national security threat posed by the secret history of the war. But to have to assess the risk to national security posed by the publication of documents that could not be identified was an impossible task.

▪ ▪ ▪ ▪ ▪

In the end Mardian and his aides concluded that the *Times* publication threatened the nation's security for several reasons. The four volumes detailing diplomatic negotiations focused on unresolved, ongoing, important issues that were highly controversial in the United States and abroad. They also detailed the evolution of the Johnson administration's policies toward a negotiated settlement and the sporadic diplomatic contacts between the United States and North Vietnam. In addition the four volumes traced numerous efforts by several other nations to bring the two antagonists to the conference table. For example, the volumes described separate efforts by two Canadians, Blair Seaborn and Chester Ronning, to bring about settlement talks; the initiatives undertaken by Poland and code-named Marigold; the overture named Sunflower, which involved a direct U.S. approach to North Vietnam in Moscow, and parallel attempts by British Prime Minister Harold Wilson and Soviet Premier Alexei Kosygin to begin peace talks; a series of peace moves from early 1967 through early 1968 in which Norway, Sweden, Rumania, and Italy took turns as intermediaries; and an attempt by Henry Kissinger, acting as a private citizen at the behest of the U.S. government, to arrange talks with North Vietnam through two French go-betweens.

Leslie Gelb and Richard Moorsteen prepared the four volumes on the assumption they would be used as background papers if and when negotiations began. Although the Paris peace talks started six months before the volumes were completed, they were immediately sent to the American delegation upon completion. Moreover, once Kissinger became Nixon's national security adviser in January 1969, he used the volumes as a basis for developing policy. Indeed, Gelb has even maintained that the detailed negotiating strategy followed by Kissinger in secret talks was partially derived from recommendations contained in a study based on the four diplomatic volumes.[35]

Mardian and his aides concluded that if the *Times* published material contained in the final four volumes, it would gravely injure diplomatic efforts to end the war and to secure the release of the prisoners of war. He believed, as he said years later, that publication of this material would embarrass the political leaders of foreign countries. He pointed to Sweden to illustrate his point: "Sweden ostensibly was hosting anti-Vietnam conferences in Sweden, and putting on a face to the North Vietnamese that they were against us, but at the same time [they] were doing our bidding." Indeed, Mardian, in a not atypical way, even went so far as to claim that Sweden was "whoring for us" by publicly condemning us, and yet they were "carrying our baggage to the North Vietnamese."[36]

Mardian was not alone in this view that the four diplomatic volumes contained highly sensitive material. When he prepared the volumes Gelb treated the four diplomatic volumes as especially sensitive and permitted only three or four staff members access to them. During the litigation over the government's claim for a prior restraint, Paul Warnke, a former Pentagon official in the Johnson administration, told twenty newsmen at breakfast that public disclosure of diplomatic moves detailed in the diplomatic volumes could create such serious problems that the Nixon administration's lawsuit against the *Times* was warranted.[37] Ellsberg also believed the four volumes were sensitive, so much so in fact that he withheld them from Neil Sheehan, a critical fact that the Nixon administration did not seem to be aware of as it determined its response to the *Times* publication, even though the *Times* had stated on page 1 of its first report that it did not have the four diplomatic volumes.[38]

Although Mardian and Mitchell were unaware of it at the time, most of the events covered in the four negotiating volumes were, as one student of the subject concluded, "described in some detail and with remarkable accuracy in contemporary newspaper accounts and in such books as Kraslow and Loory's *Secret Search for Peace in Vietnam*," which was published in 1968.[39] But it is uncertain what impact that knowledge would have had on these two Justice Department officials. As they viewed it, there was a critical distinction—as there surely is—between a reporter or scholar claiming that Sweden or Canada or Poland acted as an intermediary and the publication of secret government documents that proved the point. The former permitted the United States and foreign leaders to deny—or not comment on—the validity of the claim, reducing the degree of political embarrassment to compromised foreign leaders and enhancing the possibility that foreign governments would continue to act as go-betweens. The latter undeniably established the intermediary's role, created severe political embarrassment for foreign leaders within their own countries, eroded confidence in the ability of the United States to keep highly sensitive information secure, and generally so strained diplomatic relations on all sides as to undermine the likelihood that others would participate in confidential and risky actions as part of the peace process.[40]

Defense and intelligence officials told Mardian that, in addition to the highly sensitive material in the four diplomatic volumes, other parts of the Pentagon Papers would compromise intelligence interests if published. Mardian remembered that the National Security Agency pored over the study and "kept coming up with more and more reasons why this particular information couldn't be published." He recalled great concern among intelligence officials that the publication of some documents within the study would reveal covert information sources. He explained: "the disclosure of the communique would disclose the nature and location of our intelligence gathering—in other words, the fact that we knew of a troop movement within a matter of minutes from the time it began meant that there could be only one way that we could have that information."[41] Laird recently agreed with Mardian's recollection. He maintained that there were a dozen or so paragraphs (some of which were published, although he will not specify which) that ran a high risk of revealing important intelligence information.[42]

Although defense and intelligence officials are characteristically averse to risk and easily alarmed by the disclosure of classified material, there was sufficient cause for concern in this case to make responsible officers deeply uneasy and apprehensive. These officials really did not know the entire scope of what was contained within the Pentagon Papers; they were completely surprised by the *Times*'s sudden publication of the material; they did not know what the *Times* would publish next; and they were compelled to assess the possible threat to intelligence secrets under great time pressure. Thus, Mardian's conclusion that the *Times* reports seriously threatened intelligence matters was completely understandable, and it is not surprising, especially given their biases, that Mardian and others with whom he consulted were gravely concerned.[43]

▪ ▪ ▪ ▪ ▪

Even though Mardian concluded that further publication by the *Times* would harm national security interests, a lawsuit against the newspaper seeking a prior restraint was by no means inevitable. It was always possible to decide that continued newspaper reports might retard the peace process and harm some intelligence interests but that these potential injuries were too uncertain and difficult to assess. Also, in the absence of specific and concrete evidence that further publication would directly threaten lives (as in the publication of the sailing time and course of a troop ship), it was possible to decide against a prior restraint lawsuit because of the fear that the administration could well lose its effort to stop the *Times* and be sorely embarrassed.

But these alternatives were not to be. Mardian did not believe that the government should have to risk harm to the nation's security at the hands of unelected newspaper editors who were making independent judgments about which secret documents to publish. Rather than focusing upon the risks of such a major and unprecedented suit, Mardian concentrated on the injuries that might result from publication and on the fact that prior court decisions had not foreclosed the possibility of securing a prior restraint. Mardian's decision was also colored by his attitude toward the media. He considered the press arrogant and often wrong. He thought the press's role in our political system fell far short of presuming the authority to declassify top secret documents relating to a war in progress. In addition Mardian was from the western United States, had been a Goldwater supporter, and was deeply suspicious of what he viewed as the liberal eastern press. Any remaining uncertainty about the need to stop the Pentagon Papers series would have been further discounted because the *Times* was the publisher.[44]

Given Mardian's views, a prior restraint emerged in his eyes as the only effective legal remedy. A criminal prosecution would take many days to begin, and a trial might not be held for months, perhaps a year or more. And even if the *Times* were convicted, the imposed penalty would only deter the paper from publishing similar material in future situations. This alternative was obviously impractical.

Mardian also viewed a prior restraint order as a means of gaining the time needed to assess the real dangers of the situation. As he recalled years later, a prior restraint action was a way of saying: "Hey! Give us a chance to find out how damaging it is before you go any further."[45]

Mardian's office on that Monday was chaotic, resembling a crowded railway station at rush hour, with admirals, generals, and national security officials coming and going. There were more people to consult, and more research to do, than could be accomplished in the few hours remaining before the *Times* went to press again. No one in the administration (least of all Mardian) thought the newspaper would respond favorably to an informal request to delay its planned installments while government officials assessed the defense implications. Swift legal action seemed the only recourse.

■ ■ ■ ■ ■

But Mardian was only an assistant attorney general. There would be no lawsuit without Mitchell's approval.

Mitchell spent very little time reviewing the alleged national security injuries flowing from the *Times* reports, for he did not see how he could give the matter his own special attention. As he saw it: "There's so God damn many things going on in the Justice Department that it's just another one that you take as it comes along." Mitchell's schedule on that Monday included a drug conference at the White House in the morning, a noon meeting with Haldeman, and lunch with Nelson Rockefeller, governor of New York.[46] Along the way he huddled with Herb Klein to discuss "what was coming next and how we should handle it."[47] Consequently, Mitchell never paused long enough to review relevant legal precedents or the actual evidence that the *Times* series might threaten national security in some significant way. Consequently, when Mitchell approved Mardian's assessment that the administration should try to enjoin further publication, he relied upon Mardian's assessment of the relevant law of prior restraint and of the national security risks.[48]

Mitchell's minimal involvement in what he later termed this "monumental law suit" against the *Times* was typical of him. He had not wanted to become attorney general and was not primarily interested in running the Justice Department. Indeed, the political commentator Richard Harris quoted Mitchell at the time as saying: "'This is the last thing in the world I wanted to do.'"[49]

Unlike many men who appear reluctant to accept high government office, Mitchell was perceived by many people—such as William Safire, who knew and admired Mitchell—as meaning what he said.[50] Mitchell had been a successful bond lawyer in New York, earning more than $200,000 a year in the mid-1960s.[51] At the time of his appointment he felt he already possessed "all the things I ever wanted. I'm a fat and prosperous Wall Street lawyer, which is just what I always wanted to be."[52] In addition

Nixon told Safire that Mitchell was "worried about his wife, Martha. You know, she's had this problem for years, but I told him the hell with it, come down and she'll be all right. Or at least no worse than she was in Rye." According to Safire, Martha Mitchell had "no drinking problem, but a yen for attention and a habit of pouring her heart out to strangers on the telephone late at night." But Nixon "needed" Mitchell. "Nixon saw in John Mitchell a man . . . who, in age, self-confidence, and sense of authority, was at least Nixon's equal. . . . Mitchell was tough." Mitchell was "the rock upon which Nixon built his church." When Nixon's long-time California friend Robert Finch turned down the offer to become attorney general, Nixon turned to Mitchell, who gave in and accepted what the Nixon campaign had characterized as the law-and-order job within the administration. Between his own interests in politics and Nixon's reliance on him Mitchell quickly became deeply involved in many matters outside the Justice Department—so much so that he was viewed as "'the second most powerful man in America.'"[53]

In a general sense Mitchell shared Mardian's assessment of the *Times* affair. Like Mardian, Mitchell saw no reason to risk the nation's security, particularly when Rogers and Laird both claimed that the Pentagon Papers contained material that "would jeopardize the American Government's relationship with other governments" if disclosed. As Mitchell recalled years later, the decision to seek a prior restraint against the *Times* was "a very simple thing . . . [since] nobody in the government believed that the newspapers had *carte blanche* to publish anything they wanted to that was inimical to the best interest of the United States."[54]

▪ ▪ ▪ ▪ ▪

As convinced as Mardian had become, and as powerful as Mitchell was within the administration, no legal action against the *Times* was conceivable without Nixon's express approval. Nixon's anger at the *Times* was certainly intense on Monday morning, but there is no evidence that he considered the possibility of trying to enjoin the *Times* until the Justice Department made the suggestion. As Mardian has remembered the situation, he had more than one conversation with Haldeman during the day, and Haldeman was skeptical about a prior restraint action. Mardian felt that he first had to persuade Haldeman and, through him, Nixon.[55] In the end Nixon was persuaded and gave his approval by late Monday afternoon.

In his memoirs Nixon stated that he approved the action against the *Times* because the National Security Agency was "immediately worried" that some of the "more recent documents could provide code-breaking clues"; the CIA was "worried that past or current informants would be exposed"; the State Department was "alarmed" because the study "would expose Southeast Asia Treaty Organization contingency war plans that were still in effect"; and the international community was shaken because the published study contained material relating to the secret role of various governments who served as diplomatic go-betweens. In addition Nixon asserted that the *Times* publication came at a "particularly sensitive time because Kissinger's secret trip to China was only three and a half weeks away, secret negotiations with North Vietnam were underway in Paris, and the SALT talks were on-going." Although Nixon portrayed these considerations as important, he insisted in his memoir that there was "even a more fundamental reason for taking action to prevent publication." He stated that there was an important principle at stake in this case: "it is the role of the government, not the *New York Times*, to judge the impact of a top security document. . . . If we did not move against the *Times* it would be a signal to every disgruntled bureaucrat in the government that he could leak anything he pleased while the government stood by."[56]

Given that Nixon completely reversed himself between Sunday morning and Monday afternoon, the reasons he offers in his memoirs clearly fail to reflect the evolution of his own thinking. Rather, it seems to represent a summary of the views that Mardian and others put forward and that were perfectly acceptable as "public" positions. It is of course possible that Nixon and his aides received oral reports during Monday indicating that the National Security Agency, the CIA, and the State Department were worried that further publication by the *Times* might injure national security interests. But if Nixon's decision to sue the newspaper was based primarily on such concerns, he would almost certainly have insisted that someone explain the issues in some detail. After all, he would have recognized immediately that a legal attack against the *Times* would be an international event with serious political and public relations consequences. Before incurring such costs, he would at least have wanted to know what the most critical national defense risks were—how grave and how imminent. But we know that neither Nixon nor anyone else within the White House received a briefing on security matters that day. It is difficult to believe that Nixon, who paid such close attention to detail—and must have realized, because of his own prior legal work, that the administration faced a very difficult legal fight—would authorize a prior restraint action against the *Times* solely because an assistant attorney general had decided that it was necessary.

Nor is it persuasive that Nixon gave his approval primarily because of the "important principle" he identified. Nixon had already known, on Sunday morning, that the *Times* had publicly compromised the "principle" that only the government has the authority to declassify documents: indeed, he had told Haldeman on Sunday morning that it was "criminally traitorous" for someone to leak the papers and for the *Times* to publish them. Nevertheless, despite these strong statements, Nixon's reaction to the *Times* publication on Sunday morning was unequivocal: his administration would do nothing.

It is equally unpersuasive that Nixon approved the legal suit because of Kissinger's pending trip to China, or the secret negotiations with North Vietnam, or the SALT talks. Nixon certainly gave these matters high priority—his intense interest in foreign affairs is well known. Moreover, his popularity was low, and he felt the need for some dramatic success in foreign affairs in order to bolster his domestic political support. His ability to carry forward his new diplomatic initiatives would depend greatly on maintaining the confidence of both China and the Soviet Union in the capacity of the United States to protect confidential communications. But Nixon must also have been somewhat sensitive about these diplomatic considerations on Sunday morning, when he decided to do nothing. Moreover, there is no evidence that he expressed—on either Sunday or Monday—these concerns to those aides he most trusted. Haldeman's notes make no mention of them. Mitchell, who was aware of the new diplomatic initiatives, does not recall any discussion of what impact the *Times* publication might have on them.

It would be foolish to deny that Nixon's approval of the legal action against the *Times* may have reflected some apprehension on his part about future unauthorized disclosures of intelligence secrets or current diplomatic initiatives. Such a feeling of apprehension may have developed as Nixon reflected on the entire set of issues over the course of the day. But, given the specific sequence of events of Sunday and Monday—particularly Kissinger's call to Nixon on Sunday—it seems unlikely that national security and diplomatic factors alone caused Nixon to accept Mardian's recommendation. What seems more plausible is that these factors made a prior restraint suit against the newspaper credible and publicly defensible in Nixon's mind but that Kissinger's pressure, especially his contention that Nixon would appear weak if he did nothing, made the major difference. As Nixon's biographer, Stephen Ambrose, concluded: "Nixon hated to appear weak."[57]

Once Nixon decided to take some legal action against the *Times*, he did not concern himself with the pros and cons of a criminal prosecution as opposed to a civil action for a prior restraint order. Nor did he request a review of the precedents for such a move or of the evidence supporting the claim that the *Times* series jeopardized national security. He did not even consult more than one or two White House aides before approving the action. In other words there was essentially no formal or even informal review of all the considerations. Whatever other factors entered into Nixon's decision, Kissinger's call seems to have been the single strongest catalyst.

■ ■ ■ ■ ■

By early evening Mitchell and Mardian had gone to Mitchell's Watergate apartment to review a draft of a telegram that asked the *Times* to cease publication of the Pentagon Papers series. As Mitchell and Mardian worked, Nixon met in the Oval Office with Kissinger, who had just returned from California, and Kenneth Rush, U.S. ambassador to the Federal Republic of Germany.[58] (Rush later joined Mitchell and Mardian at the Watergate once his meeting with Nixon ended.) Although the subject of Nixon's meeting with Kissinger and Rush is not known, Nixon probably brought Kissinger up to date on his decision to sue the *Times*. Kissinger concedes he did not object.[59] When Nixon's forty-five-minute meeting with Kissinger and Rush ended about 6:45 P.M., he met shortly with his secretary, Rosemary Woods, and had brief telephone conversations with George Schultz, Secretary of Labor, and John Ehrlichman. Then, at 7:19 P.M., he had a three-minute telephone conversation with Mitchell, during which Mitchell likely informed him of the telegram he had sent the *Times* a few minutes before.[60]

Mitchell's short, four-paragraph telegram to Arthur Ochs Sulzberger stated:

> I have been advised by the Secretary of Defense that the material published in the *New York Times* on June 13, 14, 1971 captioned "key texts from Pentagon's Vietnam Study" contains information relating to the national defense of the United States and bears a top secret classification.
>
> As such, publication of this information is directly prohibited by the provisions of the Espionage law, Title 18, United States Code, Section 793.
>
> Moreover, further publication of information of this character will cause irreparable injury to the defense interests of the United States.
>
> Accordingly, I respectfully request that you publish no further information of this character and advise me that you have made arrangements for the return of these documents to the Department of Defense.[61]

Although Mitchell's telegram left unstated what the administration would do if the *Times* did not comply with the government's request, he must have assumed that *Times* officials would realize upon receiving such a telegram that the administration was prepared to take legal action unless the newspaper complied. Nevertheless, Mitchell did not leave important matters to chance. He wanted the *Times* to know that the government was prepared to go to court if it had to, and he also wanted to put as much pressure on the *Times* as he could in the hope that the newspaper would voluntarily stop publishing the Pentagon Papers series.

Either just before or after Mitchell sent his telegram, Mardian telephoned Sulzberger in New York, only to discover that he was in London. He spoke with Harding Bancroft, read Bancroft the telegram, and asked him for a response. Bancroft told Mardian he would have to call him back because he had to consult with others before a decision could be made.[62]

At the same time Mitchell telephoned Herbert Brownell.[63] Mitchell called Brownell not only because of his prominence within the firm but because Brownell was a senior statesman of the Republican party and had been close to Thomas Dewey and Richard Nixon. In addition Mitchell and Brownell had just seen each other at Tricia Nixon's wedding two days before.

Mitchell and Brownell have offered different accounts of that conversation. Mitchell confessed he did not remember the specifics of the call but insisted that "basically it was, 'Herb old boy, your client has got no case and you better either pull it or we're going to have to sue you, one or the other.'"[64] Brownell's version of the call is markedly different. According to Brownell, Mitchell told him that the government would sue the *Times* if it did not stop publishing the Pentagon Papers; that the government's suit would be based on the president's executive order establishing the classification system, an order that Brownell drafted as Eisenhower's attorney general; that Brownell's authorship of the executive order created a conflict of interest for the firm and if it chose to represent the *Times* the government attorneys would move to disqualify it; and that the government might call him as a witness to testify about the history, purpose, and meaning of the executive order.[65]

Regardless of which version of the telephone call is more accurate, Mitchell was obviously trying to intimidate the *Times* through its lawyers. Mitchell wanted the firm to instruct its client that it had no right to publish classified material that related to national defense and that if it persisted in publishing the material the firm would not be able to represent the newspaper in any legal proceeding the government initiated.

▪ ▪ ▪ ▪ ▪

The common belief at the time was (and still is) that the administration sought an injunction against the *Times* for a prior restraint in order to intimidate the press. In *The Politics of Lying* David Wise cited the prior restraint action as a prime example of the Nixon administration's "unprecedented effort . . . to downgrade and discredit the American press."[66] A 1971 report of the American Civil Liberties Union written by Fred Powledge characterized the prior restraint action as the "most dramatic" part of the Nixon administration's campaign against press freedoms.[67] The following year, Sanford Ungar reported that the "strong presumption of legal observers . . . [was that] it was impossible to view the crisis over the Pentagon Papers in perspective without considering the overt hostility of the Nixon administration toward the press and the inhibiting effects the hostility produced."[68]

This interpretation is perfectly understandable. Nixon viewed the press as the enemy and hated it. As William Safire confessed after years of working closely with Nixon: "I must have heard Richard Nixon say 'the press is the enemy' a dozen times."[69] By the time Nixon became president his acrimonious and distrustful relations with the press were long-standing and well known. Indeed, many of his confrontations with the press had become common political reference points. Perhaps the most famous of these were his "Checkers" speech in 1952 (when he tried to save his position as Eisenhower's vice-presidential running mate in the face of reports of a secret slush fund) and his "last press conference" (after he lost the 1962 California gubernatorial election) in which he told the press: "You won't have Nixon to kick around anymore."[70] Nixon's actions after he assumed the presidency also lend credence to the view that the prior restraint action was part of an offensive against the press. In the fall of 1969 Vice President Spiro Agnew delivered several speeches that encouraged the public to distrust and discredit the national press services. This attack was reinforced by a number of hostile inquiries aimed at the major television networks by Dean Burch, whom Nixon had recently appointed to head the Federal Communications Commission. Federal investigators also subpoenaed the files, including unused photographs, of national news magazines as part of ongoing criminal investigations. Reporters were brought before grand juries and asked to reveal their sources. When these actions are viewed in light of Attorney General Mitchell's best-remembered public statement ("You'd be better informed if, instead of listening to what we say, you watch what we do") the administration's purpose in suing the *Times* may seem self-evident.[71]

Nevertheless, all the evidence reviewed in these pages suggests that it is a misconception to interpret the Nixon administration's decision to sue the *Times* as one more action intended—either entirely or mainly—to strike yet another blow against the press. Once legal proceedings began, some members in the administration certainly began to discuss the lawsuit in precisely such terms. But these considerations were not initially responsible for driving the administration to undertake legal action.

Mardian's recommendation, endorsed by Mitchell, is inexplicable unless one accepts the fact that national security considerations were at the heart of their concerns. If their main motive had been to intimidate the press, then there were other—far less risky—legal remedies available. They could, for example, have begun a grand jury investigation to determine how the *Times* had secured the classified study. (Later in the summer, the administration in fact began such an investigation.) Or a grand jury investigation might have been launched to examine whether publication violated any criminal espionage statutes. Either of these approaches would have been a powerful and frightening weapon to use against any newspaper. Either would have intimidated the press as much as a prior restraint action—perhaps even more. The administration may not have prevailed in such proceedings, but its chance of prevailing would probably have been greater than the pursuit of a prior restraint action.

Nixon had his own reasons for approving Mardian's and Mitchell's recommendation. He did so not because he had been persuaded that an injunctive action was necessary to protect national security or because he viewed the legal attack as another weapon in his battle against the press. Rather, Kissinger persuaded him that he had to take some action against the *Times* or run the risk of appearing weak, especially in the eyes of the Soviets, North Vietnamese, and Chinese. In addition Nixon may also have feared that his failure to act could undermine diplomatic initiatives unrelated to Vietnam and encourage other serious leaks. Mardian, Mitchell, Nixon, and Kissinger had various reasons for wanting the administration to take action against the *Times*. But none of their fundamental concerns included waging war against the press in an attempt to intimidate it. In this sense the dominant view, which has sought to characterize the national security concerns pressed by the government as a pretext, needs major reconsideration and revision. Moreover, insofar as the Pentagon Papers actually did include materials that many—Ellsberg, Warnke, Gelb, Mardian, Laird, Rogers—considered highly sensitive, there is clearly a need to review the actual strength of the government's claims in the lawsuit—claims that have received far too little serious treatment.

PART TWO

The *New York Times* Case

CHAPTER SIX

The *Times* Is Restrained

On Monday morning, June 14, 1971, Defense Secretary Melvin Laird publicly stated that he had asked the Justice Department to evaluate the legal ramifications of the *Times* Pentagon Papers series. That caused the *Times* officials to become even more anxious than they had been.[1] When the government had not announced its intentions by early evening, James Goodale, the *Times* in-house counsel, decided it was safe to go home. Shortly thereafter, Assistant Attorney General Robert Mardian telephoned Harding Bancroft, executive vice president of the *Times*, and told him that the government would sue the *Times* the next morning if it did not immediately suspend publication of the Pentagon Papers series. Bancroft told Mardian he would have to consult with other *Times* officials before he could give an answer.[2]

Bancroft telephoned Goodale, Abe Rosenthal, the managing editor, and Sydney Gruson, the executive assistant to the publisher. When the men got together in the *Times* executive offices on the fourteenth floor they disagreed over how to reply to the government's request. Goodale and Rosenthal argued that the *Times* had to publish the series, Bancroft and Gruson that the *Times* should suspend publication.[3] Bancroft telephoned Louis Loeb, the newspaper's attorney. In keeping with the advice he had given the *Times* during the previous weeks Loeb urged the newspaper to suspend further publication. He told Bancroft to inform Sulzberger of the developments and of his recommendation.[4]

Bancroft telephoned Sulzberger, who was asleep in his London hotel, and summarized the telegram Attorney General John Mitchell had sent the newspaper that evening and the position taken by Mardian during Bancroft's call with him. Bancroft also told Sulzberger that Loeb opposed further publication. Rosenthal could contain himself no longer. He shouted into the speaker phone. "Punch, this is Abe. I think you should talk to Goodale." Goodale strongly urged that the *Times* continue to publish the series as planned. Sulzberger asked Goodale if further publication would increase the newspaper's legal liability, and Goodale answered, "Not by five percent." The publisher told them to "go ahead" with the next installment.[5]

Rosenthal went to the city room on the third floor. Over 150 people were waiting to learn whether the *Times* would publish the next installment. Rosenthal announced, "Go ahead," and the crowd cheered. Meanwhile, Bancroft called Mardian and informed him that the *Times* was "respectfully declining" to comply with the government's request that it voluntarily cease publication of its Pentagon Papers series.[6] Bancroft also sent Mitchell a reply telegram which stated that the *Times* believed that the threatened legal action was "properly a matter for the courts to decide, [that] the *Times* would oppose any request for an injunction, [and that the *Times* would] of course abide by the final decision of the court."[7]

Goodale telephoned Loeb. He told Loeb that the *Times* was turning down the administration's request to cease publication of the series and asked him to have Lord Day & Lord assign an attorney to represent the newspaper in court in the morning. Loeb told Goodale to call Herbert Brownell, the most influential partner at the firm. Brownell was waiting for Goodale's call: Loeb had just briefed him about Mitchell's telegram and Mardian's conversation with Bancroft. But Lord Day & Lord could not represent the *Times* in the impending lawsuit, Brownell explained, because he had drafted the executive order that created the classification system, and he had signed a memorandum indicating that the executive order was constitutional. Brownell said that John Mitchell had telephoned him and indicated that the government's lawsuit would cite Brownell's executive order as authority for the injunction the government would seek. And, Brownell said, according to Mitchell, the government would almost certainly make a motion to disqualify Lord Day & Lord from representing the *Times*; such a motion would embarrass the newspaper.[8]

Several facts suggest that Brownell was less than forthright in his conversation with Goodale. Mitchell did not corroborate Brownell's version of their telephone call. His purpose in telephoning Brownell, he claimed, was to give notice that the administration would sue the newspaper if it did not voluntarily stop publication.[9] He denied intimating that government lawyers would move to disqualify Lord Day & Lord from representing the *Times*. In addition the fact that Brownell drafted the executive order in the 1950s would not necessarily justify a motion to disqualify his firm from representing the *Times* in the lawsuit. Finally, it is not at all clear how such a motion, if it were made, would embarrass the *Times* or the law firm, or why the embarrassment would be greater than the awkwardness that both would feel if the law firm walked away from the case at such a critical moment.

What is more believable is that Brownell and Loeb were angry at the *Times* for rejecting their advice not to publish the classified material in the first place and for refusing to suspend publication when Mitchell asked it to. Brownell was also a prominent member of the Republican party, had a working relationship with Nixon since Nixon's days as Eisenhower's vice president, had attended Tricia Nixon's wedding in the White House Rose Garden just two days earlier, and was embarrassed at the prospect of seeing his firm oppose the Nixon administration in such a visible case.

When Goodale finished his telephone conversation with Brownell about eleven o'clock he had to find a lawyer. Goodale's first thought was to get Alexander Bickel, with whom Goodale had had lunch that day at the University Club. Bickel, a Yale law professor, and Floyd Abrams, a young partner at a Wall Street law firm, were representing various news organizations in a case involving the right of a reporter to keep his news sources confidential from government prosecutors engaged in a criminal investigation. The case was scheduled to be argued before the Supreme Court during the October 1971 term, and Bickel had come to the lunch to discuss the case with several representatives from news organizations.[10]

Bickel was born in Bucharest, Rumania, in 1924, came to the United States at the age of fourteen, and became a naturalized citizen in 1943. He served in the army during World War II, then graduated Phi Beta Kappa from City College of New York in 1947. After graduating summa cum laude from the Harvard Law School he clerked for Supreme Court Justice Felix Frankfurter, with whom he maintained a close relationship. Bickel joined the Yale Law School faculty in 1956 and quickly established himself through his writings as a prominent constitutional law scholar. By 1971 he had a reputation as a "liberal Democrat" in politics and a "constitutional conservative" in legal philosophy. He was well known, occasionally being mentioned as a possible appointee to the Supreme Court.[11]

Goodale suggested Bickel to Bancroft, but Bancroft preferred Herbert Wechsler, a Columbia Law School professor, who had successfully represented the *Times* before the Supreme Court in *New York Times v. Sullivan,* a landmark case in which the court concluded that the First Amendment to the United States Constitution provided qualified protection to news organizations against libel claims.[12] But Wechsler told Bancroft he could not accept the case because of a teaching commitment in Europe. Bancroft then told Goodale to call Bickel. While the *Times* operators tried to reach Bickel, Goodale telephoned Abrams and told him that the *Times* would not be represented by its regular counsel; would he agree to work with Bickel in representing the *Times*? Abrams agreed, provided Bickel did so, and assuming he could obtain approval of his partners, which he expected he could secure. A few minutes later the *Times* secretaries located Bickel at his mother's apartment on Riverside Drive in Manhattan. Bickel agreed to take the matter on. Goodale told him to call Abrams. Later, about 1:15 A.M., Abrams picked Bickel up in a taxi, and the two went to Abrams's law offices in lower Manhattan.[13]

The two went to the firm's library. Their only lead concerning the possible legal claims the administration might assert was Mitchell's reference to the Espionage Act, contained in his telegram. They pulled the appropriate volume and soon discovered that the espionage law was not the easiest law to understand. Moreover, they could not understand why Mitchell thought the *Times* had committed espionage, at least as that crime was defined in statutes. As Abrams has recalled, they essentially said to one another: "what does he know that we don't know?"[14] Abrams and Bickel worked through the night reading various statutes and judicial opinions discussing free press, prior restraints, and the espionage laws.

▪ ▪ ▪ ▪ ▪

On Tuesday morning, June 15, Michael D. Hess was shaving in his New York apartment when his wife called to him that Whitney North Seymour, Jr., was on the telephone. Seymour was the United States Attorney for the Southern District in New York, which included Manhattan; Hess headed the civil division within the U.S. Attorney's office. Seymour recounted for Hess a telephone conversation he had just finished with Assistant Attorney General Robert Mardian, who had said that Mitchell had ordered Seymour's office to take legal action against the *New York Times* for publishing the Pentagon Papers material. Mardian and other Justice Department attorneys had worked through the night preparing legal papers, which he said would arrive by courier at Seymour's office in the morning. Seymour told Hess to go to the office and begin preparing himself to present the government's case against the *Times*.[15]

Hess was a talented, thirty-year-old attorney who had shouldered substantial responsibility before. Nevertheless, he had never handled a case that came close to equaling this one. He dashed to his office, where he received five legal documents sent from Mardian: a proposed two-page order in which the government requested the court to enjoin the *Times* from further publishing the Pentagon Papers series and ordered the newspaper to deposit the classified documents with the court until the court resolved the dispute; two affidavits, one signed by J. Fred Buzhardt, general counsel for the Defense Department, the other signed by Mardian; a seven-page "complaint" in which the government set forth the basic facts of the dispute, defined its legal claims against the *Times*, specified the judicial relief it sought, and identified the defendants—the *New York Times* Company and twenty-two *Times* executives, editors, and reporters; and a seven-page memorandum that presented the government's legal arguments in support of the request for a prior restraint.[16]

Hess was in no position to do more than make stylistic changes in the legal papers. All that he knew about the case was what he had read in the newspapers, and he had no time to study the materials since he needed to rush to court as fast as possible.

▪ ▪ ▪ ▪ ▪

Abrams and Bickel arrived at the *Times* offices on West Forty-third Street about 9:30 A.M. Abrams was given a message that a government lawyer had called giving the *Times* notice that it should have an attorney in court at noon. Abrams telephoned the Manhattan U.S. Attorney's office and learned that Hess was responsible for the case. Abrams tried to persuade Hess to delay the court appearance until later in the day, but Hess refused.[17]

During the morning Bickel and Abrams met with *Times* editors and executives. Bickel presented to the group a significant question. Should the *New York Times* concede that the First Amendment to the constitution permitted the government to obtain a prior restraint in narrowly defined circumstances but insist that those circumstances were not presented by this case? Or, alternatively, should the newspaper argue that the First Amendment prohibited all prior restraints?[18] The literal wording of the First Amendment prohibited Congress from making any law that abridged free speech or the freedom of the press.[19] But the Supreme Court had never interpreted the amendment to forbid all abridgements of speech, and during the entire history of the Court only Justices Hugo Black and William O. Douglas maintained such a position. Moreover, although throughout its history the Supreme Court had strongly disfavored prior restraints in contrast to post-publication sanctions, it had consistently stated that as a theoretical matter the First Amendment permitted prior restraints.

Bickel told the *Times* officials that he strongly opposed espousing the position that the First Amendment prohibited all prior restraints. He gave two reasons for his position. First, he personally believed that, as important as press freedoms were to the democratic process, the government needed some residue of power to limit press freedom if the nation's security was to be protected. Second, the case would be won or lost ultimately in the United States Supreme Court. Bickel was confident that four of the nine justices would rule in favor of the *Times*. Justices Black and Douglas would do so because they opposed all prior restraints. Based on his reading of Justices William Brennan and Thurgood Marshall, Bickel expected that they too would vote against a prior restraint in this case. But to prevail the *Times* needed a fifth vote, and Bickel said that the *Times* would likely get that vote from either Justice Potter Stewart or Justice Byron White, both of whom considered the absolutist's position extreme and might be offended if the *Times* asserted it. He contended that the *Times*'s chances of ultimately persuading one or both of these justices to rule in its favor would be strengthened if the *Times* conceded that the government could enjoin publication in limited circumstances but insisted that those circumstances did not exist in this case.[20]

Times officials had mixed reactions to Bickel's presentation. Some initially thought that the *Times* should claim that the First Amendment should be construed to bar all prior restraints. The First Amendment gave the press constitutional standing, the amendment's unequivocal wording prohibited all restraints on the press, and although the Supreme Court had construed the First Amendment to permit prior restraint theoretically, no American court had granted the government a prior restraint against the press. But loyalty to principles weakened in the face of strategic choices that could affect the judicial outcome. Thus, with some expressed misgivings, the majority of *Times* officials went along with Bickel's recommendation. Bickel thought this the most important decision the *Times* made throughout the entire litigation.[21]

▪ ▪ ▪ ▪ ▪

About noon Michael Hess walked into a courtroom in the federal courthouse just off Foley Square in lower Manhattan. Bickel and Abrams, accompanied by Goodale, arrived about the same time. The room was crowded with lawyers and observers. The presiding United States District judge was Murray I. Gurfein, gray-haired, stocky, and sixty-three years old.

Gurfein had graduated from Harvard Law School. In the 1930s he became a key assistant to District Attorney Thomas E. Dewey and helped smash labor racketeering and exposed waterfront gangsterism. Gurfein served in Army Intelligence during World War II and was later an assistant to Robert H. Jackson, the United States Chief Counsel, at the Nuremberg war crimes trials. He had been in private practice and had been active in the Republican party, as well as various Jewish organizations.[22] Nixon appointed Gurfein to the district court, and Gurfein had taken his oath of office just a few days before the government sued the *Times*. To date he had sworn in some new citizens and heard a few motions. The Pentagon Papers case was literally his first.

The proceedings got off to a peculiar start. Once Gurfein learned that the government was requesting a temporary restraining order, and that the attorneys were present, he invited Hess to begin his argument. Hess had barely begun, when the clerk of the court interrupted and told Gurfein he could not hear arguments until the government had filed the appropriate papers and obtained a number for the case. Gurfein reacted with impatience. But the clerk persisted until Gurfein relented and told Hess to follow the clerk's instructions. The lawyers did not reappear again until the early afternoon.

The hearing consisted only of oral argument by the lawyers; no witnesses were presented, no testimony was taken.[23] Hess argued first because the government had the burden of persuading Gurfein to grant an injunction against the *Times*. Adhering to Mardian's guidance, Hess contended that the *Times* publication of the classified Pentagon Papers violated a provision of the federal espionage laws and that this criminal statute authorized Gurfein to enjoin the *Times*.[24] Hess claimed that criminal proceedings—the alternative to a restraining order—would take months to prepare and would obviously not protect the national security from the irreparable injury that would be caused by continual publication of the entire *Times* series. He maintained that only an injunction would offer adequate protection and that the administration was entitled to the injunction because the disputed documents were properly classified top secret in accordance with a valid executive order. Hess asserted that, by definition, information classified top secret meant that its unauthorized disclosure could result in exceptionally grave injury to the national defense. He stated that the *Times* was not authorized to possess or to publish the disputed documents, that the *Times* publication had already prejudiced the national defense, and that further publication by the newspaper would irreparably injure the national defense. In support of this position Hess drew Gurfein's attention to Secretary of State William Roger's statement that several friendly nations had expressed "concern over the disclosures in the articles." He also offered Gurfein the affidavits signed by Buzhardt and Mardian, although they contained only general allegations and provided no concrete example of specific information that the government considered to be a danger to the national security.[25]

During Hess's argument Gurfein stated that he had served in the military, that he had experience with intelligence codes, and that he thought it was possible that the government could ultimately prevail. Hess was impressed by Gurfein's obvious sympathetic disposition toward the government, and by the time he completed his argument Hess was confident that Gurfein would restrain the *Times*.[26]

Bickel made two main points on behalf of the *Times*. He maintained that any plausible conception of the separation of powers doctrine barred the government from suing the *Times* because of inherent power. He contended that the suit could go forward only if Congress had passed a statute authorizing it, and it clearly had not done that. He also argued the government had cited no particular part of the espionage laws that could form a reasonable basis for its lawsuit and that no other statute had been invoked. Bickel conceded that the First Amendment permitted prior restraints in limited circumstances but argued that the material published by the *Times* was well outside the scope of such circumstances. Consequently, the Nixon administration's request for an injunction should be viewed as a "classic case of censorship."[27]

Gurfein was in an extraordinary situation. For the first time since the very adoption of the Constitution the U.S. government was seeking a prior restraint with respect to the freedom of the press. Moreover, Gurfein had only a few hours to decide the motion before the *Times* would go to press with its fourth installment of the Pentagon Papers. Gurfein invited the lawyers into his chambers, and he told Bickel that he wanted the *Times* to consent to a temporary restraining order, which would last only a few days, until he had an opportunity to hold a longer hearing in the case in order to reach a decision. Gurfein added—by way of pressure—that he assumed "we are all patriotic Americans," obviously implying that the *Times* would be unpatriotic if it refused.[28] Bickel replied that he had no authority to consent and would have to consult his client. Goodale went to a public telephone in a courthouse corridor and called *Times* officials. He informed them of Gurfein's request and said that he, along with Bickel and Abrams, was opposed to consenting to the imposition of an injunction. Goodale was told to sit tight: he would be called with an answer within a few minutes. Goodale hung up, and dozens of people pushed up against the phone booth waiting to find out what the *Times* would do. Twenty minutes passed, but no call came. Goodale telephoned again, to say that he needed an answer immediately. He repeated his view that the *Times* should not agree to Gurfein's request. Shortly afterwards, Goodale was told not to consent, and he returned to Gurfein's chambers to report the decision.[29] Gurfein proceeded to hear additional arguments from the attorneys and then granted the government a temporary restraining order barring further publication. He refused, however, to order the *Times* to deposit the disputed documents with the court. He then scheduled another hearing for Friday morning.

Gurfein's short memorandum in support of his judgment stated that this legal proceeding presented "serious and fundamental" questions that were both procedural and substantive in nature and that he had granted the restraining order because he believed that "any temporary harm that may result from not publishing" while he decided the motion "is far outweighed by the irreparable harm that could be done to the interest of the United States Government if it should ultimately prevail." He denied the government's request that the *Times* turn over the disputed material to the court because he "did not believe that . . . [the *Times*] will willfully disregard the spirit of the restraining order." He expressed confidence that the administration had brought the action against the *Times* in "good faith" and insisted that he was expressing "no opinion on the merits."[30]

Prior case law gave Gurfein considerable discretion in deciding whether to grant the government's motion. While earlier decisions indicated that a prior restraint should be available only in limited circumstances and that the government had the heavy burden of justifying the need for such extraordinary relief, they most certainly did not offer clear detailed guidance. More to the point, they also offered no help with respect to the circumstances in which a *temporary* restraining order, which might be required as a preliminary step, would be appropriate. Thus, given this lack of clarity in the law, as well as the complexity of the case at hand, Gurfein was well within the discretion the law gave him.

It was particularly noteworthy that Gurfein did not require the government to identify even one specific document the *Times* possessed that would gravely injure the nation's security if published.[31] Instead, he accepted as sufficient the broad and conclusionary statements contained in the government's affidavits and repeated in Hess's oral argument. His willingness to act as he did was a reflection of his initial partiality toward the government, his belief that the government had commenced its suit in good faith, and his conviction that a brief suspension was necessary to allow for a proper presentation of the evidence and arguments.

Gurfein's memorandum did not address any of the important legal questions raised by the government's request for a temporary restraining order. He made no statement concerning the legal requirements that he thought the government had satisfied to secure a temporary restraint. He did not comment on whether the executive branch of government could seek a prior restraint without statutory authorization, or whether Congress had authorized such action. He said nothing about whether publication of the documents violated Section 793(d) of the espionage acts, or even whether the statute was at all applicable to the press. He did not address the government's far-reaching claim that it was entitled to a prior restraint merely because the *Times* was publishing classified material. He gave no indication that he considered prior restraint to be an exceptional form of relief. Finally, he failed to specify the kind of evidence the government would be required to submit in order to prevail.

It is uncertain why Gurfein was not more forthcoming on the legal claims presented by the parties and on the legal basis of the temporary restraining order he had granted. What seems likely, however, is that he was uncertain what he thought about these legal issues, and he had no time to think through the complicated issues if he was going to enjoin the *Times* before its next edition went to press. He might well have also feared the prospect of having stated something he would soon regret if he said more in his memorandum. He may well have decided that the best—the most prudent—course for him to follow was to grant the temporary order and not to try to support it with legal analysis.

The *Times* decided not to appeal Gurfein's order, because its lawyers believed it most unlikely the *Times* would prevail in such an appeal.[32] The *Times* also decided to obey Gurfein's order and did not publish Wednesday's installment. This was consistent with the earlier telegram to Attorney General Mitchell, stating that the *Times* would comply with the rulings of the court. Bickel also offered two additional reasons for it. The *Times* might abhor Gurfein's decision, but he felt strongly that the newspaper had to comply, and then seek a reversal in accordance with the available judicial processes. Otherwise, the *Times* would be openly flaunting the entire judicial process and disparaging the rule of law.[33] He also argued that it was critical to follow an impeccable course of conduct in order to increase the chance of ultimately winning before the Supreme Court. These views were persuasive.

In place of the Wednesday installment of the Pentagon Papers there was a headline that read: "JUDGE, AT REQUEST OF U.S., HALTS TIMES VIETNAM SERIES FOUR DAYS PENDING HEARING ON INJUNCTION."[34]

▪ ▪ ▪ ▪ ▪

The day's legal proceedings displayed the different strategies that the *Times* and the administration were pursuing and would continue to pursue throughout the litigation. The *Times* focused on shaping a strategy that would maximize the odds of final victory. The administration—essentially Mardian at this stage of the case—had at least two concerns. It clearly wanted to win the case. But it did not want to be in a position of proving specific facts establishing that continued disclosures of the Pentagon materials would harm national security interests—or even to explain in detail the security considerations that prompted legal action in the first place. Instead, the government, once it decided to sue the *Times* for a prior restraint, was eager to win on the basis of a broad principle that would restrict the right of the press to publish classified information. Such a result would constitute a dramatic departure from accepted legal norms, as well as the practices and traditions underlying the American press, and its relationship with the government.

As a result Hess did not offer to identify and present particular documents that government officials believed would seriously injure military plans, intelligence capacities, and diplomatic efforts aimed at ending the fighting in Vietnam and securing the release of the prisoners of war. Nor did he emphasize that government experts had been unable to identify all the documents the *Times* had already published as truly official government documents, or that they needed more time to determine the actual or likely scope of the security breach. Indeed, Hess even failed to point out that government officials had not yet had time to review the entire voluminous study in order to assess its full implication.

Mardian's strategy did not prevent the government from obtaining the temporary restraining order it sought. But it was—for many reasons—a misguided course to follow. Bickel's initial set of decisions and the arguments underlying them proved to be sound and effective. Mardian, by contrast, chose a line of argument that lent itself to powerful attack and demonstrated vividly how crucial to any legal case are the first set of moves. Without a clear and concrete presentation of relevant evidence, the government's case was—as we shall see—exceedingly vulnerable.

CHAPTER SEVEN

On the Eve of the *Times* Trial

The legal attack against the *Times* developed quickly in the wake of district judge Gurfein's grant of a restraining order on Tuesday. Melvin Wulf, the legal director of the American Civil Liberties Union (ACLU), and Norman Dorsen, a New York University law professor who was one of three ACLU general counsel, decided that the ACLU should try to intervene and join the *Times* in resisting the government.[1] Intervention of this kind would have allowed the ACLU equal standing with the initial parties, thus giving it the right to make motions, present witnesses, engage in cross-examination, offer objections, and appeal. This type of participation is obviously very different from the friend-of-the-court (*amicus curiae*) role, which ordinarily permits only the submission of written briefs.

Several reasons prompted the ACLU's action. Wulf considered the case to be "a great event in American history in general and in constitutional history in particular."[2] It had the potential of redefining the entire relationship between the government and the press and could thus have profound consequences for the public's ability to be informed about the affairs of its government. Since the ACLU considered itself, as Dorsen characterized it, somewhat of a "specialist" on free speech and free press issues, with "decades of experience" as well as a "certain fervor" in this field, Dorsen and Wulf believed the ACLU could make a contribution to the case.[3]

In addition Wulf, like many others, was troubled by the choice of Alexander Bickel as the lead lawyer for the *Times*. Indeed, Wulf went so far as to characterize the selection of Bickel as a "mistake."[4] Unlike Thomas

Emerson, a colleague of Bickel's at Yale, Bickel had no notable scholarly reputation in First Amendment theory or the rights of a free press. Unlike Herbert Wechsler, who was at Columbia Law School and had represented the *Times* in the seminal *New York Times v. Sullivan* libel case, Bickel was not known as a strong defender of the press. And in contrast to several other academic lawyers, Bickel had no litigation experience.

Wulf was also concerned by Bickel's conservative conception of the judicial function. Bickel was a strong proponent of judicial self-restraint, and he tended to favor technical legal doctrines that permitted courts to dispose of cases without ruling on the substantive issues in dispute.[5] Wulf feared that Bickel would emphasize the argument he used on Tuesday—that the government could not sue the *Times* because Congress had not passed a law authorizing it to do so. A legal victory based on this argument might simply invite Congress to pass such a law. Wulf, for his part, wanted to seize the opportunity to gain a decision that would protect the broadest possible right of the press to publish and restrict the government's power to censor.

Wulf was worried that the *Times* might not resist the government as vigorously as he thought it should. Wulf believed that Bickel and Abrams should have immediately rejected Gurfein's request to consent to a temporary restraining order rather than first consult with officials at the *Times*. Bickel also failed to define in the narrowest possible way the circumstances under which courts might enjoin publication, and this left the door open for much broader and vaguer grounds on which to grant a prior restraint. All of these concerns persuaded Wulf that the ACLU's participation in the lawsuit was necessary to assure the presentation of an extremely strong position against the prior restraint. On Wednesday afternoon, the ACLU filed a motion to intervene. Judge Gurfein scheduled oral argument on the motion for 10 A.M. the next morning.

Meanwhile, after the Tuesday hearing, Michael Hess began preparing a government motion that would permit government experts to examine all the classified documents possessed by the *Times*. It seems likely that Robert Mardian directed Hess to make this motion, probably to see whether the documents might help to identify the person who had leaked them. Hess expected his motion would be vigorously opposed precisely because disclosure might reveal the identity of the source and because protection of sources was vital to a free press. The chances of prevailing, therefore, would almost certainly be stronger if Hess argued, as he did, that the government had to know exactly what information was contained in the documents because the government had the burden of proving that further publication of the classified material would injure the national security. Gurfein scheduled this motion for the same time as the hearing on the ACLU's motion.[6]

Two complete sets of the Pentagon Papers, accompanied by armed Defense Department security guards, arrived in New York late Wednesday afternoon. One copy was sent to the United States Attorney's Office and was placed on a large table in a room adjacent to the office of Whitney North Seymour, Jr. Seymour thought that the offices, bristling with security guards, looked like an "armed camp."[7] The second copy went to Judge Gurfein's chambers. No government official—Mitchell, Mardian, Seymour, or Hess—admitted to knowing who ordered this; Seymour and Hess stated explicitly that they did not even know the study had been forwarded to Gurfein. But Gurfein's clerk at the time, Mel P. Barkan, remembered that Defense Department personnel deposited the papers in Gurfein's chambers and left.

Gurfein was astonished that the forty-seven top secret volumes had been left unguarded in his office. He was concerned that nighttime security arrangements had not been made for the documents, and this question in turn prompted him to wonder how much of a threat to national security the documents actually posed.[8]

The delivery of the documents to Gurfein's chambers on Wednesday was clearly irregular. Without notice to the *Times*, and without legal basis, the most critical evidence in the case was delivered unannounced and unrequested to the judge's chambers a full day and a half before the hearing. In addition Gurfein's copy included all forty-seven volumes, even though the *Times* had announced on the very first day of its series that it did not possess the four volumes describing the diplomatic history of the war from 1964 to 1968.

Gurfein examined the documents prior to the hearing, but his clerk, Barkan, does not recall the judge's reaction.[9] Gurfein never told the lawyers for the government or the *Times* that a copy of the papers had been delivered to him. Why Gurfein did not order the immediate removal of the documents or why he did not disclose their presence to the *Times* attorneys are two question to which we do not have answers.

▪ ▪ ▪ ▪ ▪

At ten o'clock Thursday morning Gurfein convened a hearing to decide the ACLU's motion to intervene and the government's motion to permit government officials to inspect the top secret documents possessed by the *Times*. Wulf argued in favor of the intervention motion. From the moment Wulf rose to argue Gurfein made his position clear: "I told you the other day [Tuesday] that I would be delighted to have the American Civil Liberties Union file a brief as amicus. I am going to deny your motion for intervention."[10] From then on Gurfein made little effort to disguise his impatience with Wulf.

MR. WULF: Won't you hear us, your Honor?

THE COURT: I can't hear you on this because I don't think there is anything to argue. Do you claim you have an intervention as of right or as of discretion?

MR. WULF: As of right, your Honor.

THE COURT: As of right? I deny that. Next. As of discretion.

MR. WULF: We also move under that provision, your Honor.

THE COURT: I know you do. . . . I believe that the counsel for the *New York Times* can adequately represent the interests of the *Times* and the public. I don't think they are in conflict.[11]

Although the exchange between Gurfein and Wulf continued, Gurfein never wavered. Gurfein, disposed to see ACLU lawyers as publicity seekers, was unpersuaded by the ACLU's major contention: that the *New York Times* would not adequately protect the interests of its readers. Although the ACLU's legal memorandum contended that the "thrust" of the *Times* legal position was not "sufficiently broad to clearly and conclusively protect the rights" of those who sought to intervene, Gurfein brushed this point aside: "I don't believe that the *Times* is in here avowedly for the purpose of selling newspapers, but for the purpose of asserting that the general public has a right to read and hear."[12] In Gurfein's view there was little if any difference between the legal interests of the *Times* and those of its readers, and Wulf failed to define that difference.

In addition Gurfein did not believe there was a substantial distinction between the ACLU and any other readers of the *Times* who might wish to intervene. He told this to Wulf with evident frustration: "if I let you in, I would have to let every citizen in. The only ground you have is that you read the *New York Times* and that you have a constitutional right to read it. But there are 200 million people with the same right." And since Gurfein was obviously not about to allow other readers to intervene, he saw no reason to admit the ACLU. It was apparent that Gurfein's ruling was final. Nonetheless, Wulf continued to argue, and Gurfein finally interrupted. "Let me ask you a simple question. Should I allow 200 million people to intervene?" To which Wulf answered: "No, sir. I would be quite satisfied if you just allowed our motion to intervene and denied any others which might be filed." Gurfein pressed again: "Suppose the other 199 million come tomorrow? What do I do?" Wulf responded: "You can deny those, your Honor." "I see," answered Gurfein.[13]

Throughout the argument Gurfein did not ask the *Times* lawyers whether the *Times* favored or opposed ACLU intervention, and they did not say a word one way or the other. Given their silence, however, it seems safe to assume that the *Times* was at best neutral or quite possibly opposed to the intervention. As for the government, it was certainly opposed. But Gurfein was so openly hostile to the ACLU motion that Hess simply sat quietly in the corner of the courtroom, looking out the window.[14]

Gurfein then turned to the government's request to inspect the classified documents possessed by the *Times*. Hess argued that the documents were the property of the United States and that they had been either "stolen or embezzled." He stated that the government was not now asking for their return but only for the opportunity to examine them closely. This was essential because the government had to prove at the Friday hearing "why [the documents] should not be published, why they should be enjoined, why it will hurt the national interest to have them published. In order to do that we have to know what documents the *Times* has and what documents they intend to publish." Given that the *Times* has "not stated with particularity what documents" it has, the government would be litigating "in the dark" unless the motion was granted. Hess added that if the government eventually persuades Gurfein to grant a preliminary injunction, the "Court cannot frame an injunction unless the Court knows what needs to be enjoined."[15]

Floyd Abrams argued for the *Times* and strongly opposed the motion. "There is absolutely no need whatever for the Government to have these papers," Abrams asserted.[16] The government already knew enough to draft a complaint and to secure a temporary restraining order. Under these circumstances, no urgency existed that required the *Times* to produce the documents at this stage of the litigation.

Gurfein asked Abrams if the *Times* would give the government a list of documents with sufficient description to permit government officials to identify them. Abrams said yes and then immediately added: "Wait a minute, sir, I want to make sure I am making my position very clear." The government's complaint referred to "two kinds of documents . . . one supposed 47-volume series and one summary with respect to the Tonkin Gulf." The *Times* would be willing to identify documents that were part of these two specific documents. As for any other government documents the *Times* possessed, Abrams replied: "We are absolutely unprepared, sir, to go through our files and make available to the Government, or to advise the Government of anything which is outside the scope" of the issues as framed by the government's complaint. "A newspaper has a great many sources of information," said Abrams, a great many documents, a great many employees, a great many secrets, which is the essence in good part, your Honor, of journalism." Gurfein made it clear he was asking only for a list of documents that the *Times* had received from the "same source" and that formed part of the basis for its Pentagon Papers reports. Abrams said he would consult with his client on the subject. He then returned to his argument and stressed that any government inspection of the documents ran the risk of disclosing the identity of the person or persons who had supplied the documents. Many of the photocopies possessed by the *Times* had handwritten notations on them, which might facilitate the identification of its source.[17]

Hess countered that the government would not object if the *Times* blocked out any handwritten notations on the papers—a step that could easily resolve the dilemma.[18] But Gurfein paid virtually no attention to this point and Hess, oddly enough, did not pursue it. This was a major error. Since the government did not know what documents the *Times* possessed, the right to examine the specific materials would undoubtedly have helped the government lawyers prepare for the Friday hearing. Hess should have pressed this point vigorously. But he failed to do so, and at the end of the hearing Gurfein told the lawyers he would simply reserve judgment on the government's motion.

■ ■ ■ ■ ■

The Pentagon Papers arrived at the United States Attorney's office on Wednesday, and Hess immediately assigned two assistants to help him study them. The aim was to identify documents that could be used to support the contention that further publication would injure national security. Given the voluminousness of the documents, Hess knew they could not hope to read everything (or even a substantial portion) before Friday. Instead, they tried to grasp the overall organization and to focus on those parts that seemed most likely to contain the most relevant information. Their efforts met with little success. The study's organization was far from simple, and the relatively young lawyers had no experience in intelligence matters, diplomatic relations, or military affairs. They received no help from national security officials. In addition they discovered photocopies of newspaper articles and presidential speeches and could not understand why such materials—already in the public domain—were classified. They began to wonder whether the top secret report actually did contain information that seriously threatened the national security.[19] About six o'clock Thursday evening Hess received a list of the documents the *Times* possessed. But the list was of no real help, because it showed that the *Times* had nearly the entire study, as well as some materials that the lawyers could not identify at all.[20]

Early Thursday evening Mardian and Fred Buzhardt met with Hess and Seymour, who had just returned to his New York office from Washington. They were joined by three Washington officials, Dennis Doolin, Admiral Francis J. Blouin and William Butts Macomber, whom Mardian had chosen to be witnesses the next day.[21] Seymour asked the prospective witnesses to identify the specific documents in the Pentagon Papers study that would jeopardize national security. Buzhardt replied, "They cannot tell you. The information is classified." Seymour was flabbergasted.

"Impossible as it may be to believe," Seymour has written, "the Defense and State Department representatives simply would not explain to the government lawyers which of the documents in the forty-seven volumes of the Pentagon Papers presented specific risks to national security, although they were absolutely positive that such documents existed." For hours Seymour tried to persuade Buzhardt and Mardian that their position was absurd. But they were "adamant." In addition they told Seymour they would "*not even* let [the witnesses] tell the judge, unless everyone else was cleared out of the courtroom." After "wasting precious hours in argument" Seymour finally persuaded Buzhardt, Mardian, and the witnesses to agree to describe "the nature of the sensitive documents, in broad categories." But "never once would they agree to identify specific documents," or explain why public disclosure would have serious consequences.[22]

Although allowing the witnesses to take the stand, be sworn in, and testify about the national security dangers in general terms was an improvement, it certainly left Seymour with a potentially fatal problem. The *Times* would surely argue that the government's request for a preliminary injunction should be denied unless the government proved that publication of specifically identified information would cause significant damages. Under these circumstances, if Gurfein decided the government had such a detailed evidentiary burden, then the government was bound to lose. Seymour's only recourse was to argue that the case was controlled by a legal theory that did not require specific proof in terms of particular and identifiable pieces of information relating directly to national security concerns.

The friction between Mardian and Seymour that Thursday evening was partly personal. Mardian viewed Seymour as arrogant, condescending, and not a very effective courtroom lawyer. Mardian also resented the independence that Seymour and his office had traditionally asserted.[23] For his part, Seymour considered Mardian brash and high-handed, even a "dangerous man" who had a "national security paranoia" that led him to be suspicious of anyone (including government lawyers) outside the national security community.[24]

As much as Mardian and Seymour may have disliked and distrusted one another, there was a more important reason for their being at odds. Mardian, with the support of Attorney General Mitchell, wanted not only to win the Pentagon Papers litigation but to use it to remake American law. He wanted to challenge the untested assumption that the government could obtain such relief in only strictly limited circumstances, and then only when it proved by specific evidence that further publication would cause irreparable injury fairly immediately after publication. Instead, the strategy was aimed at securing a prior restraint order merely because the material in dispute was classified. Mardian wanted to shape the government's evidence in such a way that Gurfein would be compelled to rule in favor of the government purely because the documents were classified top secret, and he believed Gurfein would take that step if it were the only legal ground available to him. Seymour was instructed to follow this line.[25]

Seymour considered Mardian's strategy very risky and far too sweeping in its implication. He wanted concrete, detailed, and relevant evidence but was simply unable to persuade Mardian and Buzhardt to change their minds. He then tried to convince them that the government must at least prove that the documents were *properly* classified top secret. But Mardian believed that the government was entitled to an injunction once it established that the documents were classified—there was no need for the judiciary to determine whether the assigned classification was proper or not. Seymour was completely unpersuaded by Mardian's views.[26]

Eventually Mardian capitulated and agreed that the government's case should rest on proving that the documents were properly classified. We do not know exactly what considerations led Mardian to shift his ground. Nor is it clear what kinds of evidence the government team thought—at that moment—would be sufficient to carry the day. Thus compromised, and with very little time to prepare even the rudiments of so complex a case, the government's lawyers focused on the next morning's proceeding.

CHAPTER EIGHT

Inside the White House, Part 1

President Richard Nixon had his hands full during the third week of June. The economy was "sluggish." Republicans and Democrats alike were demanding that the administration deal effectively with growing unemployment and inflation. The Paris peace talks to end the Vietnam conflict were stalled. The Strategic Arms Limitation Talks (SALT), aimed at curtailing the arms race, seemed deadlocked. Kissinger's negotiations with China—which would, within the month, produce a historic diplomatic breakthrough—were at a critical stage. Discussions with the Soviets concerning tensions in Berlin seemed promising even if they were not consummated.[1]

Given this set of complex issues, one might have expected Nixon to avoid getting deeply involved in the Pentagon Papers case. He had already authorized the legal action against the *Times*, ordered that possible criminal charges be assessed, and received word by mid-afternoon on Tuesday, June 15, that Judge Gurfein—his appointee—had temporarily enjoined the *Times* from further publication. Matters were going Nixon's way, at least for the moment, and there was little more the president could realistically accomplish, now that the case was in court. Once having entered the arena, however, Nixon found it impossible to pull back. More and more he allowed himself to be consumed by what he referred to as the "*Times* deal."[2]

▪ ▪ ▪ ▪ ▪

Having authorized the litigation for reasons that had little to do with his attitudes toward the press as such, Nixon's long-standing battle with the press soon provided him with additional impetus—fueled by anger and outrage—once the struggle with the *Times* was actually underway. Even his closest associates were surprised by the ferocity of his reaction. Apparently, it was not enough that Nixon had already ordered that no member of the White House staff was to grant the *Times* an interview. When he met Haldeman on Tuesday morning he emphasized the importance of freezing the *Times* out, making a special point of insisting that Kissinger "return [. . .] *no* calls."[3] As the day wore on Nixon amplified his directive. In the early afternoon he told Haldeman to tell Ronald L. Ziegler, the president's press secretary, that *New York Times* reporters should not be included in any pool of reporters that was in his presence or on any airplane with him. He also told Haldeman to persuade Senator Barry Goldwater to "take on the *Times*." Nixon wanted Goldwater to charge the *Times* with "reckless disclosure of secrets" and a "shocking breach of security."[4]

An hour and a half later Nixon brought the "*Times* deal" up again in a meeting with Haldeman, Colson, and Kissinger. He told them that "[we] need to get across [to the public the] feel[ing] of disloyalty," that the *Times* is "putting [the] press interest above [the] national interest." He also directed them to arrange for some "hard hitting speeches in Congress" attacking the *Times*. The president told Kissinger to "mobilize some of the old estab[lishment] to hit [the] *Times*." He also wanted someone to "get LBJ's people to speak out—Acheson, Rusk, and McNamara."[5]

During a mid-afternoon meeting the same day Nixon expressed his concern about the situation's effects on public relations. He told his aides that the administration needed a "team"—suggested that maybe William Safire head the team or that Ray Price, a Nixon speech writer, be asked for a suggestion. Someone should be found to "handle this whole situation on an overall basis, to develop a basic position . . . [to] launch an attack." We need to explain why this injures national security and why secret documents must be secure. This point needs "to be thought through," he emphasized. And as if to assure that there was no dissent on the question, Nixon stated: "we do believe in the security of secret documents."[6]

Nixon also told his aides that he wanted the Pentagon Papers referred to as the "Kennedy/Johnson papers on the war." This would emphasize that the previous two Democratic administrations were responsible for the protracted war in Vietnam. The American people must be made to see that the *Times* publication amounted to a "family quarrel" and was equivalent to washing "dirty linen" in public. Nixon wanted to make clear that his administration would not "get into" a sordid dispute about the origins of a war that American soldiers were still fighting. The suit against the *Times*, therefore, was a way of keeping "the linen"—essentially Democratic linen—appropriately out of sight. His own administration, after all, had "nothing to hide": not a single document from his own period as president was in the top secret study, and he had in fact "developed a new policy [toward the war], and it's working."[7]

Soon afterward, at 3:45 P.M. that same afternoon, Nixon told Ehrlichman and Mitchell that the *Times* publication was "treasonable." Indeed, he suspected that the dates of publication had been deliberately chosen to coincide with the congressional debate over the McGovern-Hatfield amendment, which proposed the withdrawal of U.S. troops by the end of the year. Nixon stated that "no cause justifies breaking the law," although he failed to specify which law he believed had been violated.[8] Ehrlichman's notes of the meeting do not indicate whether Mitchell agreed or disagreed with the idea that the *Times* had violated any federal criminal law or had committed treason. During this same meeting Nixon also told his aides to "get" Daniel Ellsberg, who, perhaps with others, was already suspected of having been the source of the leak. Nixon suggested that the administration use either a congressional committee or a grand jury to investigate Ellsberg.[9]

The next morning, the president met with Ziegler shortly before Ziegler was to have a session with the press. Nixon described in detail how he wanted the "Pentagon" issues presented. What we are trying to do, he said, is "to protect the integrity of government" and the administration's "ability to conduct gov't." These considerations "require some classification," especially since (in a possible allusion to the highly secret negotiations Kissinger was conducting with China—which Ziegler apparently did not know about) "many discussions [are] going on now" that require complete secrecy.[10]

Later in the afternoon, Nixon returned again to the administration's need to define the issues at stake rather than allow the *Times* and the rest of the national press to define them. There is no question that the public has the right to know, Nixon told Haldeman, how the United States became involved in Vietnam. But, he insisted, we must maintain the "integrity of government." The publication of the classified material is "massively endangering security." Once again Nixon characterized the *Times* as a "lawbreaker [and] disloyal."[11]

At other moments throughout the day Nixon reminded Haldeman "to carry out his directive [with regard to th]e NYT—never in office, on pool, on plane, etc. No one is to raise this [with the President]." Nixon told Haldeman that "nothing else we do will give more pressure" to the *Times* than restricting its reporters' access to news sources. Finally, someone should "analyze the Kennedy stuff," presumably the material that Nixon hoped would implicate Kennedy directly with Diem's assassination, and "find a way to let the Kennedy segment out."[12]

By Thursday members of Congress and former government officials had attacked the *Times*. General Maxwell D. Taylor, a major figure in the Pentagon Papers study and ambassador to South Vietnam from the summer of 1964 to the summer of 1965, reported on television that the *Times* had initiated "a practice of betrayal of government secrets." Averell Harriman, who served as President Johnson's delegate to the Paris peace talks, told newsmen at a Wednesday breakfast meeting that the *Times* had published "a lot of miscellaneous documents" that had "misled" the public.[13] Democratic Senator John G. Tower from Texas questioned whether the *Times* publication of top secret material was "within the excellent and responsible motto of which the *New York Times* prides itself—'All the news that's fit to print.'"[14]

But Nixon was not yet satisfied. He told Haldeman to arrange for some influential Republican members of Congress to begin "whacking [the] Dems for partisanship." He ordered Haldeman not only to cut *Times* reporters off from all administration sources but to "do everything we can to destroy the *Times*." He added that he was "not sure Mitchell shld delay [the] Grand Jury [investigation]" and emphasized that we "must play boldly—don't be afraid of risks." It was, he said, the "same way in [the] Hiss case; all will get jittery [and] want to pull back. . . . Don't fight it defensively—take the offense." This is "an opportunity," and "we can beat 'em if we work it right."[15]

As the day wore on Nixon wanted to know whether Bryce N. Harlow, a former Nixon adviser who was then working as a lobbyist for Procter and Gamble, had yet persuaded Johnson to issue a statement criticizing the *Times*.[16] He demanded evidence of "hard line attacks on" the *Times*. He even told Haldeman at one point that he was considering arguing "the case before [the] Supreme Court to indicate the importance of it."[17] Still later that day, the president began to turn more of his attention on the actual leak of the documents and focused on Ellsberg as well as on the members of the national security staff. At this point Kissinger burst into an explosive attack on Ellsberg, acknowledging that he was a "genius [and the] brightest student [I] ever had" but adding that Ellsberg had "shot at peasants" in Vietnam and that he was "always a little unbalanced." He used drugs and had "flipped" from "hawk to peacenik in early '69." Kissinger stressed that he had not seen Ellsberg for a year and a half, presumably not since January 1969, except for a chance meeting at MIT in February, when Ellsberg had "heckled" him. According to Kissinger, Ellsberg clearly "stole" a set of the Pentagon Papers from the RAND Corporation. As if that were not enough, Ellsberg had also "married a wealthy girl," Patricia Marx, the daughter of a successful toy manufacturer.[18]

All of these points—Kissinger knew—would strike home forcefully with Nixon. Anyone who was intellectual, "unbalanced," disloyal, and then married for money was more than beyond the pale.[19] Nixon's anger was instantaneous.[20] Haldeman later described the scene:

> In four and a half years in the White House I listened, often with smiles, to many Kissinger rages, but the Pentagon Papers affair so often regarded by the press as a classic example of Nixon's paranoia was Kissinger's premier performance. . . .
>
> I was in the office when one of the angry speeches was made. As I remember, it ended with charges against Ellsberg by Kissinger that, in my opinion, go beyond belief. Ellsberg, according to Henry, had weird sexual habits, used drugs, and enjoyed helicopter flights in which he would take potshots at the Vietnamese below.[21]

Quite apart from the "performance" portrayed in this episode, Kissinger's charges were obviously hyperbolic and in some cases false. Ellsberg, for example, had been Kissinger's colleague, not his student at Harvard. Nor is there any evidence that Ellsberg ever shot at peasants. And Kissinger had of course met with Ellsberg as recently as ten months before at Nixon's San Clemente compound when Ellsberg had strongly urged him to read the Pentagon Papers. But true or false, Kissinger's missiles found their target, and had the desired effect.

▪ ▪ ▪ ▪ ▪

Events continued to fan Nixon's anger all week. As he prepared to travel to Rochester on Friday, June 18, he became even more convinced that the *Times* had consciously planned its publication of the documents to coincide with the critical congressional vote on the McGovern-Hatfield amendment requiring the withdrawal of all American troops from Vietnam by the end of the year. In fact the first few installments of the Pentagon Papers did seem to give the sponsors of the amendment a boost, increasing the chances that the legislation might pass. At this point, Nixon warned the congressional leaders that he would break off the Paris peace talks if the amendment were approved because Congress would have crippled the president's ability to negotiate. Senator Hugh Scott, the minority leader, predicted—correctly, as it turned out—that the amendment would be defeated.[22]

But there was still more in store. Mike Mansfield, the Senate majority leader, announced within days of the first *Times* installment that a Senate committee would hold public hearings on how the United States had become involved in the war. Mansfield told newsmen that he had been "surprised, shocked, and astounded" by the published secret documents because it was now apparent that President Johnson had decided to expand the war without informing Congress.[23] Significantly, Mansfield also made it clear that the hearings would not be simply retrospective in nature but would also examine the Nixon administration's Vietnam policies.[24] Nixon and his aides were certain that Mansfield would ask for a full copy of the Pentagon Papers from the administration. This would place Nixon in an extremely difficult position. On the one hand, if the administration were to give top secret materials to Congress, a precedent would be set, allowing classified documents to be available on request to congressional investigating committees. On the other hand, if the administration refused, it would come under powerful criticism for denying Congress important information. It would also heighten suspicion that the administration did indeed have something to hide.

Nixon was further annoyed by sharp press and congressional criticism that he was systematically disregarding the public's legitimate right to know how their government became militarily involved in Vietnam.[25] Sixty-two members of the House of Representatives signed a letter addressed to Defense Secretary Laird and Attorney General Mitchell asking that the Pentagon Papers study be made available to Congress and protesting what they considered to be the administration's harassment of the *New York Times*. Senator George McGovern, a candidate for the Democratic party nomination, criticized the Nixon administration for intimidating the *Times* and cutting off the free flow of information to the people. Although Senator William Fulbright had a substantial portion of the classified material in his office safe, and Congressman Pete McCloskey had returned the Pentagon Papers to Daniel Ellsberg months before, both made public requests that the *New York Times* turn over a copy of the classified material to Congress since the administration had refused to do so. Arthur Ochs Sulzberger, the *Times* publisher, and others in the press criticized the Nixon administration, asserting that the classified material published by the *Times* was "a part of history that should have been made available long ago."[26]

This criticism—especially from leading members of the Democratic party—irked Nixon.[27] From Nixon's point of view he had actually helped the Democrats by allowing the suit against the *Times* to go forward, since the Pentagon series was inevitably damaging to the reputations of two Democratic administrations, Kennedy's and Johnson's. Nonetheless, Democrats continued to pillory Nixon, Mitchell, and others. Few congressional Republicans missed the irony of these developments; but they could do little to help and remained bewildered and frustrated.

Nixon, meanwhile, was more and more convinced that he had done the right thing. He was now certain that he had a responsibility as president to protect the classification system and the integrity of classified documents. In his view the *Times* had resorted to vigilante tactics, assuming that it had obligations that transcended the national security laws.[28] At the same time the president was increasingly frustrated because government officials could not determine the precise scope of the security breach. They had not been able to trace the identity of all the documents the *Times* had published, and they were still unable to discover which documents in addition to the actual Pentagon Papers the *Times* or Ellsberg possessed. Finally, Nixon began receiving information that Ellsberg was acting in concert with others. The episode began to take on an air of conspiracy, challenging the president's capacity to govern. One report submitted to Nixon at that time even suggested that a copy of the Pentagon Papers had been given to the Soviet embassy in Washington.[29]

▪ ▪ ▪ ▪ ▪

It is possible to see how Nixon's attitude and feelings evolved during that first week of litigation. On Monday Nixon wanted to punish the *Times*. By Thursday his intention was to "destroy" the newspaper and to use the "*Times* deal" as an "opportunity" to "beat 'em"—by which he presumably meant his life-long political enemies. At the end of the week he was determined not to back down: he would persist and remain on the offensive until he had won.

The ferocity and intensity of the president's mood was certainly not lost on his White House aides. Nixon met with Haldeman, Kissinger, and Ehrlichman on Thursday afternoon; afterwards, the three aides had a short meeting with other White House staff members. At one point Richard Moore said: "Why is he doing this?"—referring to the possibility that Nixon would, over the reservations of Mitchell, make a strong public statement to describe the legal case against the *Times*. Ehrlichman answered: "He sees it as one of those opportunities that comes along in four years when he can tell where the forces are running and can be channeled in a desirable direction." To which Haldeman added: "Or highly desirable direction." John Scali followed up these statements with another question: "What forces does he think he can move [and] to what objective?" Ehrlichman's answer was disarming: "I honestly don't know. But it has consumed him." No one contradicted Ehrlichman and no one answered Scali's question.[30]

CHAPTER NINE

The *Washington Post* Publishes

For days just prior to June 13 the offices of the *Washington Post* were riddled with rumors that the *Times* was about to publish a major story on the war. Robert McNamara, who had been alerted by *Times* columnist James Reston, notified friends at the *Post* that the *Times* was about to publish something "detrimental to him," but McNamara "did not furnish details." A *New York Daily News* reporter, Stan Carter, told Chalmers Roberts of the *Post* that the *Times* was about to publish something that "could end the war."[1] On Saturday afternoon, just hours before the *Times* went to press with its Sunday edition, Reston saw Donald Graham—the son of the *Post*'s publisher—and told him the *Times* was about to publish a story on the origins of the war based on classified documents.[2] By the time Graham passed this information on to the *Post*'s national desk the *Post* editors and reporters had already received the *Times* Sunday edition on the teletype.

Benjamin C. Bradlee had become managing editor of the *Washington Post* in 1965 and executive editor in 1968. He, Katharine Graham, and many others at the newspaper had set their sights on transforming the *Post* from a good newspaper into one of the nation's great newspapers. Bradlee would say on occasion that what he wanted was for people to say "'the *New York Times* and the *Washington Post*' in the same breath." By 1971 Bradlee had not yet succeeded in his mission. "We had the perception of what we wanted it [the *Post*] to be and we weren't there yet."[3]

When Bradlee learned about the *Times* story he was exasperated, possibly "desperate."[4] The *Times* had done it again. This was not essentially a matter of substance. As David Halberstam has noted: "neither he [Bradlee] nor [Abe] Rosenthal, after all, had been so fascinated by the question of how and why the United States had gone to war in Vietnam as to assign a team to find out."[5] Instead this was a question of how, from his perspective, potentially "uninteresting" material had been turned into a provocative "scoop" of national and international proportions. Bradlee took it personally and felt again like the editor of a newspaper that would be seen as a distant second to the *Times*. Bradlee told his editors to rewrite the *Times* report and to credit their rival.[6] He also told them to get him the classified history because he was determined to catch up with the *Times*.[7]

On Sunday Marcus Raskin called Bradlee. Raskin's book *Washington Plans an Aggressive War*, coauthored with Richard Barnet and Ralph Stavins and based in part on a portion of the Pentagon Papers, was then in production. Raskin had not expected Ellsberg to find an outlet for the Papers before his book appeared, and he was apparently "shaken" by the unexpected *Times* publication. He wanted to meet with Bradlee on Monday. Bradlee quickly agreed: "The score was thirty-six to nothing, and we were trying to get even."[8]

At breakfast Raskin told Bradlee that they had finished a book based on the Pentagon Papers, and they offered to let the *Post* serialize it. Bradlee expressed interest, if for no other reason than he wanted direct access to the source materials. But Raskin said they no longer had the original documents.[9] Bradlee persuaded them to let him read their manuscript without having to make a commitment on behalf of the *Post*. Bradlee found the book unsatisfactory, and Chalmers Roberts, who read the book at Bradlee's request, called it "just atrocious." In Bradlee's opinion the authors were too intent upon proving that America had committed war crimes in Vietnam.[10]

Also on Monday, Philip L. Geyelin, the editor of the *Post*'s editorial page, received a call from a friend in Boston. The friend, whose identity is not known, said that he had about two hundred pages from the Pentagon Papers—and that some of the material concerned events that the series in the *Times* had not yet covered. He offered to send the documents, and within a few hours they arrived at the *Post*. Murrey Marder, a diplomatic reporter at the *Post*, immediately read the parcel and thought it could form the basis for a good story. But before the *Post* could go to press, the *Times* published the same material in its Tuesday edition.[11]

Bradlee's best hope for getting a full copy of the Pentagon Papers was Ben H. Bagdikian, the *Post*'s assistant managing editor for national affairs. Bagdikian knew Ellsberg through the RAND Corporation and thought Ellsberg was the most likely source of the leak. The articles in the *Times* paralleled important points and arguments that Ellsberg had been making to Bagdikian for a long time. So, Bagdikian began making telephone calls to locate Ellsberg.[12]

Ellsberg felt both elated and furious by the *Times* publication on Sunday: elated because the material was out but furious because Sheehan had not told him in advance. Ellsberg felt that the lack of notice placed him in possible jeopardy, since the FBI, if it suspected him as the *Times* source, might then locate the additional copies of the Pentagon report that Ellsberg had hidden in different locations.[13] Then, when the government obtained a temporary restraining order, and the *Times* complied without dramatizing the censorship by leaving a blank space on page one where the next article would have appeared, Ellsberg's anger and disappointment increased.[14]

On Wednesday Ellsberg tried to make the papers public through the three major television networks, but none of them would agree to do so. Because the networks were licensed by the Federal Communications Commission, they were vulnerable to governmental investigation and retaliation in ways that the press was not. This vulnerability had already been made all too clear by Vice President Agnew's assault on the media as well as by the Federal Communications Commission itself.[15] The networks may also have believed the volume and complexity of the Pentagon Papers surely did not lend themselves to video presentation—at least not without many days of special preparation.

Once the television networks turned down Ellsberg on Wednesday, he had a lengthy telephone conversation with Bagdikian. Bagdikian tried to assure him that the *Post* would present the material in a serious manner. Ellsberg wanted a commitment that the *Post* would begin its series with the pre-Kennedy era. He insisted on this because he did not want the *Post* to scoop the *Times*'s fourth installment, which concerned the significant build up of the United States involvement in Vietnam during the Kennedy years. Ellsberg also believed the public might realize that Nixon's Vietnam policies were doomed to fail, if it understood that these policies were essentially no different from the unrealistic strategies of all prior administrations extending back to the 1940s.[16] When Ellsberg felt satisfied that he had an adequate commitment from Bagdikian, they made arrangements to meet in Boston that evening.

Bagdikian returned to the *Post*'s offices and met with Eugene Patterson, the managing editor, since Bradlee was out of town. Although Bagdikian had assured Ellsberg that the *Post* would definitely use the papers, he himself did not have the authority to make such a guarantee. He now asked Patterson: "If I can get a solid chunk of the Pentagon Papers, will we publish them Friday morning?" Patterson said yes. But Patterson also told Bagdikian that he had to check with Bradlee to gain final approval. From National Airport, Bagdikian telephoned Bradlee. Bradlee told Bagdikian to get the papers—and added that if the *Post* did not publish them, he would resign as executive editor.[17]

We do not know where Bagdikian actually went after he arrived in Boston, or whether he met with Ellsberg or perhaps with someone else who was assisting Ellsberg.[18] We do know, however, that by the next morning, Bagdikian had more than 4,000 pages of the Pentagon Papers stashed in a large box, tied with a simple cord.[19] He bought two seats on the return plane trip; one for himself and one for the box. For knowledgeable reporters, however, Bagdikian's box was no mystery. Stanley Karnow, a former *Post* correspondent, accidentally met Bagdikian on the plane and instantly drew the right conclusion. "Oh, you've got it," he said.[20]

▪ ▪ ▪ ▪ ▪

Bradlee was waiting at his home in Georgetown when Bagdikian arrived about 10:00 A.M. Three *Post* reporters were also there: Chalmers Roberts, Murrey Marder, and Don Oberdorfer, whom Bradlee had chosen because of their knowledge of the subject and their ability to turn out good copy quickly. Before long, Philip Geyelin, who was in charge of the editorial page, and Meg Greenfield, his deputy, both arrived. The first task was to sort the documents, organize them chronologically, and divide them according to different presidential administrations.[21] At that point the group began what turned out to be six hours of intensive study.

At mid-day Roger Clark—a relatively young lawyer from the firm of Royall, Koegell, and Wells—arrived at Bradlee's home. Ironically, the senior partner of Clark's firm had been William P. Rogers, who was now serving as President Nixon's secretary of state. Rogers in fact had previously been the *Post*'s chief lawyer. After Rogers's departure the *Post* continued to retain the same firm, and Clark was dispatched when the newspaper called for legal assistance.

As soon as Clark was briefed on the situation at the *Post* he telephoned his colleague, Anthony Essaye, and asked him to study the espionage statutes that were at issue in the *New York Times* case and might be applicable to the *Post*. Later in the afternoon Essaye also went to Bradlee's to join the entire group—as did Frederick Beebe, chairman of the board of directors of the *Washington Post* Company. Beebe had come to Washington to attend a party at Katharine Graham's home, but when he got wind of what was happening he went immediately to Bradlee's.[22]

By mid-afternoon Clark, Essaye, and Beebe were challenging Bradlee's view that the *Post* should clearly publish a story based on the classified papers it now possessed.[23] Clark said that the administration would certainly sue the *Post* for a prior restraint order and would be successful. He also warned that publication might violate one or more of the provisions of the espionage laws. He did not argue that publication would definitely constitute a crime, because he saw the same ambiguities Goodale had perceived in the espionage laws. But Clark thought that a criminal prosecution was likely and that there would be serious risks ahead for the *Post* and those associated with it.[24]

In addition Clark pressed Bradlee on the question of potential harm to the nation's security. The *Times* had taken three months to review the material and prepare it for publication. By contrast the *Post*, with more than half of all the documents in hand, was racing to turn out a story within twelve hours. How could one be certain that some of the information might not seriously injure national security interests? If such injury did occur then the *Post* might lose not only the prior restraint suit but also the follow-up criminal prosecution.[25]

Bradlee disagreed violently. The substance of Clark's advice was objectionable enough from Bradlee's point of view, but his tone made matters far worse. He was aggressive, strident, and inflexible. Bradlee expected advice that would help the editors minimize—if not eliminate—the legal obstacles. Instead, he found that the lawyers were themselves an obstacle.[26]

If Clark was so strident and aggressive, he was at least partly reacting to the considerable pressure of the moment: he knew very little about the actual legal problems that publication of the classified secret papers might entail; he had no experience with such questions; and he was being asked to give an immediate assessment of the situation. Under these circumstances he was understandably concerned about the hazards and the substantial "unknowns." He may also have felt that nothing less than a very forceful stance would make any impression at all on Bradlee.

Clark was not alone. Frederick Beebe was also against publication. Beebe was chairman of the board, and, according to David Halberstam, he was "the single most respected and admired figure in the entire company." He had been associated with the *Post* for a long time, had worked closely with Bradlee in making the *Post* a national newspaper, and probably had more influence with Graham than anyone else. Beebe's concerns were different from Clark's. The *Post* had "gone public" only two days before, and more than a million shares of stock had just been offered for sale. One clause in the agreement provided that the stock offering could be canceled if the company suffered a "disaster" or "catastrophic event." The agreement did not define these terms. No one knew, therefore, whether an injunction barring further publication or criminal charges brought against the newspaper would be construed as catastrophic or disastrous. But even the possibility of such an outcome heightened the already strong sense of jeopardy involved in proceeding along Bradlee's determined course. Finally, Beebe was concerned that if the *Post* did publish the Pentagon materials, that action might well undercut the pending application for a renewal of broadcast licenses for the television and radio stations owned by the *Washington Post* Company.[27]

Although Beebe was opposed to publication, Bradlee sensed that his attitude and tone were very different from Clark's. Beebe seemed ambivalent because he knew that the Pentagon Papers would represent a major story for the *Post*. Beebe also knew that the *Post*'s failure to publish that night would be common knowledge in the morning and, as a result, the paper's reputation would be injured. Much of what they had all worked so hard to achieve for the *Post* would be lost. Bradlee realized that Beebe was genuinely torn and was doing his utmost to decide upon a responsible course of action, taking into account the conflicting aspects of the problem.[28]

Bradlee was at fever pitch over the issue of publication. The *Post* was at a crucial stage in its development. It had steadily gained strength over the years. It now had the resources and the talent to become a major national newspaper, and the Pentagon Papers would allow the *Post* to take a giant stride toward its goal. Bradlee was desperate to take that stride in order to demonstrate to everyone that the *Post* was a newspaper with courage, determination, ambition, and will power—that it was a force to be reckoned with.[29]

It was only a matter of time—literally hours—before word would seep out to the greater Washington community that the *Post* had the Pentagon Papers. If the *Post* did not publish, everyone would assume that—unlike the *Times*—the *Post* was intimidated by Nixon and Mitchell. The failure to publish was not simply a matter of missing an opportunity; it would constitute a blow from which the paper might not fully recover.[30]

There were also personal motives and energies involved. Bradlee saw himself as a fighter, and publishing the Pentagon reports meant that he and his colleagues had nerve, they had courage. In Bradlee's mind, not publishing was tantamount to being a coward, and Bradlee recoiled at the idea. Also, Bradlee actually relished the idea of a court battle with the Nixon administration.[31] He would probably have felt differently if Kennedy were president, for he admired Kennedy and they were friends. But there was no love lost between Nixon and Bradlee, or between Nixon and the *Post*.

So as the afternoon wore on, Bradlee became more and more incredulous at what was taking place in his own living room. Just a few days before he was exasperated that the *Times* had proven yet once again that it was the premier newspaper in the nation. Now because of a set of unforeseen events, the *Post* was in a position to accomplish something that—even a day before—had seemed impossible. And yet Bradlee's own lawyers were insisting he not publish the Pentagon documents, and the chairman of the board of directors was siding with them.[32]

Bradlee made no progress in his efforts to change the views of Clark, Essaye, or even Beebe. He felt instinctively that the chances of avoiding serious legal liability were much stronger than the lawyers indicated, but he could not understand why they were so strident if they were so wrong. He decided to get a second legal opinion, and he telephoned his old friend Edward Bennett Williams. Williams was not in his office—he was in Chicago trying a divorce case. Bradlee then called Jim Hoge, editor of the *Chicago Sun-Times*, and said that he had an "emergency." Would Hoge "send a copy boy down to the courthouse with a note to Williams to call me?" Hoge should emphasize that the problem was "really important." Shortly thereafter, Williams received the note that stated: "Please ask for a recess ASAP. Need to talk to you NOW. URGENT."[33] Williams soon returned the call, and the two talked for about fifteen minutes. Bradlee summarized the situation and described the arguments on both sides. Williams listened without interruption—something that, as Bradlee said many years later, "was quite unlike Williams." When Bradlee finished, Williams asked if that was everything. Bradlee replied: "Yeah. That's it. I can't do anymore." Williams: "You just have to publish. Never mind the law, you just have to publish. They'll never get you. They'll go after you, but they'll never get you."[34]

As Bradlee reflected on Williams's reaction years later, he thought that each of them had responded to the situation instinctively, with an "animal reaction." Both of them felt that the political climate at that moment, the growing strength of the *Post*, Nixon's attitude toward the press, and the implications of failing to publish, all required the paper to move ahead immediately. Years later, Bradlee said that his telephone call to Williams was "the most important call I ever made."[35]

Bradlee now felt more determined than ever and more confident about avoiding serious legal consequences. He decided he could not share Williams's advice with anyone that night, but he was now ready to go the next round—indeed, the full distance—as he rejoined Clark, Essaye, Beebe, and the others.

The argument continued—without any progress. Press time was approaching, and the editors were holding four pages in the first edition. As the pressure mounted, and the need for resolution increased, someone suggested that the *Post* not publish the Pentagon materials that night but wait until the next day. At that time they could notify Attorney General John Mitchell that they had the papers and were intending to go public the next day. Alternatively, they could print a notice alerting readers that the *Post* now had a copy of the Pentagon study and that it was preparing to begin publication soon. These ideas were not immediately dismissed by anyone at the meetings. Indeed, as the discussion wore on, one option or the other appeared to offer the only way out of the impasse.[36]

At that point the reporters took a dinner break. They had been working all afternoon in another room and were completely unaware of the struggle that was taking place between Bradlee and the others. When they learned that the story might not go forward that night, and that the *Post* might actually notify the government in advance, they exploded. "That's the shittiest idea I've ever heard," Don Oberdorfer blurted out. Chalmers Roberts accused Bradlee, Beebe, Clark, and the others of "crawling on your belly" to Mitchell: "If you don't want to risk running it, then the hell with it, don't run it." Roberts threatened that if the *Post* did not go to press with the story that night, he would resign, take his retirement two weeks early, and make a public statement dissociating himself from the decision. These outbursts had an immediate and powerful effect, especially on Beebe. The fact that Chalmers Roberts was so unequivocal and vehement made a strong impression on everyone, particularly because he was viewed as a "traditionalist figure," "the epitome of the establishment reporter."[37]

Bradlee again took the initiative and insisted on going ahead without delay. But Clark remained resolute in his opposition. Beebe was more moderate in tone and substance, but he also continued to oppose publication.

▪ ▪ ▪ ▪ ▪

That evening, Katharine Graham, the publisher of the *Post*, was giving a party at her Georgetown home for Harry Gladstein, who was retiring as the paper's circulation manager. Graham does not remember precisely when she first learned that Bagdikian had obtained a substantial portion of the Pentagon study, but she is sure that she heard the news from Bradlee earlier in the day. She knew that reporters and editors were at work on the story, but she did not join the group at Bradlee's because she believed that the "process was working," and there was no reason for her—in her role as publisher—to be any more intrusive than she ordinarily would be.[38]

Toward the beginning of the party James Daly, the newspaper's general manager, urged Graham to telephone Bradlee for a progress report. Four pages were being held for the Pentagon Papers article, and Daly was more and more concerned as press time drew near. Graham put him off: she was not worried, and she had always left legal and related matters to others. Even now, as the *Post* was on the verge of publishing classified secret documents that the government had temporarily blocked the *Times* from printing, she had not considered the potential legal consequences ahead. She had simply assumed, as she later remembered, that "we were just going to publish."[39]

In addition Graham did not believe it was necessary to become more involved because she knew that Beebe was at Bradlee's. She considered Beebe an "able lawyer," a "wise" and "decent" man, who was both "liberal" and "editorial" minded. But her bond with Beebe went deeper. She felt they were "almost interchangeable." It was her impression that they always saw things the same way and agreed. They had worked closely together for many years, and she considered Beebe "wonderful," "really fabulous."[40] With Bradlee directing matters, and Beebe—whom she trusted absolutely—fully involved, Graham felt confident and saw no reason for concern.

Eugene Patterson, the managing editor, knew that a serious dispute was underway at Bradlee's. After Patterson arrived at Graham's he took her aside and warned her about the struggle. Graham was surprised that a serious dispute over publication was brewing. She was immediately taken aback: if Bradlee and Beebe were on different sides, the issues were obviously far more difficult and important than she had suspected. Patterson told her she would have to make the final decision, and this "stunned" her.[41]

Somewhere between 7:00 and 7:30 that evening, Graham began her toast to Gladstein. She had barely begun when she was interrupted: "They want you on the phone." She answered that she would "come when I'm through," but was told "They want you now."[42] Graham shortened her toast and hurried to her library to take the call.

The telephone conversation was chaotic. Beebe, Bradlee, and others were each on a different extension with each pressing his own point of view. Beebe explained why he thought the financial and legal considerations weighed against publication, but he also made it clear that a decision not to publish would create major problems with their best reporters and the entire newsroom. Bradlee, of course, argued for immediate publication. Meanwhile, Paul Ignatius, the president of the paper, who had recently been secretary of the navy, was with Graham and repeatedly urged her to "wait a day, wait a day, wait a day."[43]

Graham was impressed by two points that Bradlee made. Now that the government had gained a temporary restraining order against the *Times*, it was important for the *Post* to support the *Times* in this historic struggle against censorship. Bradlee also made it clear that many people in Washington already knew that the *Post* had a cache of Pentagon documents and that by morning the word would be all over town. The *Post*, therefore, ran the risk of seeming to be intimidated by Nixon and Mitchell. The government would, in effect, win a de facto victory, and the cause of press freedom would be severely damaged. The *Post* would be gravely embarrassed, and its reputation would be greatly compromised.[44]

The turning point in the conversation came when Graham again solicited Beebe's views. He told her that, all things considered, he would not go ahead that night. Graham was instantly struck by what Beebe did *not* say, as well as by the way in which he carefully balanced his argument. He did not say that publication would gravely injure the newspaper or the entire *Post* company. He did not say that waiting another day would yield better or definitive answers. He gave the impression that the decision was a close call, and that there were good arguments on both sides. He also gave Graham the feeling that the decision was genuinely hers to make, that either course of action could have serious risks and consequences, and that although he had his own preference, he believed the final choice should reflect her own views. The moment could hardly have been more tense. More was understood than explained. There was a brief silence, and then Graham said: "Okay, go ahead."[45]

Graham's decision, which she later described as not "the most cerebral decision in the world," reflected her momentary distillation of all the conflicting feelings, arguments, and considerations expressed under such pressure in that single complex telephone conversation. Graham assumed that publication would cause the government to sue the *Post* for an injunction; that there might be difficulties with the stock sale; and that there might also be repercussions for the company's electronic broadcasting stations. But she was deeply worried about the morale and commitment of her editors and reporters and about the reputation of the paper. She also knew that this was a rare "make-or-break" opportunity to thrust the *Post* forward toward becoming a national newspaper of the first rank. Interestingly, she was not worried about national security issues, because she trusted the reporters and editors to eliminate any questionable material.[46]

But Graham's judgment to approve the publication included factors well beyond important points made by Beebe and Bradlee. She felt that Nixon had unfairly criticized—and actively disliked—the *Post*. His animosity was not new. It reached back to the 1950s, when he was vice president. At that time he had dropped his personal subscription to the *Post*, presumably to protect his family from the *Post*'s criticism of him and from what he considered to be Herblock's gratuitously cruel cartoons. Once Nixon had been elected president, Graham tried to make herself available to many within the administration, essentially inviting them to call her if they felt that the *Post*'s coverage was unfair. But these overtures were not accepted and seemed not to be appreciated. Before long, Graham began to feel that the upper leading members of the administration viewed her (to use her own words) as the "living devil"—one of those idols that you "stick pins in."[47] By the time of her conversation with Bradlee and Beebe, she was already angered by the administration's apparent campaign against the *Post* and other newspapers. Hence, when Graham made her decision that night, she was not worried about what Nixon, his aides, or cabinet members might think of her and the *Post*: she already knew. Like Bradlee, she may even have relished the idea that Nixon and his aides would have no choice but to sue the *Post*.

▪ ▪ ▪ ▪ ▪

Once Bradlee put down the phone, he went "roaring back" into the room and shouted, "We go!" Reporters and editors were elated, and Beebe seemed relieved, as if Graham's decision seemed clearly right, now that she had made it. But the hour was very late, and they had missed the first edition, whose four "Pentagon pages" had been filled with photographs and promotions. There was still time to make the second edition. Roberts was an expert on the 1954 Geneva Accords dealing with Vietnam, and he had been working all day on the documents that dealt with the Eisenhower years. His story was ready and was sent ahead in time for the second edition.[48]

At this point Clark raised a new objection against publishing that night. He called Bagdikian, who was already at the news offices with the last pages of Roberts's article. Clark demanded to know if there had been any collusion between the *Post* and the *Times*. Had Bagdikian obtained the 4,000 pages of Pentagon Papers from someone at the *Times* or from the same source that had supplied the *Times*? If so, Clark warned that publication would violate Judge Gurfein's order against the *Times* and would subject the *Post*, its editors, and its reporters to serious contempt penalties.[49]

Bagdikian would not identify his source to Clark. He insisted that the source was confidential and would remain so. Clark insisted that Bagdikian return to Bradlee's home for more discussion. Bagdikian finally agreed and returned to Georgetown. The conversation was acrimonious. Clark insisted that the attorney–client privilege would protect the confidentiality of any disclosure by Bagdikian, and Bagdikian then volunteered that he presumed that Ellsberg had been the source of the material he had obtained, and that he assumed that Ellsberg had also given it to the *Times*. To Clark, this was tantamount to collusion, assuming that Ellsberg had also been the *Times* source. Clark consulted by phone with William R. Glendon, one of the senior partners in the law firm's New York office. Glendon agreed with the potential danger of contempt charges, and that led Clark to call Bradlee, who had by then left with Beebe and the others for Graham's house. Thus began another round of discussions: Bradlee talked with Graham and Beebe, and shortly after midnight, with only minutes to spare, Graham decided once again to publish. The first copies of the *Post* second edition rolled off just in time. A four-column headline was emblazoned above Roberts's story: "DOCUMENTS REVEAL U.S. EFFORT IN '54 TO DELAY VIET ELECTION."[50]

Although Bradlee thought Clark was "great once he got going," he also thought that Clark's midnight intervention concerning possible collusion bordered on being obstreperous.[51] Yet Clark's concern had merit. Gurfein's order barring publication applied not only to the *New York Times* Company and the twenty-two named individuals but also to "all other persons in active concert or participation with them." Whether Ellsberg was covered by this sweeping and open-ended injunction—and whether the *Post* would be liable if Ellsberg proved to be the single common source—were important legal questions that simply had to be asked and confronted. If Clark had not pressed those questions, and if Gurfein ultimately imposed severe penalties on the *Post*, Clark would clearly have been open to serious criticism for not alerting his clients to this particular set of additional risks.

▪ ▪ ▪ ▪ ▪

The *Post* took fourteen hours to publish, the *Times*, three months. What explained the discrepancy? "Because we had to and they didn't," said Bradlee: "I guess it's as simple as that."[52] What drove the *Post* to publish that Thursday? Would another day or two have made any substantive difference, particularly because the article concerned actions that had occurred seventeen years earlier, during President Eisenhower's tenure? From the public's point of view, the information would be important historical information. It also had an added current relevance in the context of the increasingly fierce dispute concerning publication of the Pentagon Papers. But whether the public learned about these matters on Friday morning, June 18, 1971, or whether the news surfaced on Saturday, Sunday, or even later, had very little to do with anyone's urgent "need to know."

Instead it seems obvious that the great push to publish had mainly to do with the other considerations already discussed earlier in this chapter: the desire to achieve national prominence in the same league as the *Times*; the need to exhibit determination and courage rather than timidity in the face of the Nixon administration; and finally, the unusual opportunity to step in at a moment when the *Times* was observing Judge Gurfein's restraining order so that the *Post* would be seen as having picked up the torch as the defender of freedom of the press.

For the *Post*, as well as for Bradlee, this was a crucial moment. The episode concerned not the publication of timely information but the capacity to scoop, to command attention, and to demonstrate the kind of heroism associated with those who stand up against powers that threaten to intimidate. Bradlee and Graham, as well as the reporters and editors, correctly saw that this was a major institutional test, an act of self-definition on which the paper's future would depend.

When Bradlee later looked back on the Pentagon Papers case, he thought the decision to publish that Thursday night changed not only the public perception of the *Post* but, more important, the self-perception of everyone associated with the *Post*. It allowed them to believe they could undertake important, controversial, and risky ventures—that they could fight for themselves, and defend themselves. Publishing the Pentagon Papers meant they were entering combat in a national arena "really for the first time." It made them feel there "was no limit to what we could do if we stayed bold and stayed right."[53] In Bradlee's view the Pentagon Papers case made possible the *Post*'s reporting of the Watergate scandal, which significantly contributed to the end of Nixon's presidency.

Katharine Graham's view was more equivocal. It was certainly important in her mind, but she was (and is) less certain about how important. She does not think that Bradlee is necessarily incorrect in seeing the Pentagon story as the most important experience in the *Post*'s development, but she is simply not certain.[54]

There is one sense, of course, in which Bradlee's opinion is incontrovertible. He regarded this entire series of events as critically "formative" to his own evolution as executive editor, and that fact was an essential factor in the *Post*'s continued progress. It became a springboard that enabled the emboldened newspaper to unravel and expose the Watergate affair. As a result the *Post* continued its path to becoming a stronger, more resourceful, more vital, nationally acclaimed journal.

CHAPTER TEN

The Friday Hearing: The Public Session

By ten o'clock in the morning on Friday, June 18, people filled every seat and stood two or three deep in the aisles in the large federal courtroom in lower Manhattan. The crowd was excited, with countless people shaking hands, exchanging greetings, and waving to each other across a sea of heads. It was not festive, but it was not solemn either. Rather, there was an edge of excitement and anxiety in the air as the crowd waited for the historic hearing to begin. Judge Gurfein had scheduled the hearing to consider evidence to decide whether to continue the injunction barring the *New York Times* from publishing any further reports based on the secret Pentagon Papers.

Whitney North Seymour, Jr., and Michael Hess, representing the government, were seated at one of the two tables assigned for counsel. At the other, Alexander Bickel was flanked by Floyd Abrams, Lawrence McKay, and William E. Hegarty, all partners of Cahill, Gordon, Sonnett, Reindel & Ohls. The audience fell silent when Gurfein entered the courtroom: "I understand from the clerk that there are some petitions for intervention. I will hear those first, very briefly, indeed."[1]

Thomas Emerson, a respected and well-known Yale Law School professor, rose first. Emerson and Gurfein had known each other for over thirty-five years, having met in the 1930s, when Gurfein followed Emerson as the assistant to Walter Pollack, an attorney who represented the Scottsboro Boys in their first appeal to the U.S. Supreme Court. During the succeeding years Emerson had established himself as a leading scholar of the First Amendment. After the government had secured its temporary restraining order against the *Times* Marcus Raskin of the Institute for Policy Studies asked Emerson if he would represent Robert Eckhardt and twenty-six other members of the House of Representatives, who wanted either to intervene on behalf of the *Times* or to file an *amicus curiae* brief. Emerson agreed.[2]

Emerson knew that Gurfein had previously denied motions to intervene by the American Civil Liberties Union and the Emergency Civil Liberties Union. He hoped, however, that he might have more success, because his clients were members of Congress, with a special claim for access to the Pentagon Papers based on their constitutional duties. But Gurfein soon dashed Emerson's hopes. "I am going to deny [your motion] for the same reason that I denied" previous intervention motions (3). Gurfein said he assumed that Emerson must be representing individual members of Congress who were not petitioning on behalf of the House or the Senate per se. Consequently, Gurfein did not believe that intervention would "serve any useful purpose," because the counsel for the *Times* could adequately protect the interests at stake (3).

Emerson asked if he might have "a moment" to argue, to which Gurfein answered, "surely" (3). Members of Congress, Emerson said, had a "quite different" interest in the case from that of the civil liberties groups: senators and representatives had a constitutional duty to vote on pending legislation, which currently included legislation that called for an end to the war. Access to the Pentagon Papers would place members of Congress in a far better position to evaluate the soundness of such legislation. Congress was unable to obtain the necessary information from the executive branch—indeed, Emerson stated that anyone "who depends on the executive to tell what is going on is in a bad way" (4). The Pentagon Papers were "as directly relevant as anything could be" to the important matters pending before the House and Senate (4).

Gurfein was unimpressed. He asked Emerson if he was contending that in any case between private parties, or between the government and a private party, a single Congressman has the right to intervene because there might be something that might affect his judgment on pending legislation (5). Emerson replied that he was not basing his argument on such a broad premise: instead, the particular government documents in dispute were "important," they were no longer exclusively in the control of the executive branch, and they were "absolutely essential to an intelligent decision" that his clients would have to make (5). But before Emerson could finish, Gurfein interrupted to say he would not permit intervention. The Congressmen could file an *amicus* brief if they wished. Emerson indicated that they would do so, and then sat down.

Morton Stavis rose next and asked Gurfein for "a half minute of the Court's time" (6). He explained that he represented a variety of groups such as the Vietnam Veterans Against the War, the American Friends Service Committee, and the War Resisters League, who were opposed to the war and had been on the "forefront" of opposing the war for a long time (6). Stavis claimed that his clients had a right to know what was in the classified documents so that they could more effectively advocate their position. He asserted that this interest was different from the *New York Times*'s interest, which was limited to a right to publish, and that therefore his clients' motion should be granted.

Gurfein moved quickly to deny Stavis's motion. But then, as if suddenly aware of how swift and abrupt his rulings might appear, Gurfein said he would explain his position again, because he agreed that the "public has an interest in this case." Indeed, every "person in the United States is interested in this case," and if he permitted "everybody opposed to the war" to intervene, he would have to permit "everybody in favor of the war, if anybody is in favor of a war," to intervene. "I thought I would state that," he said, "so that you could see my decision is not arbitrary" (7–8).

That ended the applications to intervene. During the thirty minutes it took Gurfein to dispose of these initial motions neither Seymour nor Bickel said a word, nor did Gurfein ask either one of them to comment. Time was passing, and the hearing had yet to address any matters that were central to the case.

▪ ▪ ▪ ▪ ▪

Bickel then stood and told Gurfein that he had "a new matter I would like to put before your Honor." Bickel told Gurfein that the *Washington Post* had published that morning the first of several articles based on the Pentagon Papers. Bickel explained that this report appeared under a headline that stated "DOCUMENTS REVEAL U.S. EFFORT IN '54 TO DELAY VIET ELECTION" and that the news story was based on materials that made up part of the Pentagon Papers study. Bickel stated that the Post clearly possessed the same documents as the *Times*. Furthermore, the *Washington Post* "runs a news service to 345 clients," including the *New York Post*, which had also just printed a major story under a bold headline "MORE WAR SECRETS." "This story is out," Bickel insisted. "Without any exaggeration, we can assume [that] this story . . . will be made available by every news medium in the United States to the public" (9–10).

Bickel argued that the *Washington Post* publication "radically changes the posture of the case" (10). It was apparent that the government's effort to keep the Pentagon materials secret was ineffective. Whatever national security considerations may have originally existed—and Bickel made it clear that he was not conceding that any did exist—had now vanished. There is "nothing for your Honor to protect with a temporary restraining order," and there is no possibility that the government will secure a permanent injunction (13). In short the case is moot (14). Continuation of the temporary restraining order would injure readers of the *New York Times*, since the order removed their access to important information in the newspaper of their choice. In addition the injunction was now working a direct injury on the *Times*, because publication of the Pentagon documents by the rest of the national press meant that the "story is gone" (18).

Bickel's announcement had a dramatic effect and stunned Gurfein as well as everyone else in the crowded courtroom. But his legal arguments were nonetheless far from decisive. He had asserted that the secret materials were now essentially in the public domain—spreading throughout the national press. But his only tangible evidence was that morning's publication by the *Washington Post* (and its clients). The Pentagon documents had "spread," but there was nothing to indicate that they had spread beyond the capacity of the government to control.

Bickel's second point was also unpersuasive. The *Post* was publishing reports apparently based on "the same" documents possessed by the *Times*, thus making the temporary restraining order moot, but Bickel could prove only that the Post had *some* of the same documents. He could not determine the real extent of the overlap. If it turned out—as was indeed the case—that the *Times* had a far more complete copy of the entire report, then the government's case against the *Times* was not moot. Equally important, Bickel did not know whether the government would sue the *Post*. If it did so and if it were successful—and if the Pentagon Papers had not been circulated beyond the *Post* and the *Times*—then the injunction against the *Times* would continue to be an effective way of protecting the confidentiality of the classified secret documents.

Gurfein asked the government lawyers whether the government intended to sue the *Washington Post* for an injunction. Hess told Gurfein that he had only learned of the *Post*'s article that very moment. The *Post*'s second edition had been out for hours, but Hess and Seymour, unaccountably, had not been informed.

Hess then stated that the case against the *Times* was not moot merely because the *Post* had published one news report. The Pentagon study was massive, and once the full report had been submitted as evidence Gurfein would see immediately that the newspapers had published only an extremely small percentage of the whole (16). Hess made only a feeble response to Bickel's claim that the temporary restraining order against the

Times was unfair: he said that the *Times* had placed itself in this predicament by "opening up the subject, being the first to announce that they were going to publish and coming into this court and asking this court to decide. . . . We would say that they put themselves in this unique position" (17). At that moment Hess noticed Mardian was trying to catch his attention. Hess asked Gurfein for a moment to consult with Mardian, after which Hess announced that the Justice Department would make an immediate review of the *Post*'s publication and take whatever legal action was required (17).

Bickel was now angry and asked Gurfein for permission to speak: "We are not in this court because we came . . . seeking its approval of our publishing enterprise. We are in this court because the Government brought us in this court" (18). Bickel continued. Publication by the *Post* demonstrated the ineffectiveness of using a prior restraint to protect the national security in this case, and the *Post* was now in a position to "scoop" the entire Pentagon Papers story while the *Times* was forced to remain idle. The government has claimed that "grave danger to the national security would occur if another installment of a story that the *Times* had were published. Another installment of that story has been published. The republic stands and it stood for the first three days" (19). The courtroom crowd roared its approval, and Gurfein quickly reacted: "I don't see anything funny about that." Bickel agreed: "I am surprised that it is a laughing matter" (19).

Bickel sensed that he was making headway with Gurfein and pressed his point that the injunction against the *Times* was transparently ineffective. "This story is out. We have information that Congressman McCloskey has a copy and is about to put it in the *Congressional Record*. Every news medium in the United States has access to exactly what the *Times* is alleged to have" (19). Gurfein confessed that Bickel posed "a very difficult problem," but he did not explore it further at that time (20). He said that he did not have the Pentagon Papers study (which was untrue, since a full copy had been delivered to his chambers on Wednesday); he wanted to examine the materials so he might make some judgment about the possible risks posed to national security. But the judge did not pursue that path of inquiry either.

Instead, Gurfein began a twenty-five minute exchange with Bickel, during which the judge accused the *Times* of being unpatriotic, of having compromised intelligence codes, and of basing its right to publish on an extreme and untenable legal claim. Gurfein said that a "free and independent press ought to be willing to sit down with the Department of Justice and screen these documents that you have or [that] the *Washington Post* has or [that] anybody else has as a matter of simple patriotism to determine whether the publication of any of them is or is not dangerous to the national security" (20).

He explained that he was concerned about several matters. The *Times* had paraphrased coded messages, and this action might permit another country to break the code. The *Times* had printed documents sent to the United States by a foreign nation—documents which therefore did not "belong to the United States under the rules of international law." The *Times* may have printed information that revealed "methods of intelligence gathering" (20). Gurfein said that he thought that all "patriotic citizens"—"the press as well as anybody else"—would want to keep this information confidential "to protect what is dear to all of us, the security of the country" (21). In evident frustration, if not impatience, Gurfein told Bickel that he did not "understand, though, frankly, why a patriotic press should not be willing to subject these papers" to prior government review to assure that the national security would not be harmed (21).

Bickel replied that Gurfein's suggestion that the *Times* "sit down pleasantly with the Government and go over our story and our materials . . . is utterly inconsistent with the First Amendment" (23). Daily, Bickel told Gurfein, the *Times* and the national press published "massive amounts of material" that was of the same character as the material in dispute in this case. The idea that the national press should cease deciding for itself what to publish and should first seek government comment or consent before publication would be totally inconsistent with the requirements of a genuinely free press—or with the rights of the press under the Constitution. Bickel conceded that during a war, or a "pitch national crisis," such as the Cuban Missile Crisis, the press could not responsibly decide to publish information directly relevant to national security without seeking government comment (23–24).

The actual difference between Gurfein's position and Bickel's, at least as modified by Bickel's two important concessions, was in fact not very great. Gurfein was clearly not asking the *Times* to consult daily with the government concerning what it should print. He also knew that the press withheld sensitive information from publication because of national security concerns and that it did consult with the government about such information prior to publication. But he wanted to know why the *Times* was so unwilling to "sit down" with the government in this particular instance. Given Bickel's concession—that the *Times* would consult with the government during a war or a national crisis—Gurfein wanted to know whether those circumstances did not apply in the current case, since the Vietnam War was manifestly still in progress. This was a completely understandable question. Bickel did not explain why one or both of his two exceptions were not relevant, and Gurfein neglected to press him on the point.

Gurfein did, however, challenge Bickel specifically on the issues of codes. "With all due respect, I may say that neither you nor I nor the *New York Times* is competent to pass on . . . what will lead to the breaking of a code" (22). Bickel tried to assure Gurfein that the *Times* had not published any material that compromised a code. "It is absolutely out of the question" (23). Bickel said that the government had made no claim that the *Times* had printed anything that "broke a code, compromised a code, came within five miles of an existing code" (22). He also claimed that "the security of codes . . . [was] insured by their being changed with extreme rapidity" (23).

But Gurfein refused to drop the subject. "Do you have reason to believe that" the *Times* has not compromised a code? he shot back (25). Bickel was taken aback. The government had the burden of proving that the *Times* had compromised a code. But here was Gurfein trying to impose this burden on the *Times* and asking it to prove that it had not published anything that could aid in the breaking of a code. After a minute of fumbling for the right words Bickel replied: "It is not our burden to prove that we have not published something that offends against the national security" (26).

Gurfein then turned his fire to another subject. He accused the *Times* of making the untenable claim that the Constitution forbade all prior restraint (27–28). This accusation was clearly unwarranted: Bickel had made it crystal clear on Tuesday that prior restraints were constitutionally permissible in limited circumstances. Moreover, Bickel had repeated this position in the legal brief submitted to Gurfein on Thursday. Bickel was agitated: "I've spent some years of scholarship, if I may say so, resisting the idea of absolutes and I am not now turning around and embracing it" (28). Gurfein backed off and soon stated that he would take "under advisement" the *Times* motion to vacate the temporary restraining order because of the *Washington Post* publication (29).

This lengthy exchange between Gurfein and Bickel was, from a legal point of view, superfluous. The purpose of the hearing that Friday was to determine whether the temporary restraining order should be lifted or whether the government should be granted a preliminary injunction that would continue to prohibit publication. Without question, the government had the burden of proof, and it was clear that the government would be presenting witnesses to support its claim. That was the heart of the case, and Gurfein had set aside the day for it. It was legitimate for Gurfein to explore whether the *Washington Post* publication made the government's lawsuit against the *Times* moot, but the other issues were essentially at the margin. Gurfein's inexperience may have been the problem—or he may well have been probing to see whether the *Times* would voluntarily permit government officials to review its documents prior to further publication. Whatever his reasons, Gurfein conveyed the strong impression to the courtroom audience that he was partial to the government and impatient with the *Times*.

▪ ▪ ▪ ▪ ▪

The judge then turned his attention to the government lawyers. Hess rose and said he wished to remove any doubt over whether legal proceedings would be initiated against the *Washington Post*: "the Government will move against those articles [published in the *Post*] so that the readers of the *Times* will not be allegedly the only ones suffering" (30). Hess also said that Seymour would be sharing the argument with him that day, to which Gurfein replied, "Delighted to have the distinguished United States Attorney" (30).

Seymour then took over from Hess and made his opening argument. He began by trying to place the *Times* in a bad light. Twice, he told Gurfein, the *Times* had turned down requests to suspend publication of the classified material. The first had been made by Attorney General John Mitchell in "a very polite telegram" (32). The second was Gurfein's own, during Tuesday's hearing. The government had sued the *Times* because the newspaper had been intransigent and did not ask for the classified study pursuant to the Freedom of Information Act, which Seymour conceded would have been unavailing.

To Seymour the case presented "a very simple" legal issue, namely "whether, when an unauthorized person comes into possession of documents, that person may unilaterally declassify those documents in his sole discretion" (31). The United States's concern in this matter was "fundamental" and involved military, defense, intelligence, and diplomatic matters (34). Although it might not be obvious to the "layman," it was clear "to the trained intelligence man" that the *Times* had already published information that was "harmful to the interests of the United States," most specifically its relations with other countries (36). Seymour insisted that the Pentagon Papers contained information that has "current vitality" and whose disclosure would "adversely affect" military alliances, diplomatic efforts, and military and defense strategies and plans (34).

The government would offer the Pentagon Papers as evidence. The documents were at hand, in the courtroom, under the custody of Brigadier

General Jacob Glick of the Marines. In addition the government would produce several witnesses, whom Seymour described as military and diplomatic "career officers" (not political appointees, and therefore presumably unbiased [36]). Then, after some preliminary testimony, the government would request that the public be excluded from the hearing and that the court reconvene *in camera* (that is, hold a hearing from which the public was barred).

Seymour said he was prepared to assume that the *Times* had commenced publication in good faith, unaware that it would seriously injure the national security (34–35). But since it had acted unilaterally to declassify critical documents, and had made no effort to determine if the government had any objection to their doing so, the government's only option was to sue (35). Seymour said that he was ready to proceed with the government's proof, "unless Mr. Bickel would like to make a[n opening] statement" (37).

Bickel made two quick points. First, he complained that Hess had previously indicated he would provide the names of government witnesses and the general subject matter of their testimony. Yet he had submitted the names only minutes before, and the list gave no indication of the topics to be covered. Bickel said that he felt "handicapped" as a consequence (38). Seymour replied that the government would gladly agree to an adjournment, provided that the temporary restraining order continued. Gurfein made light of Bickel's objection: "having been in government yourself, Professor Bickel, you know they have done a remarkable job in getting three named persons in two days" (40).

With respect to the government's desire to hold part of the hearing *in camera*, Bickel stated there was nothing in the documents that required a closed hearing. But if there was to be such a hearing, Bickel asked that Max Frankel, a *Times* correspondent, and Harding Bancroft, a *Times* vice president, be allowed into the hearing room to assist with the cross-examination of government witnesses (38). Gurfein granted this request.

At that point Norman Dorsen, Victor Rabinowitz, and Morton Stavis, attorneys representing parties filing *amicus curiae* briefs, objected that they would be barred from attending the hearing *in camera*. Collectively, they made several points. They argued that no such hearing should be held unless the government makes some minimal showing warranting such an unusual procedure. They claimed they would not be able to participate effectively in the proceedings as *amici curiae* unless they had a representative in attendance. Moreover, Bickel's failure to object to a hearing *in camera* made it clear that interests of the *Times* were different from those of the groups represented by Dorsen and others. Consequently, they renewed their motions to intervene. Gurfein again denied the motions and also turned down the request to attend the closed hearing.

Seymour now called Dennis James Doolin to the stand. Doolin stated that he had been a senior analyst with the Central Intelligence Agency, specializing in Chinese affairs before assuming his current responsibilities in May 1969 as deputy assistant secretary of defense for international security affairs. Doolin said that the office with which he was now associated had prepared the secret report on the Pentagon Papers. He described the study and its origins, saying that only fifteen copies of the study had been made when it was completed and that security precautions were taken to protect them after distribution.

Although Doolin had not been involved in the preparation of the study, he had taken up his current position at the Pentagon before the work was finished (56). Doolin had become familiar with the Pentagon Papers study after Senator Fulbright wrote to Defense Secretary Laird asking that the study be declassified and released to the Senate Foreign Relations Committee. Doolin was charged with reviewing the documents to recommend whether or not to declassify. He had recommended against declassification. Fulbright later made several similar requests, and Doolin had evaluated each one. He had also studied the list of documents possessed by the *Times* and compared it with the contents of the Pentagon Papers: most of the *Times* documents were part of the study, but others were not identifiable.

Seymour asked Doolin a series of questions about the study, and Doolin replied that, of the forty-seven volumes classified top secret—sensitive, information from only two volumes was already in the public domain. He added that everything in the study was properly classified, because government guidelines required that any particular set of documents must be given the classification level of the most sensitive document within the set. For example, the several historical sections that formed part of the Pentagon study were based on material that was both classified and unclassified (79).

Could Doolin state whether public disclosure of the study "would compromise the present or future military or defense plans, intelligence operations or jeopardize international relations" of the United States (88)? He could—and he had in his "possession information concerning specific fact situations which are intimately related" to the classified study (89). At the same time he had been ordered by Fred Buzhardt not to discuss "these subjects in open court" (89–90). Seymour told Gurfein that the government was prepared to prove *in camera* that the classification of the disputed documents was not arbitrary (93–94).

Seymour then asked about the Command and Control Study on the Tonkin Gulf Incident, a document the *Times* had listed on its inventory. This paper was classified top secret but was not part of the forty-seven volume study. Access to the paper was limited to individuals who worked for the Joint Chiefs of Staff, which meant that Doolin had therefore not read the report. Finally, Seymour asked Doolin if the *New York Times* was authorized to have access to either the Pentagon Papers study or the Tonkin Gulf study, to which Doolin answered no (83–86).

Gurfein indicated that he had a serious question he wanted answered. It was his impression that the classification rules favored declassification in order to make information available to the public. As a result the government had a duty to take the initiative in declassifying even top secret documents. Had the government taken the initiative to declassify any part of the Pentagon Papers? No, said Doolin. The executive order that defined the classification system did not require this to be done for documents classified top secret. Also, he did not think such distinctions could feasibly be made, because the study continuously wove together material that was appropriately classifiable with material that might be declassified (73).

Gurfein was not satisfied with this explanation. He pressed Doolin to explain how the duty to declassify affected the different classifications of top secret, secret, and confidential. Doolin did his best, without much success. Gurfein repeated his view "that whatever can conceivably be declassified for the purposes of public information should be declassified as rapidly as possible" (99). He did not think top secret documents were exempt from these rules, but even if they were, Gurfein suggested that the government ought to respect the general policy preference favoring declassification. Could the task of sifting the materials really be so difficult?

Seymour stepped in at this point and said that the government had a witness available who was an "expert on the intricacies" of the classification rules (78–79). He also asked Doolin some questions that set the stage for introducing the entire Pentagon Papers study into evidence. The volumes were contained in two large cardboard cartons, marked as government's exhibits 7 and 7A. Seymour asked that they be sealed and that only Gurfein have access to them. Requesting that the documents be kept from public examination was perfectly reasonable under the circumstances, but asking that they should also be kept from the *Times* attorneys was very different—especially since Seymour had told Buzhardt and Mardian the previous evening that the *Times* had a right to confront and cross-examine witnesses. Gurfein was now being asked to do precisely what Seymour had said could not be done: namely, to accept evidence that could not be examined by the defense.

Surprisingly, Gurfein granted the motion that the study "be sealed and be for the Court's eyes only" (63). Even more surprising, Hegarty, who was the most experienced trial lawyer among the *Times* attorneys and was responsible for Doolin's cross-examination, said he had "no problem" with Gurfein's ruling (64).

Hegarty's lapse was extraordinary. Without hesitation he had just consented to a decision that barred him, his clients, and their experts from examining the central piece of evidence in the entire case. For all he knew at this stage of the proceedings, government witnesses might make reference *in camera* to dozens, perhaps hundreds, of pages or documents within the Pentagon Papers that they claimed would injure the national security if disclosed. If they did so, Hegarty would be essentially helpless to test these claims or cross-examine witnesses in any detail at all. Furthermore, this ruling meant that Hegarty would be prevented from having access to the four volumes that traced the diplomatic history of the war from 1964 to 1968. Ellsberg had considered these volumes so sensitive that he did not make them available to Sheehan. Former Assistant Secretary of Defense Paul Warnke believed that the publication of information in these volumes would unquestionably injure the national security and should be enjoined.[3] The problem, moreover, was more than one of access: since the four diplomatic volumes were clearly very sensitive—and potentially harmful if published—they could well become the centerpiece of the government's argument for continuing the injunction against the *Times*.

Francis Blouin was called next. Blouin was a career officer who had graduated from the Naval Academy in 1929. He was the deputy Chief of Naval Operations for Plans and Policy within the Joint Chiefs of Staff, a position he had held for three years (100–1). His primary responsibilities included the planning of policy and military operations and the coordination of relations with other parts of the executive branch on military matters.

Blouin testified that he was familiar with the Tonkin Gulf study, that it was classified top secret, and that its circulation was limited to the Joint Chiefs of Staff. Although Blouin did not know how many copies of the study were in existence, Seymour pointed out that the front page of the study indicated that there were only forty copies. Blouin said that public disclosure of the study's content would "very definitely" damage present and future military and defense plans as well as intelligence operations (103). He said he could describe these consequences in detail.

Blouin had learned only on Wednesday night that he should read the Pentagon Papers so that he could appear as a witness on Friday. He had, therefore, "a little better than 24 hours to get acquainted with" the materials (104). On the basis of his examination he believed that further publication of the report would be a "disaster" for military and defense plans as well as intelligence operations (104). He also said that the *Times* had already printed information damaging to intelligence operations. Blouin did not think that the "ordinary layman would detect" this information in the news reports, but a trained intelligence officer would derive "a great deal of benefit" from them (105). Gurfein asked Blouin whether the government had taken steps to declassify the Tonkin Gulf study (105). Blouin answered that he did not know, since declassification was not part of his responsibility.

Hegarty postponed cross-examining Blouin, and so Seymour proceeded to call William Butts Macomber, deputy undersecretary of state for administration. His principal responsibilities included finance and personnel (106), and he had held his position for about a year and a half. Macomber described himself as a career employee of the State Department, "having spent my entire professional life [there], with very few exceptions," since 1953 (106).

Macomber said that he too had been asked to familiarize himself with the Pentagon Papers on Wednesday (114). He had no doubt that the newspaper had already "jeopardized international relations" and that further publication would "compromise" current and future military, defense, and intelligence operations, as well as international relations (111). Macomber made the general point that the confidentiality was essential to diplomacy, including diplomatic efforts to secure "an enduring and just peace in the world," but he offered no specific examples (112). In response to a question asked by Gurfein, Macomber stated that the Pentagon Papers study contained information relevant to current "sensitive diplomatic matters and treaty matters" and that if it were disclosed it would have an "impact" on those matters (113). As with Doolin and Blouin, Seymour indicated that Macomber would offer details *in camera* (113–14). At that point Gurfein called for a luncheon break.

The hearing did not get under way again until 2:45, at which point the government's last "public" witness, George MacClain, was called. MacClain was director of the Pentagon's Security Classification Management Division. He was a career officer who had joined the department in 1955 and had held his current position since 1963.

MacClain then proceeded to complicate matters considerably. He began by saying that Doolin's testimony was incorrect with respect to top secret documents. These materials were eligible for declassification, although the rules governing such action were complicated. When Gurfein asked for a detailed explanation, MacClain had considerable difficulty making the matter clear. Gurfein interrupted: was there a manual that set forth all the rules? MacClain said there was, and he offered Gurfein his personal copy. Gurfein asked MacClain what safeguards existed to minimize the use of classification to suppress information for political purposes. MacClain seemed offended by the question. "Sir, the basis for classifying information both by the Executive Order and the Department's regulations is that the information be so related to the interest of national defense that the unauthorized disclosure of the information would be harmful to those interests" (148). Gurfein pressed. Who had the authority to classify or declassify? "Officials or their successors in interest or those who are higher in their own chain of command are the ones who should address that question" (148). Gurfein kept probing. "Obviously the Secretary of Defense has no time to review this stuff. Who really does it" (149)? "Staff personnel," MacClain said, and Gurfein then dropped the subject (149). Another twenty minutes were spent questioning MacClain, without real consequence. The public hearing was then recessed, so that matters could begin *in camera*.

▪ ▪ ▪ ▪ ▪

As the session ended, the government had reason to be confident that it would prevail, and the *Times* lawyers could take very little comfort from what had so far occurred. Gurfein seemed to accept the idea that the government could win its case by proving that the disputed documents were properly classified, a task that did not appear to be difficult. Gurfein had even indicated that he would undertake his own study of the classified material. The *Times*, meanwhile, could make no such independent review of the evidence. In addition Gurfein was respectful of the government witnesses, deferential toward Seymour, and hostile toward Bickel and his team. For the press the omens were far from auspicious.

CHAPTER ELEVEN

The Friday Hearing: The Closed Session

In America public access to judicial proceedings is the norm. It helps protect parties from unfairness at the hands of the state, and it aids the public in staying abreast of how the courts function. As in nearly every area of the law, however, even this fundamental rule has its exceptions.

But whether the Pentagon Papers case was the kind of case that justified such an exception was anything but clear. When U.S. Attorney Seymour stated that the government wanted an *in camera* hearing he offered no support for this extraordinary request. The mere fact that the disputed documents were classified was insufficient, since it was widely recognized, even by the Nixon administration, that the government frequently classified documents that presented no national security threat. In addition the government's legal theory did not require a closed hearing. The government had claimed it was entitled to an injunction if the disputed documents were properly classified. Because the executive order establishing the classification scheme broadly defined the specific classification categories, it was almost a certainty that the government would be able to prove that the documents were properly classified and that it would be able to accomplish this without revealing information harmful to the national security.

Nevertheless, the *Times* lawyers did not object to the request for a closed hearing. Alexander Bickel said only that he did not think a closed session was necessary; he did not insist that Seymour offer some minimal evidence proving a closed hearing was required. It was left to Norman Dorsen, who represented the American Civil Liberties Union as *amicus curiae*, to urge Gurfein to require proof of the necessity of a closed hearing. But Gurfein denied Dorsen's suggestion, as well as his renewed motion to intervene. Indeed, Gurfein's dislike of the ACLU was so evident that he even taunted the prominent law professor: "run upstairs [to the United States Court of Appeals for the Second Circuit]," he said, "and see if you can get a reversal of my order."[1]

The *in camera* hearing began about 4:30 in the afternoon and ended at 8:40 that evening. Seymour, Hess, Mardian, and Buzhardt represented the government at the hearing. Bickel, Hegarty, Abrams, Max Frankel, and Harding Bancroft were the *Times* representatives. Guards were posted at the closed doors to keep everyone else out.

Once the closed hearing was completed, the 162-page transcript was sealed, and the defendants and the public were denied access to it. With very few deletions, the transcript was made public in the late 1970s. A few passages that had been initially excised were made public in the late 1980s. Lines here and there remain censored, but it is unlikely that their content would alter the substance of the transcript in any meaningful way. The transcript is not published, and it is unlikely that more than a handful of individuals have ever read it.[2]

▪ ▪ ▪ ▪ ▪

Dennis James Doolin was the government's first witness during the closed hearing. He was also potentially the government's strongest witness, because he was more familiar with the Pentagon Papers than either Francis J. Blouin and William Butts Macomber. But his hour-long testimony turned into a disaster.

Seymour, mindful that Doolin and the other government witnesses were under orders not to offer specific references to the Pentagon Papers, asked Doolin to describe, in general terms, some examples of how further publication would injure the national security.[3] Doolin stated that the Pentagon Papers contained information that would have a "tremendously serious impact" on current military operations and plans and on contingency military plans if disclosed (4). He claimed the Pentagon Papers included documents that revealed that the government of Thailand was giving assistance to the Royal Lao government, a revelation the Royal Lao government repeatedly denied (5). The *Times* disclosures hurt the South East Asia Treaty Organization, he claimed, adding that the Pentagon Papers contained "references . . . to certain SEATO operational plans, Plan 5 in particular," which he stated "is still in existence" but did not explain (10).

Doolin claimed that further *Times* disclosures would seriously harm diplomatic efforts to end the war and free the prisoners of war. He said that the Pentagon's study contained documents detailing "sensitive negotiations with other governments" the United States had been using as intermediaries to "get Hanoi to move on the question of prisoners of war" (5). Doolin described these third-party countries as "allies," "neutrals," and "hostile" to the United States (5). He alleged that the disputed documents contained "extremely privileged communications" with these governments and that as a result of the *Times* publication it was now "difficult, if not impossible," for the United States to ask these countries to pass on to Hanoi "sensitive" probes regarding the mutual exchange of prisoners, or even to get a list of the prisoners (5). Although Doolin did not specify the documents he had in mind, he presumably meant, at minimum, the four volumes that traced the diplomatic history of the war and probably other documents in other volumes as well.

He also said that the study included intelligence material, which he summarized as "signal intelligence, electronics intelligence, [and] communication intelligence," that revealed that the United States was not only reading the other side's "traffic" but how it was able to read it (6–7). Doolin did not state that further disclosures would permit the breaking of any U.S. code. His point was different; it was that information in the study indicated how the United States obtained intelligence information about the North Vietnamese and the Viet Cong and that its disclosure would directly harm intelligence activities. Doolin stated that this material had a higher and far more restrictive classification than top secret.

Doolin claimed that the *Times* reports threatened the Nixon administration's Vietnamization program, which was intended to permit phased withdrawal of U.S. troops so that South Vietnam forces would eventually be alone in opposing the North Vietnamese and the Viet Cong. The reports would undercut the willingness of the Australians, the New Zealanders, and the Thais to maintain military forces in Vietnam and possibly quicken the rate at which they withdrew their troops. Doolin said that these developments "could have a very adverse impact" on the rate of withdrawal of U.S. troops, thus causing more American soldiers to remain in Vietnam for longer, which in turn "could endanger the lives of American servicemen" remaining in Vietnam (8).

Seymour did not ask Doolin to provide one reference to the Pentagon Papers that supported the government's allegations, and Doolin did not volunteer any citations. But Gurfein asked Doolin to anchor these allegations in the Pentagon Papers. After Doolin had stated that it was his "considered opinion" that further *Times* disclosures would cause the Thais to accelerate the rate of their troop withdrawal from Vietnam, Doolin told Gurfein: "I could mention other items, but there is one particular area that frankly is so sensitive that I can't mention it even within this room and I could only mention it on a personal basis." Gurfein ignored Doolin's suggestion that he exclude the *Times* representatives from the courtroom and asked Doolin if he had any specific references to documents.

But having asked this important question, Gurfein did not give Doolin a chance to answer. He may have felt self-conscious about having interrupted Seymour's direct examination of Doolin, for he instantly apologized to Seymour: "I don't mean to take over the examination, Mr. Seymour, you go ahead." Perhaps hoping that Doolin would disregard Robert Mardian and Fred Buzhardt's admonition to refuse to provide references to the documents, Seymour said to Gurfein: "Go right ahead, your Honor. We want to get the facts out that the Court needs." But Gurfein continued to defer: "I suppose you are coming to it now. Let's relate . . . these categories you have given us" to the study. At that moment Hegarty objected to Doolin's statement that he was prepared to tell Gurfein about extremely serious matters in private; Gurfein agreed with Hegarty and told him he did not "want to hear it" on that condition. Seymour continued to ask Doolin questions but did not ask him for specific citations (8–9).

Within a few minutes Gurfein interrupted again. This time he wanted to know from Doolin whether there wasn't "anything" in the study that was "just of historical significance." Doolin agreed there was but that it would take several people "trained in the trade," by which he presumably meant national security officials, to identify purely historical information that had no current significance. As an example of what he meant, Doolin said that Admiral Blouin had that day pointed out an item of significance that he would have missed because he, Blouin, worked exclusively in the military area. Even then Doolin continued to insist it would be "very difficult" to segregate the historical information because of the "political, military, intelligence mix of data" in the study (11–13).

Gurfein was troubled. He was sympathetic to the government's position and respectful of the government's legal claims and witnesses. But he did not think it would be as difficult as Doolin implied it would be to identify purely historical material with no current national security import. Gurfein said it was his "feeling" that the government was "not trying to suppress what the public should properly know." But he told Doolin that there was "no question" that "a lot of errors can be hidden under the guise of security" and that the task at hand was to decide whether there was any way of separating "errors" from valid security matters. Responding to Gurfein's comments, Seymour asked Doolin whether in his judgment the continued classification of the Pentagon Papers was intended to avoid personal or political embarrassment. Doolin said "No" (14–15).

Gurfein then switched gears and asked Doolin another question. If the Pentagon Papers study was extremely sensitive, why did two former secretaries of defense, Robert S. McNamara and Clark Clifford, each have a copy? If they wrote their memoirs, might they not rely upon these documents and thus reveal, perhaps inadvertently, information that was terribly damaging to the national security? Doolin confessed he did not know why McNamara and Clifford had copies. But he maintained that they "couldn't use" them for their memoirs because they remained classified (18–21).

The opening twenty minutes of Hegarty's cross-examination was inconsequential. Then Hegarty reminded Doolin that Gurfein had asked him shortly before to identify particular documents to illustrate his point that the Pentagon Papers study contained "extremely privileged communications" between the United States and other countries. Hegarty wanted Doolin to pinpoint the documents. Doolin said he "certainly" could do that. But that missed his basic point, he answered: the disclosure of any classified document seriously harmed diplomacy (28).

Gurfein interrupted and asked Doolin: "can you point to specific documents which fit the category, for example, of compromising communications with certain governments about release of prisoners from Hanoi?" (28). Doolin did not answer. Instead, he made somewhat garbled remarks that nevertheless deserve to be quoted because of their ultimate impact on Gurfein:

> As I said, your Honor, on that point there is material in there on sensitive discussions that we have had with other governments and we cannot now, in my judgment, and I think it is an expert judgment, go to Stockholm [Sweden], a country we have very chilly relations with at this time but who had been helpful to us on the prisoner issue, and if this got out that they are doing things for us on the prisoner issue, it would be extremely damaging to the parties concerned and I can't see how we can expect a Swede in a situation like that to continue helping us if we can't keep secrets. (28–29)

Hegarty then asked Doolin to cite a Swedish government communication on the prisoner issue in the study. Seymour objected; Hegarty's question was "unfair." Doolin could not be expected to go through the 7,000-page study and find all the references to Sweden. Seymour's objection had to baffle Hegarty. Hegarty was asking Doolin the same question—more or less—that Gurfein had asked a few minutes before and that Seymour had encouraged Gurfein to ask. Hegarty must have been confident that

Gurfein would overrule the objection and direct Doolin to answer the question. But Gurfein did not say this. Instead, he said that it was "beyond human capacity" to expect Doolin to cite to a particular document. Doolin could only be asked, Gurfein said: "Do you recall in the study [whether there] was . . . some communication between the government of the United States and the Kingdom of Sweden which appears concerning the private intercession by the Swedish government with Hanoi?" Given Doolin's testimony, as quoted above, Gurfein and Seymour must have assumed that Doolin would answer yes, that the Pentagon Papers did contain such documents referring to Sweden. But Doolin said "No" (29–30).

Gurfein was flabbergasted: "There is none?" he asked. And a moment later the judge interrupted Doolin and asked: "Why did you mention Sweden then?" And with still another interruption, Gurfein told Doolin: "I want to get two things straight. One is that there is no doubt that a breakdown of any security system, and this was a breakdown of the security system, . . . will cause repercussions. . . . Number two, beyond that generalized trouble that you get from a breach in security, are there specific items, indeed volumes, which press upon our relations with other governments at this time?" (30–31). Doolin answered "Yes," but he was flustered, and, instead of simply citing the last four volumes of the study, he fueled Gurfein's impatience with more perplexing remarks that made little sense: "Because with this material, sir, that is already on the record in terms of private communications and others that we know are in the possession of the *New York Times*, you are not going to get further representation" (30). And a minute later, Doolin testified: "Again, your Honor, and I am trying to be helpful, you have to look at all of this in the context of the totality of the study, in terms of the decision process taking you into it, in terms of what we did in points of time as we went up in terms of our involvement, and it just gives the other side frankly just one hell of a jump ahead" (32).

From that moment on Gurfein had no use for Doolin's testimony. When Doolin said that the study contained targeting data Gurfein questioned: "What good is a targeting study of 1968 [in] 1971?" (31). When he asserted that the study contained information about the "force structure" that would be harmful if revealed, Gurfein shot back: "We put that in the paper every day." Doolin countered: "but here you are talking about specific planning documents that tell you what you are going to do with that force." Gurfein, impatient, fired in return: "Every day on television I can find out almost the entire order of battle of the United States Army and Marines." And then, to make sure that Doolin did not miss his point, Gurfein mimicked a TV news reporter: "I am here with the First

Division at so and so and we are doing this." Gurfein lectured Doolin: "Warfare today is different from what it was in the days when there was really security. Everybody and his brother knows what everybody is doing today" (39).

A moment later Gurfein again impatiently told Doolin: "I will give you one more chance. . . . Is there anything you would like to add to your testimony for the enlightenment of the Court" that relates your general allegations to specific parts of the Pentagon Papers (40)? Doolin said yes but explained nothing. He confessed: "I could explain it, but I can't." Seymour immediately tried to rescue Doolin: "In fairness to the witness, he is under orders not to explain" (42). Gurfein's insistence on being offered specific and concrete evidence finally collided with Mardian and Buzhardt's order forbidding the witness to give such testimony.

Two minutes later Doolin left the stand. His testimony, which had lasted a little more than an hour, had a profound effect on Gurfein. Up to the last minutes of Doolin's testimony, Gurfein had been openly respectful and sympathetic toward the government. But Doolin's failure to refer to specific documents to substantiate his reference to Sweden transformed Gurfein. He became suspicious and impatient; he challenged every allegation Doolin made; and his suspicions now began to seep through the government's entire case.

There was a final irony of Doolin's testimony: Sweden's role as an intermediary was documented in the Pentagon Papers.[4]

■ ■ ■ ■ ■

During his testimony Doolin mentioned several times that Admiral Blouin, the government's next witness, would be able to provide references to the Pentagon Papers relevant to defense and military matters. Blouin did provide a few specific references of the kind that Doolin did not. But Blouin's testimony failed to repair the harm that Doolin's had caused the government's case; in fact, Blouin's testimony may have increased the harm.

Blouin's testimony focused on both the Tonkin Gulf study and the Pentagon Papers. Blouin was the government witness best informed about the Tonkin Gulf study, which had been prepared by the Weapons Systems Evaluation Group for the Joint Chiefs of Staff, and the distribution of the study had been limited to within the Joint Chiefs. Blouin claimed that the study contained a "detailed description of the decision making process in our government" and "quite a detailed description of the National Military Command Center," which shed light on the system's "faults" and "good parts." Blouin stated that he saw "no useful purpose in publicizing" this information, since it could help an enemy "draw a pretty good picture . . . as to where the key command and control centers" were, and that this information would make it "relatively simple" for an enemy to "sabotage the communications at the right places" (63–64). To illustrate his concern, Blouin offered this example: Russian submarines armed with nuclear weapons could more strategically position themselves off our coast because they would know how long it might take our military command to decide to react (62). Blouin also claimed, without explaining, that the Tonkin Gulf study gave clues as to how we gather intelligence information about adversaries (47).

Gurfein was skeptical. At one point he told Blouin: "Let's face the fact . . . [the enemy] knows we are reading him." Later, after Blouin referred to a situation from 1958, he said: "I hope our communications are not that static, Admiral." But as skeptical as Gurfein was, the Tonkin Gulf study concerned the *Times*. Hegarty initially objected to Blouin's testimony about it because the *Times* had only a three-page summary of the study. But when Gurfein asked Hegarty to permit him to review the summary so that he could compare it to the full study, Hegarty refused. Consequently, Gurfein said that he would permit Blouin to testify on the assumption that the *Times* had the entire study. By the end of Blouin's testimony, however, the *Times* altered its position and submitted the summary to Gurfein to examine (47, 63, 66).

The balance of Blouin's testimony focused on the Pentagon Papers, which he saw for the first time only on Wednesday evening. He told Gurfein that no one within the Joint Chiefs of Staff, including the officers who headed the separate armed services, had ever seen the study before.

Blouin's focus was military matters. He claimed that the Pentagon Papers was "full of highly sensitive material" pertaining to war plans, covert war plans, the length of time it takes to generate an air strike, the number of air craft used in particular operations, the "so-called 34-A operation . . . that is so sensitive that I know many flag and general officers [didn't] . . . know exist[ed] even when they . . . had duty in Vietnam," the listing of bombing targets, the rules of engagement that defined the constraints under which our military forces operate in a wide variety of circumstances, contingency military plans in the event that the withdrawal program was not successful, and plans for troop deployment as the size of the U.S. military forces decreases (50–52, 56–59).

Blouin then did what Buzhardt had told Seymour the government witnesses would not do: he offered Gurfein ten specific references to the Pentagon Papers to support his general points (54).[5] In addition Blouin referred Gurfein to twenty-five pages that he claimed contained "old messages" that might assist someone in breaking intelligence codes used at that time. He even implied that this material in conjunction with other material and the assistance of computers might help someone break a current code (55).[6] But Blouin conceded that he was no expert on codes (55). Blouin told Gurfein that he could provide many more details if he had more time to examine the study and that he was certain that the office of the Joint Chiefs would have citations for the judge if it had time to study the report.

Blouin made no comment on the references he provided. He did not describe or characterize them in any way. He simply gave the references with no explanation as to how or why they supported the general themes of his testimony.

As odd as that was, what was even more peculiar was that Gurfein did not ask Blouin one question about the references. After all, Blouin had just indicated that these specific page references to the Pentagon Papers related to a whole host of highly sensitive and significant military matters, and Gurfein did not ask for clarification, explanation, or elaboration.

By comparison to Doolin, Blouin was a responsive and forthcoming witness. He spoke clearly; he was not argumentative; he particularized the military considerations that supported his overall judgements; and he provided a handful of references to pages in the study he claimed illustrated his points. Gurfein seemed unimpressed. He even expressed deep skepticism that the national security would be injured by disclosures of the kind cited by Blouin. This was true in part because Gurfein doubted that much of what Blouin claimed was secret was in fact secret. Gurfein thought that the Vietnamese obviously knew that the United States was trying to break their codes and that the United States used surveillance methods against it. He mocked Blouin's claim that the rules of engagement were important secrets by asking Blouin if by secret rules of engagement he meant the prohibition against bombing Haiphong Harbor "and things like that?" (57). He gave the clear indication that he doubted the so-called 34-A operation was current, or that the rules of engagement were current, or that the contingency military plans were current, or that the study compromised current intelligence capacities.

Gurfein's attitude toward Blouin was a direct reaction to Doolin's testimony. He treated Blouin's answers with the same suspicion he had displayed after Doolin had made him feel he was being misled and taken for granted. But Blouin's general attitude toward the government's need for confidentiality also fed Gurfein's skepticism. Blouin made it clear that he thought the press already reported so much information that the government operated in a "fishbowl." Blouin said "[I] deplore much of what I read" in the press. He said that the "way we do business in our country . . . [is to] live by the open book." Blouin indicated he disapproved of that characteristic; he said his critical feelings were due to the way he was "brought up." He complained that he thought "we make it too easy" for the Soviets, and presumably others, to learn about critical defense matters (49, 59, 70). Gurfein gave the strong impression that he objected to Blouin's willingness to keep from the public a wide range of information. He told Blouin that perhaps he had to adjust to operating in a fishbowl, that it was not just a prying press that disclosed classified material but "everybody and his brother" who wrote a memoir. He informed Blouin: "I read with great interest every word said by President Kennedy during the Cuban missile crisis. It was none of my business, but there it was" (49).

It is also quite possible that Gurfein's growing impatience with the government may have been fueled by yet one more factor. During Blouin's testimony Seymour told Gurfein that, within the time constraints of the litigation, the government could not separate the documents within the Pentagon Papers study into two stacks—those that could be released and those that could not. Such a sorting out would take much more time than the government had. The crux of Seymour's explanation was that the government wanted an injunction covering the entire Pentagon Papers study and that the government would not help Gurfein identify purely historical documents that could be made public forthwith (53–54).

Gurfein repeated throughout the day that while the government was not trying to suppress information the public should have, there must be some information in the study that was so historical that it could be made public without jeopardizing the national security. When he made such comments, Seymour did not directly inform Gurfein that the government opposed the judge's effort to separate out the material. Now, toward the end of a long day, Seymour told Gurfein that the government rejected that approach, and that it wanted every page protected. Gurfein was likely irritated. He was disposed toward the government, but he needed its cooperation on a matter that he obviously considered of impeccable reasonableness. And now the government was turning him down, no matter how reasonable he thought he was being. If Doolin had made Gurfein feel manipulated, Seymour may have made him feel betrayed.

▪ ▪ ▪ ▪ ▪

William Butts Macomber was the most polished and forceful of the government witnesses. He was poised and confident; he answered questions directly and with a sense of authority. He skillfully held his own when questioned by Gurfein or cross-examined by Hegarty. Indeed, while on the stand he was so much in command that he almost seemed to conduct a tutorial on the interaction between the press and diplomatic initiatives in a democratic society.

Macomber began by offering three examples of how the *Times* publications on Sunday, Monday, and Tuesday had already injured the national security. First, the *Times* reported on the so-called Seaborn mission. Seaborn was the Canadian representative on the International Control Commission who often went to Hanoi and would press some negotiating points on behalf of the United States with Hanoi officials. Macomber said that Seaborn had been helpful, and that he had been under difficult circumstances. The *Times* publication of a telegram sent by a U.S. official to Seaborn spelling out a negotiating position was embarrassing for Seaborn and for the Canadian government, for it appeared that Seaborn was "working for us" and that he and other Canadian officials were at our "beck and call." Macomber said that the *Times* disclosures have prompted tough questioning by the opposition party in the Canadian Parliament and has put the Canadian government on the defensive. More important, the *Times* report would make Canada "reluctant" to help the United States in the future and would make it "almost impossible" for the United States to ask third-party countries to help with sensitive matters that would be politically embarrassing if the request and the subsequent diplomatic actions were publicly reported (76–77).

Second, Macomber said that the *Times* publication sparked a "political storm" in Australia. Some published documents implied that the "Australian government didn't really go to Vietnam because they were asked to by the Vietnamese government" and because of obligations under the SEATO treaty, even though that was the public explanation offered by the Australian prime minister. Instead, the Pentagon Paper documents implied that Australian troops went to Vietnam because of "United States maneuvering." Macomber stated the *Times* story "broke at the time the opposition party" was having its annual meeting and that the current prime minister "has been politically embarrassed." Indeed, the Australian prime minister had characterized the disclosures as "absolutely appalling." In Macomber's view there was little doubt that the *Times* report had undermined "our relations with an extremely important ally" (77).

Macomber's third example was the *Times* publication of a "message" sent by Harold Wilson, who was prime minister of Great Britain at the time, to President Lyndon Johnson. Macomber condemned it; it was "absolutely unacceptable" to publish confidential communication between long-standing and trusted allies (78).

Macomber expressed deep concern that the *Times* might publish additional injurious information. As an example of what he had in mind, he cited a lengthy and candid 1968 communication from the U.S. ambassador to the Soviet Union, Llewellyn Thompson. Macomber said that Thompson prepared this report in response to a request that "he give the United States Government his best judgment about what the Soviet Union would do if we took certain steps that would escalate our activities in Vietnam." Thompson's communication was addressed to then Secretary of State Nicholas de B. Katzenbach and was marked "eyes only." Macomber said that Thompson "has long been considered and is still considered as outstanding an expert as we have in the Soviet Union. It is generally regarded in Washington and elsewhere that what Ambassador Thompson thinks is going on in the Soviet Union is pretty much what the United States government thinks." Macomber claimed that it would be very beneficial to the Soviets to know what we thought of them and what we would expect of them (79–80). Macomber even speculated that the publication of the Thompson message would have a rippling effect and might restrain all U.S. ambassadors from being perfectly candid in their reports.

Macomber testified that the *Times* reports would injure the United States's ability "to do something about the POW's." The nations "that have the most chance of accomplishing something are the ones that stand to lose the most" if their efforts on our behalf become public. Macomber cited the Soviet Union as an example. He explained that the Soviet Union had "somewhat different objectives in the world than the mainland Chinese" and was in a "somewhat more vulnerable position as far as international communist public opinion is concerned" (81–82). He said that the Soviet Union could not be counted on to help the United States with Hanoi at all if the Soviets believed that whatever they said or did might be splashed across the pages of the *Times*.

Macomber made three additional points. The "one thing the Arabs and the Israelis agree on is if they are going to talk with us about peace out there, they can only do it if they have absolute guarantees that we aren't going to put it in the papers." He claimed that negotiations over Berlin required total secrecy if tensions were to be relieved. The "SALT talks would be dead" if their substance were disclosed (98).

Gurfein did not challenge Macomber's claims that the *Times* had already published information that had injured national security or that further *Times* publications would injure other national security interests. He expressed no dissatisfaction with Macomber's level of specificity, nor did he belittle the examples offered by Macomber as insignificant. He did not question whether Macomber's examples were so hypothetical as to be of little relevance.

What Gurfein was interested in was Macomber's views on a set of related theoretical questions. During a fifteen-minute exchange that separated Seymour's direct examination and Hagerty's cross-examination, Gurfein asked Macomber about a range of issues. Was the classification system used to bury "mistakes?" Were "policy questions" that belong to the "political area" "disguised" as national security questions and classified? How does one accommodate the need for confidentiality in diplomacy and the democratic process, which emphasizes the citizen's need to be informed about domestic as well as foreign affairs? What was the average citizen's recourse for obtaining information that was improperly withheld by the executive branch? Did the State Department have a process for routinely declassifying information (85–88)? How severe was the leak of the Pentagon Papers?

Macomber answered Gurfein's questions directly and respectfully, conveying the impression throughout of being thoughtful, reasonable, and sensitive to both the needs for security and the public's need to be informed. Macomber conceded that the classification system was abused to hide political blunders. But he insisted that this was "a very difficult problem," and that it was not a new problem: "The problem of diplomacy fitting into a democracy has been with us from the beginning" (85). Moreover, "it is incredible to suggest that the people that have taken the responsibility for the basic decisions in Vietnam are not politically accountable. The burdens that the last President and this President have borne on that make it very clear that the principle that I am speaking for today has not been carried to the point where the leadership has managed to escape the bruises that grow out of this kind of policy" (86).

Macomber agreed with Gurfein that mistakes that were political in nature should not be suppressed, but he asserted that "information taken out of context put out by people who are not in a position to know the entire thing" is not the answer either. He contended that in this case the *Times* officials "can't possibly know that a derogatory remark they are printing in the paper is jeopardizing a completely different kind of operation of great importance they know nothing about." He said that it was not a "question of judgment or goodwill; it is a question of whether they have adequate information" (87–89).

Macomber denied that the public was deprived of basic information it needed. The State Department had a program for declassifying documents similar to that of the Defense Department. Moreover, the State

Department was subject to "constant pressure from the Congress, from the press and from the public for disclosures." He stated that "it is my feeling that the pressure is so great that I don't say you cease to worry about the executive covering up too much, but the pressure is so great that he can't hope to cover up very much more than the absolute essentials." He contended that if the ability to conduct confidential diplomatic negotiations is thrown out, "we [will] have irreparably damaged the chance of free government to endure and some of these other questions [will] become academic." It is "obviously," Macomber told Gurfein, "a question of competing principles and pressures and through our history I think in an uneasy way we have handled it pretty well" (88).

As for the leak of the Pentagon Papers, Macomber said he knew of no comparable leak. "We can't say this is the first serious leak but the size of this, the magnitude of it is unprecedented in my judgement." What's more, the leak is not being published "by a small weekly newspaper but one of the great newspapers of the world," which has an impact "all over the world." Macomber also emphasized that this was "a slow motion leak," unlike others that were usually reported all at once leaving the government with no option but to respond to what has already been published. Here the "world is watching to see whether the U.S. government has the capacity to prevent this thing in circumstances when they are forewarned it is happening" (89).

▪ ▪ ▪ ▪ ▪

Once the giving of testimony was complete, Gurfein heard legal arguments from Bickel and Seymour for a little more than an hour, until 8:40 P.M. At 9:50 Gurfein returned to the bench after a break for dinner and opened the courtroom doors to the public. During this session Gurfein heard from Norman Dorsen on behalf of the American Civil Liberties Union and additional arguments from Seymour and Bickel.[7]

Dorsen, who waited in the courthouse all day to argue on behalf of the ACLU, had barely spoken when Gurfein asked him how long he expected to take. Dorsen said twenty minutes; Gurfein shot back: "take 10." Gurfein also snapped that he did not need "the rhetoric" and that Dorsen should "give it" to the press, from Gurfein's viewpoint Dorsen's intended audience, later (160).

Dorsen emphasized that a primary purpose of the First Amendment was to ensure an "informed citizenry," which was the basis of the democratic process. "Nothing so diminishes democracy as secrecy. Self-government is meaningful only with an informed public," he told Gurfein. Dorsen conceded that the First Amendment tolerated prior restraints, but he insisted that such restraints could be lawfully imposed "only with matters directly affecting military operations." To illustrate his point, Dorsen said that the public need not know the precise location of troops but that it had to know about policy decisions that could lead to the shipment of troops or the initiation of war (161–62). Dorsen stated that, because he had been barred from attending the *in camera* hearing, he did not know what the government witnesses had said. The question boiled down to whether to trust the government experts or not, and on that point he warned Gurfein not to "allow the experts to govern." He said that the "experts don't know everything" and that it was appropriate for the judiciary to insist on protecting the press's right to publish unless the government's evidence met the requirements of the constitution, which he doubted it did (163–64).

Bickel argued at length during the closed hearing as well as during the public session. Bickel dismissed Doolin's testimony as conjecture; all the dangers identified by the assistant secretary of defense were hypothetical in nature and fell far short of the Constitution's requirements for a prior restraint. Bickel attacked Admiral Blouin's conclusions that further publication would injure the national security as unreliable because he had made it clear that he thought the court should enjoin further publication merely because it was "just better" not to make the information public and that further publication served "no useful purpose" (151). Bickel then said that he and Macomber had been classmates at Harvard Law School, and he characterized Macomber as essentially concerned about political embarrassment for either United States or foreign political leaders (156–57). Bickel said that the government had failed to prove that the *Times* publications undermined any United States codes or any other intelligence interests or activities. He emphasized that the government witnesses seemed worried mainly about matters that were either already public or historical.

Bickel repeated his claim that the president did not have inherent authority to ask the court for an injunction in this case. In response to a question from Gurfein, however, Bickel conceded the government could bring such a lawsuit even though there might not be a statute expressly forbidding the publication of sailing dates or information pertaining to atomic weapons. Gurfein then asked what the difference was between those circumstances and the one presented by this case. Bickel's answer was befuddled. He seemed to suggest that the difference was that in the case of sailing dates or atomic weapons an emergency existed, and in this case there was no emergency. But when Gurfein suggested that the issue of whether the government was authorized to sue the *Times* for an injunction seemed to boil down to how one assessed the government's claim,

Bickel equivocated and did not make it clear why he did not agree with Gurfein. In the end Gurfein seem unpersuaded by Bickel that the government could not as a matter of law ask the federal courts for an injunction under the circumstances of this case.

Seymour restated a position he had previously asserted. He contended that the government was entitled to a preliminary injunction once it established that the disputed documents were properly classified, which he believed it had done. He claimed that the *Times* was not authorized to possess the disputed stolen documents and that it had not availed itself of the remedy Congress had created when it adopted the Freedom of Information Act. He told Gurfein that he and the other government lawyers had been unable to identify any other incident in which a newspaper had published the complete text of classified documents. He tried to discount the fact that there had been no previous efforts by the government to obtain a prior restraint by arguing that the press normally surprised the government by publishing the objectionable material all at once. To the extent that the First Amendment limited the government's right to obtain injunctive relief in this case, Seymour agreed with Bickel that the troop ship example in the *Near* case was an appropriate guide. But he claimed that the government's evidence satisfied that requirement.

As the arguments ended, Gurfein gave little indication as to how he would rule. He suggested that the government probably had the right to sue the *Times* absent a statute. He said that the government had done a "good job" in presenting evidence that the disputed material was not improperly classified. He stated that the government had a heavy burden to carry if it were to prevail. Although he appeared to accept Bickel's suggestion that the troop ship example was the appropriate guide, he also seemed greatly troubled by the publication of verbatim messages between governments and by the claims that the *Times* already had and might in the future compromise intelligence interests. He appealed, even at this late hour, once again, to the *Times*'s sense of patriotism.

As he left the bench well past eleven P.M. he told the lawyers that he would "try to work out something in the morning." He advised them to call his chambers about eleven to "see how I am doing" (195). With that, the hearing ended. Gurfein left the courtroom and the courthouse and went home.[8]

CHAPTER TWELVE

Gurfein's Decision

Gurfein returned to his chambers about eight o'clock the next morning. By that time he knew that the *Washington Post* was enjoined during the night from publishing additional reports based on the Pentagon Papers. He told his law clerk, Mel P. Barkan, not to interrupt him while he dictated his opinion to his secretary. When the 4,000-word opinion was typed Gurfein reviewed it with Barkan, but they made only a few stylistic changes.[1]

The lawyers arrived at Gurfein's chambers in the early afternoon. By that time the hallways and staircases close to Gurfein's chambers were crowded with reporters and members of the public. Gurfein told the lawyers that he was dissolving the temporary restraining order and denying the government the preliminary injunction it sought. He indicated that the newspaper was free to print what it wished except for one document. That document, Gurfein explained, would make it unlikely that an unidentified third country would act as an intermediary between the United States and North Vietnam if disclosed. For reasons that are not known, Gurfein must have thought that the country in question was a more potential vital link to North Vietnam than the many other countries whose identities were also revealed in the Pentagon Papers. Although the document and the identity of this third country are still not known, it is likely that the country was the Soviet Union. Gurfein asked if the *Times* would agree not to publish this document. Gurfein said that if the newspaper did not accede to his condition, he would issue the appropriate order. The *Times* agreed.[2]

Gurfein also announced that he was continuing the restraining order until the government had an opportunity to seek a stay from the Second Circuit court of appeals. Gurfein informed the lawyers that the clerk of the court was in his office waiting for the order to be filed and that Irving Kaufman, a court of appeals judge, was waiting upstairs in his chambers to consider the government's request that the restraining order be continued pending the anticipated appeal. After Gurfein gave the lawyers a copy of his opinion they left his chambers.

Barkan took the original opinion and order with him as he left the chambers. He was supposed to go directly to the clerk's office to file the documents. But he was so exhausted that he absent-mindedly left the courthouse with the legal documents. Barkan crossed the street in front of the courthouse, descended the stairs to the subway, deposited a subway token, and headed for an uptown train. It was only then that he realized that he still had the original opinion and order. Because the government could not appeal until he filed the papers, Barkan raced to the courthouse. Once this formality was completed, Barkan went home.[3]

▪ ▪ ▪ ▪ ▪

Gurfein's opinion began with a brief review of the factual circumstances that gave rise to the legal dispute, a summary of the legal proceedings that had occurred, and a short description of the claims made by the government and the *Times*. He stated that this case was "one of first impression" and that the lawyers in the case had been unable to identify any case "remotely resembling" the one at hand. He asserted that the government sued the *Times* "in absolute good faith to protect its security and not as a means of suppressing dissident or contrary political opinion."[4]

Gurfein's opinion then addressed the *Times*'s legal argument that the government lacked the authority to obtain a prior restraint in this case. Gurfein's discussion of this issue was far and away the longest section of his opinion. The *Times*, he wrote, contended that the government had "no inherent power" to seek an injunction against the *Times*, that such power could be derived only from a statute, and that no statute authorized the government to seek such judicial relief against the *Times* in this case. The government, he stated, responded that it did have statutory authority for the injunction and that, alternatively, it had the inherent "right to protect itself in its vital functions" and thus could seek to enjoin the *Times* even in the absence of an authorizing statute.[5]

Gurfein noted that the government relied upon Section 793(e) of the espionage laws as authority for the action against the *Times*. After quoting the provision in full he observed that, since the word "publication" did not appear in the statute, it was most unlikely that Congress intended this provision of the espionage laws to cover media disclosures. But he noted that the absence of the word was not conclusive as to the statute's meaning. Nevertheless, Gurfein contended that a careful reading of this and related statutes indicated that it was "truly" an espionage section that prohibited secret or clandestine "communication" of national defense information.[6]

Once Gurfein concluded that Congress had not passed a statute that authorized the executive branch to secure a prior restraint, he discussed whether there was "inherent power in the Executive to protect the national security." He stated that the *Times* had conceded that the executive branch had inherent power under the Constitution to "restrain serious breaches vitally affecting the interests of the Nation" and that he believed that the government had inherent power to obtain "injunctive relief against a newspaper that is about to publish information or documents absolutely vital to current national security." But Gurfein wrote that he did not believe that the evidence offered by the government during the hearing *in camera* established that a security breach existed that vitally affected the interests of the nation. That conclusion left Gurfein facing what he termed a "delicate question." Does the president have inherent authority to "protect the functioning of his prerogatives—the conduct of foreign affairs, the right to impartial advice and military security—" when the security breach is less than vital to national security? But Gurfein stated that he did not have to decide this question because he was denying the government the injunction it sought on the ground that the government's evidence "did not convince" him that the publication of "these historical documents would seriously breach the national security."[7]

Gurfein devoted only the last few pages of his opinion to his conclusion that the First Amendment barred the government from securing a prior restraint in this case. He observed that the First Amendment did not prohibit all prior restraints and quoted approvingly from Chief Justice Hughes's majority opinion in *Near v. Minnesota* that "no one would question but that a government might prevent actual obstruction to its recruiting service or the publication of the sailing dates of transports or the number or location of troops." Gurfein then stated that the *Near* examples indicated that a prior restraint could be secured in only limited circumstances. Without any additional analysis or review of the evidence, Gurfein claimed that this case did not present a "sharp clash" between vital security interests and the right of the *Times* to publish the disputed material, because "no cogent reasons were advanced as to why these documents except in the general framework of embarrassment . . . would vitally affect the security of the Nation."[8]

Gurfein ended his opinion with a strong affirmation of the importance of protecting the press's freedom. "The security of the Nation is not at the ramparts alone," he wrote. "Security also lies in the value of our free institutions. A cantankerous press, an obstinate press, a ubiquitous press must be suffered by those in authority in order to preserve the even greater values of freedom of expression and the right of the people to know." In addition he observed, "these are troubled times. There is no greater safety valve for discontent and cynicism about the affairs of Government than freedom of expression in any form. This has been the genius of our institutions throughout our history. It has been the credo of all our Presidents. It is one of the marked traits of our national life that distinguish us from other nations under different forms of government."[9]

▪ ▪ ▪ ▪ ▪

Why did Gurfein rule against the government? What Gurfein stated in his opinion was undoubtedly true; the government had failed to support its serious allegations with references to the Pentagon Papers sufficient to satisfy Gurfein. But why did Gurfein conclude that the government had failed to satisfy its evidentiary burden?

Throughout the hearing on Friday Gurfein seemed confused or uncertain about fundamental questions that he had to resolve before he could decide whether or not to grant the government the injunction it sought. These were, in effect, primary questions that Gurfein had to settle before he could decide what evidence was relevant or necessary to the resolution of the dispute and what standard to use in assessing its adequacy.

For example, the government had contended that it should prevail if it proved that the documents were properly classified. The *Times* argued that the government's claim for a preliminary injunction had to be measured against the First Amendment, which required the government to prove that further publication would gravely injure the national security. Because these were drastically different legal claims, Gurfein had to decide which of these two competing legal rules should govern the case. If he adopted the government's view, the relevant evidence for resolving the dispute would be different from the evidence otherwise required. If he endorsed the *Times* approach, he would have to decide a multitude of other questions. Regardless of which legal rule he decided should govern this dispute, he had to resolve this matter before he could decide what evidence was relevant and whether it was legally sufficient.

Gurfein was also confused about whether he was going to read through the Pentagon Papers on his own and identify documents that injured the national security or whether he would consider only the documents identified by the government witnesses. On the one hand, he stated that he was going to read the study himself. On the other hand, Gurfein expressed great impatience with the government witnesses for not pinpointing documents that supported their general allegations and at one point impatiently told Doolin that he was going to give him just one more chance to specify the documents. Obviously, before Gurfein could decide that the government was not entitled to the injunction because its witnesses had failed to identify key documents that supported its claims, he had to decide whether he was going to take the initiative and read through the Pentagon Papers on his own.

Gurfein also suggested during the Friday hearing that he thought the government's entitlement to an injunction might be affected by how the *Times* gained possession of the classified material. If Gurfein had decided that how the *Times* gained possession of the top secret documents was relevant to his decision, the *Times* might have lost no matter how weak the government's evidence was.

By the time Gurfein dictated his opinion on Saturday morning he had resolved these important issues. He had decided that the government could not prevail simply by proving that the documents were properly classified and that the *Times*'s right to publish the papers was not affected by how it got them. He had concluded that the First Amendment limited the government's right to enjoin the *Times* and that the government had the burden of proving that further publication would injure the national security. He also decided that he would limit his reading of the classified documents only to the ones identified by the government witnesses.

These were incredibly important conclusions that set the stage for Gurfein to decide what evidence he should consider in deciding how to resolve the dispute and whether the evidence that he considered relevant warranted an injunction. Indeed, Gurfein could not even begin to think intelligently about the evidence—what was relevant and whether it was legally sufficient—until he had resolved these issues. Thus, if we are to understand why Gurfein ruled against the government we must understand why Gurfein decided these central issues the way he did.

The fact that Gurfein came to these conclusions was to some extent explicable by prior cases. The government's legal claim that it was entitled to an injunction if it proved that the disputed documents were properly classified was unsupported by earlier cases. As already indicated, such a conclusion would have constituted a radical departure from established expectations of what the law was, as well as the working assumptions of the daily press, not to mention many government officials. Thus, it is likely that Gurfein, who was not steeped in First Amendment law and had not had time to study many First Amendment cases before making his decision, had learned enough during the previous hectic days to conclude that the government's legal position was novel, extreme, and at odds with settled expectation as to what the law was.

Prior case law probably also persuaded Gurfein that the question of how the *Times* came into possession of the classified documents was irrelevant to the matter. There was certainly no support in the case law for such a linkage, and it seems likely that Gurfein concluded that he should ignore this consideration in deciding the government's request. It also seems likely that prior cases persuaded Gurfein that the government's entitlement to an injunction had to be measured against the press's rights as guaranteed by the First Amendment and that the First Amendment imposed upon the government the burden of proving that further publication would injure national security.

As important as these conclusions were, the resolution of these issues still left Gurfein having to resolve two other fundamental questions before he could reason his way to a conclusion. Gurfein had to decide whether he would assess only the government's references to the Pentagon papers or whether he would assume responsibility for reviewing the entire study himself. He also had to decide whether the government's evidence was legally sufficient.

Once Gurfein decided that the government had the burden of proving that further publication would injure the national security, he might well have concluded that he would review only the references that the government witnesses offered. This would be an entirely justifiable conclusion. But there was a problem with this line of thinking. Gurfein had stated during the Friday hearing that he would assume responsibility for reviewing all the documents. Seymour had indicated that he was going to rely upon Gurfein's statements, which might have meant that the government was not going to identify all the Pentagon Papers passages it was concerned about because it assumed that Gurfein would review the entire study on his own. Case law permitted Gurfein to restrict his review to the government citations, but it did not require it. What Gurfein had to consider was whether in fairness to the government he could renege on his representations that he would review the entire study and limit his examination only to those citations offered by the government.

The other major issue left open by prior case law was what standard Gurfein should apply in deciding whether the government's evidence was sufficient to warrant an injunction. In his opinion Gurfein indicated that his assessment of the government's evidence was guided by Chief Justice Hughes's majority opinion in *Near v. Minnesota*.[10] The Supreme Court did not invoke the doctrine of prior restraint until the *Near* case, when it invalidated a Minnesota statute aimed at curbing obscene, lewd, malicious, scandalous, and defamatory publication. Thus, the Court in *Near* was not faced with circumstances remotely related to national security, and its comments on the propriety of a prior restraint to protect some national security interests were totally unnecessary to the resolution of the case.

Gurfein stated that Hughes's examples indicated "how limited is the field of security protection" provided the government by the First Amendment. But Hughes's statement left open several critical issues. First, what kind of injury to the national security must the government allege and prove to be entitled to a prior restraint? The examples indicate that a prior restraint may be granted to protect the life of troops. But that cannot be the only injury sufficient to warrant a prior restraint. Preventing the death of civilians or of prisoners of war would seem to be equally deserving of a prior restraint. Would the disclosure of military plans that would not result in the immediate death of any soldiers but might contribute to the possible defeat of an army at some future but unascertainable time be legally sufficient? Would the threatened disclosure of information about U.S. intelligence activities in a foreign country warrant a prior restraint even though no lives were threatened? Would the threatened publication of classified information that might help a third country build a nuclear weapon be subject to a prior restraint? Would the threatened disclosure of secret negotiations aimed at ending an armed conflict involving U.S. soldiers warrant a prior restraint? Neither Hughes's brief statement nor subsequent decisions provide unambiguous, straightforward answers to these questions.

Hughes's brief statement also left undefined what kind of relationship must exist between the disputed publication and the predicted injury to national security. This inquiry really involves two related ones. In order for the government to secure a prior restraint, how quickly must the injury follow publication, and how likely must it be that the injury will in fact follow from publication. Hughes's examples shed little light on these inquiries. If the sailing times of a troop transport are made public, the departure time could be changed so that there would be no injury. If the time were published after the troop ship left port, it could return to port or change its course if there was concern that the announcement of its departure endangered the ship. If the location of ground troops were revealed, whether that might result in certain death depends upon such factors as the position of the enemy forces, the availability of escape routes, the ability to lift the troops from their position by helicopter, the ability of air power to protect the troops from ground attacks. Unless one knew about each of these circumstances as well as others, one would not be able to say with any certainty that the publication of the information about transport ships or troop location would result in injury. Similar doubts exist about how immediately after disclosure injury would result. If the transport ship never left port, there would never be an injury, let alone an immediate one. If the ground troops were able to escape following publication of their position, there would be no direct injury. If the air force were able to forestall an attack, injury would be delayed, perhaps avoided.

Third, Hughes's examples did not address the issue of whether the legal standard for the granting of a prior restraint would vary depending upon the magnitude of the potential harm. For example, if the government alleged that publication would cause the death of one soldier, should a court insist that the information be of such a nature that its disclosure would cause the death directly and immediately before granting a prior restraint? But if the government claimed that the information in question would increase the risk of a nuclear holocaust if disclosed, should a court apply a less demanding standard and not insist that publication result in an immediate and direct consequence?

Last, Hughes's examples seem to anticipate that the government would be able to identify the specific injury to national security that would result from a denial of a prior restraint. It did not anticipate a situation presented by the Pentagon Papers case in which the government stated that it did not know the full extent of the security breach and thus could not predict the extent of injury to national security. Case law certainly did not require Gurfein to factor this consideration into his decision as to whether or not to grant a prior restraint. But it also did not explicitly forbid him from doing so either.

The fact that these issues were unresolved was no surprise. The government had never before tried to restrain the press prior to publication. Moreover, these questions involved a myriad of considerations, and it would be difficult for case law under any circumstances to develop a set of concrete rules that governed all eventualities. But regardless of whether the open-ended nature of prior cases was a surprise, the key point was that Gurfein had substantial discretion in deciding these critical issues, as well as the ultimate question as to whether to grant the government an injunction. Prior case law and the nature of the government's evidence were certainly important factors, but they did not completely explain Gurfein's decision. Thus, a fuller, more complete explanation of why Gurfein ruled the way he did requires consideration of other factors.

As we have seen, Gurfein had been extremely irritated by Assistant Secretary of Defense Doolin. Doolin had given Gurfein the impression that further disclosures would cause Sweden to cease acting as an intermediary between the United States and North Vietnam and then testified—incorrectly, as it turns out—that the Pentagon Papers did not include any documents that revealed that Sweden had played this role. He probably felt misled, taken for granted, or worse, manipulated by the government.

In addition each government witness conveyed the impression that he thought that routine news reporting about defense, military, diplomatic, and intelligence matters was improper even though not necessarily very harmful to the national security because it did not further the public's understanding of public affairs. Admiral Blouin's statement that the government functioned daily as if it were in a "fishbowl" typified this theme. This attitude, which the witnesses did not try to disguise, likely caused Gurfein to place little reliance on their unsubstantiated conclusions that further publications of the Pentagon Papers would seriously harm the national security. After all, if the officials believed that every day the press published too much information about defense, military, diplomatic, and intelligence matters, what credence could Gurfein now give to their view that further disclosures from a classified history would injure the national security?

Furthermore, unlike Macomber, who testified with a sense of authority and confidence, Doolin and Blouin were not strong and forceful witnesses. Admittedly, this is a difficult factor to assess, but, given the overall circumstances in which Gurfein found himself in this case, it was probably of real significance as he tried to determine what he thought of the evidence. The government was asking Gurfein to find that further publication by the *Times* would injure national security, and to a large extent it was asking Gurfein to reach this finding not so much because the documents in dispute made this conclusion obvious but because the government witnesses said they did. Unless Gurfein was impressed by the witnesses, unless he was willing to put his trust in what they said, the government could not prevail.

Mardian also likely contributed to Gurfein's decision to resolve key issues against the government. During the Friday hearing Mardian sat right behind Seymour and Hess, and, although he did not participate in the proceedings directly, he whispered in their ears, passed notes to them, and glared. To government and *Times* lawyers alike, as well as to Gurfein and his law clerk, he seemed arrogant, if not scary.[11] By itself, this might have been inconsequential, but, when it is joined with all the other circumstances, Mardian's impact on Gurfein's sympathy for and trust in the government cannot be minimized.

As already noted, Mardian had ordered the government witnesses not to offer specific references to the Pentagon Papers to support their general allegations. He was hoping to force Gurfein to rule in the government's favor on the extreme theory that it was entitled to an injunction merely because the documents were properly classified. As uncertain as Gurfein was about what legal rule should govern this case during the Friday hearing, he knew that he wanted to read documents that were linked to the government's general claims. He wanted to know what was so alarming about these documents, and he wanted help from the government's witnesses as he tried to determine this. But the witnesses were not forthcoming. Indeed, they refused to help the very judge they were trying to persuade to rule their way.

The government's insistence that no portion of the Pentagon Papers could be declassified within the context of the litigation also contributed to how Gurfein resolved the outstanding issues. This was a mindless position for the government to take. The government conceded that two volumes of the top secret study contained only documents that were already in the public domain. The government could have easily consented to the disclosure of these documents as well as others. But it did not, even after Gurfein repeated his request several times.

The Friday hearing converted Gurfein. It caused his attitude toward the government to change. He ceased being sympathetic and became skeptical. As much as any other factor, this attitude change explains why Gurfein decided not to review the Pentagon Papers beyond the few references offered by the government witnesses and why he concluded that the government's evidence was legally insufficient.

▪ ▪ ▪ ▪ ▪

Mardian and Seymour were responsible for the errors and misjudgments that paved the way to the government's defeat. Others may have made contributions of their own—Buzhardt had a hand in curbing what the witnesses would say; the witnesses themselves had some responsibility for agreeing to be witnesses with the restrictions imposed upon them; Attorney General John Mitchell was surely consulted by Mardian about the government's legal theory and strategy—but Mardian and Seymour were mainly responsible for what happened, and between them, Mardian had far and away the greater share.

Although Seymour was not responsible for the action being filed or the drafting of most of the legal papers that the government submitted, he did take the lead during the critical Friday hearing, and as a result he bears some responsibility for the government's weak showing that day. Seymour failed to point out to Gurfein that prior cases left him with considerable discretion in deciding how to decide critical legal questions. He could have emphasized that prior decisions did not specify what evidence was legally adequate, or whether the degree of harm to national security affected the nature of the evidence the government had to offer. Seymour also might have argued how different this case was from the hypothetical ones referred to by Chief Justice Hughes in *Near.* Unlike Hughes's examples in that case, the disputed documents in this case were too voluminous to permit a quick assessment. The government did not know exactly what the *Times* would publish next or what harm might flow from publication. If he had taken this tack, he could have asked for more time and a longer hearing at which the witnesses could fully explain the implications. This would have given Seymour a chance to try to reverse Mardian and Buzhardt's strategy. Gurfein might well have denied this request, but, given what Seymour knew of the limitations he was laboring under, it is a wonder he did not try to obtain an adjournment.

Mardian's responsibility for the government's loss, however, was much greater than Seymour's. Mardian decided that the government would press an extreme legal theory. He selected the government's three main witnesses and was responsible for preparing them. He limited their testimony. He was probably the one who insisted on not helping Gurfein identify documents that could safely be declassified.

It may be that the government could not have prevailed no matter how many things Seymour and Mardian had done differently. But that was not certain. The Pentagon Papers study did contain some sensitive documents, and it is not inconceivable that Gurfein might have been persuaded that the *Times* should be barred from publishing them. This is especially plausible, given how partial Gurfein was toward the government. If the government witnesses had testified without restraint, if they had been authoritative and confident in their presentation, if they had provided Gurfein numerous references to the Pentagon Papers that they claimed supported their general allegations, if Seymour had emphasized the discretion Gurfein possessed and how unique this case was, Gurfein might have ruled in the government's favor.

What Gurfein decided and what he said in his opinion likely reverberated throughout the remainder of the litigation. Gurfein was known to be sympathetic toward the government, and, since Nixon had just appointed him to the bench, it was widely assumed that he would be disposed toward the administration. As a result, when Gurfein ruled against the government, it was likely believed that he reached this conclusion only because there was nothing in the Pentagon Papers to warrant an injunction. It was going to be difficult for the government to recover from this defeat, and, to the extent that the government had made serious errors and misjudgments that contributed to its loss, it had much to regret.

▪ ▪ ▪ ▪ ▪

In the wake of Gurfein's decision the government's choice was to appeal to the United States Court of Appeals for the Second Circuit or abandon its effort to prevent disclosures from the Pentagon Papers. The government did not consider this much of a choice. Thus, no consideration was given to discontinuing the lawsuit against the *Times*.

Appeals judge Irving R. Kaufman was in his office that Saturday afternoon waiting for the government and the *Times* attorneys. Kaufman was nationally known for sentencing Ethel and Julius Rosenberg to death in 1951, after a federal jury had convicted them for passing information to the Soviet Union that was useful for the building of a hydrogen bomb. The central question presented to Kaufman was narrow: whether or not to continue the restraining order that barred the *Times* from further publishing its planned excerpts from the classified Pentagon Papers. If Kaufman refused to continue the stay, the government's action against the *Times* might be at an end, as would its parallel legal action against the *Washington Post*. If he maintained the restraining order, presumably a panel of three appellate judges would decide the case within a few days.

After hearing oral arguments Kaufman recessed the proceedings to write a two-and-a-half-page opinion, which he made public about four o'clock that afternoon. Kaufman continued the restraining order until twelve noon on Monday.[12] This also happened to be the day, as Kaufman surely knew, that an evidentiary hearing would be held in the government's action against the *Washington Post* in a Washington federal court.

Kaufman's opinion was defensive and apologetic. Kaufman claimed that he had no choice but to grant the requested stay if a panel of three appellate judges were going to have an opportunity to hear the case. Otherwise, he stated, the lawsuit would be moot, which would be tantamount to deciding the case in favor of the *Times*, which he did not think that he, acting alone, should do. Thus, Kaufman claimed that "institutional considerations," a term he did not elaborate on, compelled his conclusion. Kaufman then noted that his decision should not be interpreted as indicating his views on the merits. He even stated that his continuation of the stay did not mean that he would have "granted the temporary restraining order in this first instance."[13]

There was no reason for Kaufman to include these later comments in his opinion. Gurfein had denied the government a preliminary injunction and had continued the restraining order only long enough to give the government a chance to seek review before a Second Circuit judge, which turned out to be Kaufman. If Kaufman thought he owed *any* deference to Gurfein's decision, it would have been to Gurfein's findings of fact, which went against the government and continuing the stay. In short Kaufman had ample discretion to discontinue the stay, but he obviously did not want to, and he did not want to assume responsibility for continuing it. Instead, he apparently wanted to give the misleading impression that his hands were tied and that he had no choice but to continue Gurfein's injunction.

PART THREE

The *Washington Post* Case

CHAPTER THIRTEEN

The *Post* Is Restrained

Mardian first learned that the *Post* had published a report based on the Pentagon Papers when Alexander Bickel made the announcement in court. Mardian likely telephoned Attorney General Mitchell at that point, and they probably agreed that the government had no choice but to sue the *Post* or risk having Gurfein dismiss the suit against the *Times*. That meant that the Justice Department had to review the *Post*'s report, prepare the necessary legal documents, and decide whether to sue the *Post* in Washington, D.C., or New York.

There was one important reason to sue the *Post* in New York: Gurfein. Gurfein had been openly sympathetic toward and solicitous of the government all week long and equally hostile toward the *Times*, even going so far as to repeatedly put in question the *Times*'s patriotism. Nevertheless, Mardian decided to sue the *Post* in Washington. His reason was simple; he disliked Whitney North Seymour, Jr., and did not think Seymour was an effective courtroom lawyer.[1] By suing the *Post* in Washington, Mardian could avoid dealing with Seymour altogether.

About three o'clock Friday afternoon, Assistant Attorney General William H. Rehnquist telephoned the *Post* and spoke with Ben Bradlee, the *Post*'s executive editor. The conversation was brief, formal, and polite. Rehnquist said that the government considered further Pentagon Papers reports a violation of the espionage laws and irreparably harmful to the national security. Rehnquist requested the *Post* to stop the series and to return the documents to the Defense Department. Bradlee, with "hand and legs . . . shaking," declined.[2] Rehnquist then told the *Post*'s lawyers to meet the government's lawyers at the federal courthouse at 5:00 P.M. that afternoon.[3] Mitchell also sent a telegram to the *Post*, similar to the one he sent to the *Times*: the *Post*'s possession of the classified documents was illegal, and its publication of material seriously threatened national security.

▪ ▪ ▪ ▪ ▪

Lawyers for the government and for the *Post* met at the courthouse. Within a few minutes the case was assigned, by a process designed to assure random results, to Judge Gerhard A. Gesell.

Gesell was born in 1910 and was the son of the prominent child psychologist and pediatrician, Dr. Arnold Gesell. Gesell had graduated from Yale College in 1932 and Yale Law School in 1935. For six years he served as a trial lawyer with the Securities and Exchange Commission. In 1941 he joined the prominent Washington law firm of Covington & Burling and stayed there until President Johnson appointed him to the district court bench in 1967. Gesell and Katharine Graham were friendly as young adults, although they rarely saw each other by 1971.[4] And, as it happened, in 1971 Gesell lived across the street from Bradlee and on occasion bumped into him when Gesell walked his dog.[5]

Gesell was a confident and impatient judge who was used to exercising an unusually firm hand over the courtroom. He brought sharp intelligence and broad experience to cases that came before him and would insist that attorneys before him make their points quickly.

Mardian was not overjoyed by Gesell's selection. He thought of Gesell as a "tough son-of-a-bitch" who was "anti-government."[6] The *Post*'s lawyers were delighted.

Gesell spent a few minutes examining the government's complaint and the two supporting affidavits signed by defense department officials.[7] The government's complaint against the *Post*, which named fifteen defendants, including Katharine Graham, Frederick Beebe, Benjamin Bradlee, and Chalmers Roberts, essentially mirrored the one filed in the *Times* case. It contained several allegations: the *Post* illegally possessed portions of the top secret–sensitive Pentagon Papers; it had published an article based on the study; it knew its report was based on the same classified material that was the subject of the government's lawsuit against the *Times*; its report had already prejudiced and "irreparably" injured the defense interests of the United States; it intended to publish additional reports that would inflict "immediate and irreparable harm" on the United States.

Gesell met with the attorneys without a stenographer. He asked them to summarize what the dispute was about. Just as Judge Gurfein had asked the *Times*, Gesell asked the *Post* to agree to defer publishing any further articles based on the classified documents until he held an evidentiary hearing on the matter, which he said might be the next day, Saturday, or on Monday. The *Post* declined.[8]

At six o'clock, Gesell began a hearing on the government's request for a restraining order with a stenographer present. Kevin T. Maroney argued first. He maintained that the court should grant a temporary restraining order because the disputed material was classified. He said that the government would eventually offer evidence on how the *Post*'s publication would injure national security but that it did not need to do so to obtain a restraining order (2–4).

Under questioning by Gesell, Maroney conceded that the only relevant statutes were the federal espionage statutes and that a court does not ordinarily enjoin the commission of a crime. But Maroney contended that a criminal prosecution was not an adequate remedy since the harm the government wanted to prevent would be inflicted upon publication. Maroney also asserted that the *Post*'s entire position presumed that it had sufficient knowledge and experience to decide what information could be declassified without injuring the national defense. Maroney said that no matter how well intended the *Post* was in making its judgments, and no matter how well informed its editors and reporters were, they did not know as much and could not know as much about how the disclosures would affect the national security as the secretary of defense (4–8).

Roger Clark argued next. He claimed that under the government's theory any newspaper in the country that threatened to publish classified information would be vulnerable to a temporary restraining order. He said that the government's position was inconsistent with the First Amendment and relevant case law and would "undermine the traditional relationship" between the press and the government (13). He characterized the Pentagon Papers as historical and asserted that it was inconceivable that the report on the 1954 Geneva Accords had injured the national defense.

Gesell said that the *Post* was in a weaker position than if it were the only newspaper publishing reports based on the Pentagon Papers, since denying the restraining order against the *Post* might cause Gurfein to dissolve the restraining order against the *Times*. Gesell also stated that characterizing the Pentagon Papers as historical undermined the claim that the public had a compelling interest in immediate disclosure. Gesell implied that he saw little harm to the public interest if it had to wait one, two, or three additional days before it was able to read the *Post*'s reports (16–17).

Clark responded that the government's request for an injunction should be decided on the basis of the papers before the judge in this case, without regard to the consequences to the *New York Times* case. He warned that judges would be "treading on dangerous grounds" if they tried to distinguish between "cold" and "hot" news situations and that such efforts would soon result in judges enjoining "hot" news (22).

Gesell ended the hearing at about 7:00 P.M. so he could study the relevant statutes and case law. He told the lawyers he would have a written decision by 8:00 P.M. that night, roughly an hour before press time at the *Post*. That would give the *Post* adequate time to make any changes that might be necessary, and it would give the government time to go to the appeals court to apply for a stay if that were necessary.

■ ■ ■ ■ ■

At 8:05, Gesell announced his decision: "The *Post* will be allowed to publish and the request for a temporary restraining order is denied." Gesell also warned the *Post* that it "stands in serious jeopardy of criminal prosecution."[9]

Gesell gave several different reasons for his decision. He did not have "precise information suggesting in what respects, if any, the publication of this information will injure the United States." A restraining order in this case would not prevent the classified material from ultimately being made public, no matter how impressive the government's evidence might be. He did not believe that the Constitution permitted any prior restraints. He could not grant a temporary restraining order because Congress had not passed a statute authorizing it.[10]

Gesell's reasons for denying the restraint must have given little comfort to the government. Only one of them—that he had "no precise information" indicating how further publication would injure the national security—suggested that the government might have secured a temporary restraining order if it had provided some detailed evidence. The other reasons suggested that the government could not obtain a restraining order no matter what evidence it offered. It would seem that Gesell thought the only remedy available to the government was a criminal prosecution.

Gesell's denial of a temporary restraining order was entirely proper, given that the government had failed to provide any evidence whatsoever to support its general allegation that further publication would injure the national security. But Gesell's conclusion that the government could not prevail no matter what evidence it offered was untenable. Gesell had no basis to believe as of Friday evening that the courts could not restrain the leak of the Pentagon Papers. The government was proceeding against the two newspapers that it knew had the classified material. If the documents were distributed to other newspapers, the government could initiate suits against them. So long as the government could keep on putting its fingers in the dike and plugging up the leaks, the injunctions were effective. If the distribution eventually overwhelmed the government's efforts, and the government was no longer able to contain the leak, the courts could dissolve the injunctions.

Gesell's suggestion that the government could not prevail because he was unable to assess the impact of disclosures on national security and the consequences of an injunction on the press and the public was unpersuasive. Judges are always making judgments on a less-than-perfect empirical basis, and they routinely make them by assessing factors or variables that are not quantifiable or comparable. Gesell did not indicate why he thought that the government's request for an injunction was unique or especially hard. His claim that the Constitution did not permit such relief was inconsistent with the general body of First Amendment law. Indeed, as we have already seen, even Chief Justice Hughes's opinion in *Near v. Minnesota*, to which Gesell actually referred, specifically stated that a prior restraint could be obtained in limited circumstances. Finally, Gesell's statement that injunctive relief could be granted only if Congress had passed a statute authorizing it, and that Congress had passed no such statute, was at least debatable.

In the wake of Gesell's decision the *Post*'s editors, reporters, and printers worked frantically to prepare the Saturday edition for the presses, which was supposed to contain a Pentagon Papers article written by Murrey Marder. It claimed that the Johnson administration stopped the bombing of North Vietnam between 1965 and 1968 for short periods of time not because it believed that the pauses would result in peace talks. Rather, it stopped the bombing to placate domestic and world opinion. As Bradlee has recalled, "we were desperate to get the presses going and then desperate to get [the copies printed.] We felt that [if we could publish] a thousand copies . . . [that] would constitute publication for that day and that it would be academic for . . . [the court] to stop that issue because it was in effect out."[11]

■ ■ ■ ■ ■

Once Gesell announced his ruling, Maroney and the other government lawyers rushed to the appeals court. A panel of three appellate judges, which consisted of Circuit Judges Spottswood W. Robinson, Roger Robb, and J. Skelly Wright, however, did not begin a hearing until 9:45 P.M. that evening, about one hour and forty-five minutes after Gesell announced his ruling. Maroney argued that Gesell's decision constituted "an abuse of discretion," and he asked the court to take "the bare minimal step of preserving the status quo for a few days until the lower court takes testimony." Clark argued that the court should affirm Gesell's ruling. Judge Wright accused the Justice Department lawyer of "going a little far," after Maroney compared the *Post*'s publication of the reports based on the Pentagon Papers to "a 1941 newspaper report which was allegedly the first public indication that the United States had broken Japan's secret diplomatic code." Judge Robb quizzed Roger Clark about whether the *Post* would have published U.S. military plans for D-Day during World War II if it had them in advance. Clark answered that he did not think the comparison was fair or appropriate.[12]

The judges concluded the hearing at 10:20. While they deliberated, Frederick Beebe, the chairman of the board for the *Post* company, was at the courthouse on an open phone to Bradlee. Beebe pressed Bradlee to print as fast as possible. "How many have you got for Christ's sake, how many are out," he shouted into the phone. Bradlee would answer: "You know, we would have to guess, really." But Bradlee also reassured Beebe that all the presses were rolling.[13]

At 1:20 A.M. Saturday a split panel announced its decision. Robb and Robinson voted to reverse Gesell's order and to order him to hold a hearing and to render a decision by five o'clock in the afternoon on Monday, June 21, 1971. Because the *Post* had already distributed many copies of its Saturday edition, the two judges permitted the *Post* to continue to publish the Marder report. Otherwise they enjoined the *Post* from further news reports based on the Pentagon Papers pending the completion of the hearing before Gesell. Judge Wright dissented and voted to affirm Gesell's order.

Later that morning Robb and Robinson wrote an opinion in support of their decision, as did Wright.[14] Robb and Robinson's *per curiam* opinion stated that they were "aware" that the government had not set forth "particular elements of prejudice to the national defense" and that the Pentagon study covered events only through 1968. But they claimed that the documents concerned military and diplomatic matters pertaining to the Vietnam War, and the government may have been hampered in making specific allegations because it did not know precisely what documents the *Post* had. Under these circumstances, they concluded, it was not possible to say "one way or the other" whether the disputed material was "essentially historical in character or whether any of it has a present impact on vital matters affecting national security." Because they feared that a denial of a temporary restraining order "may possibly threaten national security," they believed that the proper discharge of judicial responsibility required "some inquiry into the matter." Aware that their decision would prompt the criticism that it permitted the government to intimidate the press by injunction, the two circuit judges stated that they believed that the "brief pause in publication is clearly outweighed by the grave potentiality of injury to the national security."[15]

The two circuit judges also stated that Gesell's action was "improper." They concluded that Gesell erred when he wrote that the Constitution did not permit prior restraints. "Freedom of the press, as important as it is to us, is not boundless." Prior restraints are appropriate in a narrow area involving national security, and this case "may lie within that area." The opinion implicitly rejected Gesell's assertion that it was impossible to assess and balance the competing interests affected by an injunction. It criticized Gesell for concluding that a court will not enjoin the commission of a crime, because there were "recognized exceptions approved by the Supreme Court." Robb and Robinson also claimed that the espionage laws did not "foreclose all possible resort to injunctive relief to protect such information in such exceptional circumstances as would justify prior restraints under *Near*." They did not claim that Congress had passed a law that authorized prior restraints. They took a more moderate position; in the absence of a statute prohibiting such relief the executive branch had authority to seek a prior restraint from the courts to guard the national defense.[16]

Judge Wright dissented. He stated that this "is a sad day for America," because the government's effort to censor the Pentagon Papers was the first time that "the executive department had succeeded in stopping the presses." He lamented that the "long and sordid war in Southeast Asia" had already done enough "harm to our people," and he argued that it should not now be "used to cut out the heart of our free institutions and system of government." He stated that prior restraints, which he described as a "potentially deadly" governmental "weapon," were "even more serious than subsequent punishment" because they were imposed "before the speech at issue has even seen the light of day." Wright claimed that the "key" issue was that the government had the burden of going forward and justifying the grant of a prior restraint. "In the case," he wrote, "the executive department has made no allegations—to say nothing of convincing showings—that troop movements or recruitment are threatened. Neither obscenity nor overthrow of the government is at issue. All that is at issue is what the district court termed 'essentially historical data.'" Wright complained that all that the government had alleged was that the disputed material was classified and that its disclosure would adversely affect the nation's security. "Surely," he maintained, "we must demand more. To allow a government to suppress free speech simply through a system of bureaucratic classification would sell our heritage far, far too cheaply." He asserted that the majority's position that no real harm was caused by a few days of delay "cheapens the First Amendment," since all of the "presumptions must run in favor of free speech, not against it." He rejected the government's claim that it was better to rely upon the judgment of government officials rather than newspaper editors. That "misses the point," he exclaimed. "The First Amendment is directed against one evil: suppression of the speech of private citizens by government officials. It embodies a healthy distrust of government censorship. More important, it embodies a fundamental trust of individual Americans. Any free system of government involves risks. But we in the United States have chosen to rely in the end upon the judgment and the patriotism of all the people, not only of the officials."[17]

The government had obtained a temporary restraining order and now had a chance to prove the truth of its allegation at an evidentiary hearing. But it could not have been very sanguine about prevailing, given that Gesell was the judge. Gesell had been openly hostile toward the government's claim for relief on Friday, and his reasons for denying the temporary injunction were so broad that they all but decided the merits of the case even before the hearing began.

CHAPTER FOURTEEN

On the Eve of the *Post*'s Trial

On Saturday morning the *Washington Post* confronted this choice: should it ask Chief Justice Warren E. Burger of the Supreme Court to vacate the appeals court injunction, or should it return to district judge Gesell's courtroom for a hearing the appeals court had ordered completed by late Monday afternoon. Given Gesell's denial of the temporary restraining order, the *Post* knew that its chances of prevailing before him were excellent. But if the *Post* returned to Gesell's courtroom, it might ultimately be at a disadvantage because of legal developments in the *Times* case. District judge Murray Gurfein had stated he would decide the *Times* case Saturday afternoon. It was possible that he would decide to allow the *Times* to continue with its reports and that the federal appeals court in New York would affirm his decision. The *Times* would renew its series on Sunday while the *Post* remained enjoined, a predicament the *Post* wanted to avoid. Thus, the *Post* probably waited until after appeals Judge Irving Kaufman continued the injunction against the *Times* until Monday before it decided to forgo its appeal to the Supreme Court.

Over the weekend Gesell held two conferences with lawyers for the *Post* and the government to prepare for the Monday hearing. The government asked that its officials be permitted to examine the classified documents the *Post* had. As in the *Times* case, it claimed it needed to know precisely what documents the *Post* had if it were to prove that further publication would injure national security. Gesell denied the request. He feared, as had Gurfein, that permitting government officials to examine the documents might reveal the identity of the *Post*'s source or sources, thus implicating important press rights. But Gesell did order the *Post* to prepare an inventory of its documents and to give it to the government by Sunday evening.

Once the government identified its witnesses, and it became apparent it would use some of the same officials it had presented in the *Times* case, the *Post* requested that it be permitted to examine the transcript of the *Times in camera* hearing. The transcript would give the *Post* some idea of what these officials would say in its case, and it would assure they did not change their testimony. Gesell denied the request, without offering a reason. But Gesell told the *Post*'s lawyers that they could renew the request during the hearing on Monday.

During the weekend conferences Gesell instructed the government lawyers to "particularize the documents it considers will create irreparable injury if published, and to particularize the reasons for its position document by document."[1]

Gesell and the lawyers also agreed that the government would present its evidence by way of affidavit and that the *Post* would be able to cross-examine any or all of the government officials who submitted such an affidavit. Although this was a departure from the usual practice of having witnesses testify, it had the advantage of saving time, which was a consideration, since the appeals court had ordered the hearing completed by five o'clock. Gesell directed the government attorneys to let the *Post* lawyers read the affidavits (but not to take a copy) by Sunday night so they could prepare their cross-examination.

During the conferences Kevin Maroney, the government's lead lawyer, said that the government wanted to offer the Pentagon Papers study into evidence on the condition that only Gesell could examine it. Because Judge Gurfein had accepted the Pentagon Papers study into evidence in the *Times* case on that condition, Maroney may have hoped that Gesell would do the same. Maroney also said he wished to offer into evidence on the same basis an affidavit by Vice Admiral Noel Gayler, the director of the National Security Agency. Gesell stated that he would not accept the documents into evidence on that condition. The *Post* had a constitutional right to examine any document the government wished to submit in support of its claim for relief, and if the government refused to permit the *Post* to read the documents, Gesell would not admit them into evidence. The government was unwilling to permit the *Post* access to the documents and thus for the moment indicated that it would not offer them into evidence.[2]

▪ ▪ ▪ ▪ ▪

Three affidavits formed the core of the government's evidence. The detail in these documents suggests that they were written to persuade a skeptical judge like Gesell that further disclosures by the *Post* would harm national security. It is also obvious that Gurfein's decision in the *Times* case had so jolted Robert Mardian and Fred Buzhardt that they had decided to permit government officials to make detailed allegations.

Deputy Assistant Secretary of Defense Dennis Doolin signed a three-page affidavit.[3] Although Doolin's affidavit in the *Post* case included specific page references to the Pentagon Papers, something he did not provide in the *Times* case, the affidavit had obvious weaknesses.

Doolin's affidavit made six points. The first referred to a 1965 memorandum written by Maxwell Taylor to President Johnson entitled "Assessment and Uses of Negotiations Blue Chips," in which "Taylor listed six items that Hanoi would like from us and five items that we would like from them." Doolin wrote that Taylor had discussed these items "candidly in terms of trade-offs" and that North Vietnam would have a "major advantage in any negotiations" if the memorandum was disclosed. But Doolin did not identify what the six "blue chips" were. Nor did he attach Taylor's memorandum as an exhibit to his affidavit. Since Gesell had refused to admit the Pentagon Papers into evidence, it was impossible for Gesell to know what the six "blue chips" were. In addition it was doubtful that a six-year-old negotiating posture was still secret or current or both.

Doolin's second point was that the North Vietnamese had "repeatedly stressed the importance of keeping their contact secret and repeatedly complained of leaks to the press." Doolin sought to bolster his point by referring to one incident in which the "Vice Minister of Foreign Affairs" had told a Canadian official that the so-called LaPira peace feeler was "genuine" but that "Hanoi had to denounce it" when it became public. Doolin asserted that negotiations with Hanoi had to be confidential if they were to be fruitful.

Doolin may well have been correct that North Vietnam had complained about news leaks concerning negotiations. His point that real progress would be made only if secrecy could be maintained may also have been accurate. Doolin's claim, however, did not depend on any particular document within the Pentagon Papers study. Rather, it encompassed the disclosure of any diplomatic contact with Hanoi. As much as the government may have wished to suppress all diplomatic reporting, no court would sustain such a position because it would fundamentally contradict the needs of democracy.

Next, Doolin focused on the Seaborn initiative, which had been raised during the Friday hearing in the *Times* case. Canadian officials were embarrassed by the *Times*'s disclosures of Seaborn's activities as an intermediary. By the time Doolin wrote his affidavit in the *Post* case, however, he knew that the Seaborn initiative had been described at length in books on the war and was thus in the public domain. Yet he raised it again as an example of material that would injure the national security if disclosed. Doolin weakened this point further, however, by expressing contempt for routine press reporting of diplomatic matters: "it is obvious to me that if we cannot have guarantees of secrecy in sensitive areas of negotiations—secrecy that the North Vietnamese themselves demand—then we might as well transact all our business through either classified ads or letters to *The New York Times*."

Doolin made three additional points. Doolin stated that one volume of the Pentagon Papers study contained "detailed information" describing the "overthrow of President Diem by Generals Duong Van Minh, Tran Van Don, Le Van Kim, and others." He asserted that "these same individuals are now deeply involved" in the South Vietnamese elections scheduled for October 1971 and that "General Minh, who is expected to be the leading opposition candidate to President Thieu in these elections, could claim that disclosure of the above specifics by the United States at this time was designed to discredit General Minh and thereby assure the election of the 'puppet regime of President Thieu.'" Doolin went further and alleged that the disclosure of this material could result in "political chaos . . . causing possible coup attempts and certainly creating an unacceptable condition of instability" that could affect "future redeployment plans." Second, Doolin reiterated a point he had made in the *Times* case, that the Pentagon Papers detailed the use of third-party countries by the United States to negotiate with Hanoi over American prisoners of war. He stated that these countries would be embarrassed if their diplomatic efforts were disclosed and that they might refuse to assist the United States in the future if "confidentiality cannot be guaranteed." If that happened, he warned, "more of our men may die in North Vietnamese prisons." Last, Doolin claimed that "specific SEATO planning is mentioned" in the classified study, and as an example he referred to Operation Plan 5. Doolin alleged that if the "story of their [Thai] ground and air combat role in Laos in the mid-1960's (which they deny) was disclosed, this could cause their withdrawal from Laos, weaken an already mediocre Lao army, cause Thai reassessment of their role in Vietnam, accelerate removal of the Black Leopards, and endanger Vietnamization (and, consequently, the lives of American troops still in Vietnam)."

By comparison to Doolin's first three points, these claims arguably had current importance. A serious disruption of the political processes in South Vietnam or the withdrawal of Thai military forces could have important consequences for the military situation in South Vietnam as well as the overall Vietnamization program. If third countries refused to act as intermediaries between the United States and North Vietnam, the possibility of securing better conditions for American prisoners of war or their release might be diminished.

But these allegations were also quite hypothetical. Further disclosures about the Diem coup might disrupt the political process in South Vietnam, but no one could predict that with any degree of certainty. Further reports on the military activities of the Thai forces in Laos might cause the Thai forces to be withdrawn, which might affect the military situation in South Vietnam, but that was not certain. News reports on the role played by third countries in negotiating with Hanoi might keep third countries—the same ones or others—from acting as intermediaries in the future, and that might have a serious impact on negotiating an end to the fighting or the release of the prisoners of war, but that was speculative.

The government submitted a ten-page affidavit signed by Melvin Zais, a lieutenant general who was director of the Operations Directorate of the Joint Staff of the Joint Chiefs of Staff.[4] Zais replaced Admiral Francis Blouin, who had been the government's military expert in the *Times* case and whose testimony was a major disappointment to Mardian. Zais stated that he began his review of the forty-seven volume study on Saturday, June 19, with an eye toward assessing the "military consequence" of further publications by the *Washington Post* and the *New York Times*. On page 2, he wrote: "I am able, at this time, to state without equivocation and with a firm conviction that the publication of the 'History' in the *Washington Post*, the *New York Times*, or any other news publication, would, in my judgment, have a potential for causing exceptionally grave damage to the national security of the United States and grave danger to the well-being and safety of its deployed armed forces in Southeast Asia."

Zais supported his conclusion with three points that included specific citations to the Pentagon Papers and a number of general claims that made no reference to pages within the classified history. Zais identified several documents that he stated exposed "two major military operational plans which had been used in 1964 and in 1965 for planning of emergency deployments of United States ground combat forces into Southeast Asia." He explained that these deployment plans were to be used to meet "any military offensive moves against the United States by the armed forces of the People's Republic of China." Zais conceded that these two specific plans were "no longer in use," but he claimed that "the discussions relating to these plans do reveal possible total force commitments and planned areas of operations which are valid for future operations." He asserted that this information, "if disclosed to an enemy planner, would, if combined with other intelligence generally held by the intelligence communities of foreign countries, seriously compromise current war planning for Southeast Asia . . . [and would cause U.S. forces, were they deployed] in response to military actions by the armies of the People's Republic of China, . . . to assume greater risks and potentially accept greater loss of life."

Zais referred to several pages of the study that he alleged would provide "foreign military planners with an authoritative insight in deployment times for the movement on major United States units." He claimed that the information would be of "great value to a potential enemy planner in accurately estimating the United States capability to react in response to his major force deployments or comparable strategies . . . [or in determining] our deployment times for reinforcing United States armed forces in combat." He also referred to several pages in the study that he claimed described the "planning for and the past conduct of certain covert operations in North Vietnam." He stated that the disclosure of these plans might foreclose their use "in alleviating a situation where the survival of withdrawing [U.S.] forces under attack" was at stake.

Zais supplemented these claims with a statement that the study included other "numerous examples," which he did not identify, that discussed "contingency plans and procedures," how we "structure the composition of our forces," and our "tactics" and "techniques" used to meet military threats. Although Zais claimed that the disclosure of this information would injure "future planning and operations" and "compromise world-wide contingency planning," he emphasized that he was primarily concerned about the impact of these disclosures on "the current posture of our deployed forces in Southeast Asia."

The rest of Zais's affidavit made two points. First, additional Pentagon Papers reports might seriously harm the Vietnamization program. He argued that the "one major assumption that is implicit in the current withdrawal rate [of U.S. combat troops] is that the planned support which we expect from our allies and from the Republic of Vietnam will continue without major change." He speculated that further reports might create political consequences that will cause the governments of South Korea, Japan, Thailand, the Philippines, and South Vietnam to change their troop commitments or alter how U.S. forces are allowed to use military bases within their respective countries. Those consequences, he claimed, would have a serious impact on the Vietnamization program and the security of U.S. forces.

Second, Zais claimed that the United States used air bases in Thailand for B-52s, which were "essential to the safety and well-being of the United States forces now deployed in Southeast Asia." He implied that further disclosures from the Pentagon Papers might have serious political repercussions in Thailand, which in turn might cause the Thai government to curtail the use of these air bases by the United States so that the safety of U.S. military forces in Southeast Asia was threatened. Zais did not offer any specific citation for this claim.

The government's third affidavit was signed by William B. Macomber, who had been the government's most impressive witness in the *Times* case.[5] Macomber's affidavit filled twenty-five legal-size pages. In contrast to Macomber's refusal to provide Judge Gurfein with specific references in the *Times* case his affidavit included many citations to the Pentagon Papers.

Macomber stated that he had "intensely" reviewed the classified study since Wednesday, June 16, and that in his opinion further publication "would result in injury to the United States and benefit to foreign nations of such magnitude as to constitute irreparable harm." Macomber emphasized that he was not "referring to such minor problems as embarrassment or inconvenience. I am referring to the mortal danger such disclosures constitute to the diplomatic process itself." He claimed that without secrecy there can be "no meaningful American diplomatic process," which would mean that the United States would lose "an essential part of its national security effort and its principal instrument for resolving disputes by peaceful means and seeking a just and enduring peace." Macomber even asserted that the injury caused by further disclosures would be far greater than the destruction of a troopship "where no more than a few hundred lives are involved."

Macomber's affidavit emphasized two points. The first was that secrecy was the lifeblood of diplomacy. Without that prerequisite, he claimed, foreign nations would not engage in meaningful negotiations with the United States. Macomber maintained that such a consequence would not only cause irreparable harm for the course of developments in Southeast Asia but gravely damage the Strategic Arms Limitations Talks, the ongoing "Four Power" talks over Berlin, the Paris Peace Talks, and the various efforts to secure peace in the Middle East. Macomber argued that this had special relevance to the Vietnam War, because the United States often needed the assistance of third-party countries to negotiate with North Vietnam. He claimed that these countries were sometimes allies of the United States, but often not. If it became known that they had helped the United States, they would be politically embarrassed and perhaps unwilling to help in the future.

Macomber illustrated his point by referring to twelve of the diplomatic initiatives detailed in the four volumes of the study that traced the diplomatic history of the war. He gave the code name of each of the episodes—Seaborn Mission, Mayflower, XYZ, Pinta Rangoon, Ronning, Sunflower, Marigold, Packers, Ohio, Aspen, Pennsylvania, and Killy—the dates for each initiative, and a brief description of each overture. He claimed that these diplomatic efforts, which began in May 1964 and ended in February 1968, were aimed at reducing or ending the fighting in Vietnam, gaining the release of the prisoners of war, improving the conditions of the prisoners, or "getting food and medicine and other relief packages through to our prisoners of war." He warned that the United States's "apparent lack of ability to preserve the confidential character of sensitive communications . . . seriously undermines our efforts to make such arrangements."

The "second type of problem" identified by Macomber was the "stifling effect" that the *Post* and the *Times* publication had "on the candor with which officers of the United States Government must express their views internally in order for the policy-making process to function properly." Government officials had to feel free to speak their minds without restraint in order to enhance the possibility that wise decisions would be made. To support this well-worn argument that favored secrecy and confidentiality in government, Macomber cited about a half dozen communications contained within the classified study. His point was that these disclosures would injure the interests of the United States, discourage others from putting their candid opinion, advice, and assessments in writing, and that a combination of these consequences would seriously harm the government.

Macomber stated that he could not "over-emphasize the breadth, intensity, and severity of the harm which would be caused to the national security" if the *Post* and other newspapers were permitted to continue to publish reports based on the top secret study. He added that he was "deeply concerned that disclosure of materials contained in the study could seriously complicate, perhaps even destroy, our current efforts to withdraw from Vietnam with minimum assurance that the situation will not unduly deteriorate."

Macomber's affidavit explained why further disclosures might injure the national security and provided page references to the classified study to support his position. This was much more than he had done in the *Times* case.

▪ ▪ ▪ ▪ ▪

Somewhere between Saturday afternoon and Monday morning lawyers for the *Post*, Roger Clark and Anthony F. Essaye, wrote an eleven-page memorandum of law. Like the *Times*, they conceded that the First Amendment permitted a prior restraint in some limited circumstances. But unlike the *Times*, the *Post* lawyers focused solely on the right of the press to publish free of government censorship. They did not argue, as the *Times* had, that the government was barred from seeking a prior restraint because Congress had not passed a statute authorizing such legal action.

The *Post*'s legal memorandum made its points crisply and succinctly. The government was entitled to a preliminary injunction only if it proved that it was likely to ultimately succeed in the case and that the failure to grant interim relief would result in grave and irreparable injury. To win interim relief, the government had to prove that further publication would result in a "serious, immediate and substantial threat to its ability to wage war, imminent risk of death to American military personnel, or a grave breach of the national security." Mere embarrassment to political leaders of the United States or foreign nations was insufficient. Moreover, no injunction should issue to protect the capacity of governments—in general—to deal with one another on a confidential basis or of government officials to "speak and write candidly." The *Post* contended that the government's best and most appropriate remedy for unwanted leaks was "increased vigilance within the Executive Department," which might prevent the unauthorized disclosures in the first place, rather than a prior restraint.[6]

The *Post* attacked the government's central legal contention "that the classification of a document by the Executive is controlling upon this Court, absent a finding that such classification is arbitrary and capricious." The *Post* responded: "Nothing could be further from the fact. . . . The question is whether a prohibition on publication . . . constitutes a violation of the First Amendment. The use of labels—even the label 'Top Secret–Sensitive' by the Government—does not relieve this Court of its duty to determine independently, on the basis of all the facts adduced, whether the injunction the Government seeks would impinge upon defendants' First Amendment rights."[7]

In contrast to the *Times* the *Post* vehemently objected to the government's request for an *in camera* hearing. "Having embarked on a course of censorship unparalleled in the history of the Republic, the Government now seeks to frustrate the very judicial process which it has itself invoked." The *Post* claimed that Gesell should not hold a hearing closed to the public "before this Court [requires] . . . the Government, at the very least, . . . to prove in public the nature and degree of the harm it claims it has already sustained." This was especially true, the *Post* claimed, since Judge Gurfein had just denied the government a preliminary injunction after holding an *in camera* hearing.[8]

In addition to its legal memorandum the *Post* submitted a dozen affidavits signed by Ben Bradlee and some of the newspaper's more prominent editors and reporters including Bernard D. Nossiter, Murrey Marder, Ben H. Bagdikian, George Wilson, and Chalmers M. Roberts. In general the affidavits made three main points. The information that the government was trying to suppress was already in the hands of many people, a development that would ultimately make any injunction ineffective. Bradlee's affidavit gave particular force to this point. He stated that on Monday, June 14, he was given a book manuscript that contained "major, verbatim quotations" from the Pentagon Papers, that the authors of the manuscript told him that they had the classified material quoted and referred to in the manuscript, and that their manuscript was in the hands of publishers.[9] Bradlee also stated that the *Washington Post* had received about 150 pages from the Pentagon Papers. He also stated that on Wednesday, June 16, he read the galley proofs of former President Johnson's book, which was scheduled for publication in November 1971, and that the book contained "extensive, verbatim quotations" from the classified documents included in the study. Finally, Bradlee stated that it was a matter of public record that Representative Paul McCloskey, a Californian Republican, had claimed on Friday, June 18, that he had an immense volume of the materials involved in this case.

The second general point made by the affidavits was that officials of the executive branch of the government routinely and purposefully make classified information available to reporters and editors in Washington.[10] The *Post*'s premier diplomatic correspondent, Chalmers Roberts, expressed the point this way: "It is a regular practice through all four administrations I have covered in this area to leak to newsmen material thus classified when the Government official involved deems it in his or his administration's interest to do so. It has also been the practice over the same period for Government officials to leak such material to newsmen because they felt it should be printed in the public interest which they conceived to be of a higher order of importance than the classification."[11]

The affidavits made a third point. Journalists develop a close working relationship with government officials, who in turn learn to trust a reporter's judgment and discretion. As a result reporters and editors had considerable experience reporting on national security matters and could be trusted to sift through highly classified material and not publish material that would not harm the national security.

CHAPTER FIFTEEN

Gesell's Decision

Judge Gesell arrived in his chambers at 6:30 Monday morning, June 21, and read the legal briefs and affidavits submitted by the government and the *Post*. At eight o'clock he took the bench and made several announcements: he had held two conferences in the case over the weekend; there would be an *in camera* hearing despite the *Post*'s objections; he would take a short luncheon recess at noon; he would cease taking testimony at four o'clock; and he would render a decision by five o'clock that afternoon, as the court of appeals had ordered. He also stated that several congressmen wanted to intervene into the action, but he was denying their motion mainly because of the *in camera* hearing.[1]

The public hearing lasted until about ten o'clock. During that time the government presented two witnesses, George MacClain, a security classification official, and Dennis Doolin. Both were witnesses in the *Times* case. The purpose of their testimony was to establish an evidentiary basis for the government's claim that it was entitled to a preliminary injunction merely because the Pentagon Papers remained properly classified. In this regard MacClain's testimony was essentially unnecessary because it was mainly limited to explaining how the classification worked, which was already explained in the executive order. Doolin's testimony was more to the point. He tried to establish that the study remained properly classified by describing the several reviews he conducted of the study.

During this otherwise uneventful segment of the hearing the government lawyers took positions that agitated Gesell. The government wanted

Gesell to suppress all forty-seven volumes of the study, including the volume that contained only public statements of former Presidents Kennedy and Johnson. Gesell told Kevin Maroney, who represented the government, that he thought this was ridiculous. Yet Maroney insisted that was what the government wanted because it could not distinguish, given the hectic pace of the litigation, between material that believed it presented serious national security threats and material that could be safely disclosed to the public (24–25). He was obviously afraid that if he conceded that these distinct volumes could be exempt from an injunction, Gesell then might require the government to identify additional material that could be declassified without jeopardizing the nation's security. Since the government did not want to do that, it was in the unenviable position of claiming that the court should enjoin even the publication of public presidential speeches. Maroney then took another difficult position. Gesell had directed him to prepare an order pertaining to who was permitted to attend the *in camera* hearing and what restrictions would be placed on them. Maroney submitted the proposed order at the very end of the public session. Gesell expected the order to be uncontroversial: he had previously told Maroney that all the named defendants would be permitted into the closed hearing, but Maroney tried to exclude at least some of them, possibly all; the transcript is unclear. Gesell was annoyed: "I have ruled that all defendants in this case have a right to be present. I don't see how I can exclude defendants in a lawsuit from hearing the testimony. If you have any notion as to how I can do that, you can let me know" (68). Maroney agreed to alter the proposed order.

William R. Glendon, the lead attorney for the *Washington Post*, then said he had another objection, to which Gesell responded that they had better examine the order paragraph by paragraph. Maroney's proposed order permitted only the government to present witnesses during the closed hearing. Gesell was understandably astonished. "I am going to hear the evidence on both sides *in camera* if the parties want it" (68). Maroney said the *Post* had no right to present testimony since it had opposed the government's request for an *in camera* hearing. Gesell replied sarcastically that he would agree to bar the *Post* from presenting witnesses during the *in camera* hearing provided the government had no objections to the *Post*'s witnesses testifying about national security issues during a hearing open to the public. Predictably, that was not acceptable to Maroney. He then relented and agreed that the *Post* would be permitted to present testimony during the closed hearing.

■ ■ ■ ■ ■

The closed hearing ran from ten until two in the afternoon, with a thirty-minute recess for lunch. In accordance with the prior agreement the affidavits signed by Doolin, Melvin Zais, and William B. Macomber were treated as testimony in support of the government's request for a preliminary injunction. That meant that Doolin, Zais, and Macomber would not testify unless the *Post* lawyers wanted to cross-examine them. After the courtroom's doors were closed and locked, Gesell directed those attending the closed hearing to identify themselves for the court stenographer. He also directed that "all notes or other writings" kept during the hearing be surrendered at its conclusion. At that point William Glendon called Doolin to the stand.

Glendon asked Doolin about General Taylor's 1965 memorandum that spelled out "six blue chips" that the United States could use in negotiating with North Vietnam. After Glendon asked a few preliminary questions Gesell interrupted the cross-examination and told Maroney that it was "meaningless to me that Volume IV(c)(7)(a), Pages 112 and 114, would give the North Vietnamese a major advantage in any negotiations." The references were to the Pentagon Papers, which were not in the courtroom, and neither Doolin nor his affidavit defined what the so-called blue chips were.[2] Maroney agreed to have the classified study brought to the courthouse, and it arrived before Doolin left the stand. After Gesell examined Taylor's memorandum he said:

> Now, gentlemen, let me just get your help on this. Here are the six blue chips that are revealed by this top secret document, and let's just consider them.
>
> "Cease bombing the north; see [*sic*] military operations of the Viet Cong Unit; stop increasing our forces in the south; withdraw our forces from the south; give amnesty to the Viet Cong; give economic aid to the north."
>
> Now, I grant you those are perhaps blue chips, but they are the kind of blue chips that I would think today any high school graduate could put down. There is nothing in here of an intimate secrecy about blue chips." (In Camera, 132)

Gesell's scorn was unmistakable, and neither Doolin nor Maroney were able to mollify him.

Glendon next turned Doolin's attention to the "LaPira peace feeler" and the Seaborn affair. Upon questioning Doolin admitted that he had no idea what the "LaPira peace feeler" was. Glendon was amazed: "Don't you know what the LaPira peace feeler was?" Doolin responded: "No, I don't." It was also apparent that Doolin did not know that the substance of the "LaPira peace feeler" had been detailed in books tracing the diplomatic history of the Vietnam War. He even assumed the same position—that it had not been publicly reported—with regard to the Seaborn mission, even though he was told during the *Times* case that the Seaborn mission had previously been publicly reported. Gesell was exasperated. He turned to Maroney: "I don't understand this position, Mr. Maroney." Gesell was perplexed because it seemed that the critical information was already in the public domain and that the government's contention was that it is much better "if we conduct our affairs in private" (In Camera, 105E–G, 106).

Maroney gave a two-part answer. He claimed that there was information within the classified material that was not yet in the public domain. He emphasized: "certainly *The Washington Post* and *The New York Times* don't have an avid interest in these documents because the material is already in the public domain. They are looking for stories which are news, not a rehash of what is already in the public domain." Maroney also claimed that it was much more harmful to diplomatic efforts if the precise text of a cable was published in a newspaper than if part of its contents was summarized to which Gesell said: "I grant you that" (In Camera, 107–8).

Moments later Gesell told Doolin that he was interested in his statement "that prisoners are going to be killed" if countries that had acted as intermediaries were identified (In Camera, 114). Doolin told Gesell that he had misread his affidavit. Doolin said he had previously stated that some prisoners may die if there were further disclosures. Gesell asked for an explanation. Doolin explained that all he meant was that the longer American soldiers were imprisoned, the more likely that more will die. Since third countries were useful as negotiators with North Vietnam, their continued diplomatic efforts on behalf of the United States increased the possibility that some prisoners may be released more quickly than would otherwise be the case (In Camera, 114–15).

Gesell asked Doolin what he meant by his statement during the public portion of the hearing that the classified material contained information about current troop movements. Doolin said that he did not mean to give the impression that the Pentagon Papers related to current troop movements. He said that he was referring to the build-up of American troops in Vietnam presumably from 1965 through 1967. That answer annoyed Gesell. Gesell had the impression that Doolin was referring to current troop movements and that he thought the courtroom audience had that impression as well. Gesell even admitted that Doolin's statements made him wonder if this high government official had intentionally misled everyone (In Camera, 117–18).

By the time Glendon completed questioning Doolin Gesell's impatience with the government was obvious. He had told Maroney over the weekend, as well as all morning, that the government had to offer specific documents that implicated current military or diplomatic matters. Gesell characterized the government's evidence up to that point as hypothetical and general, which did not "measure" up. It all boiled down to the fact that the government thought that secrecy was better, Gesell said. And in referring to Doolin, Gesell added, "that is the way this man feels." Gesell then stated: "That is the way everybody who is involved in intelligence feels, that is the way that everybody in the State Department feels, that is the way that everybody in the Pentagon feels, and if that is what we are talking about, there is no need to take testimony" (In Camera, 125).

Minutes later Maroney returned to this point. He said the judge had to respect the judgments of those who represented the Departments of State and Defense because they had superior knowledge of relevant factors. Gesell was irritated. "I don't want to seem cantankerous," he told Maroney, but if that were true, there would be no need for a hearing. Gesell told Maroney that he read the court of appeal's order to mean that he had to decide these issues and not simply accept the judgments of executive branch officials (In Camera, 133).

As in the *Times* case, Doolin had been a dreadful witness. He did not testify about facts that Gesell thought important. He did not know about matters that even he had brought up himself. Worse yet, he gave Gesell the impression he was misleading him.

Glendon next called Macomber to the stand. Macomber was articulate, well informed, sure of what he knew, confident of his opinions and judgments, moderate in his expression, and willing to concede the limits of his point. Macomber was also respectful of the judge and opposing counsel while insisting that he be permitted to complete his thought or a summary of facts he believed to be important. All in all, he was impressive and commanding.

In the end, however, Macomber's testimony did not measurably strengthen the government's claim for an injunction, at least when compared to Gesell's request that the government support its general allegation with reference to specific pages or documents in the Pentagon Papers. Macomber's central point was thin: the lifeblood of diplomacy required secrecy and that further publication from the Pentagon Papers would gravely threaten diplomatic initiatives affecting the Vietnam War, the Middle East, and the SALT talks. But Macomber's point did not depend upon any particular document or documents within the Pentagon Papers study. It was a general, overall point: secrecy is important to effective diplomacy, and unauthorized disclosures threatened it.

Macomber tried to strengthen his point by claiming that the leak of the

Pentagon Papers was unique and that the *Times* and the *Post* were two of the largest, wealthiest, and most powerful newspapers in the world. He maintained that the world was closely watching this lawsuit and that the outcome would affect all aspects of diplomacy.

But Gesell was unpersuaded. The government was not entitled to a prior restraint unless it proved that disclosure of identified documents would gravely injure national security. Even then, Gesell had doubts. He wondered why the executive branch did not maintain such strict restrictions that leaks were impossible. Alternatively, he questioned the utility of an injunction, given that much of the information was already in the public domain and that the *Post*'s source could leak it to other newspapers.

Macomber tried to answer Gesell. He told the judge that the executive branch could not prevent all leaks and that more stringent restrictions aimed at accomplishing that end would tie the government up in knots. He insisted that the government needed another way of dealing with unauthorized disclosures if diplomacy was to function and that resorting to the courts, as the government had done in this case, was the best alternative. He did not think that judicial injunctions would be ineffective in this case, but even if that proved to be the case, there was no reason to decide that so prematurely.

Gesell respected Macomber and was interested in what he had to say. But Gesell's reaction to Macomber left unchanged his assessment that the government's evidence was weak.

▪ ▪ ▪ ▪ ▪

Only three other significant things happened during the *in camera* hearing. First, the government renewed its motion to have the *Post* permit government officials inspect the classified documents. When the *Post* repeated its objection, Gesell ruled that he was going to assume that the *Post* had the entire study. This was important because it meant that Gesell assumed that the *Post* had any document the government cited as threatening national security. It is not at all clear why Gesell made this ruling at this juncture in the proceedings. The government made no new argument in support of its position, and there seemed no new reason for the government to inspect the documents. What is possible, however, is that by the time Gesell had heard Doolin and Macomber's testimony, he thought that he had heard the government's best evidence, which he thought inadequate. With that in mind, he may have decided that he would give the government the benefit of the evidentiary ruling and assume that the *Post* had the entire study.

The government altered its position respecting the affidavit of Vice Admiral Noel Gayler, director of the National Security Agency. In the morning Maroney had stated that the government would submit Gayler's affidavit on the condition that only Gesell would read it. Gesell refused to accept the affidavit on that condition, stating that the defendants' attorneys and perhaps the defendants themselves had a right to read the affidavit. As the hearing went on, perhaps hoping to strengthen the claim for an injunction, Maroney offered to submit Gayler's affidavit on the condition that the defendants' attorneys and defense experts be permitted to read it. The *Post* agreed to these conditions, as did Gesell, but not before he commented that he did not think that the affidavit involved "such monumental problems" as Gayler thought, thus indicating that he did not think the affidavit substantially strengthened the government's evidence (In Camera, 214).

Gayler's affidavit remains classified today, but, given that the National Security Agency, dubbed the "Puzzle Palace," is concerned with codes, it seems inevitable that Gayler's affidavit claimed that the disclosure of certain documents or specified information contained in certain documents would compromise intelligence codes either currently in use or in use at some earlier time. Indeed, Gesell made a brief comment during the hearing that all but established that fact. Gesell stated that he did not think that the "security aspect" of Gayler's affidavit was all that pressing since over the weekend the *Post* had stated it was not going to publish the precise times that messages were sent. He also said that if the *Post* actually had a particular message referred to by Gayler that would compromise the SIGINT intelligence system, he was sure that the *Post* "in its own good conscience" would not disclose it (In Camera, 216).

The last matter of significance that occurred during the *in camera* portion of the hearing was the *Post*'s refusal to call Lieutenant General Melvin Zais to the stand. This surprised Gesell. Zais's affidavit contained many serious allegations, which Zais supported with specific references to the classified study. Since Zais's affidavit was the equivalent of testimony, it was the most serious obstacle standing in the way of a *Post* victory.

We do not know exactly why the *Post*'s lawyers did not want to cross-examine Zais. They probably calculated, however, that they were better off leaving Zais's impressive affidavit unanswered than risking the possibility that the general would make a powerful impression on Gesell that they could not undo under the strict time constraints of the hearing.

▪ ▪ ▪ ▪ ▪

With the lawyers for the *Post* deciding not to call General Zais and the attorneys for the government not calling any witnesses, the *in camera* hearing was concluded earlier than Gesell expected. He took a short recess before reconvening in public.

The last part of the proceedings was devoted to oral argument. Congressman Robert Eckhardt from Texas argued first. Gesell had granted him and other members of Congress status as *amici curiae*, and they had filed a legal memorandum in support of the *Washington Post*. Gesell was deferential toward Eckhardt, having expressed concern during the early part of the *in camera* hearing that it should end in time for Eckhardt to have an opportunity to present an oral argument.

Eckhardt's argument was unexceptional. He emphasized that the responsibility for curtailing unauthorized leaks rested with the executive branch of government, and the courts should not come to its aid. He asserted that Congress had a special interest in reading the disputed Pentagon study, that it was relevant to the responsibilities assigned it by the Constitution, and that the court should take this special claim into account in deciding whether to grant the government an injunction. He asserted that any disruption of diplomatic affairs caused by the disclosures was the "price" that had to be paid if the government was to retain a vital democratic character (232). After ten minutes, which was all that Gesell had allotted him, Eckhardt thanked the judge for the opportunity to present his argument and sat down.

Maroney was next. Maroney repeated the legal arguments he had made throughout the proceeding. He claimed the government was entitled to an injunction because the documents in dispute were classified, because in the opinion of State and Defense Department officials further disclosures would seriously harm national security, and because the government's evidence satisfied the legal standard established by the Supreme Court in the *Near v. Minnesota* case. Maroney also told Gesell he was authorized to state that the government was engaged in a full review of the classified documents and that it intended to make public as many of them as possible. Maroney said the court should grant an injunction, which would permit this proposed review to go forward. Finally, Maroney asserted that an injunction would only slightly injure the public or the press. He reasoned that since the *New York Times* had kept the public waiting three months while its reporters and editors reviewed the material and decided what to publish, the *Post* could hardly argue that the public would be seriously harmed if it had to wait awhile longer while the government reviewed the documents. Apart from his announcement that the government was engaged in a review of the classified material there was nothing new in Maroney's remarks.

Glendon was the last to argue. Like the others, his argument was a review of points made many times before. He insisted that the issue was whether the government was entitled to a preliminary injunction, a legal question that had to be decided by reference to traditional legal standards. The mere fact that the documents were classified was no reason to grant a preliminary injunction, since the classification system swept so broadly that it resulted in the classification of documents already in the public domain, such as presidential speeches and newspaper articles. As for the government's evidence that further disclosures would harm the national security, Glendon claimed that the government's predictions of harm were entirely hypothetical in nature and thus legally insufficient. Glendon tried to undermine the government's witnesses by insisting that there was no evidence that the first three *New York Times* articles resulted in any injury to the national security. When Glendon finished Gesell thanked everyone and said he would announce his decision at 4:30 that afternoon.

▪ ▪ ▪ ▪ ▪

Gesell reconvened the proceedings on time and announced that he was denying the government the preliminary injunction it sought. Given the signals Gesell had sent off during the day's proceedings, his ruling was no surprise.

Gesell's opinion in support of his judgment ran about six and a half pages in the transcript. Although he may have written the opinion during the recess and just read it into the record, it is more likely, given the sentence structure, redundancy, and imprecision in thought, that he made extensive notes during the break and that these notes guided him while he announced his judgment and presented his supporting reasons.

Gesell stated that the government had made a "responsible and earnest appeal" in this case, which he said presented "the raw question of a conflict between the First Amendment and the genuine deep concern of responsible officials in our Government as to implications both immediate and long-term of this breach of confidentiality" (269–71). Although he stated the disputed material was properly classified top secret when it was first written, some of the material was no longer sensitive and not properly classified. Claiming to be tracking the text of the executive order that defined top secret, Gesell stated that the government had not proven that there would be "a definite" break in diplomatic relations, an armed attack on the United States or an ally, a war, or a compromise of military or defense plans, intelligence operations, or scientific and technological materials (269).

Gesell conceded that further publication "may interfere" with delicate diplomatic relations, but if that were true, he asserted, it was "not so much because of anything in the documents, themselves," but rather because "it will appear to foreign governments that this Government is unable to prevent publication of actual Government communications" (267). But, Gesell asserted, the "degree and significance" of this injury "cannot be measured" (267–68). Moreover, Gesell observed that the right of the press to publish cannot be "adjust[ed]" to "accommodate the desires of foreign governments" to be protected from embarrassing disclosures or to the wishes of "our diplomats that they . . . be protected against either responsible or irresponsible reporting" (271).

Besides making these important points, Gesell took the government to task for making no effort to distinguish top secret material from other material, much of which he noted was already in the public domain. While conceding that the leak in this case was "unusual" because of its size, he noted that affidavits submitted by the *Post* "detailed" how government officials selectively and frequently use classified material in dealing with the press. Gesell acknowledged that Maroney had, at the close of his oral argument, represented that the government "was engaged in declassifying some of the material and requested time to complete this process with the thought that permission would then perhaps be given to the *Post* to publish what is ultimately declassified out of the whole," but he concluded that "any effort to preserve the status quo," given that the government had failed to meet the evidentiary burden the First Amendment imposed upon it, "would be contrary to the public interest" (268–71).

Gesell noted that because the disputed material related to the "longstanding and often vitriolic debate" over the Vietnam War, the question presented by the case was of "paramount public importance" and an order suppressing the material "would feed the fires of distrust" (270). He stated there was a "a growing antagonism between the executive branch and certain elements of the press," that this hostility had "serious implications for the stability of our democracy," which depended on its citizens being informed about their government. Gesell criticized the appeals court for imposing upon him the "role of quasi-censor" and for failing to define the legal standard he was to apply in this case, a case he described as one of "first impression" (266).

Gesell's opinion also contained two questionable factual assertions. Gesell stated that no "contemporary" troop movements were involved.

But Lieutenant General Zais's affidavit made that allegation, and it was unchallenged; thus, Gesell had no basis for this conclusion.[3] Also, Gesell stated that further disclosures would not compromise "our intelligence." That too was of doubtful accuracy. Vice Admiral Gayler's affidavit alleged that further disclosures could harm intelligence interests. Although Gesell had indicated that he was confident that the *Post* would not make any such disclosures, the disputed classified documents apparently contained information that could compromise some intelligence secrets if disclosed.

1. President Lyndon B. Johnson meeting with key Vietnam War advisers in February 1968. Clockwise from lower left: Walt Rostow, special assistant to Johnson (with hands on table); Vice President Hubert Humphrey; General Maxwell Taylor; Defense Secretary-designate Clark Clifford; Undersecretary of State Nicholas Katzenbach; Secretary of State Dean Rusk; Special Envoy Cyrus Vance; President Johnson; Secretary of Defense Robert McNamara; Chairman of the Joint Chiefs of Staff General Earle Wheeler.
Credits: AP/Wide World Photos

2. During the months before Secretary of Defense Robert McNamara commissioned the Pentagon Papers study, he was under enormous strain as he considered that the United States would not be able to achieve a military victory in Vietnam and that he was unable to bring about a change in the administration's war policies. In February 1967 McNamara stated at a news conference that U.S. air attacks on North Vietnam would not humble Hanoi but that they were a necessary adjunct to the ground operations.
Credits: AP/Wide World Photos

3. Robert McNamara retired as secretary of defense on February 28, 1968. Choked with emotion, he briefly spoke at the White House after being praised by President Johnson: "I cannot find words to express what lies in my heart an[d] I guess I better respond on another occasion."
Credits: AP/Wide World Photos

4. Secretary of State Rusk answering questions about the Pentagon Papers case shortly after the Supreme Court decision.
Credits: AP/Wide World Photos

5. Leslie Gelb directed the task force that prepared the forty-seven-volume Pentagon Papers study.
Credits: AP/Wide World Photos

6. Morton Halperin supervised the task force that prepared the Pentagon Papers study.
Credits: AP/Wide World Photos

7. Daniel Ellsberg, who made the Pentagon Papers available to the *New York Times*, went underground the day after the government sued the *Times*. While the FBI searched the country for him, Ellsberg was interviewed by CBS news anchor Walter Cronkite. The interview was filmed at a secret location and broadcast on Wednesday, June 23. *Credits:* AP/Wide World Photos

8. Although a civilian while in Vietnam in the mid 1960s, Daniel Ellsberg often donned a combat helmet and joined the combat troops. In this photograph Ellsberg takes aim during a clearing operation in the demilitarized zone.
Credits: AP/Wide World Photos

9. Daniel Ellsberg and Anthony Russo. Russo worked with Ellsberg in making the Pentagon Papers public.
Credits: UPI/Bettmann

10. Daniel Ellsberg held an impromptu news conference outside the federal courthouse in Boston after his arraignment. Ellsberg's wife, Patricia, is behind him and to his left.
Credits: AP/Wide World Photos

11. Searching for evidence, FBI agents confiscated papers that Daniel Ellsberg stored at a warehouse in Beverly Hills, California.
Credits: AP/Wide World Photos

12. Offices of Dr. Lewis Fielding (second floor, far right) in Beverly Hills, California. The White House Plumbers Unit broke into Fielding's office in the fall of 1971 in search of information about Ellsberg.
Credits: AP/Wide World Photos

13. Reporter Neil Sheehan, Managing Editor A. M. Rosenthal, and Foreign News Editor James L. Greenfield in the offices of the *New York Times* after it was announced that the *Times* won the Pulitzer Prize for Public Service for publishing the Pentagon Papers. Sheehan, who obtained and wrote most of the stories about the Pentagon Papers for the *Times*, was not cited in the award.
Credits: AP/Wide World Photos

14. Prepared page of the Pentagon Papers series is wheeled from guarded storage area, where it had been held, into composing room of the *Times*.
Credits: Edward Hausner/ NYT Pictures. 229 West 43d St., 9th fl., New York, NY 10036

15. In January 1971 President Richard M. Nixon responded to questions of four correspondents on national television. He identified his major achievement as starting to bring the American combat role in South Vietnam to an end. *Credits:* AP/Wide World Photos

16. Henry Kissinger, President Nixon's national security adviser.
Credits: AP/Wide World Photos

17. President Nixon with his chief of staff, H. R. Haldeman, walking from the Executive Office Building to the White House.
Credits: AP/Wide World Photos

18. Robert C. Mardian being sworn in as assistant attorney general in charge of the Internal Security Division of the Justice Department by Justice Potter Stewart in November 1970.
Credits: AP/Wide World Photos

19. In May 1971 Attorney General John Mitchell stated that he believed there were enough laws to handle "these particular mobs" who protest the Vietnam War.
Credits: AP/Wide World Photos

20. Assistant Attorney General Robert Mardian photographing antiwar demonstrators from the window of Attorney General Mitchell's office in the Justice Department in May 1971.
Credits: AP/Wide World Photos

21. The day after the *New York Times* began its Pentagon Papers series, Secretary of Defense Melvin Laird told the Senate Foreign Relations Committee that he had asked the Justice Department to investigate how the *Times* had obtained the Pentagon Papers, which he said were "highly classified" and should not be made public.
Credits: AP/Wide World Photos

22. Secretary of State William P. Rogers told reporters on the day the government sued the *New York Times* that the American people doubted what the government said about the war because they believed the government had misled them in the past.
Credits: AP/Wide World Photos

23. President Nixon's top domestic adviser in 1971, John Ehrlichman, facing news reporters (in 1973) after entering a plea of not guilty to burglary, conspiracy, and perjury charges resulting from the break-in at the office of Daniel Ellsberg's psychiatrist. At left is Ehrlichman's attorney, Joseph Ball.
Credits: AP/Wide World Photos

24. Charles W. Colson, a Nixon assistant in 1971, who urged Nixon to use the Pentagon Papers affair to deepen the conflicts within the Democratic party.
Credits: AP/Wide World Photos

25. Arthur Ochs Sulzberger, president and publisher of the *New York Times*, answering queries about the Pentagon Papers controversy at a news session at Kennedy Airport after he returned from England. *Credits:* Barton Silverman/ NYT Pictures. 229 West 43d St., 9th fl., New York, NY 10036

26. Whitney North Seymour, Jr., the United States attorney for the Southern District in New York, who pleaded the government's case in the United States district court and the court of appeals. *Credits:* AP/Wide World Photos

27. Professor Alexander Bickel (left), the *Times*'s lead attorney, arriving at the district court in Manhattan on Friday, June 18, along with Floyd Abrams (sunglasses), an attorney from the Wall Street firm of Cahill Gordon; Max Frankel, the *Times*'s Washington correspondent; Tom Wicker, associate editor; Harding F. Bancroft, executive vice president; and James C. Goodale, in-house counsel and vice president.
Credits: NYT Pictures. 229 West 43d St., 9th fl., New York, NY 10036

28. United States district judge Murray I. Gurfein arriving at the federal courthouse in Manhattan on Saturday, June 19, the day he rendered his decision in the *Times* case.
Credits: AP/Wide World Photos

29. Benjamin Bradlee, executive editor of the *Washington Post*, receiving a telephone call from the Justice Department asking the newspaper to voluntarily halt its Pentagon Papers series (Friday, June 18).
Credits: NYT Pictures. 229 West 43d St., 9th fl., New York, NY 10036

30. United States district judge Gerhard A. Gesell, the trial judge in the *Post* case, in his office.
Credits: AP/Wide World Photos

31. Deputy Undersecretary of State William B. Macomber was a key government witness.
Credits: AP/Wide World Photos

32. Dennis James Doolin, a government witness of the Pentagon's International Security Affairs unit.
Credits: AP/Wide World Photos

33. Major General Melvin Zais saluting during change of command ceremonies in Vietnam in 1969. Zais later was the government's main military expert in the *Post* case.
Credits: AP/Wide World Photos

34. Katharine Graham, publisher of the *Washington Post*, and William Glendon, the newspaper's lead attorney, outside the district court in Washington, D.C., after a day of proceedings.
Credits: AP/Wide World Photos

35. Attorneys for the *New York Times* leaving the Supreme Court after presenting oral argument on Saturday, June 26. From left to right: Lawrence McKay; Floyd Abrams; Alexander Bickel; James Goodale; and William Hegarty.
Credits: AP/Wide World Photos

36. Erwin N. Griswold, solicitor general of the United States, argued on behalf of the government in the court of appeals and in the Supreme Court.
Credits: AP/Wide World Photos

37. The justices of the Supreme Court who decided the Pentagon Papers case. From left to right: Associate Justices John M. Harlan, Thurgood Marshall, Hugo L. Black, Potter Stewart, Chief Justice Warren E. Burger, and Associate Justices Byron R. White, William O. Douglas, Harry A. Blackmun, and William J. Brennan.
Credits: AP/Wide World Photos

38. Katharine Graham, publisher of the *Washington Post*, and Benjamin Bradlee, executive editor, reacting to the Supreme Court's decision denying the government a preliminary injunction and permitting the *Post* and the *Times* to continue publishing excerpts from the Pentagon Papers.
Credits: AP/Wide World Photos

PART FOUR

The Courts of Appeals

CHAPTER SIXTEEN

The Second Circuit

While the government argued its suit against the *Washington Post*, it appealed Judge Gurfein's order in the *Times* case. Court of appeals judge Irving Kaufman had restrained the *New York Times* until Monday, June 21, when the government's appeal was scheduled for review by a three-judge panel. That meant that the government's lawyers had Saturday and Sunday to prepare a memorandum of law and to figure out a strategy for prevailing in the wake of its disastrous presentation before district court judge Gurfein.

Whitney North Seymour, Jr., and his assistant, Michael Hess, knew that the evidence they had presented was extremely weak. To offset the weak evidentiary record, Seymour decided that the government would prepare a special appendix, which would summarize the *in camera* testimony presented before Gurfein and offer additional citations to the Pentagon Papers that allegedly supported the government's claim that further publications endangered the national security.[1]

This approach had obvious advantages. It would allow the government to beef up its weak evidentiary record, which would supposedly aid the appeals court in assessing the strength of the government's overall allegations. It would also provide the appeals court with several remedial options that would be satisfactory to the government: grant an injunction on the basis of these citations; remand the matter to Gurfein with an instruction to enter an injunction; or direct Gurfein to hold a new hearing, during which the government would present testimony pertaining to all these citations.

Seymour faced two obstacles in implementing his strategy. First, he and Hess could not identify additional references to the Pentagon Papers without the aid of the government officials. That kind of cooperation would require a change in attitude on the part of Mardian and Buzhardt. Seymour telephoned John Dean, White House counsel, and asked him to intercede. Seymour wanted Dean to persuade the government's national security officials to tell him and Hess what they needed to know in order to prepare the appendix.[2] As it turned out, little pressure was required to get Mardian and Buzhardt to change their minds, since they were shocked by Gurfein's decision denying the government an injunction. Sometime on Saturday, the government officials were unmuzzled, and Seymour and his assistants got to work collecting additional citations to the classified material and organizing them into some coherent, presentable format.[3]

Second, Seymour faced a legal problem. As a general rule, it is highly inappropriate during an appeal to supplement the factual record, since the appeal is supposed to be based on the facts developed at trial. If these rules were applied to the government's appeal in the *Times* case, the government would be stuck with the weak evidentiary record presented to Judge Gurfein. Seymour believed, however, that he had some basis for pursuing his strategy. During the Friday hearing the government had introduced into evidence the entire forty-seven-volume Pentagon Papers study. Gurfein had indicated more than once during the hearing that he was going to review the entire study before deciding the government's motion for an injunction. When Gurfein denied the government injunctive relief, and stated that he had not reviewed the entire study, Seymour believed that he had a basis for claiming that the purpose of the special appendix was to guide the appeals court through the study and that Gurfein's failure to review the entire study, after he stated he would, was reversible error. Putting aside how tenable this was, Seymour thought this was the only conceivable strategy the government could pursue if it were to prevail before the Second Circuit.[4]

▪ ▪ ▪ ▪ ▪

The government's legal brief filed with the appeals court centered on three main issues. The first was whether the government had the right to sue the *Times* for a prior restraint. Alexander Bickel, the *Times*'s lead attorney, had placed great emphasis on the claim that the government could not sue the *Times* for an injunction absent a statute authorizing such action. In response the government contended that the executive branch had inherent authority to seek such relief against the *Times*, since such a suit was "in aid of the Constitutional Duty of the Federal Government to provide for the national defense and conduct its foreign affairs."[5] It claimed that such inherent authority had been previously recognized by courts.

Alternatively, the government claimed, as it had before Judge Gurfein, that its request for injunctive relief against the *Times* was authorized by a provision of the espionage act, Section 793(e). The government maintained that Section 793(e) made the *Times* criminally liable for the possession and publication of the Pentagon Papers and authorized the courts to grant a prior restraint barring the *Times* from further publication. It conceded that Section 793(e) did not explicitly refer to publications by the news media, but it contended that Congress intended 793(e) to apply to news reporting by the press when it was read in conjunction with another provision.[6]

The government's brief conceded that the First Amendment limited the government's claim for injunctive relief against the press, but it claimed that the government was entitled to an injunction under the leading case of *Near v. Minnesota*. The brief contended that the disputed documents remained properly classified, that the court should defer to government officials who claimed that further disclosures would harm the national security, and that the government's evidence established that further disclosures would "constitute a particularly grave risk to the security and defense of the United States."[7]

Finally, the government's brief argued that Judge Gurfein's failure to read through the complete study was reversible error. The brief stated: "With the greatest respect, we submit that the actual volumes of classified documents were the heart of the Government's case and no intelligent finding of fact could be made without giving them fairly thorough study. Indeed we submit that it was plain error to reach the factual conclusions adverse to the Government's contentions without reading the Government's central exhibit. The Top Secret study itself was the core of the entire proceedings."[8]

The brief maintained that Gurfein's statement in his opinion that the government had "'an opportunity to pinpoint what it believed to be vital breaches to our national security'" was misleading. It claimed that Gurfein had pressured the government to keep the *in camera* hearing as brief as possible. In addition the brief charged that the atmosphere in the courtroom was coercive and intimidating, complete with "murmurs," and an accusation by a would-be intervenor, that "any *in camera* hearing would be a 'star chamber proceeding.'" Under these circumstances, the brief argued, the government had no opportunity to present a "page-by-page discussion" of the classified report and was forced to rely on Judge Gurfein's personal review of the entire study. At the close of the brief the government lawyers referred to the "Special Appendix to this brief" and requested that it be sealed.[9]

The first part of the appendix was a five-page summary of the *in camera* testimony of government witnesses Doolin, Blouin, and Macomber with page references to the transcript. There was nothing startling or inappropriate in these pages. The second part of the appendix, however, was controversial. Entitled "Potential Impact of Publication of Exhibits 7 and 7A on the National Security of the United States," it provided page references to the Pentagon Papers study and the Tonkin Gulf Command Study, which the government witnesses did not present to Judge Gurfein. This section of the appendix was in turn split into two parts entitled "Current Military Operations" and "Current Diplomatic Relations." The emphasis on "current" in these headings was a deliberate attempt by the government lawyers to counter the criticism that the Pentagon Papers did not affect current matters.

The part on "Current Military Operations" began with a four-page single-spaced narrative claiming that further publication by the *Times* "would impede" the current rate of withdrawal of U.S. troops from the Republic of Vietnam and "seriously jeopardize" the "safety and security of our forces . . . unless our withdrawal rates were slowed to compensate for this weakening." It recounted the fact that the United States had been withdrawing its military forces for the previous eighteen months "at the fastest rate possible consistent with capabilities of the South Vietnamese armed forces in taking over the combat role and consistent with the retention of adequate military security for the United States forces remaining." It stated that the Vietnamization program was premised on the assumption that the "planned support which we expect from our allies and from the Republic of Vietnam will continue without change" and that this military balance was a "delicate" one that had "a high risk of being upset." Following these claims were six paragraphs in which more detail was presented. The government contended that "political and other consequences" of further publication "will jeopardize the military support we are receiving from foreign forces," and if the level of military strength fell "below prudent risk . . . an adverse snowballing effect could not be ruled out," especially if the North Vietnamese and the Viet Cong forces achieved a "major localized or tactical victory over the South Vietnamese forces."

The government also contended that additional disclosures would have an impact on "Thai political attitudes, both within [the] country and without," and that the United States's use of critical air bases within Thailand might be threatened because of this. The administration claimed that U.S.

tactical air units and B-52s stationed at Thailand bases were "essential to the safety and well-being of the United States forces now deployed in Southeast Asia," to the success of the Vietnamization program, and to the "interdiction program against the enemy supply routes in South Vietnam." The government maintained that without "continued support from the Republic of Thailand, air support missions would be substantially reduced, permitting the North Vietnamese to build major supply bases in preparation for mounting sizeable force attacks."

The appendix stated that additional public reports "will . . . have an impact upon the attitudes, expectations, interests, and allied solidarity of those countries of Southeast Asia, including Korea, Thailand, Japan, and the Philippines, upon whose bases and troop participation our current operation planning relies." It asserted that if publication caused these countries to reduce their support the "military risks and dangers . . . [would be] of major military proportions to the stability of the situation in South Vietnam." More particularly, it claimed that further publication "could also have an impact upon the attitudes, expectations, and interests in South Korea, and there is a possibility that the release of this information might cause the Government of Korea to withdraw [its 49,000 troops in Vietnam] . . . faster than is currently envisioned." It claimed that a change in withdrawal rates "would be extremely serious and would require" the United States to reassess its own withdrawal rates.

The appendix asserted that additional publication by the *Times* would have some effect upon the internal political processes of the South Vietnamese Government: publication would stimulate "instability" within the South Vietnamese armed forces, which might cause the South Vietnamese high command "to terminate their cross-border operations and return their participating forces to bolster the security of the homeland. Particularly in the case of Cambodia, withdrawal of these forces would allow the North Vietnamese and the Viet Cong forces to reestablish the series of base areas along the Cambodian-South Vietnamese border from which they could mount increased military activity throughout South Vietnam."

These statements were followed by five pages of references to pages within the Pentagon Papers the government claimed supported its allegations. These references were grouped under two headings. The first concerned disclosures that "would present increased risks to the safety of U.S. forces," and they were organized into ten paragraphs that focused on: plans for bombing North Vietnam, the capacity of the United States to assess enemy forces, the process of making U.S. military decisions, the reaction times of military forces once an attack order was given, current war planning for Southeast Asia and China, information about the allied effort and the "(enemy) success in combatting that effort," intelligence matters, "SEATO contingency war plans and relationships," the very survival of SEATO "as an organization," "the limited cost of an all out effort [required by the Communists] to take all of Southeast Asia," "deployment times of major U.S. units," and the integrity of U.S. codes used during various periods in 1966 and 1967.

The second group of references were collected under the heading that stated that further disclosure would "slow the U.S. program of shifting military responsibility in Vietnam to South Vietnamese forces." These citations were organized into four paragraphs covering two-and-a-half single-spaced typed pages. One paragraph asserted that the publication of certain information contained in the classified study would "endanger" the government of South Vietnam's "interest in and support of the pacification program" by:

(1) Citing overparticipation by the US in a program which should have been essentially Vietnamese in character.

(2) Documenting friction and competition between US agencies in Vietnam and Washington to the detriment of the program.

(3) Documenting efforts by the US to use foreign aid or US withdrawal as leverage to exert pressure on the GVN despite its status as a sovereign state.

(4) Criticizing the Vietnamese Government for lack of interest and emphasis on Pacification.

(5) Describing prominent Vietnamese, many of whom are still active in the government, of corruption, inability, inertia, or lack of interest in the essential program.

The paragraph ended with the prediction that further disclosures would "subject the GVN and key officials to ridicule; cause the Pacification Program to be considered as US rather than Vietnamese; result in diversion of GVN emphasis to less critical programs; jeopardize US advisor relations with their Vietnamese counterparts; and endanger other critical programs in Vietnam."

The next paragraph claimed that if the information cited were made public it would reveal "in detail US disappointment with GVN efforts in government administration and conduct of the war, and US failure to generate effective leverage on the GVN in behalf of changes felt by the US to be essential." It was argued that these revelations would make "all facets of relations with the South Vietnamese more complicated at a time when the United States is entering a very delicate phase of the withdrawal process wherein we seek to win GVN support for new programs of the utmost significance to their own survival and to the security and effectiveness of US forces which remain in South Vietnam."

The third paragraph asserted that the publication of some documents would reveal in "great detail the process involved in US decision making." It was claimed that the publication of this information would provide "a substantial advantage to the enemy and most often will tip the scales of victory in his favor" both on the battle field and in the political area. The administration claimed that disclosure of this information "could have a decided detrimental impact upon the present Vietnamization program and US deployment objectives."

The last paragraph claimed that further disclosures would reveal "GVN weaknesses" and "US attempts to influence GVN actions." It claimed that these documents would provide effective propaganda to the communists and damage many of the current leaders who are expected to continue in their leadership roles. Indeed, the administration speculated that the damage to current leaders might be so severe as to cause a "loss of leadership . . . [which in turn] could collapse the GVN and affect US programs for successful troop withdrawals."

The second controversial section of the special appendix was entitled "Current Diplomatic Relations." It was six pages long and began with an assertion that the United States "has received the cooperation of a number of third countries in carrying out delicate diplomatic missions on sensitive and vital issues." The appendix stated that the government had approached and continued to approach other countries, "some of them not friendly to the United States," for assistance in "getting food and medicine and other relief packages through to our prisoners of war . . . and in easing their conditions." It was stated that further publication would "seriously undermine our efforts to make such arrangements." This section outlined twelve diplomatic overtures by "third party diplomats" to Hanoi, overtures that began in May 1964 and ended in February 1968 and that were recounted in four diplomatic volumes of the study.

The last three-and-a-half pages of the appendix referred to portions of the study that the government claimed would "compromise other foreign relations of the United States" if disclosed. The first citations were to two top secret cables dated February 19, 1967, and March 1, 1968, that Ambassador Thompson in Moscow had sent to the State Department. The February cable summarized a "highly confidential conversation with Soviet Prime Minister Kosygin on Vietnam and China," and the administration claimed that the disclosure that a "top Soviet leader may have been accommodating to United States interests places him in a vulnerable position with respect to his colleagues and thus less likely to be accommodating in the future." The later cable was marked "literally eyes only" and contained Thompson's "careful and detailed assessment of probable Soviet attitudes toward various possible United States military actions with respect to North Vietnam and possible Soviet countermoves." The administration claimed that the disclosure of this cable could provide the Soviets with "intelligence of a most valuable type," since Thompson "is widely known as a senior authoritative official adviser on Soviet affairs."

This section of the appendix also focused on documents "concerning the period of the *coup d'etat* against President Ngo Dinh Diem in November 1963 and United States relations with the successor regimes." The government claimed that these documents reveal "the degree of direct United States pressures and influence on the Government of Vietnam some years ago" and that they also contain "a brutally frank lecture to Vietnamese generals by the American Ambassador." It was claimed that publication of this information would "diminish the stature of present Vietnamese political figures," including then President Nguyen Van Thieu and Vice President Nguyen Cao Ky.

The last references identified in the appendix refer to documents that contain criticisms of the governments and officials of Poland and Italy who had acted as intermediaries. The administration claimed that some documents included "numerous disparaging references to Poland and Polish officials" and "casts the Poles in an unfavorable light and makes it unlikely that they would act in any future peace negotiations." Other documents "imply criticism" of the Italian government, which had also acted as a go-between at the behest of the United States. Altogether, the appendix provided over 28 citations to 226 pages plus 7 full volumes of the Pentagon Papers study.

■ ■ ■ ■ ■

The *Times* submitted both a public and a sealed brief to the appeals court. The public brief focused exclusively on the law. It maintained that the government was not entitled to an injunction. This brief discussed two legal issues: (1) what the relevant First Amendment legal standard was for deciding whether the government was entitled to a prior restraint in this case; and (2) whether the government had any right to be seeking a prior restraint against the *Times* on the facts presented by this case. The *Times* brief, however, did not treat these issues equally. It devoted only three pages to discussing what the *Times* believed to be the appropriate legal standard under the First Amendment and over forty-five pages to the separation of powers claim that the government was not authorized to sue the

Times for a prior restraint on these facts. Given that the government's legal attack against the *Times* was widely assumed to pit the government's need for secrecy against the *Times*'s right to publish, this imbalance in the *Times* brief was extraordinary. Even assuming that the separation of powers arguments fully deserved the lengthy treatment the *Times* brief gave them, there was no justification for devoting only three pages to the First Amendment issues. Those issues were as important as those regarding the separation of powers, and no less complicated. Although it is not certain, it would seem that Alexander Bickel was responsible for the peculiar imbalance in the *Times* brief, given that he was the *Times*'s lead lawyer and had from the start of the litigation placed much more emphasis on the separation of powers than on the First Amendment.

The *Times* conceded, as it had all along in the case, that the First Amendment did not ban all prior restraints. It asserted that the government had a "heavy burden" when it sought such relief.[10] But the brief did not define what that burden was. Thus, it did not define what kind of injury the government had to prove to succeed, did not define how probable it was that publication would cause harm, and did not explain how quickly after publication the injury would have to follow. In short the *Times* conceded that the First Amendment tolerated prior restraints, insisted that the government seeking such relief had a heavy burden, but left undefined the legal standard it wanted the court to apply. Unless the court accepted the *Times* contention that the government was not authorized to sue, the outcome in the case would depend upon the government's evidence and the legal standard used to assess the adequacy of the evidence. The fact that the *Times* brief did not discuss the legal standard fully was a serious weakness.

The longest section of the *Times*'s legal memorandum focused on whether the government could sue the *Times* for a prior restraint. The *Times* did not contend that the government lacked inherent authority to seek a prior restraint against the press in all circumstances. Bickel resisted such absolutist positions in all corners of the law. Instead, the *Times* conceded that the government could sue the press for a prior restraint absent congressional authorizations in "extraordinary situations of extreme emergency."[11] But the *Times* did not define what it meant by "extraordinary situations of extreme emergency." It merely asserted that the facts in this case fell far short of such circumstances.

The *Times* argument was based on the observation that the Congress was the basic law-making body under the Constitution. But the *Times* brief then proceeded from that uncontroversial assertion to more debatable questions—namely, whether the executive branch had authority to sue the press and whether the judiciary had authority to grant an injunction absent a statute. In developing this argument the *Times* had some legal authority to rely upon, but it had to stretch the prior decisions to get them to support its position.

Once the *Times* got this far in its argument, it claimed Congress had passed no statute that authorized this action. By comparison to the other assertions, this one was easier to maintain. Only one provision of the espionage laws was remotely relevant, and, as written, this was a criminal statute.[12] It defined certain conduct as a crime and it did not authorize an injunction of any kind. In addition the *Times* claimed that the purpose of this law was to protect the nation from espionage, not ban a newspaper from publishing the Pentagon Papers. The *Times* argued that its conduct was well outside the parameters of this criminal statute.[13]

Even after taking into consideration the speed with which the *Times* lawyers had to write the legal memorandum, the brief dramatically shortchanged the important and complicated First Amendment issues in favor of those concerning separation of powers. And then it compounded one misjudgment with another by failing to address fully why the government did not have inherent power to seek a judicial restraint in this case.

The *Times* also submitted a sealed brief. It was sealed because it discussed the testimony of the government witnesses during the *in camera* hearing.[14] This brief dismissed without argument the government's extreme legal claim that it was entitled to a prior restraint merely because the disputed documents were classified. Even the government did not seem to take this argument seriously, the *Times* contended, for if it had it would not have presented testimony by government officials.

The *Times* next addressed the government's contention that it should prevail so long as the disputed documents were not classified arbitrarily or capriciously. The *Times* claimed that the government had failed to satisfy even this very minimal standard. In support of this contention the *Times* cited Gurfein's statements that the government's evidence did not present a "sharp clash" between the demands of national security and a free press. It also cited the testimony of the government witnesses and claimed the testimony actually supported the *Times*'s contention that the disputed Pentagon Papers were arbitrarily classified. As an example of what it had in mind, the *Times* quoted Admiral Blouin's statement that much information in the public domain "gave him the shivers" and that he "deplore[d] much of what he read" in the newspapers. The *Times* also emphasized that the government's three witnesses provided few specific references to the classified documents that supported their general conclusions, even though "Judge Gurfein constantly urged the witnesses to supply him with specific examples." As a poignant example, the *Times* quoted Gurfein's statement to Assistant Secretary of Defense Doolin that he would give him "one more chance" to provide specific references.

The sealed brief reviewed several national security topics that the government's three witnesses had used to illustrate the kinds of concerns they had. The brief dismissed as unpersuasive the witnesses' claims that further publication would cause New Zealand or Thailand to withdraw military forces prematurely and thus disrupt the planned Vietnamization program; it characterized as pure speculation their claims that further disclosures would cause other countries to stop acting as intermediaries on behalf of the United States; and it asserted that the legitimate demands of the democratic process made some disclosure of diplomatic matters important. It stated that when government officials had made public the text of communications between heads of state, there was no cry that such disclosures would destroy diplomacy. It stated that the bombing targets identified in the Pentagon Papers were stale. It discounted any harm that might result from disclosures about the command structure, since such information was already well known. It claimed that the military contingency plans and the rules of engagement were outdated. It contended that it was pure conjecture that the disclosure of the cable from Ambassador Llewellyn Thompson would help the Soviet Union.

The sealed brief ended with the point that the distribution of the fifteen copies of the Pentagon Papers belied the government's claim that it considered the study very sensitive. If the government sincerely believed that the study was properly classified top secret, it would not have given a copy of the study to Robert McNamara or Clark Clifford, who were no longer in the government.

▪ ▪ ▪ ▪ ▪

At 10:30 Monday morning, eight days after the *Times* began its series, the lawyers in the case assembled in the Second Circuit courtroom on the seventeenth floor of the federal courthouse in Foley Square. The courtroom was packed by the time Chief Judge Henry J. Friendly and Judges J. Joseph Smith and Paul R. Hays took the bench. Bickel was the first to speak, and he requested that a transcript of the proceedings be kept. Friendly agreed. Friendly then announced that the three judges had been "consulting with each other over the weekend to a considerable extent" and had decided that all the Second Circuit judges should hear the appeal because of the importance of the case. He told the lawyers that the judges would gather the next day at two o'clock to hear the arguments.[15]

Once Friendly arranged for getting the legal briefs to the other judges so they would have time to read them, Seymour raised a new matter: in addition to its legal memorandum the government had a "special appendix" that identified particular portions of the multivolume study that the government believed would gravely injure the national security if disclosed. He said that the government lawyers had been assisted by some defense officials in preparing the document and that their advice was contained in affidavits. He asked that the documents be sealed and that the government be permitted to submit them. Friendly asked if the documents amounted to anything more than "a pointer" that would help the judges, and Seymour answered "No" (7).

Bickel objected. He asserted that what the government was trying to do was to supplement the factual record as developed before Judge Gurfein and that was highly improper. He said that it amounted to the government trying to gain a "second bite of the apple" and that the admission of this evidence would deny the *Times* its right to confront and cross-examine the witnesses. Judge Hays tried to mollify Bickel by suggesting that as he understood Seymour, the government was not trying to add anything to the testimony given by the government witnesses in the *in camera* hearing. Friendly echoed Hays and stated that any additional "characterizations" of the evidence at this stage would be improper but that information that pointed out the most potentially damaging material would be of "great aid" to the court. Friendly told the lawyers that he thought that "counsel of such eminence ought to be able to work this out" (7–8).

The judicial proceedings began anew the next afternoon before all eight judges of the Second Circuit court of appeals. Because the government was appealing Gurfein's order denying it an injunction, Seymour was the first to argue. Seymour began by characterizing the case as one of "major national importance" affecting the military posture of the United States in Southeast Asia, the Mideast peace talks, the "war of nerves in Central Europe," and "sensitive discussions on strategic arms limitations." He claimed that while the "courts have mouthed the existence of an exception" to the general rule against prior restraints, this case warranted such relief for the "first time." Seymour described the origins of the Pentagon study, as well as its contents and size. He recalled for the appeal judges the atmosphere in Judge Gurfein's courtroom. The courtroom was rarely "so crowded," he said, with a "veritable cabal of the nation's press" in attendance. It was "almost like an old-fashion movie, with bursts of laughter and approval" when the *Times* lawyers "scored a point and mutterings of disapproval as the Government made its arguments." Indeed, he told the judges, the case had stirred so much hostility toward the government that he was hissed as he entered the Second Circuit courtroom that afternoon.[16]

Seymour did his best to place the *Times* in an unfavorable light. He said the *Times* maintained that it was the "sole" judge of what could be published. He said that the newspaper had the documents for three months and never once consulted the government about whether the study contained any information that might seriously harm the national security if released. He indicated that the responsible course of action for the *Times* would have been either to consult with the government or to file a claim under the Freedom of Information Act. Although Seymour conceded that the classified documents were exempt from the Freedom of Information Act, he claimed that courts could order the release of documents that were arbitrarily classified. Seymour also said that the *Times* could have used its editorial page to pressure the government into granting a request to declassify the study in whole or part. He stated that the *Times* took the position that its right to publish the secret history was totally unaffected by the fact that the top secret material had been stolen and that it, the *Times*, was unauthorized to possess it. He claimed that the *Times* seemed to think of the classification system as no more than a "cover-up to hide mistakes in government." He said that the *Times*'s position was untenable. But even assuming that there was some truth to the *Times* contention, Seymour emphasized that it did not follow that "all classified documents should be in the public domain," that there were "no secrets that should be properly classified," and that there were "no documents which were vital to the nation's security" ([June 22] 10). Seymour said that it was all but self-evident that the 7,000-page study contained some national security secrets that required judicial protection ([June 22] 11).

Seymour had a difficult time defining for the appeals judges the government's legal claim. He tried to get some mileage out of the fact that the documents were stolen, presumably to make the appeals judges hostile toward the *Times*, even though no one suspected the *Times* of stealing the documents. But as Seymour pressed the point, Judge Kaufman asked him if he was claiming that a newspaper could not publish stolen documents under any condition. Once the assertion underlying his point was laid bare, Seymour quickly denied this was his position. But he insisted it was a "proper element" for the judges to consider and that it was a "weight in the scales" ([June 22] 13–14).

Seymour also suggested that the "vice" in this case was that the *Times* had assumed the authority to declassify information. But as soon as he made the point Judge Walter R. Mansfield asked him if he was claiming that the court was bound by the classification stamp and was obligated to grant an injunction merely because the information was classified. To that question Seymour answered no, but he asserted that the classification stamp should be considered "persuasive" evidence that the information would injure the national security if made public. But this contention was difficult to maintain, since Seymour had to concede that the study contained documents that were already in the public domain. Judge Mansfield put the dilemma to Seymour directly: "But if you concede that some of the documents are not top secret even though they bear the stamp, how can we indulge in such a presumption?" Seymour tried to escape by maintaining that the documents that were not top secret were collected in two volumes, and that "every page" in the other volumes was properly classified top secret. But this was untenable, especially given that the study contained information going back to the 1940s, and Mansfield did not allow Seymour to avoid the obvious. "Do you say that each and every one of those documents today is actually of a nature that should be classified top secret?" Seymour backed down and answered: "Your Honor, I am not going to arrogate unto myself what we say the *Times* cannot arrogate unto itself." Seymour no longer claimed that the documents were properly classified but merely that they were classified and that he had no authority or knowledge to question that fact ([June 22] 14–17).

Seymour claimed that Gurfein had rushed him the day of the hearing and did not give him adequate time to prepare and present the government's evidence. When asked by Judge Friendly why he had agreed to the deadlines Gurfein had established Seymour claimed he "never" agreed to the procedures followed by Gurfein and that he would identify portions of the transcript to support his contention when they moved into an *in camera* hearing ([June 22] 27).

Seymour argued that three reasons warranted the reversal of Judge Gurfein's decision to deny the government such an injunction. First, Gurfein should have granted a preliminary injunction unless he found that the disputed material had been classified arbitrarily. Since the government had proven that the documents were initially properly classified and remained so, Gurfein's refusal to grant the preliminary injunction was reversible error. Second, Gurfein had an obligation to review the entire study and if he had, he would have concluded that further disclosures would injure the national security. Third, Seymour claimed that the government had introduced sufficient evidence to establish that further disclosures would imperil current military and diplomatic matters, thus entitling the government to an injunction ([June 22] 24–36).

To persuade the court of the government's good faith in trying to make public as much of the disputed study as national security would permit Seymour told the judges that he was authorized to announce that the secretary of state, the secretary of defense, and the chairman of the Joint

Chiefs of Staff were prepared to appoint "a joint task force to conduct an exhaustive declassification study of the documents in question." He said that the review would be conducted on an "expedited basis," that it would be "completed within any reasonable time limit the Court may wish to set," and that the government suggested a "minimum of 45 days." Seymour stated that the government would withdraw its objection to the publication of any documents it found to be "no longer relevant to national security" ([June 22] 23–24). Although Seymour never said so in so many words, he must have hoped the court would extend the restraining order until the task force completed its work. But the offer drew no questions from the judges, and Seymour did not mention the offer again during the argument.

Seymour sought to strengthen the government's position by claiming that the court should defer to the judgment of national security officials because "the sophisticated problems that are woven through these documents are not ones that the courts or lawyers or newspaper editors . . . are qualified to judge." He even went as far as to say that it would be "foolhardy in the extreme" for the judges to assume that they could make this judgment. He urged them to defer to the "professionals in the field, the intelligence men, the military men, the diplomats" ([June 22] 33).

Seymour did not precisely define the relief the government sought. But his statements indicated that the government sought three different forms of relief: first, and most preferred, an order barring all further publication of the disputed documents on the ground that their classification was not arbitrary; second, an order continuing the injunction pending a review by a government task force, as Seymour had indicated; third, and least preferred, a remand to Gurfein with instructions that the case be scheduled for a new hearing ([June 22] 25).

Seymour's argument had gone well. Although he had some rough moments when different judges had forced him to make concessions, he had outlined a coherent position that included two alternative legal claims and three alternative forms of relief. He had also placed the *Times* in an unfavorable light, given the appellate judges a legal hook on which to reverse Gurfein's judgment, cautioned them not to assume the responsibilities of national security officials, and tried to present the government as trying to solve a problem that plagued any democracy.

▪ ▪ ▪ ▪ ▪

Bickel's argument got off to a rough start. He tried to remove the shadow Seymour had tried to cast over the *Times* and objected to the government's assertion that the documents were stolen. "There is no evidence anywhere in the record, . . ." he maintained, "that the *Times* stole these documents or that anybody stole them." When Friendly asked if the *Times* would not concede that it obtained the documents "without authorization," Bickel stated that he was only trying "to get the word 'stolen' out of the discourse." But he made things worse with the flippant remark that "for all we know" former Defense Secretaries Clark Clifford or Robert McNamara might have given the documents to the *Times*. Judge Friendly jumped on him: "You aren't serious. Why don't you face the facts?" ([June 22] 38–39).

Bickel's second point went no more smoothly than his first. Bickel said: "There is a good deal of talk . . . about what the *Times* could have done or might have done" to obtain the disputed documents, an issue he thought irrelevant to whether the *Times* could continue to publish them now that it had the classified report. Friendly understood his point immediately and said: "You mean it is quite unimportant that the *Times* did not avail itself" of any of the ways Seymour had identified to get the Pentagon study? Rather than agreeing with Friendly, Bickel continued to make the point that he had just made and that Friendly had just summarized quite succinctly. Friendly eventually interrupted Bickel and said that it would not matter, of course, that the *Times* might have acted irresponsibly, if the court had no power "to do anything" in this case ([June 22] 40–41). Friendly gave Bickel an opening to argue that the executive branch had no authority to sue the *Times* for a prior restraint, given the facts of this case, a point that Bickel thought important. But Bickel ignored Friendly's invitation and continued almost incoherently for a few moments. Perhaps Bickel was nervous because of the surroundings, but he did his client little good during the opening minutes of his argument.

The remainder of Bickel's argument was better. He asserted that the government did not have inherent authority to secure a prior restraint under the facts of this case and that no statute authorized the government to seek a prior restraint under the facts of this case. Bickel stated that the judges had to decide these questions before deciding whether the First Amendment protected the *Times* in this case. But Bickel struggled to make his argument clearly. Eventually the judges' questions indicated that they understood his contention, but even then he was unable to let the matter drop and go on to others. As a result several judges kept asking him to address the First Amendment issues and to discuss what he thought the legal standard should be. Bickel resisted these inquiries. He gave short, assertive answers rather than explanatory ones, and he often tried to return to what he considered his more basic point, namely that the government had no legal authority to sue the *Times* in the first case.

Throughout Bickel's argument Judge Kaufman was his main ally. Through his questions to Bickel he effectively advocated the *Times*'s position. Time and again he would interrupt and tell Bickel something like the following: "Isn't your argument that . . ." Bickel would agree, but he would offer a caveat to what Kaufman had said, or make a subtle distinction that was not clearly worded and distracted attention from the important point that Kaufman had just stated with precision and brevity.

Bickel's argument was weak. He failed to emphasize the critical point that the First Amendment barred the government from interfering with the *Times*'s right to publish the classified information. He did not define what he considered to be the appropriate First Amendment legal standard the court should apply. Nor did he discuss any of the relevant First Amendment cases.[17]

▪ ▪ ▪ ▪ ▪

The closed hearing was next.[18] Hegarty, a partner from the Wall Street law firm of Cahill, Gordon, represented the *Times* during this phase of the proceedings. He had been lead counsel during the evidentiary hearing before Gurfein the previous Friday, and since the *in camera* hearing focused on the factual claims, Hegarty took over from Bickel.

Hegarty made a preliminary motion and asked that the special appendix be stricken. He argued that the text of the appendix closely followed affidavits that government officials had submitted on Monday in the *Washington Post* case. Although he did not say so in so many words, his point was that the appendix constituted an improper elaboration of the evidentiary record that was created before Judge Gurfein. To support his claim, Hegarty referred to one part of the appendix in which two military plans were identified. Hegarty stated that the appendix indicated that the plans were no longer in use and that Seymour could not have known that as a result of the evidentiary hearing before Gurfein. Hegarty said that someone must have given Seymour this information. That is the "vice of this appendix," Hegarty told the judges (In Camera, 5).

Friendly was unconvinced and interrupted Hegarty. It was "not uncommon" for lawyers to get advice from clients, he maintained, citing patent cases as ones in which lawyers received assistance from their clients on the "technical parts" of the brief (In Camera, 5). But before Friendly could finish his point, Seymour stood and asked if he could be heard. Seymour explained how the appendix was prepared. Immediately after Judge Kaufman had continued the restraining order on Saturday afternoon, Seymour called the Justice Department and asked for help in preparing the legal papers. He was advised that affidavits were being prepared for the *Wash-*

ington Post case and that they identified passages in the Pentagon Papers that would injure the national security if disclosed. Seymour was told that he would receive the affidavits on Sunday. As it turned out, the affidavits did not arrive until Monday morning. Seymour said that he personally supervised the "cutting and pasting" of the affidavits that yielded the appendix, which he said was an "artless" term and that brief would have been better. As for Hegarty's suggestion that he, Seymour, had learned that the military plans were no longer current from a government defense official, Seymour said he would "admit" that the "source" of that information was the *Times* itself (In Camera, 6–8).

Friendly then announced that the court would deny the motion to strike. He said that the court would treat the appendix as a brief and would use it to "point to either specific exhibits or to matters of common knowledge, and not as supplying any additional evidence which we don't already have" (In Camera, 8).

Seymour then began his argument. His first point was that Judge Gurfein had rushed the lawyers during the *in camera* hearing. To support his contention he read some of Gurfein's statements in which he urged the lawyers to hurry the presentation. Seymour did not state that Gurfein had actually prohibited the government from introducing any evidence it wished. Nor did Seymour claim that he had asked Gurfein for more time to prepare and present the government's evidence. What Seymour seemed to imply, however, was that Gurfein's statements had kept him from having the government witnesses identify as many of the study's documents as they might have and that he did not object to this because he relied upon Gurfein's suggestions that he was going to read through the entire study.

Seymour next turned to the *in camera* testimony and summarized it in a way that was as favorable to the government as he could make it. Assistant Secretary of Defense Doolin had testified that further publication by the *Times* would injure negotiations pertaining to the prisoners of war, the safety of U.S. military forces in South Vietnam, and the operational plans of the South East Asia Treaty Organization. Vice Admiral Francis Blouin had testified that further disclosures would injure numerous military subjects including "air strike information, numbers of aircraft, potential targets, command apparatus, timing systems, rules of engagement, capability to deploy ground troops, the decision-making process on which an enemy can plan timing and response, reaction times, and specifics on Thailand forces in Laos" (In Camera, 13a). Assistant Secretary of State William B. Macomber, who Seymour said was such an "effective advocate" it was a "shame" that the judges had not heard him themselves, testified about the need to keep diplomatic communications confidential (In Camera, 14).

The judges challenged Seymour's argument on a number of grounds. Mansfield did not understand how the disclosure of events that had happened several years before could have an impact on current interests. Wilfred Feinberg asked whether the diplomatic history of the war had not already been disclosed in various books and articles. Mansfield asked why the government had not taken the initiative to declassify the study earlier. Kaufman wondered whether the government's offer to review the classified report was without legal significance since it had failed to carry its burden of proof before Judge Gurfein. Hays wanted to know what good it would do to give the government time to review the study since the court would have to decide whether the *Times* could publish the material the government eventually claimed could not be disclosed. Mansfield questioned whether the government's case against the *Times* was not moot in light of the fact that the *Boston Globe* had that day published some additional documents drawn from the secret study.

Seymour tried to answer these questions. The disclosure of historical documents could have a significant impact on current interests, and neither judges nor lawyers were competent to assess the claim. Some of the diplomatic history of the war had been revealed in books and articles, but much had not been and none had been revealed through official government documents. Documents already in the public domain that were attached to government-prepared documents were interwoven throughout the whole study and could not be quickly declassified. Seymour said he did not know why the government had not taken previous steps to declassify the study, but now that it was prepared to do so the task could not be done in much less than the forty-five days the government suggested. Although such a review would not resolve all legal issues, the court's task would be easier once that process was completed. Seymour assured the judges that the government's action against the *Times* was not moot because of the *Boston Globe*'s publication: the government had already initiated a suit against the *Globe* as it had against the *Washington Post*.

Hegarty argued next. After floundering for a few minutes Hegarty tried to get the court to realize how different the government's evidence was from what he considered the evidence in the prototype prior restraint case. In the prototype case the threatened injury to national security posed by further publication would be "obvious," "dramatic," "not complicated," and "not requiring laborious research, deep preparation." In that presumed case, Hegarty claimed, the government lawyer does not have to prepare, for "it will be clear to any layman that this is a serious problem." If such evidence had been brought forward in this case, Hegarty claimed that the *Times* would have hesitated before going ahead with further publication because it is a "responsible institution" (In Camera, 32). But that is not this case, Hegarty asserted. The evidence offered by the government witnesses fell far short of this. Doolin had conceded that he had read only seven of the forty-seven volumes in deciding whether the administration should grant Senator Fulbright's request to declassify the study, and then he was only able to assert that he was concerned by the "general impact of the total study" (In Camera, 34). Hegarty portrayed Blouin as someone who was upset by what the press generally reported and thus could not be relied upon as offering sound judgment in this case. Macomber's testimony, Hegarty argued, was flawed because the predicted injuries were built on conjecture and hypothesis.

The judges challenged Hegarty as they had Seymour. Friendly wanted to know why the *Times* did not "sit down" with the government and go through the documents (In Camera, 41). Mansfield asked what Hegarty would consider a reasonable specification, and now that the government had offered dozens of specific citations, whether the *Times* would now go over them with the government, one by one. Friendly commented that he thought Mansfield's point was constructive. Hegarty responded that the *Times* had on occasion consulted with the government about possible national security matters prior to publication but that it did not believe that the Pentagon Papers posed any such problems. Hegarty said he was unable to comment on whether the *Times* would sit down with the government to go over the specific references to the Pentagon Papers study.

The hearing ended with Hegarty and Seymour disagreeing over what Gurfein had said the previous Saturday afternoon in chambers when he called the lawyers in to announce his decision. Hegarty insisted that Gurfein had stated that he had read through all the documents; Seymour claimed that he could recall no such statement. After a short recess Friendly announced that the judges had decided to continue the stay and that the court would hand down a decision, "promptly," "surely within the next two days" (In Camera, 50).

▪ ▪ ▪ ▪ ▪

The court made public its decision the next day, Wednesday, June 22. By a vote of five to three it remanded the case to Judge Gurfein for further *in camera* proceedings and ordered him to conclude the hearing by July 3.[19] The court directed Gurfein to decide whether the "disclosure of any of those items specified in the Special Appendix filed with this Court on June 21, 1971, or any of such additional items as may be specified by the plaintiff with particularity on or before June 25, 1971, pose such grave and immediate danger to the security of the United States" as to warrant a prior restraint. The court continued the outstanding stay until June 25, at which time the stay was "vacated except as to those items" specified in the special appendix and those the government subsequently specified in accordance with the court's decision.[20]

The short, unsigned opinion was joined by Chief Judge Friendly and Judges J. Edward Lumbard, Smith, Hays, and Mansfield. Judges Kaufman, Feinberg, and James L. Oakes dissented, stating in a fifteen-word statement that indicated they would vacate the outstanding stay and affirm Gurfein's judgment.

The Second Circuit decision was peculiar. An appeals court reverses a district court judgment only when it concludes that the district judge committed reversible error. If no reversible error was committed, the losing party is stuck with the result no matter how disturbing the judgment may seem in light of subsequent developments. In this case the Second Circuit did not identify any reversible error committed by Judge Gurfein. Indeed, the only reversible error that Judge Gurfein might have committed was to apply the wrong legal standard. But, given the Second Circuit's emphasis in its brief opinion on "grave and immediate danger," it is unlikely that the Second Circuit was implying that Gurfein had applied the wrong—too demanding—legal standard. What the Second Circuit appears to have decided was precisely what it was not supposed to decide. It seems to have been persuaded that the government should have a second chance to prove that further publication would injure national security, even though it found no fault with how Judge Gurfein had conducted the hearing.

The Second Circuit seems to have been persuaded to reach this conclusion because of the government's claim that it did not have time to prepare and present its case. Not knowing how Mardian and Buzhardt had muzzled the witnesses, the judges may have thought that the chronology of events since Friday supported this decision. On Friday the government had only a handful of specific references to the Pentagon Papers, and on Monday it had dozens of references. Seymour knew that this disparity had nothing to do with the expedited nature of the proceedings before Gurfein. He knew the government witnesses had provided Gurfein with only a few references because Mardian and Buzhardt had ordered them not to offer specifics. He also must have realized that he had misled the appellate judges into thinking that Gurfein had so rushed him that he had drastically curtailed the evidence he had intended to offer. He was counting on the fact that they might accept his explanation of what happened since he was the respected United States Attorney.

The judges who voted to remand the action might well have told themselves that it was better to give the government a second chance to prove its case than run the risk that the *Times* would publish some information devastating to the national security. They might even have told themselves that they doubted that the government's evidence would be adequate, but that the harm to the press and to the public caused by continuing the stay was outweighed by the risk of harm to the national security. One cannot be sure that those thoughts were on the judges' minds, but it is not implausible that they were.

CHAPTER SEVENTEEN

The D.C. Circuit

The government appealed Gesell's decision in the *Post* case while it appealed Gurfein's judgment in the *Times* case. Because the D.C. Circuit court reviewed the significant work of the vast federal administrative agencies, the court was long considered to be the second most important court in the country after the Supreme Court.

Late Monday afternoon, June 21, all nine judges of the D.C. Circuit court were waiting for an appeal in the *Post* case, knowing there would be an appeal no matter who lost. The fact that all the judges were assembled to consider the stay application, however, was very unusual and indicated the case's importance.

Once the parties presented their positions, the judges quickly agreed to hear the appeal Tuesday afternoon, the same time the Second Circuit had scheduled the government's appeal in the *Times* case. They also extended the outstanding restraining order until 5 P.M., Tuesday afternoon, and directed the parties to file legal briefs with the court by early Tuesday morning. The record on appeal to the D.C. Circuit is incomplete, and it is not known if the *Post* or the government submitted sealed briefs.

▪ ▪ ▪ ▪ ▪

The government lawyers in the *Post* case confronted the same problem that the government lawyers did in the *Times* case. Having lost in the district court, what should be the government's strategy in the appeal? There was a major difference between the cases, however. The government lawyers had had three more days to prepare for the trial in the *Post* case than they did in the *Times* case. Even though they might argue that they needed still more time to make a full and thorough presentation of its evidence, that would be a much harder argument to make in the *Post* case.

Robert Mardian assumed the responsibility for shaping the government's strategy for its appeal in the *Post* case. The government's brief presented three reasons that Gesell's decision should be reversed.[1] The president had "sole discretion" for the conduct of foreign affairs, and his decisions "should not be subject to judicial review." Gesell's decision was improper because it ran counter to the constitutional grant of power to the president. Indeed, the government went on to argue, and Gesell conceded, that further publication "may interfere with the ability of the Department of State in the conduct of delicate negotiations now in process or contemplated for the future."

The government also claimed that Gesell applied the wrong legal standard in denying the government an injunction. Gesell had required the government to prove that further publication would result in an "immediate grave threat to the national security," and he had defined such a threat as a disclosure that would result in "a definite break in diplomatic relations," "an armed attack on an ally," "a war," the "compromise of military or defense plans," the "compromise of intelligence operations," or the "compromise of scientific and technological materials." The government maintained that this was not the appropriate constitutional standard. The government was entitled to a preliminary injunction so long as it proved that the classification of the Pentagon Papers was not arbitrary or capricious. The government sought to buttress this position by emphasizing that the courts "simply are not equipped to make their own independent judgments on these questions on the basis of what must necessarily be a rather cursory review of the material, viewed in isolation and without the background necessary fully to appreciate the implications of unauthorized publication." The government's third argument was captioned "The Court's Failure to Require Production of Documents was Clearly Erroneous." This argument was based on Gesell's statement that his role as a "quasi-censor" was made "doubly difficult" because he did not know what material the *Post* had and what material it intended to publish. This was a peculiarly odd statement for Gesell to have made, since he had announced that he was assuming that the *Post* had all the documents in dispute. Nonetheless, he did make the statement, and the government lawyers tried to get whatever mileage they could out of it. In effect they argued that Gesell had only himself to blame for the state of affairs, since he refused to order the *Post* to permit government officials to examine the documents. The government's brief completely skirted the all-important legal question of the extent to which the First Amendment limited the government's claims for an injunction. Thus, the government did not address any (let alone all) of the subsidiary but important and complex questions such as, What kind of injury did the government need to prove to prevail? How likely must it be that publication would cause the threatened injury or injuries? How immediately must injury follow disclosure? If the government's brief had addressed these questions, it could have emphasized that this was a case of first impression and that legal precedents did not define a precise legal standard. It could have then argued for any one of a number of legal positions that would have been favorable to the government. But Mardian wanted to prevail on a more extreme legal theory—that the government should win merely because the Pentagon Papers were properly classified—and thus the government did not even try to get what advantage it could from these lines of argumentation.

▪ ▪ ▪ ▪ ▪

The *Post*'s brief asserted that the First Amendment protected the press from government censorship and attacked the government's contention that it was entitled to an injunction because the documents were not classified arbitrarily.[2] In sharp contrast to the *Times*'s emphasis in the Second Circuit it did not assert that the government was prohibited from suing the *Post* for a prior restraint absent an authorizing statute.

The *Post*'s first point asserted that the government could secure a preliminary injunction only if it could demonstrate that it would prevail at a final hearing and that it would suffer "grave and irreparable injury" unless it is granted such relief. Because the government had failed to satisfy Gesell on these matters in the lower court, the brief asserted that the government was now required to satisfy "substantially more demanding tests than those imposed on it in the court below." The government could prevail on appeal, the *Post* maintained, only if it demonstrated that Gesell had "clearly abused" his discretion in denying the preliminary injunction, which the *Post* argued it could not. This was the traditional legal rule, and while the *Post* understandably relied on it, it was unlikely that the appeals court judges would closely adhere to it in such a historic case. Such a standard would allow the appeals judges only a very limited scope of review, and, given the important interests at stake, it is unlikely that they would accept such restraints.

The *Post* next addressed the central First Amendment issue. It insisted that the government could prevail only if it proved that further publications would cause an immediate and grave threat to national security. The *Post* dismissed as "insufficient" the idea that "a showing of some prejudice to defense interests" was legally adequate. It scoffed at the idea that embarrassment of the government should ever justify a preliminary injunction. Instead, the *Post* claimed that the government could obtain injunctive relief only if the proven harm was "extraordinary" and "great." The *Post* cited to Chief Justice Hughes's example in *Near v. Minnesota* to illustrate what it meant by harm: the actual obstruction to the government's recruitment of troops, the sailing dates of transport ships, and the number and location of soldiers.

The *Post* contended the court could grant an injunction only in the most narrow circumstances. It emphasized that the publication had to result in immediate injury rather than set off a chain of events that might result in a serious injury sometime in the future. Against this standard, the *Post* argued, the government had failed to establish "any" legally sufficient threat to the national security. It conceded that Gesell had found that further publication might interfere with diplomatic relations, but it claimed that diplomatic relations were only "remotely" related to national security and that the injury to national security resulting from diplomatic relations was hypothetical. In addition the *Post* claimed it was "truly shocking" that the government would make the argument, since any injury depended largely upon the reaction of other governments, and many governments that might react negatively to the disclosures had "systems" of government so "alien" to our own that they "cannot understand why we do not emulate their censorial practices."

The *Post* next turned to what it considered the government's main claim, that it was entitled to a prior restraint if it proved that the disputed material had not been arbitrarily classified. The *Post* asserted that this legal standard might be appropriate if the *Post* had sought to have the documents declassified but that it was inappropriate in this case since it already had possession of the documents. Under these circumstances the *Post* argued that the government's request for injunctive relief must be assessed against the historic limitation imposed on government censorship by the First Amendment. Under this standard it was not relevant that the government had reasonably classified the disputed documents. What was relevant, the *Post* asserted, was whether further publication would immediately and gravely threaten the national security. And against the standard, the appeals court should affirm Judge Gesell's decision.

Finally, the *Post* argued that injunctive relief in this case was futile. The courts would not be able to contain the disclosure of the Pentagon Papers. It was now apparent that an "undetermined number of persons outside the Government" possessed the disputed documents and were making them public. To support this claim, the *Post* referred to Ben Bradlee's affidavit in which Bradlee stated that he had already received the classified material from "two other sources." It cited Congressman Paul McCloskey's announcement on television that "he intended to reveal the contents of unpublished portions of the report on Wednesday if the Department of Defense" did not declassify them. It mentioned an Associated Press report that morning that the *Boston Globe* had printed that day "what it said were hereto unpublished portions of a secret Pentagon study of the origins of the Vietnam war."

▪ ▪ ▪ ▪ ▪

Late Tuesday morning, Attorney General John Mitchell told Solicitor General Erwin N. Griswold that he wanted him to represent the government in the *Post* appeal that afternoon—at two o'clock—before the court of appeals.[3] Griswold demurred and told Mitchell that he had "never seen even the outside of the Pentagon Papers," that he did "not know what is in them, and I have given no real study to the applicable law." Mitchell responded: "Well, Dean, if you don't want to argue the case, I suppose I can get someone else." At that point Griswold said: "'Mr. Attorney General, if you want me to argue the case, I will do it.'"[4] Thus began Griswold's involvement with the Pentagon Papers case.

Born in 1904, Erwin Griswold graduated from the Harvard Law School in 1928, where he was president of the law review. After a short stint of practicing law in Cleveland he joined the United States Solicitor General's office in 1929. The solicitor general represented the government before the Supreme Court, and the small office of lawyers—only five when Griswold joined it—had substantial control over deciding what lower court cases to take to the Supreme Court. In the fall of 1934 Griswold returned to the Harvard Law School as an assistant professor of law and remained there for thirty-three years. Griswold was the school's dean from 1949 until 1967, when he became the solicitor general during the Johnson administration. Although it would have been quite normal for the Nixon administration to replace Griswold once it assumed office in 1969, it asked Griswold to stay on as solicitor general.

As solicitor general, Griswold had a reputation of being very particular about which cases he personally would argue in the Supreme Court. As Mitchell stated many years later: "Old Erwin always loved to pick the cases that he wanted to argue . . . [and] he didn't much need anyone else's help in picking" them.[5] Mitchell generally went along with Griswold's decisions. But there were rare exceptions when Mitchell would pressure Griswold into personally taking on a case, as he did in the Pentagon Papers case.

It was most unusual for the solicitor general to represent the government in an appeals court. But Mitchell was eager, if not desperate, to win the appeal. District judge Gurfein had already denied the government a preliminary injunction in the *Times* case, and district judge Gesell had reached the same decision in the *Post* case. Mitchell had little confidence in U.S. Attorney Seymour, who was going to argue the *Times* case before the Second Circuit that afternoon. In fact Mitchell, Mardian, and Rehnquist were so uneasy at the idea of Seymour arguing the appeal that they had even discussed the possibility of taking the unusual step of barring Seymour from arguing the case before the Second Circuit. But Mitchell decided against making such a move because it would be very controversial and would attract a great deal of public attention.[6] That meant that if the government's chances of prevailing in one of the appeals courts were to be improved, it would have to be in the *Post* case. Mitchell thought that if Griswold took the highly unusual step and argued the appeal, it might help.

▪ ▪ ▪ ▪ ▪

The oral argument before the court of appeals lasted three hours. The first two-and-a-half hours were open to the public, while the last half hour was held *in camera*.[7] Griswold emphasized in his opening remarks that nothing less than the "integrity of the institution of the Presidency" was at stake in this case. He cautioned that "this is a great case, I suppose, and great cases sometimes make bad law." Griswold argued that additional disclosures by the *Post* would gravely injure the ability of the government to protect the nation through the diplomatic process. Referring to negotiations between the United States and the Soviet Union over limiting strategic arms, Griswold asked: "What chance is there going to be to carry on SALT talks if the people on the other side think anything they might say, particularly if they put it in writing, would show up in the American press?" Similarly, Griswold spoke of the tense relations in the Middle East and asked: "What prospect do you think there is for our playing the role we think we ought to play" in seeking peace if the Constitution permitted the press to publish anything it obtained from government sources? Griswold sought to strengthen and broaden this claim by reminding the appeal judges that the president "must be able to discuss issues frankly with subordinates and . . . receive frank recommendations without the chilling effect—and I use that word with real feeling in this case—of disclosure in the press."

Griswold belabored the point that the First Amendment tolerated prior restraints in some circumstances. He referred to the copyright laws and noted that the *Washington Post* had copyrighted its Pentagon Papers series. He suggested that if "some enterprising papers obtained a copy of an unpublished manuscript by Ernest Hemingway . . . and planned to publish it, Mrs. Hemingway could enjoin the press under [the] rule of literary property." Throughout this portion of his argument Griswold repeatedly referred to the documents possessed by the *Post* as "having been stolen."

Eventually Judge J. Skelly Wright interrupted and "scolded" the solicitor general for comparing this case to a run-of-the-mill copyright case that did not involve a First Amendment claim to publish. Chief Judge David L. Bazelon joined in and asked Griswold: "Does your case depend on those documents being the property of the United States and thus copyrighted?" Griswold gave ground on both points, conceding that the government's claim for the relief did not depend on the copyright laws or the assertion that the documents had been stolen. But he insisted that his analogy to the copyright laws was relevant and that the fact that the documents were stolen was a factor to be considered and that together they established the context for the court's analysis.

Judge Roger Robb, who had joined Judge Spottswood W. Robinson in restraining the *Post* the previous Friday evening, asked Griswold if the court was not being asked to grant a "futile" injunction. What Robb had in mind obviously was the fact that the *Post* gained possession of the classified papers after the *Times* was enjoined and that the *Boston Globe* had received some portion of the study after the *Post* was enjoined. Griswold answered that the government had already initiated an action against the *Boston Globe* and that the government's capacity to contain the spread of the documents was still intact.

Before Griswold finished his argument, he announced, as Seymour was doing the same afternoon in New York, that he was authorized by the Secretaries of State and Defense and the Joint Chiefs of Staff to offer to settle the legal dispute by having a "joint task force" examine the classified material during the next forty-five days. He explained that it was hoped that this review would result in the declassification of much of the disputed material and perhaps avoid further litigation over the documents. Even if that ideal could not be achieved, a task-force review of the material would narrow considerably the documents in dispute, which would ease the task of the courts.

Glendon argued next. He insisted that the *Post* did not steal the disputed documents and that it did not know whether they were in fact stolen. He rejected Griswold's suggestion that the *Post* agree to suspend publication of the Pentagon Papers until the "task force" had reviewed all the disputed material as a form of "government by handout." Glendon told the judges that the affidavits submitted by the *Post* indicated that government officials routinely handed out classified documents and that it was widely known that the classification system was widely abused. He asserted that it was time that the judges let the *Post* publish its Pentagon Papers reports again.

There is no transcript of the *in camera* argument that followed immediately upon the close of the public session. Nevertheless, the *in camera* argument must have been of critical importance to the government. Because both sides conceded that the First Amendment tolerated a prior restraint, the outcome of the case depended upon how the court evaluated the government's evidence. The government had to convince the appeals court that its evidence was much stronger than Gesell thought and that it warranted a prior restraint. But Griswold was totally unprepared to say a word about the government's evidence. He had not had time to look at the briefs, study the government's affidavits, read the transcript, or even glance through the record. He almost certainly had nothing of substance to offer the judges on why the government's evidence was legally sufficient.

Because the secret hearing was so short, it is most unlikely that Glendon had anything of significance to say either. What did arise during the *in camera* hearing that was unexpected was an agreement by the *Post* not to publish relatively small portions of two documents. The fact that the *Post* made this concession came to light the next day when Circuit Judge George E. MacKinnon referred to it in his dissenting opinion. The *Post* was self-conscious of this disclosure because it did not wish it to appear that it was giving in to the government or accepting the government's claim that the documents contained information that might seriously harm the national security. As a result, after MacKinnon's opinion became public, Ben Bradlee issued a statement minimizing what the *Post* did and why. Bradlee said that the *Post*'s lawyers had recommended that the *Post* go along with this "to avoid needless delay in the court's consideration of the matter." As for the information in question, Bradlee said that it was no more than "very limited quotations from two documents which the *Post* did not deem to be of reportorial significance."[8]

■ ■ ■ ■ ■

On Wednesday the nine judges of the court of appeals considered their decision in the government's appeal. None of the judges who decided the appeal has published any accounts of what happened, but the reports we have suggest a day of intense activity. Sanford Ungar, the *Washington Post* correspondent, wrote that there was a "full day of deliberations" among the judges that included many "private conferences among the members of the court." He also reported that Chief Judge David L. Bazelon "summoned the lawyers to his chambers on several occasions for consultation" and that he held a "last-minute review of [the] affidavits in the case . . . in the presence of [the] lawyers for both sides." During the conferences the lawyers reported to the judges that President Nixon had announced during the day that he had decided to make the classified Pentagon study available to Congress on the condition that the Congress not disclose the contents to the public.[9] Once the court of appeals for the Second Circuit made public its decision in the *Times* case, the lawyers informed the D.C. judges that district judge Gurfein was ordered to hold a second hearing.

According to docket sheets for the court, as well as James M. Naughton's report in the *Times*, the judges held a second, private hearing that was not even announced to the public. The government's lawyers, probably realizing that Griswold's argument on Tuesday was weak, requested the hearing, which was briefly described in Sanford Ungar's book, *The Papers and the Papers*. The government wanted to strengthen its claim that further publication would compromise intelligence matters and cited to a specific radio intercept that related to the Tonkin Gulf engagement. George Wilson, the *Post*'s defense expert, was at the hearing and remembered that this same document was quoted in a public transcript of an executive session of the Senate Foreign Relations Committee in February 1968. It just so happened that Wilson had the transcript with him at that moment, and he quickly located the document. The government lawyers were flabbergasted. The only response they could muster was that the public transcript of the document had the "time group" deleted, which made it impossible for the other side to know how quickly the transmittal had been intercepted and deciphered, whereas the time group appeared in the Pentagon Papers study. It was a weak reply and the effort failed.[10]

▪ ▪ ▪ ▪ ▪

Very late Wednesday afternoon, the D.C. Circuit court affirmed Judge Gesell's order by a vote of seven to two. Seven judges—Chief Judge David Bazelon and Judges Wright, Carl McGowan, Edward Allen Tamm, Harold Leventhal, Robinson, and Robb—joined in a two-page *per curiam* opinion drafted by Bazelon. Judges MacKinnon and Malcolm R. Wilkey each wrote separate opinions dissenting in part from the majority opinion.[11]

Over half of the *per curiam* opinion was devoted to simply summarizing the history of the litigation. The balance of the opinion made several points. On the legal standard that governed the availability of a prior restraint the court had only a few ambiguous words, the essence of which was that "any prior restraint on publication comes into court under a heavy presumption against its constitutional validity." As to whether the government's evidence was sufficient to warrant granting a prior restraint, the court stated: "In our opinion the government's proof, judged by the standard suggested in *Near v. Minnesota* . . . does not justify an injunction." The court of appeals also stated that its decision to deny the government an injunction was "fortified" by the "massive character of the 'leak'" which has occurred. The court stated that there were "substantial doubts that effective relief of the kind sought by the government can be provided by the judiciary." In this statement the court was obviously referring to how the leak of the Pentagon Papers had spread to the *Boston Globe* and the *Chicago Sun-Times*, which announced on Tuesday the twenty-second that it had top secret state department documents "showing that high ranking Kennedy Adminstration officials had advance knowledge of the coup d'état that toppled President Ngo Dinh Diem of South Vietnam in 1963."[12] The court extended the restraining order until Friday, June 25, at 6 P.M. so that the government would have time to seek further relief from the Supreme Court.

The meaning of Judge MacKinnon's partial dissent was most unclear. On the one hand he stated that he would remand the matter to Judge Gesell "for a more precise ruling . . . as to several specific documents." On the other hand he stated that "courts are not designed to deal adequately with national defense and foreign policy." He wrote that he "would not reward the theft of these documents by a complete declassification," and he stated that the newspapers should have filed a request under the Freedom of Information Act.

Judge Wilkey also dissented in part. He asserted that he believed the "great bulk" of the documents in dispute were merely "embarrassing," or not even that, and hence "ready for study by journalist, historians and the public." But he claimed that a "small percentage [of the documents] which appear dangerous could be grievously harmful to this country." Wilkey made it clear that the harm he envisioned, an assertion to which the majority took exception in a footnote in its opinion, was the "death of soldiers, the destruction of alliances, the greatly increased difficulty of negotiation with our enemies, the inability of our diplomats to negotiate as honest brokers between would-be belligerents." Wilkey stated that he would remand the case to the district court with instruction that the government should specify the documents it objected to having published and that the district court should hold a new hearing only on those documents.

The *Post* would be free to publish the remainder of the documents, which he thought would be the vast majority.

■ ■ ■ ■ ■

The government was now in an odd position. It had gained a new hearing in the *Times* case before Judge Gurfein, but it had lost completely in the *Post* case. On Thursday morning, in an effort to bring the cases in line with one another, Griswold submitted a memorandum to the D.C. court of appeals asking it to rehear the government's case against the *Post*. The memorandum described the Second Circuit's order in the *Times* case directing Gurfein to hold a second hearing. It asserted that, unless the *Post* was similarly restrained, the *Times* would be unfairly treated, the government would be denied the opportunity for a full hearing on its national security claims, and the Second Circuit's order would be undermined. In addition to these considerations the government's memorandum asserted that neither Judge Gesell nor the court of appeals judges had "examined any of the documents" that the government claimed threatened national security.

The *Washington Post* lawyers submitted a short memorandum in reply. It stated that they had been notified about 10:30 that morning—Thursday, June 24—that the government was going to move for a rehearing and a modification of its Wednesday order. The memorandum asserted that the *Post* "strenuously oppose[d]" the government's application. The government has "been afforded every opportunity to prove its case, and it has failed." Indeed, the government had "had almost two weeks to come up with one instance of substantial peril to the national security derived from the 47-volume history . . . [and it had] failed to do so." The *Post* argued that the government had a "full hearing on a full record" in this case and that the "government's procedural problems" in the *Times* case should not be grounds for delay in the *Post* case. The *Post* also argued that the circuit court of appeals' concern that injunctive relief was futile had been confirmed again by Pentagon Papers reports in the *Los Angeles Times*, eight newspapers in the Knight chain, including the *Philadelphia Inquirer*, *Detroit Free Press*, and *Miami Herald*, and the *Chicago Sun-Times*. The *Post* concluded by asserting that there is "neither precedent nor reason" for asking the appeals court to rehear this matter.[13]

The Circuit court denied the government's motion for a rehearing by a vote of seven to two.[14] The court's memorandum rejected the government's charge that neither it nor the district court had examined any of the documents. After reviewing the procedural history of the litigation to demonstrate that the district judge and the appeals court had reviewed the papers the court observed that the government's "essential complaint is a dissatisfaction with our conclusion" that it has failed to sustain its heavy burden. It rejected the government's claim that it should bend its decision in this case to accommodate the outcome of the *Times* case before the Second Circuit. It maintained that it had decided the case on the record developed before Gesell and that considerations of comity may not be "stretched unduly" when a prior restraint on the press is at issue. In addition the court noted that, since that morning, the *Times* had asked the Supreme Court to stay the Second Circuit order requiring a new hearing. Given that the court had already extended the stay in the *Post* case until Friday evening, the court claimed that both the *Post* and the *Times* cases were ripe to be presented to the Supreme Court for review and thus denied the motion for a rehearing.

▪ ▪ ▪ ▪ ▪

Why did the government lose its appeal to the D.C. court of appeals? There is one obvious answer: the appeals court concluded that the government's evidence was legally insufficient to warrant an injunction. But that answer is not truly satisfying. The majority did not define the legal standard the government had to satisfy. It referred to the *Near* case as if that reference defined its meaning. But it did not state what it thought *Near* meant, and as we have already seen, the meaning of *Near* is debatable.

In addition the majority did not provide its assessment of the government's evidence. This is especially problematic, given the forceful affidavit submitted by Lieutenant General Melvin Zais in the district court. Zais made serious allegations that were partially supported by page references to the Pentagon Papers. It is conceivable that the appeal judges reviewed Zais's references and decided they did not support his allegations. But if they did, they did not say so.

We do know that the government made some significant errors that contributed to its defeat. The government weakened its chances to prevail by asserting extreme positions before the Circuit court. By emphasizing that the government had a property right in the photocopied documents, that the government was entitled to an injunction because the disputed material was properly classified, and that the government had a right to enjoin the publication of all the classified material, the government pressed legal claims that lacked precedential support and ran directly against the strong current of tradition and daily press practice. The government compounded this error by not even conceding the broadly accepted legal principle that the First Amendment limited the government's claim for an injunction and then staking out a position as to why it should prevail in this case, under this general tenet.

The government also erred by having Griswold argue the appeal. He was completely unfamiliar with the facts and the law of the case. Because he did not know the facts, Griswold could not use them, especially those in Zais's affidavit, to support the government's advantage. Because he did not have time to read the relevant cases and to reflect upon them, Griswold was not in a position to define a legal standard that was favorable to the government and took account of the First Amendment. Indeed, Griswold was so aware of how poor an argument he made that years later he characterized it as "one of the worst arguments I ever made. . . . I didn't have the slightest idea of what I was arguing about."[15]

Griswold's appearance in the case may have even backfired and cost the government some goodwill. Mitchell thought that having Griswold argue would impress the judges with the government's good faith and its belief that the national security was seriously threatened. But it is not inconceivable that at least some of the judges were offended that a totally unprepared solicitor general, who made an appallingly weak argument, would try to influence their decisions by trading on his prestige.

Finally, the government's decision to have its case presented in affidavit form before Judge Gesell possibly undermined its subsequent appeal. That decision gave the *Post* control over what government officials would testify. Thus, the *Post*'s lawyers called Doolin to the stand because they knew from his testimony in the *Times* case that he would likely be an exceedingly weak witness. They called Macomber to testify because they knew—also from his testimony in the *Times* case—that he would identify national security injuries that were most general and speculative. The *Post* lawyers did not cross-examine Zais almost certainly because his affidavit was facially impressive and because they did not know how impressive (or unimpressive) he would be since he did not testify in the *Times* case.

No doubt the government might have lost even if its strategy was flawless and its execution perfect. But neither was, and it is uncertain whether the outcome could have been different.

CHAPTER EIGHTEEN

Inside the White House, Part 2

President Nixon's initial reaction to the *Times* publication was that his administration should not interfere with the *Times* Pentagon series. By the end of that first week, however, Nixon wanted to "destroy" the *Times* and to somehow settle what he considered the score with those he believed to be his political enemies. As more days passed and the two cases were prepared for Supreme Court review, Nixon's attitude continued to harden.

Several factors fed Nixon's evolution. The unfolding of events convinced Nixon that a loosely knit conspiracy composed of liberal Democrats, congressional war critics, disaffected former government officials, and some elements of the press were determined to undermine his capacity to govern. Surely this willingness to see the opposition as "others" who were conspiring to block or impede him, or cause his downfall, was vintage Nixon. But Nixon's sense that he was confronting forces that were coordinated somehow and working against him did not come out of thin air.

As the government tried to suppress the Pentagon Papers, the leak spread from the *Times* to the *Post* to the *Boston Globe*, the *Chicago Sun-Times*, the *Christian Science Monitor*, the *Los Angeles Times*, the *St. Louis Post-Dispatch*, and other newspapers.[1] While the FBI searched for Daniel Ellsberg throughout the nation, Walter Cronkite interviewed him on television. During these days Nixon received a report that Leslie Gelb had taken with him when he left the government classified documents that he was using to write a book on the Vietnam War, and that a set of the Pentagon Papers had been delivered to the Soviet Embassy in Washington.

The press reported that several members of Congress had known for months that Ellsberg was trying to make the Pentagon Papers public, that some members of Congress had even read portions of the study, and that Senator Fulbright actually had a portion of the study in his safe, even as he requested that Defense Secretary Laird turn them over to the Foreign Relations Committee.

In addition to sensing that he confronted a conspiracy Nixon was incensed by how many of his opponents were in the struggle over the Pentagon Papers. From Nixon's vantage point his current opponents were not his general supporters who differed with him over the public's right to read the Pentagon Papers. They were his war critics, and Nixon thought of his war critics as aiding and giving comfort to the enemy. To the extent that Nixon thought of his war critics mainly as liberal Democrats, his traditional political enemy, his ire was even more inflamed. Nixon held officials of the Kennedy and Johnson administrations responsible for planning, initiating, and escalating the Vietnam War, and because he thought of them as generally trying to make him pay a high political price for a situation they created, even while he was trying to bring it to an end, Nixon became even more enraged.

Nixon also worried about the public's reaction to the lawsuits against the newspapers. He repeatedly reminded his aides that his experience in the Alger Hiss case illustrated how important it was to get public opinion on your side. Nixon was determined to win the public relations battle over the Pentagon Papers, no matter what the final judicial outcome was.[2] As the days went by the White House monitored the public opinion polls pertaining to the prior restraint actions and conducted several polls of its own to determine how the public viewed the lawsuits. Although these polls indicated that the public was not deeply troubled by the lawsuits, Nixon wanted to mount an energetic public relations campaign. He told Haldeman to designate someone to run it and develop an explanation of why the government had taken legal action in the first place. He continually gave the text of lines he wanted Haldeman, Ehrlichman, and Colson to feed the press. He directed Haldeman to get "LBJ's people" to speak out against the *Times*, people such as Dean Acheson, Robert McNamara, and Dean Rusk. He wanted the White House aides to get to work drumming up some strong editorials around the country condemning the *Times* publication of the classified material. He wanted Senator Goldwater to attack the *Times*. He wanted someone who was not part of the administration to attack the *Times* on the ground that its publication of the Pentagon Papers was motivated by a desire to affect the vote in Congress on amendments to cut off all funding for the war. He told Haldeman to identify someone more "effective" than Robert Dole, the Republican party chairman at the time, to attack the Democrats on engaging in "partisanship in foreign affairs." He repeatedly told Haldeman to get the "Kennedy stuff" out, referring to documents that might tie the Kennedy administration to the killing of Diem.[3]

Nixon was frustrated not only because he could not get the right people to support him or enough of the right people to speak out often enough but also because he had difficulty figuring out what explanation of the lawsuits would appeal to the public. He wanted to offer an explanation that would be understood and would apply to the entire study, even those volumes that contained documents that were already public. He ultimately concluded that the administration should emphasize that it had a duty to uphold the integrity of the classification system and that the press had no right to decide for itself what documents to declassify. Nixon tried to bolster his public support by getting former Presidents Harry S. Truman and Johnson to support the prior restraint actions, but they refused. At the same time Nixon worried that the public would conclude that his administration was merely trying to suppress information that was politically embarrassing. In the hope that he and his administration could walk the narrow rail he had fashioned Nixon repeatedly directed his aides to emphasize that only the government had the right to declassify documents. He also admonished them not to defend Johnson and to distance themselves from the intensifying debate sparked by the Pentagon Papers as to whether successive administrations had in fact misled the American public over Vietnam.[4]

There was another factor contributing to the hardening of White House attitudes during the Pentagon Papers affair. Both Haldeman and Ehrlichman have claimed that Kissinger contributed to the crisis atmosphere within the White House. Ehrlichman has vividly described Kissinger's contribution: "At our daily Pentagon Papers meetings Henry exhorted us to act vigorously to stanch the flow of the nation's secrets. Without Henry's stimulus during the June 13-to-July 6 period, the President and the rest of us might have concluded that the Papers were Lyndon Johnson's problem, not ours. After all, there was not a word about Richard Nixon in any of the forty-three volumes."[5]

Charles Colson also played a part in creating a tense White House. Colson believed that the Pentagon Papers gave the administration an opportunity to create political dividends for Nixon as well as the Republican party. The Pentagon Papers disclosures were damaging to many Democrats, including some who were thinking of running for the party's presidential nomination in 1972. If the administration could keep the Pentagon

Papers story on the front pages of American newspapers by criminally investigating the *Times*, the *Post*, Ellsberg, and others, the administration could inflict political damage on Nixon's possible political opponents in 1972, especially Senators Hubert H. Humphrey and Edmund Muskie.[6]

On a more ambitious level Colson thought the Pentagon Papers might divide the Democrats and create what he termed "civil war" among the wings of the Democratic party. The disclosures certainly injured the standing of the Johnson administration in the minds of many. As read by many readers, especially the influential editorial writers and columnists, the papers proved that the Johnson administration had misled and lied to the public. Thus, the papers not only revealed what and why key decisions were made—and who made them—but made many high-ranking Democrats appear as villains. As Colson understood it, this would force antiwar Democrats to put more distance between themselves and those who were being discredited. In reaction to this assault, Colson gauged, other Democrats would come to the defense of those whose reputations were under attack and who were being assaulted as amoral or as war criminals. This conflict would weaken the party.[7]

The possible political gain from the conflict was obvious. The Democrats had held the White House since 1932 except for Eisenhower's two terms and Nixon's election over Humphrey in 1968 by a relatively slim margin. Their success had depended on maintaining a broad coalition of differing interests: the South, the cities, racial minorities, unions and ethnic groups. A number of forces were pulling this coalition apart, and the support Nixon had received in the South in the 1968 election was evidence of that. It was apparent that the divisions over the war were further splitting the Democrats, and Colson's idea was to use the disclosures of the Pentagon Papers to create even greater dissension. In order to do that the Pentagon Papers story had to be kept in the public's eye. That would require further action by the administration, no matter how the Supreme Court resolved the lawsuits against the *Times* and the *Post*.[8]

▪ ▪ ▪ ▪ ▪

As the lawyers prepared the Pentagon Papers cases for appeal to the Supreme Court the whole affair had become very complicated for the administration, finding itself in court against four newspapers—the *Times*, *Post*, *Boston Globe*, and the *St. Louis Post-Dispatch*—and it was unsure when another newspaper would publish yet another report based on the classified documents. It was criminally investigating and searching for Ellsberg, and it was gearing up to investigate the linkage between Ellsberg and the news reporters who wrote the newspaper articles. It was having trouble identifying the right people to implement its public relations campaign and figuring out what they should say. The lawsuits had complicated its relationship with Congress, with which it was already at odds over the war and which was considering bills to terminate funding for the Indochina War. At the same time the administration did not want to make the documents public, and it did not trust members of Congress to keep the classified documents confidential once they had access to them.

In a different and yet highly significant way the Pentagon Papers affair became complicated in Nixon's own mind. It created a political and public relations problem that recalled for him the Hiss case.[9] It ignited his antipathy toward the press and leakers. It made him feel challenged and besieged, while tempting him to take advantage of unexpected opportunities for political gain. It triggered a sense of being attacked by ruthless conspirators who were out to undermine his presidency, which he had won in the election booth.

The result: Nixon became involved in the Pentagon Papers struggle on several different levels at once. He increasingly experienced it as a political and personal struggle over social, cultural, and political values that he considered fundamental. As his sense of balance and proportion were affected his political judgment was impaired, and only one thing seemed certain: the Supreme Court might put an end to the lawsuits against the newspapers, but that would not end the administration's involvement in the broader political struggle the lawsuits had sparked. It seemed inevitable that, no matter what the high court decided, the administration would pursue a variety of aspects of the mushrooming Pentagon Papers affair.

PART FIVE

The Supreme Court

CHAPTER NINETEEN

The Supreme Court Takes the Case

Several factors likely persuaded the *New York Times* on Thursday, June 24, to appeal the Second Circuit's decision ordering Judge Gurfein to hold a second hearing. First, the government had to appeal to the Supreme Court its loss before the D.C. court of appeals in the *Washington Post* case; otherwise, the *Post*'s resumption of its Pentagon Papers reports would render the *Times* case moot. If the *Times* did not simultaneously appeal to the high court, it would not participate in the resolution of this historic confrontation. This would be particularly irksome to the *Times*, given that it published the Pentagon Papers first and was sued first. Second, the court of appeals had given Gurfein a July 3 deadline, which amounted to a ten-day extension of the temporary restraining order. Once that hearing was completed, there could be appeals to the Second Circuit and the Supreme Court, thus prolonging the litigation until the fall. Third, the *Times* was hoping that if it could manage to present its case to the Supreme Court before its summer recess, which was fairly imminent, the Court might actually decide the case, and decide it in favor of the *Times*, before it adjourned. The *Times* assumed that Justices Black, Douglas, Marshall, and Brennan would vote to dissolve the restraining order. Thus, to win it needed to capture only one of the remaining five votes, and chances seemed good that either Stewart or White would vote its way.

The *Times* lawyers notified Solicitor General Erwin Griswold that it intended to appeal to the Supreme Court on Thursday morning. To that end the *Times* filed a twenty-page petition for a writ of certiorari, which gave the reasons the Supreme Court should review the case. The petition summarized the prior legal proceedings, identified eight legal questions it claimed the case presented, quoted the relevant statutes and rules, specified the relief the *Times* sought, and contained a short conclusion.[1]

The petition set forth five reasons for granting immediate review. The first claimed that a conflict existed between the Second Circuit and the D.C. Circuit's decisions in the *Times* and the *Post* cases. A conflict in how courts of appeals resolve federal legal questions, particularly constitutional questions, is one of the primary considerations prompting the Supreme Court to review a case. When the Court resolves a conflict between circuit courts, it does so to develop a uniform federal law. But at this point the two circuits did not appear to disagree as to what federal law was, even though they had reached different outcomes. Indeed, in reaching different results—the Second Circuit's decision to grant a second hearing and the D.C. Circuit's decision to deny an injunction as well as a second hearing—neither court defined what it considered to be the appropriate legal standard with any detail or precision. In addition the two cases had important differences that might be thought to justify the different outcomes. The *Times* had nearly all of the Pentagon Papers, the Tonkin Gulf study, and documents that government experts had been unable to identify; the *Post* had only about two thirds of the Pentagon's history. Moreover, the government had more days to prepare for the *Post*'s trial than it had in the *Times*'s trial.

Second, the *Times* claimed that "the effect of the inconsistency [between the courts of appeals] is that the *New York Times* remains under a prior restraint against publishing articles (on a subject first disclosed to the American public by the *Times*) while the *Washington Post*, as well as numerous other newspapers throughout the country, is free to publish its articles." The *Times* claimed that it was "most inequitable that some papers should be free to publish articles of this sort, while others are not," and that this inequity bore down especially hard on the *Times*, since it was the "first newspaper to report on the documents referred to in the litigation." The *Times* obviously was not suggesting that the *Post* be enjoined; it wanted to be able to publish, as the *Post* was doing.[2]

There were three transparent problems with this argument. The *Post* was not free to resume its publication of the Pentagon Papers, because the D.C. Circuit court had continued the restraining order until 6 P.M. on Friday, June 25, and it was assumed that the government would ask the Supreme Court to extend the restraint until it reviewed the case. The government had stated that it had sued all the newspapers that had published reports it believed threatened national security. The *Times* had many more classified documents than the other newspapers.

It was only with its third argument that the *Times* petition finally got to the heart of the case and its basic reason for immediate review. "For the first time in American history, a newspaper has been enjoined from publishing news. The injunction has, as of the day of the writing of this petition, remained in effect for a total of nine days. In light of the finding of Judge Gurfein that 'no cogent reasons' had been adduced by the Government which could conceivably support the suppression of the *Times*'s articles the continuation of the prior restraint in effect for yet additional hearings imposes an unsupportable burden on a free press."[3]

This was the *Times*'s most powerful claim. The government had an opportunity to prove that further publication would injure national security, it had failed to do so, and yet the *Times* was still under injunction and was facing a second evidentiary hearing that might last another ten days. To this point, the *Times* added that a free press is important to a free society, that injunctions prior to publication gravely threaten a free press, and that the Court has time and again made it clear that there is a heavy presumption against the constitutional validity of a prior restraint.

The *Times* petition included two additional arguments as to why the Supreme Court should take the case. The *Times* claimed that Judge Gurfein had not abused his discretion in denying the injunction and that his factual findings were not clearly erroneous—the legal standard the *Times* claimed the Second Circuit had to apply (but did not) to Judge Gurfein's factual findings before it could reverse his judgment. Finally, the *Times* asserted that the government was not authorized to seek a prior restraint against the *Times* because no statute authorized this legal action and the executive did not have "inherent" power to sue the *Times*.

In addition to its petition the *Times* filed a separate motion with Justice John M. Harlan, who had jurisdiction over emergency petitions originating in New York. The *Times* asked Harlan to reverse the Second Circuit's order that barred it from publishing and ordered a second hearing. In making this motion the *Times* could not have expected Harlan to grant its request, for it had assumed all along that Harlan would ultimately vote in favor of the government. But by making this request the *Times* was demonstrating it was exploring every possibility as it tried to escape the order that had restrained it for nine days.

▪ ▪ ▪ ▪ ▪

After the D.C. Circuit court of appeals affirmed Judge Gesell's ruling in favor of the *Post* late on Wednesday the government lawyers had to decide what to do next. Sometime Wednesday night, Griswold decided to ask the D.C. Circuit court to reconsider its Wednesday ruling affirming Gesell's order. He hoped he could persuade the D.C. Circuit to modify its ruling and to grant an order similar to the Second Circuit's order requiring a new hearing on the items specified in the special appendix as well as any additional items the government might specify by Friday might. Why Griswold thought the D.C. Circuit would change its ruling is not known. The D.C. Circuit court knew of the Second Circuit's order before it ruled, and the items specified in the special appendix were before Gesell when he held an evidentiary hearing that previous Monday. Perhaps Griswold thought the Supreme Court would more likely extend the restraining order against the *Post* if the government had exhausted all avenues of relief before appealing to it. In any event, first thing Thursday morning Griswold's office prepared the motion for a rehearing and submitted it to the D.C. Circuit.

A few hours later the government submitted legal papers opposing the *Times*'s requests for immediate Supreme Court review and challenging the *Times*'s request that Justice Harlan vacate the Second Circuit's restraining order. The government minimized the Second Circuit's restraining order as doing no more than preserving the status quo until the district court had time to hold a second hearing. It stated that the *Times* could continue to publish reports based on the Pentagon Papers provided it did not disclose information referred to in the special appendix or subsequent governmental listings. It reassured the Court that it would not let the restraining order against the *Post* expire and that it would ask the D.C. Circuit to reconsider its order in light of the Second Circuit's decision. The government asserted that the remand to Judge Gurfein would not undercut the newsworthiness of the *Times* reports because the information in question related to "events which took place at least three years ago and, in many circumstances, far longer than that."[4]

Sometime Thursday afternoon, the D.C. Circuit denied the government's request for a rehearing.[5] At that point the government filed papers asking the Supreme Court to review its case against the *Post* and to enjoin the *Post* from further publication pending the appeal. The government stated that the granting of the injunction would preserve the remedy provided by the Second Circuit and provide equal treatment to both newspapers. It claimed that an injunction would not injure the *Post* because the disputed reports would retain their importance until the legal issues were resolved, whereas the national interest would be gravely injured if the stay were denied. In its last sentence the government stated that it had no objection if the Court wished to treat its papers as a request for immediate full review of the case.[6]

■ ■ ■ ■ ■

The *Times* petition seeking Supreme Court review and its motion to vacate the Second Circuit's stay were submitted to the Court about noon on Thursday, June 24.[7] Justice Harlan referred the *Times*'s motion to vacate the stay to the full Court because granting the request would make the petition for certiorari moot. The justices spent "several hours" in conference without reaching a decision.[8]

By Friday, Chief Justice Burger and Justices Harlan, White, and Blackmun favored restraining both papers until the fall, when it could review both cases. Justices Black, Douglas, Brennan, and Marshall strongly opposed this. They wanted to let both newspapers publish their reports without further delay. Justice Stewart would have to break the deadlock. He opposed keeping the newspapers under restraining order until the fall, because he thought the issues too important and the public interest too deep to let the matter hang fire so long. At the same time he was against letting the newspapers publish without the high Court reviewing the case. Thus, Stewart informed Burger, Harlan, Blackmun, and White that he would vote with the other block of four unless they agreed to grant an immediate hearing in the case. Faced with this choice, Burger, Harlan, White, and Blackmun agreed to review both cases immediately.[9]

Chief Justice Burger took the unusual step and telephoned Griswold and told him that the Court had granted the government's and the *Times*'s petitions and gave him the briefing schedule.[10] The lawyers for the *Times* and the *Post* learned of the Court's orders from the clerk's office, which was the normal means by which the Court kept lawyers apprised of developments in emergency circumstances.[11]

The Court set oral argument in both cases for the next morning, Saturday, at eleven o'clock, and ordered the parties to file legal briefs before the argument. The Court stayed the remand of the *Times* case to Judge Gurfein but barred both newspapers from publishing any material that was identified in the special appendix or that the government might identify by five o'clock that afternoon as material that would inflict "grave and immediate danger" to the national security if disclosed. Justices Black, Douglas, Brennan, and Marshall dissented from the order. They favored terminating the restraining orders and permitting the newspapers to publish forthwith.[12]

The government had only a few hours to develop a final list of the disputed documents. Given that the government had twelve days since the *Times* began publishing its Pentagon Papers series, ten days since it obtained a temporary restraining order from Judge Gurfein, and seven days since the evidentiary hearing before Judge Gurfein, one might well have expected that the preparation of a list of documents to supplement those identified in the special appendix would have been comparatively easy. But it was not. The five o'clock deadline set off "feverish activity" in the Justice Department's Internal Security Division, which was handling the efforts to suppress the documents, as well as in other branches of the government. Ultimately, the list, which was itself classified, identified so many additional items that it "swept vast portions" of the Pentagon Papers into the "dangerous" category.[13]

The Court's order presented an immediate problem for the newspapers. The newspapers had to decide whether to publish reports based on those portions of the Pentagon Papers the government did not identify in the special appendix and other documents submitted to the Court by five o'clock. The *Times* and the *Post* had differing reactions. Abe Rosenthal, the *Times* managing editor, opposed publishing on these conditions because it would be surrendering editorial control over what was fit to print to nameless government officials. Ben Bradlee, the *Post*'s executive editor, thought that the "public's right to know demanded that we give serious consideration to printing [another story based on the Papers] if we could print anything of substance without violating the court order." The government's supplemental list submitted to the Court by five o'clock resolved the conflict. The list was so sweeping that it prohibited the publication of anything but, as Rosenthal put it, "a truncated version" of the *Times*'s prepared reports. Bradlee concurred. The list was so substantial "as to make it physically impossible for us to decide, in the time allowed, what we could print, even if we chose to print anything."[14]

The Justice Department criticized the newspapers for not utilizing the publishing leeway contained in the Court's order. The department's statement pointed out that the government had asked the newspapers from the beginning of the legal dispute to disclose precisely what documents each had. If the newspapers had cooperated, the statement claimed, the government would have been able to let the newspapers know exactly which documents or portions of documents were covered by the restraining order. The Department maintained that the newspapers had no one to blame but themselves for their predicament.[15]

▪ ▪ ▪ ▪ ▪

Exhibits in a case are normally forwarded to the reviewing court by the lower court. In this case that meant that the Pentagon Papers study admitted into evidence in the *Times* case would be shipped from New York to the Supreme Court. But the government claimed it was unable to make adequate security arrangements for the trip. It was eventually agreed that the Solicitor General's office would send a copy of the study from the Pentagon to the Supreme Court.

By the time the study arrived at the Supreme Court Justice Brennan had gone home to join his wife for dinner. Brennan had left instructions with one of his clerks, however, to telephone him as soon as the documents arrived. As Brennan finished his dinner, his clerk telephoned and in an excited voice told Brennan that the documents were accompanied by armed guards. Brennan could not recall another occasion when armed guards accompanied court exhibits. He quickly left home and arrived at the courthouse about seven o'clock. He found Justice White already studying the classified documents in a conference room. Justice Brennan spent three hours reviewing the material before returning home. No other justice joined him and Justice White, and it is unlikely that any of the other justices examined the disputed documents before the oral arguments the next day.[16]

CHAPTER TWENTY

The Briefs

Instead of having the usual several weeks to write their briefs and to prepare for oral arguments, the lawyers had about twenty hours. Solicitor General Erwin Griswold faced a particularly formidable challenge. He had become involved in the case only two days before, and now he had to make sure public and confidential briefs were prepared, and he had to prepare himself to argue the government's side in the morning. Griswold assigned the writing of the government's public brief to his assistant, Daniel M. Friedman; he assumed the responsibility for preparing the sealed brief.

Griswold arranged for a complete set of the Pentagon Papers to be sent to his office. When they arrived, they were accompanied by an army staff sergeant, "who sat beside them." The sergeant complained that Griswold's secretary did not have the proper security clearance. Griswold responded that he was "in charge" in his office, that he needed his secretary's help, and that the sergeant should report the matter to his superior. To Griswold's surprise the officer left and did not return.[1]

Griswold had arranged for three government security officials to report to his office to review with him the portions of the Pentagon Papers they believed would seriously threaten the national security. The three officials were: Vice Admiral Noel Gayler, director of the National Security Agency; William B. Macomber, deputy undersecretary of state for administration; and Lieutenant General Melvin Zais, director of operations for the Joint Chiefs of Staff. Macomber had been a witness in both the *Times* and the *Post* case, and Gayler and Zais had each submitted affidavits in the *Post* case. Because Griswold had very little time to write the secret brief, he limited each interview to thirty minutes. It was during his discussion with Admiral Gayler that Griswold "felt that about half of my case, as I had analyzed it so far, went out the window." Griswold had thought that the "publication of the plain text of any coded telegram would be serious, since it would provide information for breaking the code." When he voiced this opinion to Gayler, the Admiral "laughed" and said: "That has not been true since about 1935."[2]

As the three officials spoke, Griswold wrote down on a yellow pad the page references they gave him. Some of the references were to large portions of the classified study, including one reference to the four volumes tracing the diplomatic history of the war from 1964 to 1968. After the meetings were over Griswold selected forty-one items to "study . . . as carefully as I could in the limited time available." After examining the items Griswold "felt that there were only a few that had any chance of finding favor before the Supreme Court," and he eventually "reduced these to eleven items," which he summarized in his closed brief.[3]

Griswold began the sealed brief with a point he believed truly significant, a point that had contributed to the government's decision to sue in the first place but had hampered the government throughout the litigation.[4] The government did not know, even at this late stage of the litigation, precisely what documents the *New York Times* and the *Washington Post* possessed. The brief stated that the newspapers had submitted inventories that listed the documents they possessed but that the inventories were "not very helpful because they do not, in general, identify particular documents . . . and [because] there are various versions of some of these documents, and the inventories do not show which version the papers have."

The brief emphasized that the complete forty-seven volume study had been introduced into evidence in the *Times* and the *Post* cases and that Judge Gesell had proceeded on the assumption that the *Post* possessed the entire study. The brief stated that the references in the special appendix and in the supplemental listings submitted by the Departments of State and Defense were to the forty-seven volume study. The brief now made clear that its purpose was "to refer to a selected few items and to show that the publication of these items could have the effect of causing immediate and irreparable harm to the security of the United States" (2–3).

The next six and one half pages focused on the eleven items Griswold felt had the best chance of convincing the Court that further publication would gravely injure national security (4). Griswold first referred to the four volumes that traced the diplomacy of the war. These volumes revealed that negotiations had been carried on through numerous foreign governments and private individuals.[5] The volumes identified the governments of Canada, Poland, Italy, Romania, and Norway and the individuals as persons who acted in their private capacity or as public officials who "sometimes [acted] with the knowledge of their governments, and sometimes without their governments being informed." It claimed that the study included "derogatory comments about perfidiousness of specific persons involved, and statements which might be offensive to nations and governments." It warned that "the hope of the termination of the war turns to a large extent on the success of negotiations," that it cannot be predicted "where the break may come and it is of crucial importance to keep open every possible line of communication," and that further publication of "this material is likely to close up channels of communication which otherwise would have some opportunity of facilitating the closing of the Vietnam war" (3–5).[6]

The brief's second point was that further disclosures might diminish the rate at which the United States withdrew its troops from Vietnam. The brief stated that South Korea, South Vietnam, and Australia have troops in Vietnam and that Thailand "allows the use of airfields from which 65% of our sorties are launched." It warned that the rate at which the United States could withdraw its troops from Vietnam depended primarily on the continued support these four nations provided. It claimed that there was "much material" "which might give offense to South Korea, to Thailand, and to South Vietnam, just as serious offense has already been given to Australia and Canada." Griswold did not identify specific pages within the Pentagon Papers to support these claims (5).

The third point claimed that the classified study contained "specific references to the names and activities of CIA agents still active in Southeast Asia" and "references to the activities of the National Security Agency." The brief did not give the references, identify the agents, or describe the activities, but it did assert that the references were to "persons and activities which are currently continuing." The brief claimed that the disclosure of such agents and activities "may not be exactly equivalent to the disclosure of troop movements," an obvious reference to Chief Justice Hughes's majority opinion in *Near v. Minnesota*, "but it is very close to it" (5–6).

The fourth point, which included volume and page references, claimed that the Pentagon study contained current SEATO military plans. One plan, SEATO contingency Plan 5, concerned "communist armed aggression in Laos," and the others, SEATO Operations Plans 4 and 6, dealt with military activities in Laos, Cambodia, Thailand, and Pakistan. The brief maintained that the disclosure of these plans would compromise military plans, constitute a "breach of faith with other friendly nations," and risk the loss of support of "friendly nations" (6).[7]

Fifth, the brief contended that the study set forth a 1967 estimate made by the United States intelligence community of the "Soviet reaction to the Vietnam War." The brief stated that the estimate was "in large part still applicable" and that its disclosure would give "Soviet intelligence insights into the capacity of our intelligence operations, and may strengthen them both by giving them better understanding of us, and by leading them to correct matters on their side" (6).[8]

The next point involved a U.S. intelligence estimate of Soviet capacity to provide "various types of weapons to North Vietnam." The brief claimed that there was "much about" this estimate that was "current" and that its disclosure would give the Soviets "information which could lead to serious consequences for the United States," although it did not state what they would be (7).[9]

The seventh point referred by page and volume to "an internal memorandum of the Joint Chiefs of Staff on May 27, 1967, containing a recommendation that a nuclear response might be required in the event of a Chinese attack on Thailand." The brief asserted that the "recommendation was never formally made," but it claimed that the disclosure of this would endanger the United States (7).[10]

Point eight referred to the three pages in the study that contained the full text of a 1968 telegram sent by Llewellyn Thompson, while he was the United States Ambassador in Moscow, to the State Department. The brief claimed that the telegram gave the "assessment of one of our most experiences [*sic*] diplomats of Soviet reaction to United States course of action in Vietnam." The brief contended that this disclosure would give the Soviets "valuable intelligence information" because it is "important to them to know what we think about them." The brief also claimed that the disclosure of the telegram would undercut Thompson's capacity as an ambassador and that this would "surely" affect the security of the United States, since Thompson was "an important and valuable member of our SALT talks delegation dealing with strategic arms limitations" (7–8).[11]

The ninth point was a one-page reference to a "confidential" discussion between the "military staffs of South Vietnam and Laos, given to us in confidence, relating to possible South Vietnamese military action in Laos with the consent of Laos military authorities." The brief claimed that the disclosure of this discussion "not only involves a breach of confidence, but also involves grave risk of reactions from other nations involved" (8).[12] The brief did not identify these other nations.

The tenth point, which remains partially classified, concerned the "important matter of communications intelligence covered by the affidavit of Vice Admiral Gayler," the Director of the National Security Agency. The brief stated that the concern here was not the integrity of U.S. codes and ciphers, for they "are now regarded as not destructible, or sufficiently nondestructible to be practically effective." Rather, the focus was on the codes and ciphers "of other countries, particularly the codes and ciphers of unfriendly nations." Without providing any references whatsoever, the brief contended that "various items in these volumes" will "make the enemy aware of significant intelligence successes," help "an enemy country . . . estimate our capacity," cause another country to "control methods of dissemination of messages . . . in such a way as to minimize our chance of successful interception." The brief stated that "cutting down successful interception by our communication intelligence will directly affect our military operations," because signal intelligence "now gives direct support to our troops today, and saves many lives. It also helps, directly in the recovery of downed pilots" (8–9).

The last point concerned the prisoners of war. The brief claimed that the United States was "currently engaged in discussions" on the prisoner-of-war issue with different governments, which in some cases "are not wholly friendly, such as Sweden and Russia." The brief claimed that these discussions were conducted on a confidential basis and their effectiveness would be diminished if that "confidence is broken" by the disclosure of material contained in the classified study, material the brief did not identify. The brief further claimed that reports by the *Times* and the *Post* had already prematurely caused a termination of discussions with one intermediary. The brief concluded this point by asserting that the "longer prisoners are held, the more will die" (10). The brief offered no specific references to the study to support this assertion.

The last three pages of the sealed brief were devoted to two matters. First, the brief brought to the Court's attention the fact that two governments, those of Great Britain and a country that was identified only as a "friendly" one, had expressed deep concern about the unauthorized leak of classified documents. In neither case did the government express concern about specific information that was disclosed. Rather, the concern was focused solely on the "principle" that confidential communications between governments should not be disclosed without consent (11–12).

Second, the brief asserted a general theme regarding constitutional interpretation. "Sound constitutional construction" was not to be "found in absolutist or doctrinaire constructions," and the First Amendment "must be construed in light of the fact that it is part of a constitution, particularly where foreign affairs are so directly involved, and where, in a very real sense, the workability and the integrity of the institution of the Presidency may be seriously impaired." The Constitution must be construed to respect and protect the fact that the president is the "Chief Executive" and the "Commander-in-Chief of the Army and Navy" and has primary responsibility for the conduct of foreign affairs. That requires that the Constitution be construed to assure the "free flow of information from foreign nations and for the free development of thought and ideas between the President and his immediate advisers." It also requires that the courts recognize that although the president "can go to great lengths" to protect the confidentiality of communications "by establishing security classification schemes, and by using great care in the selection of its personnel, . . . there will inevitably be weak spots in any system. When such weak spots occur, the Presidency is powerless to provide the required protection except with the aid of the courts." "In a proper allocation of powers," the brief asserted, "the courts should support the Presidency in a narrow and limited area where such protection is needed in the effective meeting of the President's responsibility, and in the safeguarding of American lives. This is not a question of exception to the First Amendment, but of rational interpretation of that provision wholly consistent with its history and purpose" (10–13).

In summary that was the government's sealed brief submitted to the Supreme Court, the most important brief submitted by any lawyer to any court throughout the litigation of both cases. It was relatively short as briefs go—only thirteen pages—and its writing style was direct and unadorned. It was, as Griswold has characterized it, an effort to focus the Court's attention on matters that he thought had the best chance of persuading the justices that further publication would seriously harm the national security. In that regard six of the eleven points reviewed in the brief—points four through nine—implicated no more than seventy-two of the more than 7,000 pages that composed the secret study, and, without diminishing the significance of these items, either individually or combined, it is most probable that Griswold considered the other items as more persuasive, more likely to affect the justices' assessment of the evidence. These five items—numbers one, two, three, ten, and eleven—concerned the future capacity of the United States to use foreign nations and private parties to help negotiate an end to the fighting and to secure the release of the American prisoners of war, the future of the Vietnamization process, on which the Nixon administration was relying as a way of withdrawing U.S. ground troops, and intelligence capacities and activities. Except for the reference to the four volumes tracing the diplomatic history of the war, these five items suggested that supporting material was distributed throughout much of the study.

Although the sealed brief condensed, focused, and narrowed the government's references to the Pentagon Papers, it would be inaccurate to think that the brief limited itself to eleven specific items. Six of the eleven items did refer to only seventy-two specific pages, and a seventh referred to the four negotiating volumes. Part of one of the remaining four items stated that the disputed material contained the names of active CIA agents, and although the brief did not provide specific citations, the material involved was probably limited in scope. But the remaining three and one half items, which involved the Vietnamization of the war, the release of U.S. prisoners of war, and intelligence activities and capabilities, may well have swept broadly throughout the classified material. For these critical points, Griswold did not provide specific references to volumes and pages as he did for the other items. Instead, he stated that the classified study contained "much material" that bore on the issue, or that there were "various items" in the study that were relevant to the point, or that the study contained "references" that disclosed the secrets in question.

Griswold has maintained in recent years that he sought an injunction only as to the eleven items he identified in the sealed brief.[13] But there is no support for this claim in the sealed brief. There are only two statements in the brief that characterize the eleven items. The first stated: "The purpose of this portion of the Brief for the United States is to refer to a selected few of these items and to endeavor to show that the publication of these items could have the effect of causing immediate and irreparable harm to the security of the United States." The second stated: "We now turn to a few selected items from the 47 volumes which, we submit, involve a serious risk of immediate and irreparable harm to the United States and its security" (3–4). Neither of these statements expressed or implied that the government was waiving its objection to the classified material possessed by the *Times* and the *Post* except for the eleven items discussed in the sealed brief. Nor is there any other statement in the sealed brief that expressed or implied such a waiver. The unmistakable impression was that the government offered the eleven items as illustrative of the national security injuries that would be inflicted by further publication. The question left unaddressed by the brief was whether the government was asking the Supreme Court to grant a preliminary injunction based on its submissions or to remand both cases for additional evidentiary hearings in the district courts.

▪ ▪ ▪ ▪ ▪

As Richard Stone, an attorney in the solicitor general's office at the time, has recalled, the entire office was "enlisted" to write the government's public brief.[14] This brief, which defined a moderate legal position, began by stating that the cases presented a narrow legal question: "Whether the First Amendment bars an injunction sought by the United States to prevent a newspaper from publishing material whose disclosure would pose a grave and immediate danger to the security of the United States." The brief disclaimed any effort to secure a "blanket" injunction against the newspapers or "a generalized prohibition upon the publication of broad categories of material." It also asserted that the government's entitlement to an injunction did "not depend upon the fact that all of the material whose publication the government is seeking to prevent is classified either 'top secret' or 'secret,' that all of it was obtained illegally from the government and that both the *Times* and the *Post* hold such material without any authorization from the government."[15] These assertions were significantly different from previous claims that the government was entitled to an injunction because the disputed documents were classified and stolen and because the newspapers were unauthorized to possess the classified material under the rules and regulations establishing the classification system. Griswold considered these previous claims as too broad, extreme, and unpersuasive. The decision not to press these positions almost certainly had to be Griswold's, since he was the only person in the Justice Department with sufficient standing to override Mardian's preferences.

In terms of the relief sought by the government the brief argued for an injunction barring the *Times* and the *Post* from publishing the material identified in the special appendix and the government's supplemental listings submitted to the Court by five o'clock Friday, pending new hearings in the district courts. The granting of such relief would have amounted to an affirmance of the Second Circuit's judgment in the *Times* case and a reversal of the D.C. Circuit's judgment in the *Post* case (22).

The government's legal memorandum made four substantive claims. First, it asserted that the First Amendment did not prohibit all prior restraints. This point was conceded by the *Times* and the *Post* throughout the litigation, so it is uncertain why the government lawyers gave it the lengthy treatment they did. The brief prominently cited *Near v. Minnesota* and claimed that *Near*'s examples of when a prior restraint would be acceptable "were merely illustrative and obviously there are other items of information so vital to the security of the United States that their publication may be enjoined" (8).

Second, the brief claimed that an injunction should be granted if the government proved that further publication posed "grave and immediate" danger to the national security. This was the standard the Second Circuit instructed Judge Gurfein to apply when it remanded the case to him. The government qualified this standard, however, in regard to diplomatic relations, for which the government claimed that the "grave and immediate" standard should give way to a "grave and irreparable" one, because the "effect of particular action upon diplomatic relations may be extremely severe in the long run, even though its immediate impact is not clear or great" or even possible to demonstrate (12–14, 20). As a practical matter, the government was surely correct that injuring diplomatic processes could have consequences far into the future and could be impossible to predict. It was an entirely different question, however, whether the Court would consider such an injury legally sufficient to warrant a prior restraint.

The government also clarified what it thought both of these standards should mean and claimed it should not be required to prove that the threatened injuries to the national security will result with "absolute certainty" or that the feared "disastrous consequences are inevitable," as Judge Gesell had required in the *Post* case. "It is enough," the brief maintained, "that there be a real likelihood of the event" (15). Here too the government's point was pragmatically solid. Inevitability is not provable. All the government could be asked to prove was that if certain information was disclosed the injury was likely. But how likely? Very? Remotely? The government's brief did not specify.

Third, without referring to it directly, the government's brief responded to the *Times*'s argument that the government lacked statutory authority to sue the *Times* for a prior restraint. It claimed that the authority of the executive branch of the government "to protect the nation against publication of information whose disclosure would endanger the national security stems from two interrelated sources: the constitutional power of the President over the conduct of foreign affairs and his authority as Commander-in-Chief." The brief correctly contended that it "has long and repeatedly been recognized that the President is constitutionally empowered to act with broad freedom and secrecy in the conduct of our relations with foreign powers" (12). It claimed that the preservation of confidential communications was essential to the resolution of the Cuban Missile Crisis and that the chances of success "of the Nuclear Test Ban Treaty negotiations, or perhaps more immediately pertinent, the SALT negotiations" required confidentiality. It warned that further publication of Pentagon Papers material "relating to confidential discussions and negotiations between this country and both friendly and unfriendly powers would have the gravest consequences because it could dry up vital sources of information and thwart, if not sometimes destroy, meaningful communication" (13–14).

With regard to the president's powers as commander in chief the brief contended that the president had not only "the duty of conducting military operations" but the obligation to "protect 'the members of the armed forces from injury, and from the dangers which attend the rise, prosecution, and progress of war'" (14). To fulfill these responsibilities, the brief asserted, the president has the "duty to preserve military secrets whose disclosure might threaten the safety of United States troops engaged in combat." The brief maintained that the disclosure of the classified material that had been identified for the Court and discussed in the government's sealed brief "would pose a serious danger to the armed forces" (14–15).

These claims—that the president had primary responsibility for the conduct of foreign affairs, that confidential communications was important to effective diplomacy, that the president was commander in chief, and that the disclosure of military plans would jeopardize the safety of troops—were not disputed by the newspapers. More important, they did not establish the point that the government was trying to make. The government was trying to overcome any doubt that it had the right to obtain a prior restraint against the newspapers absent an authorizing statute. But these points, well made and undisputed, did not do that.

It was only in a short paragraph toward the end of this section that the government lawyers really provided anything amounting to an answer to the *Times*. In referring to impending disclosures by the *Times* and the *Post* the government stated that "the only effective means of protecting the nation against the improper disclosure of military secrets is to enjoin their impending publication. To limit the President's power . . . to punishment of those who disclose secret information would render the [President's] power meaningless: the harm sought to be prevented would have been irreparably accomplished" (16). In short the President was constitutionally entitled to obtain injunctive relief against the newspapers absent statutory authorization because such relief was ancillary to the president's effective discharge of his constitutional responsibilities.

There was an obvious pragmatic appeal to the government's position. But establishing the government's right to sue the newspapers did not mean that the Court would grant the injunctive relief sought. All it meant was that the Court would not dismiss the lawsuit because no statute authorized the executive branch to sue the papers for an injunction. Instead, the court would decide the merits of the cases.

Fourth, the government's brief addressed the issue of how intensely courts should scrutinize the judgment of executive-branch officials in this case. The essence of the government's position was stated as follows: "In the present cases high government officials have explained the reasons for their concern; that judgment is enough to support the Executive Branch's conclusion, reflected in the top secret classification of the documents and in the *in camera* evidence, that disclosure would pose the threat of serious injury to the national security" (15). A few pages later the government offered some reasons for its contention that the Court should defer to the judgment of top officials. The government argued that often the injury that will be inflicted by the improper disclosure of a document cannot be determined by "a simple reading of the document." A person needs to be familiar with a wide range of information, and "with the intricacies and intimate details of the situation," to be able to make sound judgments whether the disclosure of a particular document will or will not seriously harm the national security. "Courts simply are not equipped to make [that kind of judgment]," the brief bluntly stated, "and they should not attempt to make their own independent determination whether the particular classification was justified" (21).

In one sense this was an entirely predictable position for the government to stake out before the Supreme Court, for it had asserted it before both Judge Gurfein and Judge Gesell, and it was a position that some Justice Department officials, most notably Assistant Attorney General Mardian, firmly supported. But in another sense it was a peculiar position for the government to assert, given what it had already stated in the brief. The government had already argued that the question framed by the cases was whether further publication would pose a grave and immediate danger to the national security. That suggested that the outcome in the cases would depend upon whether the courts thought the government's evidence satisfied the "grave and immediate danger" standard. It also implied that the government considered the courts competent to assess the legal sufficiency of its evidence. Without acknowledging any inconsistency in its positions—in fact, without acknowledging that it even had two positions—the government asserted that the courts were incompetent to assess national security evidence and that the courts had to defer to security officials.

There was nothing improper in the government asserting inconsistent alternative legal claims. But it was odd not to acknowledge that was what it was doing, especially given the tenor of the brief's opening pages.

■ ■ ■ ■ ■

Roger A. Clark wrote the *Washington Post*'s sealed brief. Under normal procedures he would have had an opportunity to respond to the eleven items Griswold identified in the secret brief. But the briefing schedule set by the Supreme Court required that all briefs be simultaneously submitted to the Court. That put Clark at a disadvantage and caused him to focus on the national security matters the government had emphasized before Judge Gesell.

Clark's eleven-page brief began with a factual paragraph that claimed that the government's evidence was "utterly devoid of any credible evidence of a threat to national security" and charged that the government had failed to "identify a single document in this historical study whose publication would present any credible risk to national security." The brief claimed that the government's "proof reflects a deep seated—almost reflex—commitment by many high Government officials to maintaining continued secrecy with respect to" the disputed material. The brief also asserted that the government's supplemental listings submitted to the Court by Friday at five o'clock—"some 100 items," which included "one entire volume" and fell into "13 broadly defined categories"—indicated that the government continued "to tilt at windmills."[16]

About eight pages of the brief reviewed the evidence offered by Doolin, Macomber, Zais, and Gayler. The brief's comments on Gayler's affidavit focused on intelligence matters and remains classified; the balance of the brief is now public.

The brief gave Doolin no quarter. By his own testimony Doolin had reviewed the study now and then over a two-year period, and he cited six matters to Judge Gesell he claimed would seriously impair national security if disclosed. The brief reviewed these matters but mocked Doolin's credibility. Doolin had cited a 1965 memorandum, written by Maxwell Taylor, that identified what Taylor thought were the "blue chips" the United States could use to negotiate with North Vietnam: cease bombing of the North, stop military activities against the Viet Cong, stop increasing forces in the South, withdraw forces in the South, give amnesty to the Viet Cong, and give economic aid to North Vietnam. The brief quoted Judge Gesell's statement that these blue chips were things "any high school graduate could" identify (2). The brief stated that Taylor's memorandum was the only document the government presented for Judge Gesell's inspection.

As for the rest of Doolin's testimony, the brief was scathing. Doolin had referred to a particular "peace feeler," but he did not know the substance of the diplomatic initiative or that it had already been described in the press. Doolin had cited the Seaborn mission and the overthrow of President Diem as examples of the harm caused by the newspapers' disclosures, but he stated he was unaware that these items had already been thoroughly vented in the press. Doolin had cited SEATO military plans, but he testified he had not read them and did not know if they were still current. Doolin stated that further disclosures could prevent other countries in general from acting as intermediaries for the United States, but he acknowledged that the press had already reported extensively on the United States's use of third countries to negotiate with North Vietnam (3).

The *Post*'s secret brief was less effective in minimizing Macomber's testimony. Macomber had testified that the *Post* disclosures threatened the lifeblood of diplomacy and that meaningful diplomacy was essential to ending the fighting in Vietnam and securing the release of the POWs. The *Post*'s brief picked at Macomber's testimony but did not attack it. It noted Macomber's concession that the Department of State had actually solicited cables from U.S. ambassadors in response to the Pentagon Papers disclosures, cables the government offered as evidence of the diplomatic row the disclosures had sparked. It cited Macomber's concession that the press had previously disclosed many of the diplomatic initiatives now relied upon by the government to illustrate its point. It claimed that Macomber had praised the State Department's declassification procedures but that he had difficulty explaining why the process he so admired had not caused some portion of the Pentagon Papers study to be declassified (4–5).

The *Post*'s brief missed the Achilles heel of Macomber's testimony, which was that there were no limits to the scope of injunctive relief he believed appropriate. In Macomber's view any disclosure pertaining to diplomatic matters was harmful and should be enjoined. Once that point was plain, the force of Macomber's claims was spent, for Macomber's views could not be honored without turning First Amendment law, freedom of the press, and normal daily newspaper reporting inside out.

The *Post* tried to diminish Lieutenant General Zais's claims by charging that Zais evidently had no understanding of the role of the press in the democratic process since he believed that "documents should remain classified unless there is a positive assurance that their disclosure will *not* weaken the resolve of our allies" in the Vietnam War. The brief also asserted that the documents Zais cited did not support his allegations. For example, Zais had claimed that the Pentagon Papers study contained 1964–65 contingency plans for responding to a Chinese offensive, but the *Post* asserted that these plans were "patently obsolete," given the "changes in U.S. forces levels in Southeast Asia during the past seven years, marked advances in military transportation capabilities in the interim, and the decided change in American foreign policy objectives as announced in the Nixon doctrine." The brief charged that documents cited by Zais "contain only vague references to the plans in question and not the plans themselves." It contended that although Zais had claimed that the study contained documents pertaining to covert operations in North Vietnam, the documents cited contained "only the most generalized discussion of covert operations plans initiated in 1963 and 1964." In fact the brief stated, "the greatest specificity as to the type of operations proposed is contained in the following passage (IV. C. 2(a), p.2): 'Instructions forwarded by the JCS on 26 November specifically requested provision for: (1) harassment; (2) diversion; (3) political pressure; (4) capture of prisoners; (5) physical destruction; (6) acquisition of intelligence; (7) generation of intelligence; and (8) diversion of DRV resources.'" The brief suggested that the government's allegations were so exaggerated and unsupported that they should be dismissed as absurd (6–7).

The *Post*'s public brief was of moderate length and devoted its first half, the beginning twelve pages, to introductory material—a listing of the legal questions presented, a summary of the litigation to that moment, and a short statement of its arguments. The second half of the brief was divided into several legal arguments the *Post* had previously made in the case. The *Post* claimed that prior case law established that Judge Gesell's denial of injunctive relief could be reversed only if the Court concluded that he had abused his discretion and that the government had not claimed such abuse of discretion or that any of the findings were erroneous. The *Post* contended that the First Amendment limited injunctive relief only to the most serious and immediate threats to the government's ability to wage war and to the lives of military personnel, and to the most grave breaches of the national security, and that the government's evidence failed to establish such injury. The *Post* dismissed the government's contention that the Court was bound by the classification system, on the grounds that such a result was directly at odds with the First Amendment.

In a succession of paragraphs the *Post* asserted without much elaboration that no statute authorized the prior restraint action; that the government had no property interest in the documents; that how the *Post* got the documents was irrelevant to the disposition of the case; that the *Post* had no remedy under the Freedom of Information Act since the government took the position that, because the Pentagon Papers study was classified, it was not subject to declassification under FOIA; and that the president had no inherent powers to sue the *Post* for a prior restraint. Finally, the *Post* claimed that so many newspapers had gained copies of the Pentagon Papers that injunctive relief was ineffective in keeping the classified documents confidential.

■ ■ ■ ■ ■

In theory the *Times* was in a worse position than the *Post*. Because the *Post* had prevailed in the lower courts, the government had the burden before the Supreme Court. In contrast because the *Times* had lost before the Second Circuit, it had the burden of persuading the Court to reverse the court of appeals' judgment. But it would be an error to place too much emphasis on the differences between the two cases. Once the Supreme Court decided to review both, it was not likely to resolve them differently.

Between Friday afternoon and Saturday morning the *New York Times*'s lawyers produced a seventy-two-page public brief and a sealed brief. The public brief is available, but the sealed brief is missing. Because the sealed brief discussed classified material, security agents took possession of all copies the *Times* had of it, as they did of the *Post*'s sealed brief, after the close of the oral arguments on Saturday. The government has declassified the *Post*'s sealed brief and placed it in the public domain, but it has stated it has not been able to locate the *Times*'s sealed brief.

The first twenty-eight pages of the *Times*'s public brief dealt with purely introductory material—the legal questions presented, the lower court proceedings, a summary of the evidence presented during the public hearing before Judge Gurfein, and a short statement of the *Times*'s legal position. The remaining forty-four pages addressed six legal arguments and stated a conclusion. The first argument focused on the First Amendment and filled only three pages. It claimed that the core value protected by the First Amendment was the free flow of information relevant to important public issues. It conceded that the First Amendment did not bar all prior restraints, but it insisted that any party seeking a prior restraint bears a heavy burden. And then, in one paragraph, the brief stated why prior restraints were so disfavored:

> Prior restraints fall on speech with a brutality and a finality all their own. Even if they are ultimately lifted, they cause irremediable loss, a loss in the immediacy, the impact of speech. They differ from the imposition of criminal liability in significant procedural respects as well, which in turn have their substantive consequences. The violator of a prior restraint may be assured of being held in contempt. The violator of a statute punishing speech criminally knows that he will go before a jury, and may be willing to take his chance, counting on a possible acquittal. A prior restraint therefore stops more speech, more effectively. A criminal statute chills. The prior restraint freezes.[17]

These comments were entirely appropriate. But it is a measure of how much Alexander Bickel emphasized the separation of powers argument over the free press argument that these critical points were made in one brief paragraph.

The next thirty-two pages of the brief dealt with one aspect or another of the separation of powers argument that Bickel so favored. The first seven of these pages argued that the president lacked the inherent power to seek a prior restraint in this case absent statutory authorization. In a dire national security emergency the president might have authority, absent an authorizing statute, to seek judicial redress. But the brief claimed that, even reading the government's allegations for all they were worth, no such emergency existed in this case. The *Times* contended that any other conclusion would grant the president or the courts the power to make substantive law that governed this dispute and that such a conclusion would trespass upon the law-making function assigned to Congress by the Constitution and thus violate the separation of powers doctrine.

The next nineteen pages of the brief, the single longest portion of the brief, was devoted to arguing that "no statutory basis for the action exists" (39). The *Times* maintained that the government had identified only Section 793(e) of the espionage laws as a basis for its actions against the newspapers. It pointed out that the government had failed to cite one case in which any court had applied this provision in any circumstance other than an ordinary espionage case. It emphasized that Section 793(e) did not use the word "publish," that it did not make publication a crime, and that the absence of the word "publish" was intentional on the part of Congress. It contended that an examination of other provisions pertaining to defense and intelligence matters and seeking to protect the nation from espionage revealed that "when Congress wanted to proscribe the act of publishing as well as communicating, delivery or transmitting, it knew how to do so and insisted on doing it with precision" (44). It asserted that Congress distinguished between publishing on the one hand and communication, transmitting, and delivering on the other because of its sensitivity to First Amendment values and the need to protect the free flow of information to the public. It also claimed that Congress used the word "publish" "sparingly, and only when it thought it crucial," which it did not think was the case when it enacted Section 793(e). The *Times* contended that the history of the espionage laws since their original enactment indicated that Congress was aware they did not criminalize newspaper reporting of defense information.

The next six pages contended that the government's evidence did not justify a prior restraint absent a statute. The brief stated that the courts could grant a prior restraint, absent statutory authorization, "only when publication could be held to lead directly and almost unavoidably to a disastrous event. The probabilities must be very high, near to certainty, and the chain of causation between the publication and the feared event must be direct. Anything less will risk having the exception swallow up the rule" (58). Against this proffered legal standard, the *Times*'s brief claimed that the government was not entitled to a prior restraint in this case. The government witnesses demonstrated again and again that

> their conception of the dangers justifying imposition of a prior restraint included diplomatic embarrassments, the possibility of internal political difficulties caused to friendly governments, the addition of a causative effect, however minor, to trains of events which are well launched and sufficiently caused by other facts, or the confirmation of knowledge about methods of operation which is either already in the public domain or presumed to be otherwise available to foreign governments. What is perhaps even more important, government witnesses in each relevant instance reasoned from publication to feared effect not directly or immediately, but along a lengthy chain of causation whose links invariably included speculation and surmise. On such data, prior restraints on the press cannot conceivably be sustained. (63)

The *Times* claimed that the vice in this case was that the government had restrained it from publishing without specific and concrete charges supported by detailed evidence and had succeeded in keeping it under injunction even though it had failed to present such evidence during a hearing. To avoid the defeat of the right to publish in the future, the *Times* contended, prior restraints should be limited to occasions in which the reason for the restraint "will fairly leap to the eye" (64–67).

The *Times* closed its brief by remarking that the relationship between the press and the government is "not a tidy one" and that every so often it "malfunctions" from the viewpoint of one side or the other. This case, the brief stated, represented an effort by the government to "redress the balance [between the press and the government], to readjust the uneasy arrangement which has, after all, served us well." The *Times* claimed that the government was seeking relief that was "outside the framework of both law and history." It asked the Supreme Court to reverse the Second Circuit's judgment and to remand the case with a direction that the government's complaint be dismissed (68–72).

CHAPTER TWENTY-ONE

The Argument

Sometime late Friday afternoon or evening, June 25, 1971, Solicitor General Griswold filed a written motion with the Court asking that part of the oral argument be held *in camera*, so as to allow uninhibited argument over the classified material. Griswold hoped that the Supreme Court would grant this motion as had the two district and circuit courts. The government's motion also included a request for permission to file a sealed brief, as it had in the circuit courts. Although Griswold's motion was reasonable, he made it without giving notice to the lawyers for the *Times* and the *Post*.[1] Giving notice to opposing lawyers is a cardinal rule of the judicial process, and whatever exceptions may have existed to this rule, they did not apply to this case.

The nine justices met Saturday morning to consider the government's motion. The discussion was lively, if not acrimonious, and lasted for well over an hour, and perhaps close to two. As described by Justice Brennan, much more was at stake than the government's motion in the Pentagon Papers case, for the justices were aware that the resolution of the motion could trigger similar requests in the future.[2]

The motion for a secret hearing conflicted with a presumption strongly favoring public judicial proceedings. Nonetheless, the government's motion was plausible. The government could not countenance a public discussion of the top secret documents because it was their continued confidentiality that was at stake. That was the very point that had persuaded the lower courts to grant *in camera* hearings, and Griswold hoped it would convince the Supreme Court.

But the justices denied the government's request by a vote of six to three. Chief Justice Burger and Associate Justices Harlan and Blackmun were the three dissenters. But the Court granted the government's motion for permission to submit a sealed brief by a vote of five to four, with Associate Justices Stewart and White joining Burger, Harlan, and Blackmun composing a majority.[3] The justices left no record of the reasons that prompted them to deny the government's request for an *in camera* hearing. Justice Douglas's notes of the conference mention only the two votes and Justice Black's warning that "no notes be taken in this conference as they would be bound to leak out somewhere!"[4]

At eleven o'clock the justices took their seats in a jammed courtroom. Chief Justice Burger announced that the Court was denying the government's request for an *in camera* hearing. That was the moment the *Times* and the *Post* learned for the first time that the government had made such a request.

Burger asked Griswold to begin his argument. Griswold had been the solicitor general for four years by this time. He had argued many cases before the Court, had seen many of the justices in a variety of circumstances, and was intimately familiar with the inner workings of the Court. His experience before the Court was impressive, and he probably was as comfortable as any lawyer could be who was about to argue before the nine justices. He began by informing the justices that the government and the newspapers had filed sealed and open briefs. Griswold also stated that he had "filed just within minutes two statements, one prepared by the State Department and one prepared by the Department of Defense, giving more detail about some of the items discussed in my closed brief."[5] This was quite unorthodox. The *Times* had previously complained that the government had improperly supplemented the factual record once already in the litigation before the Second Circuit. Now the government did it again. But the newspapers' lawyers had little choice but to remain in their seats.

Griswold told the justices that it was important to get "this case in perspective." It obviously involved freedom of the press, but it also involved, he contended, a fundamental question of whether the president can function effectively in the discharge of his constitutional duties. Griswold implied that due respect for the presidency required the courts to accept the executive branch's judgment that further disclosures would seriously harm the national security. But Griswold did not expand on this contention. He immediately turned to the question of whether the First Amendment prohibited all prior restraints. "If we start with the assumption that never under any circumstances can the press be subjected to prior restraint, never under any circumstances can the press be enjoined from publication, of course we come out with the conclusion that there can be no injunction here. But I suggest . . . that there is no such Constitutional rule, and never has been such a Constitutional rule." Griswold then spent the next several minutes referring to different circumstances in which courts would restrain speech. Griswold first cited the law of copyright, which authorized injunctions to protect a copyright. To illustrate his point, he related a story involving his son, who lived in Toronto and had sent him copies of *The Globe and Mail* of Toronto, which had printed reports on the Pentagon Papers "headed 'Copyright New York Times Service.' I have no objection to that," he told the Court. As a second example, Griswold referred to the law of literary property. He hypothesized that the novelist Ernest Hemingway was still living and that the *New York Times* had somehow obtained a manuscript of an unpublished novel. "I have no doubt that Mr. Hemingway . . . could obtain from the courts an injunction against the press printing it." Griswold also mentioned enjoining speech in labor and management relations and the commercial trade fields.

Griswold might have continued in this vein if Justice Stewart had not interrupted him with obvious impatience. "I thought at least for purposes of this case," he told Griswold, "[that] they [the *Times* and the *Post*] conceded that an injunction would not be violative of the First Amendment, or put it this way, that despite the First Amendment, an injunction would be permissible in this case if the disclosure of this material would in fact pose a grave and immediate danger to the security of the United States." Stewart went on to state that it was his impression that the dispute "basically came down to a fact case, that the issues here are factual issues."

Griswold stated that he had received the newspapers' briefs just before the argument and was then unaware that the newspapers had conceded the theoretical availability of a prior restraint. Why Griswold was unaware of this is not at all clear. Both the *Post* and the *Times* had made this concession from the beginning of the litigation. Moreover, Griswold must have understood the general outlines of the *Post*'s legal position because of his involvement in the appeal to the D.C. Circuit. Nonetheless, Griswold said he would proceed on the basis that the newspapers had made the concession.

From then on Griswold was peppered with questions by one justice or another. In response to questions from Justice Harlan and Chief Justice Burger, Griswold stated that the government confronted an "extreme difficulty" in this case in that it did "not know now, and never has known" precisely what documents the newspapers possessed. When Burger pointed out that the *Times* had given the government an inventory of what documents it had Griswold said that it was not possible to tell from the inventory whether the *Times* possessed the "same papers that we have. Part of the problem here is that a great mass of this material is not included in the 47 volumes. It is background material, earlier drafts of some papers which are materially different from what is included in the 47 volumes, and as a result we cannot tell from the inventory what is included." Griswold illustrated his point by claiming that one of the items published was a telegram sent to the Canadian government, "which has caused a certain amount of controversy publicly and internationally." Griswold contended this telegram was not in the study and not referred to in the study: "Where they got it, what it is, I do not know."

Griswold then made another point that obviously troubled him. The Court had permitted the government—by Friday at five o'clock—to submit a list of references to the classified material that it claimed would gravely injure the national security. Because the writing of the government's sealed brief took what little time he had, he had to "delegate the question of preparing the supplemental statement," even though the statement was submitted "under my signature." Griswold said that he regarded the statement "as much too broad." He even disclosed to the justices that he had rejected an effort by the Department of State after the five o'clock deadline had passed to add four more items to the supplemental lists. He emphasized that the government most relied on the "items specified in the supplemental appendix filed in the Second Circuit and on such additional items as are covered in my closed brief in this case."

It was clear that Griswold was disassociating himself from the lists submitted on Friday. But Justice White was uncertain whether Griswold was saying that the justices needed only to review the special appendix and the sealed brief to decide the government's motion. Griswold responded: "Mr. Justice, I think that the odds are strong that that is an accurate statement. I must say that I have not examined every one of the remainder of the items."

In a further response to White Griswold characterized the evidentiary hearing before Judge Gesell as "hastily conducted" and emphasized that there had not yet been a "full and free judicial consideration" of the relevant materials in this case. This prompted Justice Harlan to inquire about the pace of the litigation: What was the length of the hearing in the court of appeals for the Second Circuit? How long did the district court take to make public its decision after the evidentiary hearing? How long did the Second Circuit take to make public its decision after the close of the oral argument? How long was the hearing before the D.C. Circuit? How long did the D.C. Circuit take after the close of the hearing to make public its decision?

Harlan's questions gave Griswold an opportunity to emphasize more than he had so far that the haste of the litigation had prevented the government from presenting all its evidence. But Griswold did not make much of these matters, and Floyd Abrams, one of the *New York Times* lawyers, has said in more recent years that he believes that Griswold's failure to emphasize the pace of the litigation constituted a missed opportunity of uncertain importance.

Stewart followed Harlan in asking Griswold questions. He wanted to know whether it was important to the government's claim for relief that the disputed documents were classified. Griswold conceded that the government would be seeking an injunction even if the material was not classified, but he added that it would be "one string off my bow." Stewart caught Griswold's hedge: "I did not understand it was a real string on your bow. That is why I am asking you the question." Griswold answered: "Maybe it is not, but there are those who think it is, and I must be careful not to concede away in this court grounds which some responsible officers of the government think are important." But Stewart was not satisfied, and he cornered Griswold again: "As I understand it, you are not claiming that you are entitled to an injunction simply or solely because this is classified material." This time Griswold answered plain and simple: "No," he was not making such a claim. Stewart then asked whether the government's claim depended on the assertion that the newspapers possessed stolen government property. Griswold agreed that the government's claim for a prior restraint did not depend on this either. He further agreed that this case boiled down to a fact case: Did the government's evidence justify the restraint?

But no sooner had Griswold made the concession than he told Stewart that he thought it was "part of the setting" that the material was classified and stolen and that the Court should consider this relevant fact in making its decision. He repeated that he did not think it was irrelevant, that "the concatenation of words here is the property of the United States, that this had been classified under executive orders approved by Congress, and that it obviously has been improperly acquired."

Harlan disagreed with Stewart's statement that the dispute boiled down to a "fact case" and that the classification of the disputed documents was irrelevant. Harlan looked to Griswold for some support for this position. "I would think . . . that the question of classification would have an important bearing on the question of the scope of judicial review of an executive classification." Griswold began as if he were to take back his concession to Stewart: "I think, Mr. Justice, that is true." But that was as far as Griswold went. From then on Griswold's comments assumed that the outcome would turn on an assessment of the government's evidence, and he completely failed to pick up on Harlan's suggestion that the mere fact that the documents were classified might warrant the Court to grant the government an injunction.

Justice Brennan asked the next set of questions. He asked if the injunctions against the *Times* and the *Post* had stopped other newspapers from publishing information based on the Pentagon Papers study. Griswold readily understood what was on Brennan's mind: whether the Court should deny the injunction because it was futile to try to stop a leak that had spread so far already. Griswold answered: it was "my understanding" that the articles published by these other newspapers were basically rewritten versions of what the *Times* and the *Post* had already disclosed and that government officials had not been "able to find new disclosures of previously unpublished material in these other articles." Griswold agreed that a useless injunction should be dissolved, but he insisted that "there is nothing in this record or known outside the record which would indicate that this injunction would be useless."

Blackmun made the next inquiries. "Is there anything in the record, or any intimation anywhere, that the possession by the other newspapers is attributable to *The New York Times* or *The Washington Post*?" Since the outstanding injunctions barred the *Times* and the *Post* from distributing the disputed material to anyone, Blackmun was in effect asking whether the newspapers had violated the outstanding court orders. He was also suggesting that any question about the usefulness of injunctive relief should be put aside since the *Times* and the *Post* themselves may be responsible for the spread of the classified material.

Griswold answered: "No, Mr. Justice."

With no particular question prompting him Griswold then told the justices what government lawyers had stated in the lower courts and what had been widely reported in the press. Top administration officials were prepared to appoint a joint task force to conduct an exhaustive review of the study and to complete it within forty-five days. Upon completion the government "will withdraw its objection to the publication of any documents which it has found no longer are relevant to the national security." None of the justices expressed any serious interest in the offer.

White then made a statement that was unrelated to anything that had been said up to that point. In a very oblique way White asked if the government would pursue a criminal prosecution against the newspapers if it lost its effort to gain a prior restraint. Griswold stated that while he believed it would "technically be a crime" for the newspapers to publish the disputed classified materials, "I find it exceedingly difficult to think that any jury would convict or that an appellate court affirm a conviction of a criminal offense for the publication of materials which this Court has said could be published."

The fact that the argument was public prevented Griswold from discussing the eleven national security matters he had cited in his sealed brief. Nevertheless, Griswold made a conclusionary claim about the injury that further publication would cause: "It will affect lives. It will affect the process of the termination of the war. It will affect the process of recovering prisoners of war." A few minutes later and at the end of his argument he repeated his claim: "I haven't the slightest doubt myself that the material which has already been published and the publication of the other material affects American lives and is a thoroughly serious matter."

Griswold spent his last few minutes discussing the legal standard that he claimed the Court should use in deciding the case. He asserted that the proper legal standard was whether further publication would present a "grave and irreparable" harm to national security. He conceded that the Court's order had used the word "immediate" instead of "irreparable," but he claimed that "irreparable" was the proper standard. To support his position, Griswold stated: "In the whole diplomatic area things don't happen at 8:15 tomorrow morning. It may be weeks or months," but the injury may be serious, and that should be legally sufficient for an injunction. As further illustration of his point he said: "I cannot say that the termination of the war or recovering prisoners of war is something which has an immediate effect on the security of the United States. I say that it has such an effect on the security of the United States that it ought to be the basis of an injunction in this case."

Within his discussion of the proper legal standard Griswold criticized Gesell's ruling in the *Post* case as constituting "fundamental error" requiring reversal. Griswold quoted Gesell as stating that further publication *may* interfere with current or future diplomatic relations pertaining to the war, because foreign governments may conclude that the United States is unable to keep delicate negotiations confidential. He then characterized Gesell's reasoning as rejecting the "ability of the Department of State, and that means the President, to whom the foreign relations are conferred by the Constitution, to conduct delicate negotiations now in process or contemplated for the future." Griswold claimed that it was "perfectly obvious" that diplomatic relations have "an impact on the security of the United States." Griswold also claimed, and correctly so, that Gesell had insisted that the government prove that further publication "will" result in an armed attack on the United States or an ally or that it "will" compromise defense or military plans. Griswold criticized this standard: "I think to say that it can only be enjoined if there will be a war tomorrow morning, when there is a war going on, is much too narrow."

If the correct standard were applied to the two cases, Griswold told the justices, the government would prevail. Since Gesell had applied an improper standard, and since the government had not yet had a fair hearing in either case, he asked the Court to affirm the Second Circuit's order and to reverse the D.C. Circuit court judgment with instructions to conform its order to that of the Second Circuit.

▪ ▪ ▪ ▪ ▪

Alexander Bickel argued next.[6] As a professor Bickel had studied the Court, its history and opinions, and through his writings had established himself as a prominent constitutional law scholar. He certainly was familiar with the judicial opinions of the nine men before whom he stood and had a thorough understanding of the relevant law. But the Pentagon Papers case was Bickel's first litigation experience. He had never argued in court before he argued in front of district judge Gurfein on Tuesday, June 15. Since that argument, his experience consisted of another brief argument before Gurfein on Friday, June 18, and a one-hour argument before the Second Circuit on Tuesday, June 22.

Bickel tried to cast doubt on the government's claim that further publication of the Pentagon Papers would gravely injure national security by pointing out that "no great alarm sounded" within the government when the *Times* began to publish its series on Sunday, June 13. But Bickel had barely spoken a few sentences when Chief Justice Burger interrupted: "Mr. Bickel, aren't you going to allow some time for somebody to really see what this means before they act and [to get] some pleading drawn, and [to] get lawyers into court."[7]

Bickel turned to the government's claim that it had not had time to prepare and present its case. He told the justices that during the *in camera* hearing in the *Times* case, district judge Gurfein's "sole purpose" was to "provoke from the Government witnesses something specific, to achieve from them the degree of guidance that he felt he needed in order to penetrate this enormous record." Bickel emphasized that Gurfein "got very little, perhaps almost nothing." Nevertheless, the government lawyers, he correctly stated, never asked for more time, never complained that the proceedings were being conducted too quickly, never insinuated that they needed more time, never asked for an adjournment.

Bickel picked up on Justice Stewart's comment to Solicitor General Griswold that the newspapers conceded that the First Amendment did not bar all prior restraints. "We concede, and we have all along in this case conceded for purposes of the argument, that the prohibition against prior restraint, like so much else in the Constitution, is not an absolute." But Bickel said in a somewhat professorial manner, "our position is a little more complicated than that."

With that introduction Bickel launched into the separation of powers argument he had pressed throughout the litigation. His starting point was that the government's claim for a prior restraint was not authorized by a statute, which meant that the "only basis on which the injunction can issue is a theory . . . of an inherent Presidential power." Bickel conceded that the president had the power, in the absence of a statute, to establish a classification system applicable to the executive branch. He also agreed that the presidency was sufficiently injured by the newspaper's publication of the Pentagon Papers to satisfy the technical "standing" requirements that any party in federal court must satisfy, namely that there is a sufficient injury to warrant the exercise of judicial power. Bickel also stated that in some limited circumstances the president could seek a prior restraint barring publication. But, Bickel insisted, the Pentagon Papers case was well outside those limited circumstances.

Bickel described the circumstances in which the president could act without statutory authority in the following terms. The threatened harm had to rise to a certain "magnitude," it had to be a "feared event" of sufficient gravity, it had to present "a mortal danger to the security of the United States." The reason for a prior restraint had to "leap to the eye" upon examination of the disputed material: it had to be "obvious" upon reading the documents that "the public safety is an issue." It had to appear that the threatened harm would follow immediately upon publication. Bickel contended that when the government's evidence in this case was measured against these considerations, it obviously fell far short of the minimal constitutional requirements, and as a result the government's actions had to be dismissed.

Justice Blackmun interrupted Bickel at that point and read a few lines from Circuit Judge Wilkey's dissent in the *Washington Post* case in which he described what he thought would be the harm that would result from further publication. "When I say 'harm' I mean . . . the death of soldiers, the destruction of alliances, the greatly increased difficulty of negotiation with our enemies, the inability of our diplomats to negotiate, as honest brokers, between would-be belligerents." Blackmun then asked: "I take it that you disagree fundamentally with that statement?" Bickel said that a prior restraint was proper to prevent the death of soldiers, as in Chief Justice Hughes's troop ship example. But he stated that a prior restraint should not be granted to avoid the "impairment of diplomatic relations." Bickel stated that the diplomatic interest was insufficient to warrant a prior restraint, even if the restraint were authorized by a statute. But Bickel claimed that the government had failed to show there was anything in the Pentagon Papers that is "related by a direct causal chain, to the death of soldiers" or anything equivalently grave. The most the evidence indicates is that further disclosures might result in a "chain of causation, whose links are surmise and speculation, all going toward some distant event," which itself was not very grave.

Justice White asked the next question. He wanted to know what Bickel thought the correct legal standard was. Bickel said that his standard had two parts. First, the harm has to be some "grave event—danger to the nation." Second, the "link between the fact of publication and the feared danger, the feared event, [must] be direct and immediate and visible." Bickel conceded that the disputed material may all be properly classified but yet fail to meet his proposed standard. In fact he asserted that there was "nothing" in the disputed documents that would meet his standard for a prior restraint, since if there was, "it surely should have turned up by now."

Justice Stewart proposed two hypothetical cases he wanted Bickel to consider. The first: "Let us assume," he said, "that when the members of the Court go back and open up this sealed record we find something there that absolutely convinces us that its disclosure would result in the sentencing to death of 100 young men whose only offense had been that they were 19 years old and had low draft numbers. What should we do?" Bickel hesitated: "I wish there were a statute that covered it," he said lamely. "Well, there is not," Stewart answered. Bickel again sought to deflect the question by telling Stewart that he was completely confident that the Pentagon Papers contained no such information. But Stewart wanted an answer. He supposed that the death of 100 soldiers might not be considered a threat to the nation since there are "at least 25 Americans killed in Vietnam every week these days." Again Bickel stalled, but this time he tried to clarify and narrow the question: "It is a case in which the chain of causation between the act of publication and the feared event, the death of these 100 young men, is obvious, direct, immediate." Stewart agreed. Bickel again tried to avoid an answer: "I would only say as to that that it is a case in which in the absence of a statute, I suppose most of us would say—" Stewart lost his patience with Bickel's procrastination: "You would say the Constitution requires that it be published, and that these men die, is that it?" With that, Bickel finally gave an answer: "No, I am afraid that my inclinations to humanity overcome the somewhat more abstract devotion to the First Amendment in a case of that sort."

Bickel added that he assumed that Justice Stewart was really asking whether a prior restraint could in Bickel's view be granted only to protect the nation from an event of "cosmic nature." Stewart agreed that was what he was after. Bickel stated that he did not think that a "cosmic" event was required and that the protection of the soldiers' lives was sufficient, even though their deaths did not threaten the security of the nation. Bickel offered that such a rule would make "very bad separation of powers law," but that he would accept that outcome.

Stewart posed his second hypothetical case. Suppose that the information convinces us that further disclosures would disrupt delicate negotiations that might result in the release of prisoners of war. That, Bickel said, was "a good deal nearer to what is bruited about" in this case. He then stated that unless one could say that the causal link between publication and the delay in the release of prisoners was direct and immediate, the injunction should be denied. Stewart told Bickel that he got "a feeling" that Bickel did not think the courts should give much importance to the impairment of diplomatic or military sources. Bickel said that was correct and that in the absence of a statute that authorized a prior restraint, the president may not get injunctive relief to protect such interests.

Justice Douglas told Bickel it was "very strange" for the *Times* to argue that a statute would strengthen the executive branch's claim for injunctive relief, since the First Amendment specifically prohibited the Congress from making any law that abridged freedom of speech. Bickel was trapped. The premise of his separation of powers argument was that Congress had not passed a statute that authorized prior restraints. The plain implication was that if the Congress had passed an authorizing statute, the government's claim for a prior restraint would at least be stronger. Now he was asked to explain how that could be given the plain wording of the First Amendment. Bickel ran for cover and told Justice Douglas that he had "not really" argued that and that he was not conceding that a statute authorizing a prior restraint in this case would be constitutional.

Chief Justice Burger immediately spoke up and changed the topic. A case was pending before the Court in which a *Times* reporter had refused to identify his news sources to a grand jury engaged in a criminal investigation on the ground that the First Amendment protected the identity of news sources from forced disclosure. Bickel knew the case well, since he had written an *amicus* brief on behalf of news organizations in the case. Burger wanted to know how the press could insist on confidentiality of sources when it was denying the same to the executive branch of government. Bickel said that he thought there was an "appearance of unfairness" here, but in reality there was none, since the reporter's claim for privilege was made to vindicate the values of the First Amendment.

Burger's question was not very probing of the issues in the case, but Bickel's answer was not as persuasive as it might have been. The executive branch depends on confidential communication as much as the press. If the press needs confidentiality to report the news, the executive branch needs confidentiality to govern. Both interests can make claims on the Constitution. The difference between the two cases juxtaposed by Burger was that the government was trying to force reporters to divulge their confidential sources whereas the newspapers were not trying to force the government to disclose the Pentagon Papers. Given this difference, there was no symmetry; the government's right to force a reporter to disclose had no relationship to the government's power to bar the press from disclosing information it already had.

With Burger's question asked and answered, Bickel sat down. He had been articulate, poised, and self-assured. He had covered many important points, and he had done so with some force.

▪ ▪ ▪ ▪ ▪

Chief Justice Burger asked William R. Glendon, who represented the *Washington Post*, to begin his argument.[8] Glendon was a trial lawyer, whose everyday work seldom encompassed constitutional questions. Glendon, however, was able to offset his lack of familiarity with constitutional law theory by focusing on what had actually happened in the case, which gave strength to his argument.

Glendon began his presentation with a brief history of the *Post* litigation and the D.C. Circuit court's grant of a temporary restraining order. He stated that the circuit court had instructed district judge Gesell to determine whether further publication would "so prejudice the defense interests of the United States or result in such irreparable injury to the United States" as to warrant a prior restraint, but almost immediately Justice Stewart interrupted Glendon and asked him to define the appropriate legal standard. Glendon answered that he thought the D.C. Circuit had applied the proper legal standard in insisting that the government prove irreparable injury to the United States or to its defense interests.

Stewart expressed his doubt that Glendon's proposed legal standard would protect the lives of a hundred soldiers. Glendon said: "that is a hard case you put." But Glendon did not want to discuss a hypothetical question: "we have to measure this case in light of what we have before us."

He assured Stewart that the government's evidence was not "anything like that"; it was only "conjecture and surmise."

Chief Justice Burger asked if anyone could be certain of the consequences that might follow from further publication. Glendon said that the *Post*'s right to publish should not be suspended on the basis of conjecture "piled upon surmise." Glendon recalled district judge Gurfein's statement that government officials "get the jitters" when there is a security breach. "I think maybe the Government has a case of the jitters here. But that," Glendon emphasized, "does not warrant the stopping the press on this matter."

Glendon turned to the government's claim that it had not yet had a full and fair hearing in this case. He claimed that the government was "accorded the fullest hearing" in this case. "There was no rush and no pressure." He ridiculed the government's position as amounting to a request that it be given "one more time, just one more time," and mocked the government's evidence by saying "maybe we can find something" then.

Glendon criticized the classification of the documents. The documents were classified, Glendon stated, by "some unknown individual who is not presented to the court, whose subjective judgement could not be explored, despite the district judge asking that he be brought in." In addition Glendon ridiculed the classification system; under existing rules the entire forty-seven volume study had to be classified even if there had been just one top secret document. Once classified, no effort was made to downgrade its classification or declassify it altogether, except for a review triggered by Senator William Fulbright's request that the study be declassified and given to the Senate Foreign Relations Committee. As for the government's representation that it is now willing to have an interagency task force review the study within forty-five days, Glendon pointed out that the offer sharply contrasted with the government's position asserted only a few days before that "these documents were top secret and none could be disclosed."

Glendon stated that the disputed secret study was no more than a history, that it was entitled a history, and that from what he had seen of it, "that is what it is." The documents simply did not contain any information that threatened any current national security interest. He conceded he had not reviewed the new references the government had submitted to the Court that morning, but he did not believe they would constitute evidence that was any more persuasive than the evidence the government had previously submitted. Glendon told the Court the government had made "extravagant claims" that were completely unsupported by the evidence; this was "a case of broad claims and narrow proof."

Burger, who had displayed his disdain toward the newspapers throughout the oral argument, asked Glendon whether the *Post* had been ordered to produce for government inspection the documents it had. Glendon conceded that the newspapers had not been ordered to turn over the documents because the documents might contain clues that would help federal investigators identify the person or persons who had leaked them. But he said that Gesell had resolved this matter in a fair manner that totally removed any disadvantage the government might otherwise have, by assuming that the *Post* had all the documents. Burger went on to another topic.

Burger said that he recalled "an ancient doctrine" that a person seeking equitable relief had to have "clean hands." How could the *Post* expect the Court to be sympathetic to its position when the newspapers were hiding their sources? Glendon shot back: "We did not come into equity. The Government came into equity." The government had initiated the legal proceeding, not the *Post*, and it was the government that sought injunctive relief, not the *Post*. "You were brought in," Burger responded somewhat lamely. "We were brought in kicking and screaming," Glendon rejoined.

Blackmun drew Glendon's attention to Judge Wilkey's statement that further disclosures would result in the death of soldiers. Glendon took full advantage of his knowledge of the prior proceedings in effectively answering Blackmun. Glendon reassured Blackmun that as far as he knew there was "absolutely nothing" in the record "to justify that statement." But he then went one step farther. The majority of the D.C. Circuit judges not only disagreed with Wilkey's statement, he told Blackmun, but had taken the unusual step of amending their decision to make clear their disagreement with Wilkey.

Black made the last comment to Glendon. "As I understand the argument of both lawyers [for the newspapers], it seems to be that they have argued . . . on the premise that the First Amendment . . . can be abridged by Congress if it desires to do so." Black was correct. The concession made by both Glendon and Bickel—the First Amendment tolerated prior restraints in some limited circumstances—opened the door to Congress to pass a law that defined what those circumstances were. Glendon was cornered by Black's inquiry, just as Bickel had been by Douglas's, and he squirmed. "I did not make that argument. . . . No, Your Honor, I do not say that. . . . Never, I do not say that. No, Sir. I am sorry, Your Honor. I say that we stand squarely and exclusively on the First Amendment." However squarely and exclusively Glendon tried to stand on the First Amendment, it was not the same First Amendment that Black stood on. Glendon knew that, as did Black. Chief Justice Burger thanked Glendon for his argument, which was his signal that his time had expired and that he should sit down.

■ ■ ■ ■ ■

Burger invited Griswold to make rebuttal comments.[9] Griswold swiftly emphasized that the government was not worried about protecting past administrations or officials. It was worried about the present and the future, and by future he said he did not mean either the twenty-first century or tomorrow. He said that the government was concerned about consequences six months or a year or two years from then. He said that prior restraint cases were rare or unheard of because the government almost never had any advance notice that the press would publish certain information. In response to Justice Marshall's suggestion that Griswold was trying to turn the federal courts into a "censorship board" he said he thought that was a "pejorative way to put it" and that he did not know an alternative. Justice Black blurted out that the "First Amendment might be," by which he meant that the amendment forbids all prior restraints. Griswold was not cowed; he spoke respectfully but directly to the aging justice: "Now Mr. Justice, your construction of that is well known, and I certainly respect it. You say that 'no law' means 'no law,' and that should be obvious. I can only say, Mr. Justice, that to me it is equally obvious that 'no law' does not mean 'no law,' and I would seek to persuade the Court that that is true."

Griswold was in high gear and kept on going. He challenged the idea that the government had moved slowly in this matter. The *Times* published on Sunday, the Attorney General sent a telegram to the *Times* on Monday, and the government went to court on Tuesday. That was "pretty fast," Griswold claimed, given how the government operates. As for the claim that there had been a full hearing in the case, Griswold again insisted that was not true. "Everything about this case has been frantic," he asserted.

As for the relief the government sought he again asked that the Second Circuit's judgment be affirmed. He said that Judge Gurfein had not read the entire study, even though he said he would, and that the government had relied upon this promise. He said he could not determine from Judge Gurfein's opinion what legal standard he had used and that he hoped that a Court order requiring a new hearing would define the proper legal standard. As far as the *Post* case was concerned, Griswold modified his position. Instead of insisting that the hearing in the *Post* was inadequate, as he had done an hour earlier, he said he would be "content" to leave the evidentiary record in the case as it was but would request a remand so the evidence could be assessed in accordance with the proper legal standard, which was not used by the circuit or district court and which he hoped the Court would define.

Burger thanked the solicitor general for his comments, and the Court adjourned, giving no indication when or how it would decide.

▪ ▪ ▪ ▪ ▪

The justices met in the conference room to discuss the two cases. Justice Douglas kept notes of the discussion, and they suggest that each justice gave his views but that there was little, if any, discussion.

By tradition the Chief Justice spoke first and was followed in descending order by the next senior justice. Burger stated that Judge Gesell used an "invalid" legal standard in the *Post* case, that no judge knew all the facts, and that the cases should not have been tried on a "panic basis." He wanted to affirm the Second Circuit's judgment and reverse and remand the D.C. Circuit's judgment for a new hearing. He told his colleagues that if the *Times* and the *Post* won, he would write a brief opinion "at once and more fully during the summer."[10]

Black said he disagreed with Burger. The cases did not raise any question of fact, and the Court should "not destroy the First Amendment by providing a 'loitering' ordinance that was vague and loose." Black said the "President has deluded the public on Vietnam," and he voted to affirm the D.C. Circuit and to reverse the Second Circuit.[11]

Douglas spoke next, and his notes indicate only that he agreed with what Black had said.[12]

Justice Harlan said he agreed with Burger that the case had made a "travesty" of the judicial process. He stated that the courts were at the "heart of the democratic process" and that the central issue in the case was "the scope of judicial review over the Executive." He would affirm the Second Circuit's judgment and reverse the D.C. Circuit's judgment on the ground that "there was not an adequate hearing" in the *Post* case. He claimed that the proper scope of judicial review was "very, very limited. It goes no farther than to determine if there is a classification procedure and if that classification has been followed" in a particular case. National security involves "many imponderables," and only "men in the field" can be trusted to make sound judgments. He said he wanted to read these documents but that he would need help from his law clerks since his eyesight was so poor. If his clerk was barred from reading the classified material, Harlan said he would have to disqualify himself. He said that to write his opinion "will take time and he'll file later."[13]

Brennan stated that prior restraints "come here with a heavy burden." He agreed with the district judges in the two cases, that the government did not meet its burden. In his view the government claimed that further publication "might" or "could" result in serious harm to the national security, but the Supreme Court's decision in *Near v. Minnesota* required the government to allege and prove that further disclosures "will" inflict injuries. He also said that he saw no reason to grant an injunction in these cases, since other newspapers were publishing the material and the injunctions would be ineffective.[14]

Stewart was next. He emphasized that the executive branch has "great powers in foreign affairs" and that "secrecy" was of "great importance" in such matters. He had no doubt that the Court had the power to enjoin publication to protect the lives of soldiers or to prevent "irreparable harm" from being inflicted on the United States, but he did not know if further publication presented any such threat, and he had not yet decided how he would ultimately vote.[15]

White said he was "probably against the" United States. He stated that the "damage has already been done" to the national security and that there was not much substance to the government's claim for an injunction. The government had "abandoned the position" that the newspapers had violated any criminal statutes, but in his view the newspapers were criminally liable. White stated he would deny the government injunctive relief and allow the newspapers to publish, but he preferred that the "cases not be disposed of on the merits for a few days," presumably so he could continue to consider his judgment.[16]

Marshall said that the executive had "broad powers," including the power to establish a classification system and to keep information secret. But there was no statute governing this dispute, and the executive did not have "inherent power to stop the *Times* from printing." He would vote to reverse in the *Times* case and affirm in the *Post* case.[17]

Blackmun spoke last. He said that there had not been a "full hearing" in the cases. He thought that the Pentagon Papers contained "dangerous material that will harm the nation," that the *Times* publication was "reprehensible," and that he had "nothing but contempt for the *Times*." He told the other justices they "should unite on the criminal aspects of the problem." He would vote to affirm in the *Times* case and reverse in the *Post* case.[18]

Within minutes of the oral argument seven of the justices indicated they had reached a decision, with Justices Black, Douglas, Brennan, and Marshall voting to free the newspapers to publish and Chief Justice Burger and Justices Harlan and Blackmun voting to affirm the Second Circuit and to reverse the D.C. Circuit with an order to hold a new hearing. Justice White had stated he was "probably" going to vote against the government. He indicated he wanted a few days to consider it, but unless he changed his mind—and there was nothing in Douglas's notes to indicate he would—his vote, added to those of Black, Douglas, Brennan, and Marshall, would make a majority. Stewart was undecided. But Douglas thought that Stewart's position was close to Brennan and White's position and that he would end up voting against the government. As it turned out Douglas correctly understood Stewart; Stewart voted to deny the injunction.

As the justices left the conference it was clear to all of them that the Court would vote five to four or six to three against the government. Either way, the government was going to lose.

CHAPTER TWENTY-TWO

The Decision

Sometime before Monday morning, June 28, a firm majority of the Court formed in support of freeing the newspapers to publish their Pentagon Papers reports. In reaching this decision Justices Black, Douglas, Brennan, Stewart, White, and Marshall technically reversed the Second Circuit's decision and affirmed district judge Murray Gurfein's judgment in the *Times* case. It also affirmed the D.C. Circuit court and district judge Gesell's judgment in the *Post* case. The three dissenters, Chief Justice Burger and Justices Harlan and Blackmun, voted to affirm the Second Circuit's judgment, which had ordered Gurfein to hold a second evidentiary hearing. They also voted to reverse the D.C. Circuit court judgment and to order a second evidentiary hearing in the *Post* case.[1]

Once it became clear that a majority was established, Chief Justice Burger asked Justice Brennan to prepare a *per curiam* opinion that would announce the judgment of the Court.[2] A per curiam opinion represents the views of the Court but is not signed by a particular justice. There can be many reasons the Court uses per curiam opinions: it might consider a case too insignificant to decide by way of a full opinion, or it might believe that the justices' opinions on a particular matter are best expressed in a short, unsigned statement. In this case the reason for a per curiam opinion seems to have been that the justices lacked the time before the summer recess to hammer out a majority opinion they could endorse.

Brennan sent a draft per curiam opinion to the Court's printer on Monday, and it was set in type, printed, and circulated to all members of the

Court the same day.[3] Except for a one-word change in the last line, the draft of the per curiam opinion was the same as the final version. With the legal citations excised it read in the main as follows:

> We granted certiorari in these cases in which the United States seeks to enjoin the *New York Times* and the *Washington Post* from publishing the contents of a classified study entitled "History of U.S. Decision-Making Process on Viet Nam Policy."
>
> "Any system of prior restraints of expression comes to this Court bearing a heavy presumption against its constitutional validity." . . . The Government "thus carries a heavy burden of showing justification for the enforcement of such a restraint." . . . The District Court for the Southern District of New York in the *New York Times* case and the District Court for the District of Columbia and the Court of Appeals for the District of Columbia Circuit in the *Washington Post* case held that the Government had not met that burden. We agree. (714)

The Court did not explain the phrases "heavy burden" or "heavy presumption," nor did the Court state how it assessed the government's evidence or why it was deficient.

On Tuesday, June 29, Justices White and Stewart each sent Justice Brennan a note stating that they joined his per curiam opinion.[4] Sometime on Tuesday Burger circulated a memorandum that stated that the "printing presses have been rolling and everyone seems to be nearly ready" to make their opinions public. Burger stated he did not think it was "feasible" for the justices to hold themselves to a "rigid 'time table,'" but they should keep themselves "available for a Conference" on Wednesday at eleven o'clock in the morning and "consider an open Court session" for Wednesday afternoon to announce the judgments in the two cases.[5] At 2:30 Wednesday afternoon eight of the justices took their regular seats in the courtroom, Justice Douglas having already departed for the West Coast, and in a "hushed" room Chief Justice Burger read the per curiam opinion.[6]

■ ■ ■ ■ ■

In addition to the brief per curiam opinion there were nine individual opinions, but no opinion was joined by more than three justices. Black and Douglas joined each other's opinions, as did White and Stewart. The opinions of Brennan and Marshall were not joined by any other justice. Harlan's dissenting opinion was joined by Burger and Blackmun, who also wrote separately and whose opinions were not joined by any other justice.

Of all the opinions Black's was the most passionate and uncompromising. Black had been appointed to the Court in 1937 by President

Franklin D. Roosevelt and was the senior member of the Court. He worked intensely, even feverishly, on his opinion over the four days between the oral argument and the announcement of the Court's judgment, making stylistic changes up until the last minute.

Black's position, which was entirely consistent with his prior opinions, was that "every moment's continuance of the injunctions against these newspapers amounts to a flagrant, indefensible, and continuing violation of the First Amendment." He wrote that it was "unfortunate that some of my Brethren" accept that prior restraints are appropriate in some situations, for such a "holding would make a shambles of the First Amendment." Black claimed that his construction of the First Amendment was fully supported by the history of the writing of the Constitution and the Bill of Rights. Indeed, he claimed: "I can imagine no greater perversion of history" than the contention that history supported the claim that the First Amendment tolerated prior restraints (715–16).

Black made clear in his opinion that he conceived of the First Amendment's free press protection as essential to the democratic process. The purpose of the press was "to serve the governed, not the governors," that it had to "remain forever free to censure the Government," that it had to "bare the secrets of government and inform the people," and that it should "expose deception in government." Black tied his last point to the Vietnam War: The press had a duty "to prevent any part of the government from deceiving the people and sending them off to distant lands to die of foreign fevers and foreign shells" (717).

Black thought the information in dispute in these cases was "current news of vital importance to the people of this country." Instead of condemning the *Times* and the *Post*, as some had done, Black urged that the newspapers be "commended" for their "courageous reporting." "In revealing the workings of government that led to the Viet Nam war," he wrote, "the newspapers nobly did precisely that which the Founders hoped and trusted they would do" (717).

In his opinion Black made use of the separation of powers argument that Alexander Bickel, the *Times* attorney, had pressed so hard throughout the litigation. "The Government does not even attempt to rely on any act of Congress. Instead it makes the bold and dangerously far-reaching contention that the courts should take it upon themselves to 'make' a law abridging freedom of the press in the name of equity, presidential power and national security, even when the representatives of the people in Congress have adhered to the command of the First Amendment and refused to make such a law" (718).

This was a particularly odd point for Black to make, for it made no difference to his construction of the First Amendment whether the executive relied upon a statute or not. Black stated in his opinion, as he had several times before, that the First Amendment barred the Congress, the executive branch, and the courts from abridging freedom of speech or of the press. This was an absolute prohibition, and the First Amendment permitted no exceptions, and that was true whether the executive branch sought to restrain the press with or without a statute authorizing such restraints.

Black closed his opinion with a paragraph that opened with the observation that the word "security" was a "broad, vague generality." He asserted his belief that the "guarding of military and diplomatic secrets at the expense of informed representative government provides no real security for our Republic." He claimed that the drafters of the Constitution and the Bill of Rights sought to give the United States "strength and security by providing that freedom of speech, press, religion, and assembly should not be abridged" (719). These were not uncommon points, and he might have quoted for emphasis a prior opinion of his own or district judge Gurfein's opinion denying the government's request for a preliminary injunction in the *Times* case. Instead, he quoted a 1937 opinion written by Chief Justice Hughes, who he described in his opinion as the "great man and great Chief Justice that he was" (719). Hughes had written, as quoted by Black: "The greater the importance of safeguarding the community from incitements to the overthrow of our institutions by force and violence, the more imperative is the need to preserve inviolate the constitutional rights of free speech, free press and free assembly in order to maintain the opportunity for free political discussion, to the end that government may be responsive to the will of the people and that changes, if desired, may be obtained by peaceful means. Therein lies the security of the Republic, the very foundation of constitutional government" (719–20).[7] It is not clear why Black closed with a quotation from a Hughes opinion, but he may have sensed that this might be his last opinion, and he wanted to make amends to a man whom he grew to admire and respect but whose nomination by President Hoover to the position of Chief Justice he opposed when he was a member of the Senate representing Alabama.

Black's opinion attracted considerable press attention. This was true in part because the press so approved of what he wrote. But it was also true because his opinion contained a sharp criticism of the Vietnam War; the government had deceived the people and sent them "to distant lands to die of foreign fevers and foreign shot and shells."

The original version of this line, which was extensively quoted in the press and on television, read: "And paramount among the responsibilities of a free press is the duty to prevent any part of the government from deceiving the people and tricking them into a war where young Americans will be murdered on the battlefield." When Black's wife, Elizabeth Black, read his draft opinion on Monday evening she "objected" to the word "murdered," and in her diary she wrote that Black "thought it over all night and this morning at 4:00 A.M. he woke me and asked, 'how would it be if I said, "Send American boys to die of foreign fevers and foreign shot and shell"?'" Black's wife thought this was "great," and the substitution was made. She also stated in her diary that the new line came from the song "I Am a Dirty Rebel," which "Hugo and the boys used to sing just for fun."[8]

After Chief Justice Burger had read the per curiam opinion and the justices left the courtroom Mrs. Black went to her husband's office "and told him,'Honey, if this is your swan song it's a good one!'" Mrs. Black wrote in her diary that Justice Black "agreed that he could be proud of this one."[9] Mrs. Black's intuition about her husband's failing health was correct. Black's Pentagon Papers concurrence was his last opinion. He had served on the Court for thirty-four years, and although his spirit yearned for more, his body deteriorated quickly over the summer of 1971. On September 17 he resigned from the Court. Two days later he suffered a stroke, and six days after that, on September 25, he died.

▪ ▪ ▪ ▪ ▪

When Justice Douglas began to draft his concurring opinion is uncertain. He may have drafted some of it either before or during the oral argument. If he did not, then he worked quickly on Saturday afternoon, because the printed first and second drafts of his opinion have the date "6–26" handwritten across the top of them. That suggests they were printed on Saturday, which would have been unusual but possible, given that the Court extended its term because of the cases and was eager to decide them.[10]

Douglas's opinion was choppy and disjointed, and it lacked the passion and eloquence that Black, with whom he had served on the Court since 1939, had given his. The content of Douglas's opinion also evolved substantially during Saturday and Sunday as he worked on it.

Douglas's published opinion stated that the First Amendment leaves "no room for governmental restraint on the press." This statement was followed by a footnote that referred to opinions that either he or Justice Black had written in five different cases. The only noteworthy aspect to this statement is that it took Douglas several drafts to reach a legal conclusion for which he was already well known.[11]

Douglas's published opinion asserted that the First Amendment left no room for governmental restraints on the press. He then devoted the next two pages to supporting the assertion that there was "no statute barring the publication by the press of the material which the *Times* and *Post* seek to use." In doing this Douglas made no suggestion that a statute authorizing prior restraints would have caused him to qualify his absolutist position. Rather, he seemed to have wanted to put his influence behind a construction of the espionage laws that contended that they did not authorize a prior restraint in this case.[12]

Douglas's statutory argument was abbreviated and unexceptional, except in one regard. In the text of his opinion Douglas wrote that one provision of the espionage laws related to cryptography and prohibited among other things the publication of such information. Douglas added a footnote, which read: "These papers contain data concerning the communications system of the United States, the publication of which is made a crime. But the criminal sanction is not urged by the United States as the basis of equity power."[13] This was a remarkable footnote, for in it Douglas agreed with the government that the disputed classified documents contained information pertaining to intelligence matters and that its publication was a federal crime. He claimed that the government did not cite this criminal provision as a basis for equitable relief and left undecided whether the criminal statute could be construed to authorize an injunction to bar the publication of this material. Douglas also left unexplained how this conclusion squared with his absolutist position.

Douglas made numerous other points in the balance of his opinion. He vented his opposition to the Vietnam War by noting that the constitution did not authorize "presidential wars." He accepted that further disclosures by the press "may have a serious impact," but he asserted that such a consequence was "no basis for sanctioning a previous restraint on the press." He claimed that the "dominant purpose" of the First Amendment was to bar the government from suppressing "embarrassing information," that it was "common knowledge that the First Amendment was adopted against the widespread use of the common law of seditious libel to punish the dissemination of material that is embarrassing to the powers-that-be," and that the Pentagon Papers cases will "go down in history as the most dramatic illustration of that principle." Douglas asserted that the government sought to suppress information that was "highly relevant" to the debate over the Vietnam War. He concluded by observing that "secrecy in government is fundamentally anti-democratic" and that "public questions . . . should be [subject to] 'open and robust' debate."[14]

▪ ▪ ▪ ▪ ▪

Justice Brennan, whom President Eisenhower appointed to the Court in 1956, and his clerks had been discussing the Pentagon Papers case on and off since district judge Murray Gurfein had granted the government a temporary restraining order. Initially the focus of conversation was on the propriety of Gurfein's order. But as the days went by the conversation turned to whether there would be time for the government's case against the *Times*, and eventually the *Post*, to be reviewed by the Supreme Court before its term ended. Brennan asked at least one of his clerks to begin some research on related legal questions once it appeared that the Second Circuit and the D.C. Circuit would render decisions in time to give the parties an opportunity to seek Supreme Court review.[15] By the time the *Times* and the government had filed petitions for a writ of certiorari with the Court Brennan had already decided how he would rule in the case.

Although he accepted the possibility that the government might obtain a prior restraint barring the press from publishing news even when the Congress had not formally declared war, he was convinced that the rulings of the lower courts in the two cases meant that the government had failed to submit evidence that he believed warranted any injunction at all. Hence, he had decided that he would vote to vacate the injunctions and to free the newspapers to publish when the Court considered the petitions for certiorari. When the Court voted to review the cases on an expedited basis the only thing Brennan did not know was how the case would come out, and even that uncertainty vanished once he heard what Justices White and Stewart said at the conference following the oral argument.[16]

Brennan's opinion was noteworthy for two reasons. First, Brennan maintained that "every restraint in this case, whatever its form, has violated the First Amendment—and none the less so because that restraint was justified as necessary to afford the court an opportunity to examine the claim more thoroughly" (727). This was an important point for him to make, because he, unlike Justices Black and Douglas, who maintained that the First Amendment tolerated no prior restraints, conceded that the First Amendment permitted prior restraints in limited circumstances. Nevertheless, he insisted no injunction was proper in these cases at any stage. The reason, he claimed, was that the primary purpose of the First Amendment was to prevent prior restraints, and thus they could be granted only when the government submitted evidence warranting such relief for examination by the judiciary. In this case the government had offered "surmise," "conjecture," and "mere conclusions," which were legally insufficient to form the basis for any injunctive relief, even a mere temporary restraining order (725, 727).

Although they did not do so explicitly, Brennan's statements amounted to criticisms of district judge Gurfein and the D.C. Circuit for granting the initial restraining orders as well as the Second Circuit and the D.C. Circuit for continuing them. Brennan was sensitive to this fact, and in an effort to ameliorate his implied criticism, Brennan wrote that "it is difficult to fault the several courts below for seeking to assure that the issues here involved were preserved for ultimate review by this Court." Nonetheless, Brennan did "fault" them: "The error which has pervaded these cases from the outset was the granting of any injunctive relief whatsoever, interim or otherwise" (725).

Second, Brennan offered a remarkable legal standard for deciding when a prior restraint was permissible. He wrote: "Thus, only governmental allegation and proof that publication must inevitably, directly and immediately cause the occurrence of an event kindred to imperiling the safety of a transport already at sea can support even the issuance of an interim restraining order" (726–27). If Brennan were to grant injunctive relief, the government had to prove that publication would "inevitably" result in harm. But proof of inevitability is impossible. Even if the press threatened to publish the location and course of a troop transport ship, the government could not prove that publication would "inevitably" result in "imperiling" the transport.

When Brennan was asked years later what he meant by the word "inevitably," he laughed softly. He knew that proof of inevitability was impossible. He said that he wanted to get across the idea that prior restraints were available in only the most narrowly defined circumstances, that the burden of proof the government had to satisfy was extremely high, that the government had to establish that publication would "almost inevitably" result in the threatened injury. Thus, Brennan came about as close to asserting that the First Amendment barred all prior restraints, as Black and Douglas had done, as he could.[17]

▪ ▪ ▪ ▪ ▪

Justices Stewart and White joined each other's opinions, and though they did not assert an absolutist position, as did Black or Douglas, or insist on inevitability, as did Brennan, their opinions provided substantial protection for the press. Stewart took longer to make up his mind in this case than any other justice. When the justices met after the Saturday oral argument only Stewart failed to state how he would vote or was likely to vote.[18] By Tuesday, and it may have been earlier, Stewart had decided to rule against the government. Also on Tuesday several drafts of his opinion were printed, but they barely differed from the opinion he made public on Wednesday.[19]

Stewart stated that the president had "enormous power" in the areas of defense and international relations, power that presidents had "pressed to the very hilt since the advent of the nuclear missile age." This great power was "largely unchecked" by the Congress or the courts, which meant that "the only effective restraint [on it] . . . may lie in an enlightened citizenry," which in turn depended on an "informed and free press." At the same time, Stewart noted, it was "elementary" that the maintenance of the national defense and effective international diplomacy required "both confidentiality and secrecy." There was only one way out of this bind. "The responsibility must be where the power is," by which he meant that the executive branch must assume responsibility for assuring the confidentiality and secrecy it believed was required. In that regard Stewart advised that the "very first principle" of a classification system should be to avoid "secrecy for its own sake. For when everything is classified, then nothing is classified, and the system becomes one to be disregarded by the cynical or the careless, and to be manipulated by those intent on self-protection or self-promotion" (727, 728, 729).

Although Stewart's reasoning suggested that he might have been about to state, as did Black and Douglas, that he believed the First Amendment prohibited all prior restraints, he stopped far short of taking that position. Instead he asserted, without elaboration, that he joined the per curiam opinion because "I cannot say that disclosure . . . [of the disputed material] will surely result in direct, immediate, and irreparable damage to our Nation or its people." Stewart did state that he was "convinced" that further publication will injure the "national interest," but he presumably concluded that the injury would not be sufficiently direct, immediate, or irreparable (730).

In one paragraph Stewart referred to the "several" criminal statutes that Congress had passed to protect "government property and preserve government secrets." He noted that "several of them are of very colorable relevance to the apparent circumstances of these cases." And then in the very next sentence he stated that if the government instituted criminal prosecutions because of these disclosures, "it will be the responsibility of the courts to decide the applicability of the criminal law under which the charge is brought" (730). In one sense this was so elementary as to be completely unremarkable. But it was remarkable, precisely because it was so elementary. Of course it was the Court's duty to decide the applicability of the federal espionage laws to the *Times* and the *Post*. Why say so? What Stewart seemed to be doing was responding to the solicitor general's statement during oral argument that he did not believe the government would initiate a criminal prosecution if it lost the prior restraint actions, and he seemed to be suggesting to Griswold, the Attorney General, and other top administration officials that they reconsider that position.

Stewart ended his opinion without directly addressing the separation of powers argument that Alexander Bickel had pressed vigorously throughout the litigation. Instead, he assumed that the executive had inherent power to seek a prior restraint to protect the national interest; the only important question was whether its evidence was legally sufficient, and in this case, he concluded that it was not.

■ ■ ■ ■ ■

Justice White's first printed draft of his opinion was completed on Tuesday, June 29, and it differed from his published opinion in only minor stylistic respects.[20] Although White joined the per curiam opinion, he gave the impression in his opinion that he had to drag his tormented conscience and judgment to this result. In his first sentence he wrote that he concurred in the judgment, "but only because of the concededly extraordinary protection against prior restraints enjoyed by the press under our constitutional system." Two pages later White stated that it was "not easy to reject the proposition urged by the United States and to deny relief on its good-faith claims in these cases that publication will work serious damage to the country" (730, 733).

But rule against the government he did. And in so doing he made it clear he did not take the position "that in no circumstances would the First Amendment permit an injunction against publishing information about government plans or operations." The problem in this case was that "the United States has not satisfied the very heavy burden which it must meet to warrant an injunction against publication in these cases, at least in the absence of express and appropriately limited Congressional authorization for prior restraints in circumstances such as these." But that did not mean, White wrote, that further revelations of the classified material will be harmless. Indeed, he asserted that further disclosures "will do substantial damage to public interests" (731).

White wrote that he was persuaded to rule against the government in part because Congress had not passed a statute that was "based on its own investigations and findings" and offered the courts "guidance and direction" in deciding when to grant a prior restraint. In making this point

White was not claiming that the president lacked the inherent power to seek a prior restraint, the point that Alexander Bickel had emphasized. Rather, White stated that he feared that if the Court granted an injunction under these circumstances the Supreme Court's decision would be of "little guidance to other courts in other cases." He wrote that he was not willing to start the courts "down [such] a long and hazardous road." White also stated that he was ruling against the government because the "massive breakdown in security" had made the efficacy of injunctive relief "doubtful at best" (732, 733).

White emphasized that in denying the government injunctive relief, or even another evidentiary hearing, the Court "does not measure its constitutional entitlement to a conviction for criminal publication. That the Government mistakenly chose to proceed by injunction," he wrote, "does not mean that it could not successfully proceed in another way" (733). White did not leave his point as a general one: he devoted seven pages of his eleven-page opinion to reviewing the criminal statutes that might be the basis of a criminal prosecution against the newspapers. Midway through his analysis, and after he had discussed several provisions of the espionage laws, White wrote: "I would have no difficulty in sustaining convictions under these sections on facts that would not justify the intervention of equity and the imposition of a prior restraint" (737).

Perhaps the degree to which White was urging the government to mount a criminal investigation of the newspapers is best illustrated by his discussion of Section 793(e) of the espionage laws. The government had cited this provision as authority for its prior restraint actions against the newspapers, so the provision had already drawn some commentary by judges, especially Judge Gurfein. In a lengthy footnote White disagreed with a conclusion that Gurfein had stated that all criminal prosecutions under this complicated and multifaceted provision required the government to prove that the defendant intended to injure the United States or to benefit a foreign nation. White contended that a prosecution for the wrongful communication or withholding of a "document" that was covered by the statute required the government to prove only that the document was communicated or withheld willfully and knowingly (738, n. 9). White did stop short of stating that he believed the newspapers had already committed a crime—"I am not, of course, saying that either of these newspapers has yet committed a crime or that either would commit a crime if they published all the material now in their possession"—but neither the *Times* nor the *Post* could have conceived of White's opinion as anything but a strong recommendation that the government prosecute them (740).

That of course was what White was doing. He had inquired of the solicitor general about criminal prosecution during oral argument. When Griswold answered that he could not imagine the government criminally prosecuting the newspapers for publishing material the Supreme Court refused to enjoin, White was sufficiently agitated that he complained during the justices' conference that the solicitor general had given away the threat of criminal prosecution during his oral argument.[21] Now White was urging the government to reconsider the judgment Griswold had expressed.

Black, Douglas, Brennan, and Stewart had each said something about the special function of the press in the democratic process and the importance of maintaining strong press freedoms. In contrast White wrote not a word about the importance or function of the press in a democracy. He wrote nothing about the possible significance of the Pentagon Papers in dispute to Congress or the public. Nor did he bother to define what legal standard he applied to the government's evidence when he concluded that the government had failed to carry its heavy evidentiary burden in this case. What he did say about the press was that it had no duty or obligation to publish any additional material.

▪ ▪ ▪ ▪ ▪

Justice Thurgood Marshall had been on the Court for four years by the time he sat down to write his concurring opinion in the Pentagon Papers case. He came to the Court after having served as solicitor general, a judge on the Second Circuit court of appeals, and the legal director of the NAACP Legal Defense Fund.

Although Marshall concurred in the per curiam opinion, which premised the Court's judgment on the failure of the government to satisfy the substantial evidentiary burden the First Amendment imposed upon it, his concurring opinion took an entirely different tack. Indeed, he did not mention the First Amendment except to claim that he thought the "ultimate issue" in the case was "more basic" (741).

Marshall's opinion was internally inconsistent. Marshall rejected the claim that the president had inherent authority to seek injunctive relief against the newspapers in these cases. He also refused to accept that the president's responsibilities for the national defense and international relations vested him with that authority. In explaining this position he essentially followed the separation of powers analysis that Alexander Bickel had strongly urged. Marshall did concede that the courts might grant an injunction to restrain newspaper publication to "enhance the already existing power of the Government to act." But he maintained that the solicitor general "does not even mention in his brief whether the Government considers there to be probable cause to believe a crime has been committed or whether there is a conspiracy to commit future crimes" (744).

Although Marshall concluded that the separation of powers doctrine barred the prior restraint actions, he lined up behind the suggestion that the newspapers might be criminally liable. In citing one provision of the espionage laws Marshall referred to Justice White's opinion for a "plausible construction" of how that provision might cover this case (745).

If Justice White's opinion expressed sympathy for the government in this case, Marshall's opinion expressed disdain. After stating that the Constitution "did not provide for government by injunction in which the courts and the Executive can 'make law' without regard to the action of Congress," Marshall penned a not so subtle criticism of the Nixon administration:

> It may be more convenient for the Executive if it need only convince a judge to prohibit conduct rather than to ask the Congress to pass a law and it may be more convenient to enforce a contempt order than to seek a criminal conviction in a jury trial. Moreover, it may be considered politically wise to get a court to share the responsibility for arresting those who the Executive has probable cause to believe are violating the law. But convenience and political considerations of the moment do not justify a basic departure from the principles of our system of government. (742–43)[22]

▪ ▪ ▪ ▪ ▪

These were the opinions of the six justices who composed the majority. Five of them believed the central issue raised by the cases was the scope of protection the First Amendment provided the press. Two of those, Black and Douglas, claimed that the First Amendment prohibited all prior restraints. Brennan contended that the First Amendment permitted prior restraints only when the government proved that disclosure would inevitably, directly, and immediately result in grave and irreparable harm. Stewart and White stated that a prior restraint could issue only when the government proved that the disclosure would cause direct, immediate, and irreparable damage to the nation. Given these substantive differences among the Justices, Stewart and White were the only ones who defined the common ground. Marshall, the sixth vote, was the only one in the majority who based his decision on separation of powers analysis.

None of the justices in the majority paid any heed to the government's claim that the newspapers possessed stolen government property or that an injunction was appropriate merely because the documents were classified. Nor did any of the justices in the majority accept the idea that judges were incompetent to assess national security dangers or that the Court should defer to the judgment of government officials because national security was involved. Finally, no fewer than four of the justices in the majority—Douglas, Stewart, White, and Marshall—raised the possible appropriateness of a criminal prosecution against the newspapers.

▪ ▪ ▪ ▪ ▪

John Harlan, a grandson of the first John Harlan who served on the Court at the turn of the century, was an old and close friend of Herbert Brownell, Eisenhower's first attorney general, who probably more than anyone else caused Eisenhower to nominate Harlan to the Court in 1953. By 1971 Harlan's health had deteriorated, and over the summer of 1971 he became so ill that he resigned from the Court in September, two days before Black died, and died himself three months later. Harlan's dissenting opinion in the Pentagon Papers cases was his last. He gave Justice Brennan the impression that he was as proud of it as he was of any opinion he had written.[23] Chief Justice Burger and Justice Blackmun joined Harlan's dissent, thus making it the major dissenting opinion in the case.

The surviving documents make it appear that Harlan may have begun to write his dissent before the oral argument on Saturday, and perhaps as early as Friday, the day the Court decided to hear the cases on an expedited basis. In either event it seems that Harlan assumed before the oral argument that the government would lose, and he began sketching out his opinion accordingly. The many drafts of his opinion that have survived indicate that he worked toward a final version slowly and carefully. By the end of printed draft four he had developed all his main points, which he had begun to polish and refine, a process he completed during the next three edits.

Harlan made two main points in his opinion. First, he complained that the Court had been "almost irresponsibly feverish in dealing with these cases." He described the litigation as a "frenzied train of events that" precluded due regard for the extraordinarily important and difficult questions raised by the cases. Harlan listed what he considered the critical questions, which he stated were "as important as any that have arisen during my time on the Court." He made it clear that he lacked the time to address these questions thoughtfully and thoroughly because the Court had allowed itself to be pressured by a "torrent of publicity" that clamored for a result all "in the name of the presumption against prior restraints created by the

First Amendment." He expressed dismay and disbelief that the "doctrine prohibiting prior restraints reaches to the point of preventing courts from maintaining the *status quo* long enough to act responsibly in matters of such national importance as those involved here" (753, 755, 759).

Second, Harlan stated his substantive "reasons in telescoped form" as to why he dissented (755). The essence of Harlan's view was that the separation of powers doctrine required the courts to defer to the executive branch in matters involving foreign affairs. His argument proceeded from the premise that the president was the "sole organ in the nation in its external affairs" (756). He claimed that because foreign policy encompassed questions that were "delicate, complex, and involved large elements of prophecy," the scope of judicial review over executive branch decisions "must be exceedingly narrow" (758). Harlan defined the narrowness as follows. The judiciary "must review the initial Executive determination to the point of satisfying itself that the subject matter of the dispute does lie within the proper compass of the President's foreign relations power." It may also insist that "the determination that disclosure of the subject matter would irreparably impair the national security be made by the head of the Executive Department concerned—here the Secretary of State or the Secretary of Defense—after actual personal consideration by that officer." Harlan insisted that the judiciary "may not properly go beyond these two inquiries and redetermine for itself the probable impact of disclosure on the national security" (757). Harlan said that the lower courts in these two cases did not give the executive branch "the deference owing to an administrative agency, much less that owing to a co-equal branch of the government operating within the field of its constitutional prerogative." Thus, he voted to remand both actions to the district courts for new hearings and to permit the government time to procure "from the Secretary of State or the Secretary of Defense or both an expression of their views on the issue of national security" (758).

Harlan's claim that the courts in these cases could inquire only into whether the disputed material involved foreign affairs and whether the Secretary of State or Defense had, after personal consideration, determined that disclosure would irreparably impair national security was no less than striking. If his claim had prevailed, it would have constituted a major shift in American law and would have meant, in practical terms, that the courts' injunctive power would have been largely at the disposal of the executive. Harlan's willingness to remake the presumption of American law in such an extreme way was at direct odds with the views of the six justices in the majority. Not one of those justices had even intimated that the courts should defer in the slightest to government claims that further disclosures would seriously harm national security, let alone defer to the extent that Harlan, Burger, and Blackmun urged.

Obviously, what divided these justices was the degree of trust the judiciary should place in government and in the press. Harlan trusted top government officials not to censor the press abusively and not to keep vital information from the public inappropriately. He distrusted the ability of the press and of the courts to decide what information could be made public without injuring the national security. In contrast the majority trusted the press and distrusted the government sufficiently to reach the opposite result.

▪ ▪ ▪ ▪ ▪

Chief Justice Burger wrote a separate opinion and joined Harlan's as well. Burger echoed Harlan's theme that the litigation had been conducted in "unseemly haste." The result was that "we do not know the facts of the case. No district judge knew all the facts. No court of appeals judge knew all the facts. No member of this Court knows all the facts." Burger thought that this haste was totally unwarranted, because the cases presented complex and critical issues involving press freedoms on the one hand and the "effective functioning of a complex modern government and specifically the effective exercise of certain constitutional powers of the Executive" on the other. Whatever weight one gave to the presumption against prior restraints (and he stated that there was "universal abhorrence" to prior restraints), there was no justification for forcing judges to decide such important matters without adequate time. The Court should resist pressure to churn out a quick decision and should instead insist on the time necessary to create a "judicial atmosphere conducive to thoughtful, reflective deliberation" (748, 749).

Burger placed the responsibility for this haste at the feet of the *New York Times*. It had the documents for "three to four months," during which time its expert analysts studied them, "presumably digesting them and preparing the material for publication" (750). Whatever the *Times* might say about the pressing "right of the public to know" once the government sued for a prior restraint, the *Times* obviously thought that the public's right to know could be deferred for "purposes it considered proper." During the months that the *Times* readied its news reports, it did not inform the government that it had the classified documents and did not seek from the government any objections it might have to the disclosure of the material. Burger speculated that if the *Times* had taken "such an approach—one that great newspapers have in the past practiced and stated editorially to be the duty of an honorable press"—the government might well have agreed to declassify much of the material, thus greatly narrowing the scope of dispute (750). But Burger went further. The *Times* should have contacted the Nixon administration and disclosed that it intended to publish classified documents, not just to narrow the dispute but because it had a "duty" to disclose. The Chief Justice wrote: "To me it is hardly believable that a newspaper long regarded as a great institution in American life would fail to perform one of the basic and simple duties of every citizen with respect to the discovery or possession of stolen property or secret government documents. That duty, I had thought—perhaps naively—was to report forthwith, to responsible public officers. This duty rests on taxi drivers, Justices and the *New York Times*" (751). Burger did not state whether he thought the *Times* had a duty to respect the views of the government officials and to refrain from disclosing any material the government objected to. But that was probably what he thought.

Burger stated that the *Times* had asserted that the First Amendment barred all prior restraints, which was obviously false. Neither the *Times* nor the *Post* took this position, and Burger must have known that, given the oral argument in the case, as well as the briefs that were filed. Why Burger would mischaracterize the legal position of the newspaper is not known.

Burger asserted that only judges who claimed that the First Amendment prohibited all prior restraints were "really in a position to act" in these cases (748). What Burger meant was that only Justices Black and Douglas could responsibly decide these cases hastily because they were the only justices for whom the facts of the case were unimportant. But that was no more true than his claim that the *Times* had argued for an absolute bar to all prior restraints. Justice Marshall decided he did not have to review the facts of the case, because he concluded that the separation of powers doctrine barred the lawsuit. Nor was Burger's statement a fair criticism of Justice Harlan's opinion, which he and Blackmun joined. Harlan surely complained about the frantic pace of the litigation and claimed that he needed much more time to decide the important and complex questions presented by the two cases. But Harlan needed precious little time to decide these cases. Harlan, Burger, and Blackmun were willing to enjoin the newspapers if they concluded that the disputed information related to national defense and foreign affairs and if the Secretary of State or Defense submitted an affidavit stating that its disclosure would injure the national security. Given this view, these three justices needed almost no time to grant the government an injunction in these cases. The documents clearly related to the national defense and international affairs. And if either cabinet secretary had submitted an affidavit, it would have taken but minutes to read and to decide whether it satisfied Harlan's requirements.

Burger's criticism might seem to apply to Justices Brennan, White, and Stewart. But even here Burger's criticism is misplaced. Each of these three justices concluded that the government had the burden of proving facts that warranted a prior restraint. That meant that they had to review only the documents pinpointed by the government. Because Griswold stated that the eleven items discussed in the sealed brief were probably the government's strongest evidence, he made the task of these three justices much easier than it would have otherwise been. Whether a justice could responsibly review those eleven items within the time limitations of these cases would vary from justice to justice. Surely Justices Brennan, Stewart, and White all thought they acted responsibly.

Although Burger complained about the need for more time to decide these cases and suggested that his colleagues in the majority were irresponsible for deciding the cases quickly, the real difference between Burger and the majority was not whether the cases could be decided quickly, but who should prevail.

Burger also stated that he "should add" that he was in "general agreement" with White's claims that the *Times* and the *Post* might have violated the federal criminal law barring the "communication or retention of documents or information relating to the national defense" (752). He did not explain why he "should add" such a comment at the end of his opinion. It was unnecessary, given the reasoning of his opinion. It would seem that Burger had only one purpose in disclosing his "general agreement," which was to inform the Justice Department that he too, along with several other of his colleagues on the Court, thought that the government's failure to secure injunctive relief presented no obstacle to a successful criminal prosecution of the *Times* and the *Post*.

In the very first paragraph of his opinion Burger wrote: "There is . . . little variation among the members of the Court in terms of resistance to prior restraints against publication" (748). He repeated such sentiments on radio and television a few days after the Court's decision became public when he claimed that the justices were more or less unanimous in the way they interpreted the First Amendment. These statements were ludicrous. Black and Douglas had said no prior restraint was permitted no matter what the government's evidence. Marshall had claimed that Congress had to authorize such relief before he would even consider it. Brennan, White, and Stewart contended that the government had a heavy burden that it did not satisfy. Harlan, Burger, and Blackmun maintained that the government could obtain a prior restraint once a court decided that the disputed information concerned defense and foreign affairs and the Secretary of State or Defense submitted an affidavit stating that he had personally reviewed the material and that disclosure would seriously harm the national security. How Burger could ignore these vastly different positions, only he could explain, and he never did.

▪ ▪ ▪ ▪ ▪

Justice Blackmun began his opinion with the statement that he was "in substantial accord" with White's discussion of the possible criminal liability of the newspapers (759). Obviously, some of the justices made a concerted effort to convince the Justice Department not to let the government's defeat in this case block a subsequent criminal prosecution.

Blackmun was openly hostile to the newspapers. The *Times* had "clandestinely" prepared its reports over a three-month period and was responsible for the "frenetic pace" of the litigation. The *Post*, using as an "excuse that it was trying to protect its source of information," had burdened the lower courts by refusing to turn over for government inspection the documents it possessed. Blackmun was aghast that the courts had permitted these cases to be litigated in such a frenzy. "It is not the way for federal courts to adjudicate, and to be required to adjudicate, issues that allegedly concern the Nation's vital welfare." Blackmun professed not to understand what it was about the public's right to know or the freedom of the press that could conceivably take precedence over deliberate weighing of the issues these cases presented. "The country would be none the worse off were the cases tried quickly, . . . but in the customary and properly deliberate manner," he wrote. "The most recent of the material, it is said, dates no later than 1968, already about three years ago, and the *Times* itself took three months to formulate its plan of procedure and, thus, deprived its public for that period" (759–62).

Blackmun's "final comment" made his opinion different from the others. Blackmun quoted that part of Judge Wilkey's dissenting opinion in the D.C. Circuit in which he claimed that the disputed material contained information which if disclosed "'could clearly result in great harm to the nation,' and he defined 'harm' to mean 'the death of soldiers, the destruction of alliances, the greatly increased difficulty of negotiation with our enemies, the inability of our diplomats to negotiate. . . .'" Blackmun stated that he shared Wilkey's concern and that he hoped the newspapers had not already caused such damage. Then he wrote: "If, however, damage has been done, and if, with the Court's action today, these newspapers proceed to publish the critical documents and there results therefrom 'the death of soldiers, the destruction of alliances, the greatly increased difficulty of negotiation with our enemies, the inability of diplomats to negotiate,' to which list I might add the factors of prolongation of the war and of further delay in the freeing of United States prisoners, the Nation's people will know where the responsibility for these sad consequences rests" (762–63). No other justice had pointed so forthrightly the finger of blame, if not shame, at the *Times* and the *Post*. Burger had come the closest when he criticized the *Times* for failing to uphold what he considered an elementary "duty" of citizenship, the duty to alert responsible government officials that there had been a massive security breach and to offer to let the government help decide what the *Times* could safely publish without injuring the national security. But even Burger had not gone so far as to invite the public to rebuke the newspapers. Blackmun was outraged and enraged by the newspapers. Although he stated that he hoped "these two newspapers will be fully aware of their ultimate responsibilities to the United States of America," he plainly did not believe they were.

■ ■ ■ ■ ■

The nine opinions defined a broad spectrum of views. They differed over whether the litigation was too fast, or not fast enough, or should not have occurred at all. They quarreled over the role of the press in the democratic process. They divided over whether the press was patriotic in publishing the Pentagon Papers, or whether the government had deceived the people in getting the nation into the Vietnam War. They exchanged charges over who was responsible for putting American lives in danger in Vietnam. They argued over whether the First Amendment prohibited all prior restraints or only some. They differed over the circumstances in which such restraints were appropriate. These disagreements were important and affected the outcome and the reasoning of each justice. But perhaps the most important, overarching difference was the question of deference. Harlan, Burger, and Blackmun claimed that courts should defer to the executive branch on national security matters; the majority rejected this.

PART SIX

The Aftermath

CHAPTER TWENTY-THREE

The Impact of the Disclosures

Once word of the Court's decision reached the *Times* and the *Post*, people were jubilant. The *Post*'s managing editor, Eugene Patterson, jumped on a desk and shouted: "We win, and so does the *New York Times*." Reporters applauded and paid off bets made while the case was pending. Benjamin Bradlee posted a memorandum to his staff: "There is just no way of saying how proud I am of this wonderful newspaper and everyone on it. The guts and energy and responsibility of everyone involved in this fight, and the sense that you all were involved, has impressed me more than anything in my life. You are beautiful."[1] In New York A. M. Rosenthal, Arthur Ochs Sulzberger, and James C. Goodale held a press conference to mark the occasion. Sulzberger said that his reaction to the decision was "one of complete joy and delight" and that he "never really doubted that this day would come and that we'd win." Rosenthal told those assembled that this was "a joyous day for the press and for American society." He added that he "thought this was the way it would turn out. I prayed it would."[2]

The *Times* and the *Post* immediately continued with their Pentagon Papers reports. Over the next five days the *Times* published six articles written by Hedrick Smith, Fox Butterfield, and E. W. Kenworthy. Although one of the reports focused on how decisions made by the Eisenhower administration undercut the Geneva Accords, the others reported on the Kennedy and Johnson administrations. Apparently, the *Times* made no changes in what it had planned to publish, even though several justices had urged the government to prosecute the newspapers for violating federal espionage laws. The *Post* continued its series for four days, with articles written by Murrey Marder, Chalmers M. Roberts, and Don Oberdorfer. They reported that Presidents Kennedy and Johnson feared that the United States might be forced out of Vietnam by pro-French South Vietnamese who favored a neutralist state; U.S. military officials wanted Kennedy to increase U.S. military involvement in Vietnam; the U.S. supported the coup against Diem.

In addition to these newspaper reports three different book versions of the Pentagon Papers were published in the wake of the Supreme Court's decision. None of these editions was complete at the time, and a complete version of the Pentagon Papers is still unavailable. The first book was the *Times*'s edition of its reports, published within a few weeks of the Court decision. Published by Bantam Books, the 677-page book contained photographs, as well as an introduction by Neil Sheehan and a foreword by Hedrick Smith, the *Times* editorials on the case, and the Supreme Court's decision. Thousands of copies of the book were sold within hours of its arrival at stores, and well over a million copies altogether. The Bantam edition presented only a relatively small portion of the entire study or even of the material the *Times* had. In fact Leslie Gelb, who directed the task force study, estimated that the *Times* version of the Pentagon history quoted "about 5% of the total."[3] Nevertheless, at least in the view of one academic commentator at the time, George McT. Kahin, the *Times*'s abbreviated version of the secret history "scooped off an impressive amount of the cream from the original study."[4]

In the early fall two other book versions of the Pentagon Papers were published. The government published *United States–Vietnam Relations, 1945–1967* in twelve volumes priced at $50. When the government put its 500 copies on sale on September 27, which was almost three months after the Supreme Court decision, or roughly twice as long as the government had said it would take to review and declassify the documents during the litigation, Daniel Ellsberg purchased one of them.[5]

Beacon Press published the third version. It was called *The Senator Gravel Edition of the Pentagon Papers: The Defense Department History of United States Decisionmaking on Vietnam.*[6] Mike Gravel was a Democrat senator from Alaska who had been elected in 1968, after serving two terms in the Alaska State House of Representatives, one of them as Speaker. He had received about 4,100 pages of manuscript during the litigation from one or more individuals whose identities are not known but who apparently received the material from Daniel Ellsberg.[7] He seemed to include in the Beacon edition all the material he had.[8] His edition was published in five volumes, the fifth devoted to essays on the war and the papers. Beacon optimistically published 20,000 copies but did not sell many of them, and most of these to libraries and scholars.[9]

The government and Senator Gravel's versions included more of the Pentagon study than the Bantam edition, although neither of these was complete. The government version contained material not in the Gravel edition, especially for the pre-1960 period. It also contained many more documents than either of the other two versions. However, the government edition did not include much of the material in the Gravel version. Items omitted from the government edition but contained in the Gravel edition included communications from foreign governments, especially during the 1954 Geneva Conference; narrative material and documents pertaining to the Diem coup d'etat and clandestine naval and air attacks on North Vietnam; descriptions of South Vietnamese politics and American involvement in South Vietnamese governmental processes; assertions of American willingness to use nuclear weapons if China intervened; description of the decision, in 1964, to initiate the bombing of Laos, with the knowledge and consent of the Laotian government; assessments of Soviet actions; descriptions of the use of Canadian and other intermediaries with the North Vietnamese; information on the presence and location of North Vietnamese units in South Vietnam; and acknowledgement that North Vietnamese and Viet Cong electronic communications had been intercepted.[10]

The most significant single portion of the Pentagon Papers not made public by these different editions was the four volumes tracing the diplomatic history of the war from 1964 to 1968. Ellsberg had not made these volumes available to Neil Sheehan or to Senator Gravel. When the government decided what portions of the secret history to declassify, it decided to keep from the public all four diplomatic volumes. Even district judge Gesell, who had ruled against the government in the *Post* case, refused to order the government to declassify the diplomatic volumes when two members of Congress, John E. Moss and Ogden R. Reid, and a professor of journalism, Paul Fisher, claimed they had a right to have the documents made public under the Freedom of Information Act.[11]

The first disclosures based on the diplomatic volumes appeared in a series of columns by Jack Anderson published between June 9 and June 23, 1972. In the view of one student of the subject Anderson revealed "some of the choicest tidbits from the volumes," recounting the Soviet Union's role as a would-be mediator between the United States and North Vietnam, disclosing that the British had intercepted telephone conversations between Leonid I. Brezhnev and Alexei Kosygin during Kosygin's

1967 visit to London. The taped conversations, which the British had given to the United States, revealed that Henry Kissinger had acted as a go-between on behalf of the United States with a contact in Paris while he was a private citizen in 1967. Although the Nixon administration accused Daniel Ellsberg and Anthony Russo of leaking the material to Anderson, Anderson never named them. Anderson was so irked by the government's insistence that only it could decide what information was fit to print that he gave the still-classified material to the *Times* and the *Post*, which gave it immediate front-page coverage.[12]

There were no other revelations until January 1973, by which time the criminal trial against Ellsberg and Russo had finally begun. The federal district judge in the case, William Matthew Byrne, Jr., had ordered that the evidence in the case, including the negotiating volumes, be placed in the clerk's office, where they were open to public scrutiny. Washington *Post* reporter Sanford Ungar reported on the availability of the documents and printed previously unpublished excerpts. At that point the status of the documents was certainly peculiar. The State Department insisted that the documents were classified and expressed outrage that Judge Byrne had allowed the public access to them. But neither the State Department nor the Justice Department was able to alter the judge's order. When Judge Byrne dismissed the charges against Ellsberg and Russo on May 11, 1973, the negotiating volumes were removed from the clerk's office and returned to the Department of State.

In March 1974 Morton Halperin, the former deputy assistant secretary of defense under McNamara who had supervised the task force that produced the secret Pentagon history initially, began a legal proceeding under the Freedom of Information Act to secure the release of the diplomatic documents. By October 1977 Halperin had succeeded in getting declassified all but about sixty pages of the sensitive volumes. In 1983, after years of remaining essentially unavailable to the public and unnoticed in government archives, the documents were collected and edited by Professor George C. Herring and published by the University of Texas.[13]

▪ ▪ ▪ ▪ ▪

Did the public disclosure of the Pentagon Papers seriously harm the national security as the government had maintained throughout the litigation? Did the disclosures bring an end to the war or prompt a formal investigation into war crimes as Ellsberg and Sheehan had hoped? Did they cause a significant reform of the classification system? Did they injure the standing of political leaders and former government officials? Did they undermine the public's trust in the government?

There is no evidence that the newspapers' publication of the Pentagon Papers, followed by the three books during the summer and fall of 1971, harmed the U.S. military, defense, intelligence, or international affairs interests. The government never made public a report that sought to establish that the publications injured these various interests. No cabinet member or other high-ranking official documented any injuries in the wake of the disclosures. President Nixon did not take the press to task for injuring the national defense following the Supreme Court decision. Nor did national security adviser Henry Kissinger or any of Nixon's top White House aides offer any evidence of harm to the nation's security once the Court set the press free to publish. No such evidence is offered in any of the autobiographies written by Nixon, Kissinger, Haldeman, Ehrlichman, Dean, Colson, Price, Klein, Safire, Liddy, or Kleindienst. Indeed, all the evidence is to the contrary.

For example, Erwin Griswold provided the most explicit evidence: "In hindsight, it is clear to me that no harm was done by publication of the Pentagon Papers."[14]

Other evidence is equally unequivocal, but less explicit. In his memoirs former President Nixon devoted eight pages to the Pentagon Papers. He made it crystal clear that he detested Ellsberg for leaking the papers, that he believed the *Times* had acted "irresponsibly" when it published the papers, and that he considered the government's legal attack against the newspapers to be fully justified. In trying to engender some sympathy for the government's position Nixon briefly reported that the *Times* publication created deep concern about possible harms within the National Security Agency, the State Department, and the CIA. He also claimed that the *Times* publication came at "a particularly sensitive time," by which he meant the China initiative, the SALT talks, and the negotiations going on in Paris with the North Vietnamese. Except for the undocumented and unexplained claim that the *Times* publication caused one secret contact to dry up almost immediately, Nixon makes no claim that the publication actually injured military, intelligence, defense, or international affairs interests. If there had been such injury, Nixon surely would have mentioned it, because it would have helped him establish his general point that only the government is in a position to know what classified information can and cannot be disclosed.[15]

Henry Kissinger's memoirs seem to make the same point. Kissinger wrote that the *Times* publication was a "profound shock" to the administration, and he "encouraged" Nixon to oppose the "wholesale theft and unauthorized disclosure." In his view the publication of the documents was "selective, one-sided, and clearly intended as a weapon of political warfare." "Our nightmare at that time," he wrote, "was that Peking might conclude our government was too unsteady, too harassed, and too insecure to be a useful partner." Furthermore, the administration was conducting secret talks with the North Vietnamese, it was at "an important point in the sensitive SALT talks," and it was at the "final stages of delicate Berlin negotiations." If the *Times* publication had resulted in injury, Kissinger would have used that evidence to bolster the administration's decision to sue the *Times*. But Kissinger makes no claim and offers no evidence.[16]

Other memoirs written by top officials within the Nixon administration also make no effort to try to establish that the disclosures actually resulted in harm to security interests. The inescapable conclusion would seem to be, as Griswold said, "no harm was done."

What does that mean? To begin with, it meant that the newspapers did not publish information that resulted in the death of soldiers. It also meant that the disclosures did not injure the negotiations to end the fighting in Vietnam or to secure the release of the POWs, at least in any way that anyone could identify. Nor did the reports compromise intelligence interests or undermine military and defense plans. Nor did the newspaper disclosures destroy the willingness of third parties to continue to act as go-betweens between the United States and others on delicate and important diplomatic matters. Last, it meant that the reports did not harm the China initiative, the SALT talks, the negotiations over Berlin, or any other important pending diplomatic matter. Thus, with regard to all these important matters the government had raised time and again during the litigation, no harm was done.

But if the disclosures did not seriously harm the national security, that does not mean there was no information within the Pentagon Papers that could have seriously harmed national security interests if it were disclosed. Many individuals with differing political affiliations, loyalties, and perspectives believed that the release of the four negotiating volumes in June 1971 would have had serious harmful consequences. It may be that their collective judgment was off the mark and that would-be go-betweens and diplomatic veterans accepted such disclosures as part of the territory. But we will never know for sure because the four volumes were not disclosed at that time. In addition Erwin Griswold strongly asserted in his sealed brief to the Supreme Court that the Pentagon Papers did contain information concerning intelligence activities. He claimed that the study described intelligence activities aimed at gaining information about the North Vietnamese, referred to covert CIA activities, and identified CIA agents. It may be that this information was not current as of June 1971 or that the impact of its disclosure would have been relatively minor. But we do not know that for sure, because this information has not been identified and disclosed.[17]

All in all, it seems indisputable that the Pentagon study contained information that could have seriously harmed the national security if disclosed. That does not mean, of course, that the threatened injury was of such a magnitude as to justify a prior restraint. In addition the information in question likely formed a small percentage of the overall study. Outside of the four negotiating volumes, the potentially damaging information seems to have composed no more than 5 percent, or less than 350 pages of the complete study.

■ ■ ■ ■ ■

At least some people—and the two most notable were Ellsberg and Sheehan—hoped that the disclosure of the Pentagon Papers would hasten the termination of the war. It seems improbable that those who held such hopes had any concrete notion of how the disclosures might inititate a series of events that would bring the war to an abrupt end. Perhaps they thought the disclosures would cause an enormous public outcry demanding the withdrawal of U.S. troops and the termination of funding for the war.

But such hopes were naive. The publication of the Pentagon Papers during the summer and fall of 1971 seems to have had no impact on the course of the war. Although copies of the Bantam edition sold in large numbers, there was no discernible public reaction. No large demonstrations occurred in the wake of the disclosures as they had following the military incursions into Cambodia in May 1970. Nor was there any concerted public pressure on Congress to cut off funding for the war. Members of Congress showed little or no interest in the Pentagon Papers once the administration made them available. This was true even though they had clamored for a copy of the study while the newspapers were under injunction, claiming that access to it was relevant to their legislative responsibilities.

Nevertheless, one aspect or another of the Pentagon Papers case may have had an impact on some congressional members. During the first six months of 1971 twenty-two House and Senate votes were taken on resolutions to restrict the president's authority to conduct the war or to fix a date for unilateral withdrawal. None passed. But on June 22, one week after the administration had restrained the *Times* and a few days after it had restrained the *Post*, the Senate, by a vote of 57–42, adopted Senator Mansfield's Sense of the Senate resolution that declared that "it is the policy of the U.S. to terminate at the earliest practicable date all military operations in Indochina and to provide for the prompt and early withdrawal of all U.S. forces not more than nine months after the bill's enactment subject to the release of American POW's."[18] Though Sense of the Senate Resolutions were not binding on the executive, the administration was concerned that the Senate had passed the resolution. The disclosures of the Pentagon Papers, the administration's effort to suppress the study, and the administration's delay in making it available to the Congress likely contributed to the adoption of this resolution, but the significance of the contribution cannot be determined.

Sheehan and Ellsberg had also thought that the disclosures might prompt an official investigation into possible war crimes committed by top American officials. A considerable amount of information was already public that many felt warranted a thorough war crimes investigation. Thus, the conviction of William Calley, Jr., for premeditated murder of twenty-two South Vietnam civilians was considered by some just the tip of the iceberg that needed to be uncovered. There was even a rumor circulating around Washington that after Robert McNamara read parts of the completed study, he told a friend when the *Times* broke the story of the Pentagon Papers: "You know, they could hang people for what's in there."[19] But not surprisingly, there was no official investigation.

It was not unthinkable that at least one consequence of the entire affair would be an important change in the classification system. The problem of overclassification was legendary and the difficulty of securing declassification was well known. Indeed, months before the Pentagon Papers affair arose, President Nixon had appointed Assistant Attorney General Rehnquist to head a committee to recommend reforms in the classification system. Yet, as much as the Pentagon Papers study became the dramatic first exhibit for anyone seeking to revamp the classification, the system was not reformed.

■ ■ ■ ■ ■

The disclosures stimulated a great deal of commentary about former government officials and active political leaders. By far, former President Johnson received the most attention. One of the *Times*'s first reports gave the impression that when Johnson ran as the so-called peace candidate against Senator Barry Goldwater for president in 1964, he was planning military action in Vietnam. Johnson's defenders immediately charged that the *Times* had misunderstood the memoranda that were part of the study, that the documents were merely contingency plans, and that the drawing up of such contingency plans was routine and did not mean they would be implemented. Leslie Gelb gave a fairly typical answer to this defense. In an article in *Life* magazine he wrote: "It is true that until the President decided, everything was a contingency. But there is a clear difference between routine contingency planning which rarely involves high officials and the contingency proposals of the President's principal advisers as cited in the Pentagon papers. All I can say is that one man's contingency plan is another man's course of action, and that these plans were implemented."[20]

The uproar over Johnson's conduct as a presidential candidate and as president—what he did and did not do, whether he lied or misled the public—greatly affected him. As the government's cases against the newspapers made their way through the courts Nixon tried to get Johnson to condemn the disclosures and to praise the Nixon administration's effort to enjoin the press as the only responsible course of action it could follow. At first Nixon was told that Johnson would make such a statement. As the days passed, however, Johnson refused to do so. Eventually, Nixon was told that Johnson believed the disclosures meant that the *Times* and the rest of the liberal media establishment were out to destroy his reputation and legacy as a public servant, that he was having difficulty being coherent, that he was unable to make an effective statement.[21]

The disclosures also brought intense scrutiny to Robert McNamara and what he did and did not do while he was Secretary of Defense and since he became president of the World Bank in 1968. Many in the press claimed that the Pentagon Papers established beyond doubt that McNamara had misled, if not lied to, the American public and Congress about the progress (or lack thereof) of U.S. military forces in winning the war in Vietnam. They also contended that the Pentagon Papers established that McNamara was indifferent to the human suffering the war caused, that he was an automaton who was devoid of feeling and some rudimentary sense of morality. Others insisted that the papers proved no such claims. They claimed that the top secret study proved that the public and the Congress had been fully informed of what the government did, what it thought of what it did, and what it was planning to do. They said that McNamara was honorable, patriotic, and courageous. McNamara made no public comment on the disclosures and refused to discuss his reaction to them. But they deeply affected him, so much so that a recent biographer concluded that the *Times* reports were "traumatic" for him.[22]

As for the others—McGeorge Bundy, Walt Rostow, and Dean Rusk, to name only a few of the most prominent members of Johnson's administration—it is difficult to imagine that the publicity over the Pentagon Papers left them untouched. Perhaps they were annoyed, or even outraged, that McNamara would have commissioned such a study or that he would have done so without at least notifying them of the study or assuring that they had received a copy. Or perhaps they were tormented by the claims that the documents indicated they had lied or misled the public, or that they were arrogant, naive, or that they were ill informed about Indochina. There are no reports on how the disclosures affected them, but it seems highly unlikely that the controversy left them unaffected.

When it comes to the impact of the disclosures on the political fortunes of Hubert H. Humphrey, matters are less speculative. Humphrey had a long and illustrious career in the Senate before being elected as Johnson's vice-presidential candidate in 1964. After Johnson announced he would not seek the Democratic party nomination in February 1968 Humphrey won the nomination but narrowly lost the election to Nixon in November. Humphrey was hoping to gain—or at least considering seeking—the 1972 Democratic party nomination and make another run for the presidency. But the disclosures of the Pentagon Papers placed the Johnson administration in a highly critical light, and Humphrey's political fortunes were directly harmed. As news commentators began to assess who won and who lost as a result of the disclosures, Humphrey was considered one of the bigger political losers.

▪ ▪ ▪ ▪ ▪

The disclosures also affected the debate in the press over the war. The single most dominant theme during these frantic days just before and weeks immediately after the Supreme Court decision was whether the documents proved that prior administrations, especially the Johnson administration, had deceived the public about America's entanglement in Vietnam. The debate had many sides. The most prominent view was that the papers established beyond doubt that the Johnson administration had misled Congress and the nation about its plans for Vietnam both during the 1964 election and after. This claim was made time and again and in innumerable forums. Johnson misled. Johnson lied. His top aides, McNamara, Rusk, and Rostow, did the same. They duped the public into supporting the war. This view was taken one step further by some who claimed that the lasting impact of the documents would be to undermine the public's trust in its national leaders. This loss of confidence not only threatened the political fortunes of those involved, but it posed a threat to the democratic process.

Two replies surfaced to these charges. One was that there was nothing new in the Pentagon Papers—it was all "ancient history." There was some truth to this position. News reports, for example, from the critical years did include statements by public officials that seem descriptive of what the government was planning, even if they might be considered vague.

But whether the risks, dangers, and tragedies that war in Vietnam entailed should have been understood was not the point. The point was they were not—at least many people did not think so as they reflected on the war years from the perspective of 1971. As a result a large portion of the public felt in 1971 that the consequences of America's military involvement in Vietnam had taken them by surprise, and they were caught unaware because successive administrations had deliberately misled them with regard to Vietnam. The Pentagon Papers were thought to validate this viewpoint.

The second reply was more complicated than the first. It assumed that there were differences between what Johnson administration officials had said during the critical years and what the secret Pentagon documents indicated. But these differences were characterized as insignificant because knowledgeable reporters or legislators could have bridged them. That position implied that the full story of what the government was planning and considering was discoverable by any thoughtful and intelligent person. According to this view the gap between what had been explicitly stated by government officials and the Pentagon Papers was required by legitimate concerns and that a more frank and complete statement of the intentions of the Johnson administration would have run the risk of causing the Soviet Union or China to become directly involved in the struggle.

The flaw with these arguments was obvious. Few people are reporters or members of Congress able to smoke out the truth from public officials who did not wish to lie but who did not wish to tell the whole story.

The ferocious exchange over whether the Johnson administration had deceived the public about its plans for Vietnam was not the only debate sparked by the secret history. The disclosures of the Pentagon Papers penetrated into a broader and more complicated question of how it came to be that the United States was engaged in fighting a land war in Asia.

By the summer of 1971 the U.S. military involvement in Vietnam was widely characterized as a product of good faith but mistaken judgments, the blundering of government officials who were caught unsuspecting by the hidden dangers lurking underneath what otherwise seemed like the straightforward political, economic, and military surfaces of Vietnam. The most common metaphor used in explaining what happened to the United States was that it had walked into a quagmire. David Halberstam perhaps gave more currency than anyone else to this interpretation when he wrote *The Making of a Quagmire*, published in 1964. Halberstam claimed that the "American mission in Vietnam started out with the highest hopes and idealism. It failed for a number of reasons: not for lack of its own good intentions, not for the lack of long working hours and patience (too much patience on occasion), but because the legacy of mistakes was too large, because the die had been cast long, long ago, because the United States was unable to face reality in Indochina, and because we responded with cliches to desperately complicated and serious challenges."[23] But Halberstam urged steadfastness. Immediate disengagement was not a realistic alternative, since America was now "caught in a quagmire," and "we would dishonor ourselves and our allies by pulling out."[24]

In *The Limits of Intervention*, an influential book published late in 1969, Townsend Hoopes, who had served in the Pentagon during the Johnson administration, echoed the quagmire thesis. In recalling the late summer of 1965 Hoopes wrote: "But when the mists of summer confusion lifted, there were 170,000 U.S. troops in Vietnam, U.S. air forces were bombing the North with mounting intensity, and the enemy showed no sign of surrender or defeat. There was the President and there was the country—waist-deep in the Big Muddy. And the integrity, the trust, the credibility without which the leadership of great democratic nations cannot govern were all gravely strained by a pattern of actions that seemed an inextricable blend of high-mindedness, inadvertence, and either massive self-delusion or calculated deceit."[25]

Arthur M. Schlesinger, Jr., the prominent historian and former Kennedy aide, perhaps gave the quagmire thesis its most quoted expression in *The Bitter Heritage: Vietnam and American Diplomacy, 1941–1966*, published in 1967:

> "And so the policy of 'one more step' lured the United States deeper and deeper into the morass. In retrospect, Vietnam is a triumph of the politics of inadvertence. We have achieved our present entanglement, not after due and deliberate consideration, but through a series of small decisions. . . . Each step in the deepening of the American commitment was reasonably regarded at the time as the last that would be necessary. Yet, in retrospect, each step led only to the next, until we find ourselves entrapped today in that nightmare of American strategists, a land war in Asia—a war which no President, including President Johnson, desired or intended."[26]

It was against this position that the Pentagon Papers ricocheted when it became public. Leslie Gelb, the former task force director of the study, took the lead in arguing that the Pentagon Papers totally undermined the quagmire thesis and provided irrefutable evidence for a different thesis. One week after the *Times* published its first installment of the Pentagon Papers and a full ten days before the Supreme Court decision, Gelb wrote a guest column that was published in the *Washington Post* in which he first expressed views that he repeated many times over during the next several years. "Our Presidents did not stumble step by step into Vietnam, unaware of the quagmire. U.S. involvement did not stem from a failure to foresee consequences. Vietnam was indeed a quagmire, but most of our leaders knew it."[27]

Gelb argued that three propositions explained why the United States "became involved in Vietnam, why the process was gradual, and what the real expectations of our leaders were." First, America's involvement was "not mainly or mostly a story of step by step, inadvertent descent into unforeseen quicksand." Instead, those who led the United States into Vietnam "did so with their eyes open, knowing why, and believing they had the will to succeed." Gelb contended that our leaders since the end of World War II viewed Vietnam as "a vital factor in alliance politics, U.S.–Soviet–Chinese relations, and deterrence." They also were fearful of the domestic political reaction if Vietnam was "lost" to communism. Having for years employed "strong generalized, ideological rhetoric" to strengthen public support for the use of force to restrain the spread of communism, having "shed American blood in Korea" to contain communism, and having maintained large numbers of American troops in Europe for years at great expense, they had little choice but to take a stand against communism in Vietnam.[28]

Second, Gelb argued that the presidents "were never actually seeking a military victory in Vietnam. They were doing only what they thought was minimally necessary at each stage to keep Indochina, and later South Vietnam, out of Communist hands." Gelb claimed that the "tactic makes consummate sense when it is believed that nothing will fully work or that the costs of a 'winning' move would be too high," which he asserted was the case in Vietnam. "This decision-making tactic explains why the U.S. involvement in Vietnam was gradual and step by step."[29]

Finally, Gelb maintained that the presidents and "most of their lieutenants were not deluded by optimistic reports of progress and did not proceed on the basis of wishful thinking about winning a military victory in South Vietnam." Their strategy was not to win, not to quit, but to "persevere in the hope that their will to continue—if not the practical effects of their actions—would cause the Communists to relent."[30]

Gelb was not alone in insisting upon the fundamental invalidity of the quagmire thesis. Daniel Ellsberg wrote an article for *Public Policy*, the journal of the John F. Kennedy School of Government, in which he maintained that a succession of American presidents, fully understanding that there was a "high probability that U.S. troops would end up fighting in

South Vietnam, and U.S. planes bombing throughout Indochina," not only "failed to resist" this future but "knowingly cooperated with and prepared" it. Instead of stumbling unwittingly into a quagmire, American leaders trooped with their eyes open into what they properly understood to be "quicksand." In short, as Ellsberg wrote: "our Presidents and most of those who influenced their decisions did not stumble step-by-step into Vietnam, unaware of the quagmire. U.S. involvement did not stem from a failure to foresee consequences."[31]

The argument was echoed in the daily press. Max Frankel wrote in the *Times* in early July: "this was not a war into which the United States stumbled blindly, step by step, on the basis of wrong intelligence or military advice that just a few more soldiers or a few more air raids would turn the tide." Murrey Marder struck a similar note in the *Washington Post*: "The American march into the war in Indochina was neither the result of carelessness nor absentmindedness, but of purposefulness, the documents confirm." Writing in the *Minneapolis Tribune*, Charles Bailey agreed: "The United States did not as some opponents of the war have charged 'blunder' into its Vietnam involvement. On the contrary, the documents show that the highest officials were constantly aware that steps they were taking could lead to much greater involvement."[32]

In the fall of 1971 Arthur Schlesinger, Jr., picked up the cudgel and responded to Gelb's thesis that "the system worked."[33] Schlesinger wrote that in preparing his article he read the Bantam edition of the Pentagon Papers, as opposed to the government's twelve-volume edition or the Gravel edition, and that in his view these materials totally failed to support the position put forth by Gelb, Ellsberg, Frankel, Marder, and Bailey. Instead, he was convinced that the "Pentagon Papers . . . reinforced the view that the system did *not* work, that it failed wretchedly, and that the Vietnam adventure was marked much more by ignorance, misjudgment, and muddle than by foresight, awareness, and calculation." Schlesinger concluded his argument with this summation: "I cannot find persuasive evidence that our generals, diplomats, and Presidents were all this sagacious and farsighted that they heard how hopeless things were, agreed with what they heard, and then 'knowingly' defied prescient warnings in order to lurch ahead into what they *knew* was inevitable disaster."[34]

Gelb promptly replied to Schlesinger. Although he drew some distinctions between his views and Ellsberg's, he thought they were trying to pursue "similar issues," especially in contrast to Schlesinger's "onslaught against the anti-quagmire group."[35] Gelb first restated his position—that our leaders persisted in Vietnam because they did not believe that they had an "acceptable alternative," that they were doing what they believed was minimally necessary to keep Vietnam noncommunist, that they hoped their strategy would cause the communists to relent. He then accused Schlesinger of conceding that ignorance and misjudgment did not explain entirely how the United States ended up fighting a land war in Vietnam. But having claimed that Schlesinger had modified his position, Gelb still characterized Schlesinger as a proponent of the "quagmire" thesis. Gelb speculated that Schlesinger was unable to abandon the quagmire thesis even in light of what Gelb considered the overwhelming evidence embodied in the Pentagon Papers because of Schlesinger's belief that our presidents and their top aides espoused a "particular brand of pragmatism" that insisted that policies worked. If they knew in advance that a policy was unworkable, it was inconceivable to Schlesinger, Gelb implied, that they would adopt and continue to implement such policies. Hence, as Gelb saw it, the quagmire thesis was the only way that allowed Schlesinger, given his premises about national leaders, to make sense of how and why American leaders led the nation into the devastating and destructive Vietnam War.

Gelb offered his own modified position. The essence of the debate over how and why the United States became involved in Vietnam was not over whether the "system worked" but over values—why it was important not to lose Vietnam. Gelb continued: "Vietnam is what happened when our leaders calculated essentially the imagined costs of losing, and not the real costs of 'winning.' Vietnam is what happened when our values, international and domestic, were pushed to their logical extreme."[36] Presumably, Gelb was now claiming that whether the United States went into Vietnam aware or unaware of the costs of intervention was less important than comprehending the values that caused the intervention in the first place.

Schlesinger replied yet one more time. Although he might have agreed that the debate over the quagmire thesis was less important than an inquiry into the values that led to intervention, Schlesinger now took a different tack. Instead of merely insisting that the quagmire thesis remained standing even after Gelb's attack, Schlesinger argued that Gelb's view was entirely compatible with it. Schlesinger pointed out that Gelb conceded that government leaders might have implemented a policy of increasing intervention full of illusions, misinformation, and unfounded optimism, because the intelligence reports on which decisions were made "were sufficiently ambiguous that those who wanted to escalate also found grist for their mill." Schlesinger also implied that Gelb now accepted the possibility that national leaders might have believed that each step might well be the last when Gelb admitted that he "could well be wrong" that the presidents did not actually seek military victory in Vietnam. In other words they might have been seeking military victory and they might have believed that victory was at the end of the next step. Schlesinger did concede, however, Gelb's point that he was tied to the quagmire thesis in part because he believed that government leaders wanted policies that worked: "I will readily concede that the probability a policy won't work has always seemed to me a good initial argument against it."[37]

▪ ▪ ▪ ▪ ▪

The debate over the meaning of the Pentagon Papers continued through the summer and fall of 1971. Not surprisingly, there was no ultimate resolution—no general consensus reached. The issues were too important, the consequences too significant, for the various sides to change their minds quickly in the heat of the discussion. Nonetheless, the debate quieted, once the positions were fully expressed.

The deep substantive divisions over the integrity of the previous several administrations and the soundness of American foreign policy would again and again be the subject of spirited public debate before the fighting in Vietnam ended. But the Pentagon Papers ceased being the spark for the flame.

CHAPTER TWENTY-FOUR

Criminal Investigations and Impeachable Offenses

The day after the Supreme Court announced its decision, Attorney General John Mitchell stated that the government "was continuing to investigate the leaking of the Pentagon Papers" and "promised to prosecute anyone who had broken the law."[1] In fact the government had already indicted Daniel Ellsberg, having begun proceedings a few days before the Supreme Court rendered its decision in the cases for the *Times* and the *Post*. Mitchell's announcement signaled not only a vigorous prosecution against Ellsberg but a serious investigation of anyone associated with the disclosure of the Pentagon Papers.

Immediately following Mitchell's announcement, FBI investigators intensified their investigation of Ellsberg. Agents went as far as Morocco and South Vietnam in search of information. The most intensive searches, however, took place in Cambridge, Massachusetts, where the agents investigated Ellsberg's life-style, personality, and motives, as well as the identity of people who may have aided him in distributing the classified documents. Agents also focused on Neil and Susan Sheehan, questioned their friends and neighbors, and subpoenaed their bank account records.

The government used a Boston grand jury to try to identify the individuals who helped Ellsberg photocopy and distribute the Pentagon Papers and who received the classified documents at each newspaper. By and large, this investigation failed, because the main witnesses resisted testifying before the grand jury. Sam Poplin, a Harvard professor and friend of the Ellsbergs, claimed that the subpoena violated his First Amendment rights. Ralph Stavins of the Institute for Policy Studies, Richard Falk of Princeton University, and Noam Chomsky of MIT were subpoenaed and eventually excused from testifying because the government failed to satisfactorily answer the question as to whether the government had intercepted any telephone conversations of the potential witnesses. David Halberstam's testimony was postponed indefinitely, and K. Dun Gifford, a legislative aide to Senator Edward Kennedy, appeared before the grand jury but refused to answer any questions.[2]

Government lawyers spent considerable energy trying to get Leonard Rodberg to testify. Rodberg had been a researcher at the Institute for Policy Studies until he joined Senator Gravel's staff just before Gravel read the Pentagon Papers into the *Congressional Record* in June. Rodberg moved to quash the subpoena on First Amendment grounds. Senator Gravel supported him and moved to quash the subpoena, claiming that the subpoena interfered with his relations with his staff and thus infringed upon his constitutionally based speech and debate-clause privilege.[3]

The speech and debate clause immunizes members of Congress and to some extent members of their staffs from being forced into court to explain actions they have taken in their official capacity as a member of Congress. Late in the fall of 1971, district judge W. Arthur Garrity, Jr., ruled that the speech and debate clause privilege barred the government from subpoenaing Senator Gravel to testify before the grand jury, which it had threatened to do, and prohibited the government from inquiring into the propriety of Gravel's public disclosure of the Pentagon Papers in June. However, Garrity ruled that Rodberg could be questioned about anything he did prior to joining Gravel's staff and about his efforts on Gravel's behalf to arrange for publication of the Pentagon Papers. Gravel appealed to the First Circuit court, which enjoined further proceedings of the grand jury for a month and then restricted its inquiry. In January the court decided that Gravel's speech and debate-clause privilege covered some of Rodberg's actions as a staff member, but not his effort to locate a publisher for the Pentagon Papers. At that point Gravel appealed to the Supreme Court, which decided in June 1972 that the privilege covered only legislative acts and did not bar investigation of alleged arrangements for private publication of the Pentagon Papers. Even though the government prevailed in the Supreme Court, the legal struggle to force Rodberg to testify took so long and so much energy that it undermined the Boston grand jury's investigation into the Pentagon Papers affair.[4]

Government investigators also focused on Beacon Press's plan to publish Senator Gravel's version of the Pentagon Papers. In September 1971 two investigators, who identified themselves as Pentagon officials, visited the Boston offices of Beacon Press shortly before it was scheduled to publish the papers. They told Beacon Press representatives that the Gravel edition was more extensive than the version the newspapers had and might contain information injurious to the national security. They explained that the government wanted to prepare itself for the repercussions that would follow publication and requested that the press permit three military specialists to review the material. Beacon Press agreed to a second meeting, but Fred Buzhardt, the Pentagon's general counsel, canceled it minutes before it was scheduled to begin. A few months later the government subpoenaed all the bank records of the Unitarian-Universalist Association in Boston, which supported Beacon Press. The church moved to quash the subpoena, claiming that it violated its constitutionally protected right to freedom of religion. Before the court could decide the motion the government withdrew the subpoena.[5]

Government investigators also contacted MIT Press. During the summer Leonard Rodberg had discussed with Howard R. Webber, director of the press, the possibility of publishing Gravel's version of the study. Although Webber recommended publication to the press's editorial board, the board turned the project down. Sometime thereafter, Webber met with Pentagon officials to discuss the manuscript Rodberg had shown him.[6] In the end the Boston grand jury produced no indictments.

▪ ▪ ▪ ▪ ▪

A few days before the Supreme Court's decision was announced on June 30, 1971, a grand jury sitting in Los Angeles indicted Ellsberg for violating the Federal Espionage Act and for theft of government property. After that much of the grand jury's investigation was frustrated by Anthony Russo.[7] The government insisted that Russo testify before the grand jury about what he knew of the photocopying of the top secret documents. Although the government offered him full immunity from prosecution, Russo refused to testify. He was cited for contempt and imprisoned. After seven weeks Russo agreed to testify if the government provided him with a transcript of his testimony. Russo complied with the subpoena two weeks later and appeared at the courthouse. The government lawyer then informed him that he would not be given a copy of the transcript. At that point Russo refused to enter the grand jury room. A month later the judge ruled that the witness was entitled to a transcript of his testimony, since he was at liberty to make public what he said in the grand jury room, and that a copy of the transcript would assure accuracy. The government did not appeal the ruling and did not recall Russo.[8]

In December 1971 the government revised its indictment against Ellsberg, charging him with fifteen counts of conspiracy, conversion of government property, and espionage. Anthony Russo was named as a co-conspirator in the indictment. In July 1972 a trial jury was already empaneled in the case when the prosecutors disclosed that the government had an "interception"—a wiretap—of a conversation between one of the defendants, their lawyers, or their consultants. District judge Byrne, a former prosecutor, refused to stop the proceedings for a hearing on the intercept, as did the court of appeals for the Ninth Circuit. However, Supreme Court Justice William O. Douglas, who had jurisdiction over emergency appeals in the Ninth Circuit, agreed to hear arguments on the legal questions raised by the intercept. Douglas stopped the criminal trial until the Supreme Court could review the matter when the Court reconvened in the fall of 1972. Judge Byrne excused the jury until October. It was not until November that the Supreme Court decided not to hear the defense's argument on the interception. At that time Judge Byrne decided that a new jury should be empaneled.[9] The trial began in January 1973; the testimony dragged on for months.

On April 26, 1973, the prosecutors told Judge Byrne that they had learned that Howard Hunt and G. Gordon Liddy, two government employees, had participated in a burglary of the offices of Doctor Lewis Fielding, Daniel Ellsberg's psychiatrist, in hopes of gaining information about Ellsberg that would be useful to the prosecution. Although the defense lawyers vigorously claimed that this warranted dismissal of the charges, Byrne refused. Four days later, the *Washington Star-News* reported that Judge Byrne had met with President Nixon and John Ehrlichman several weeks earlier at Nixon's San Clemente home to discuss the possibility of Byrne becoming the director of the FBI. It also reported that two days after the first meeting, Byrne met with Ehrlichman alone in Santa Monica to have another conversation about becoming FBI director. The implication was clear: Nixon was trying to influence Byrne's conduct of the trial by dangling the FBI directorship in front of him, a position he was thought to covet. Even with this disclosure, Byrne did not declare a mistrial and dismiss the charges. But when the prosecutor announced that they had just learned that Ellsberg had been overheard in a wiretap as far back as 1969–70, Byrne finally relented and granted the defendant's motion.[10]

■ ■ ■ ■ ■

In the end the government's unsuccessful prosecution of Ellsberg and Russo was its only criminal action stemming from the Pentagon Papers affair. It is not known for certain why there were not more prosecutions, especially against the *Times* and the *Post*, given that more than a majority of the Supreme Court justices had indicated that the government might mount a successful criminal prosecution, even though the Court had denied it the injunction it sought. John Mitchell thought the government had no chance of winning a criminal prosecution against the press once it lost the civil actions.[11] That was also the position Griswold took during the oral argument before the Supreme Court. Perhaps that is all there was to the decision not to pursue the newspapers. But it may also be that the Nixon administration decided not to prosecute the newspapers in order to avoid a confrontation with the news media during Nixon's reelection bid.

Why the government did not prosecute others who may have helped Ellsberg photocopy and distribute the Pentagon Papers is also unclear. The government's investigation may not have turned up enough evidence to mount a successful prosecution. But there might have been other explanations. Nixon and Mitchell may have decided that what they most wanted out of the investigation was to create issues that divided Democrats and intimidated government officials from improperly disclosing documents.

The government's investigation into the Pentagon Papers only marginally fulfilled Nixon's hopes. It did not put an end to leaks that infuriated him. But the spectacle of a draining criminal prosecution must have caused some would-be leakers to have second thoughts before disclosing documents. The criminal prosecution of Ellsberg did keep the whole affair in the public's eye during the 1972 presidential election. But whatever role the Pentagon Papers played in the 1972 election seems to have been minimal.

■ ■ ■ ■ ■

For the Nixon administration the unintended and unforeseen consequences of the Pentagon Papers were far more serious and significant than the immediate failures of the criminal investigation. The intense involvement of Nixon and his aides in the affair created a tense and angry mood within the White House. Raymond Price, Nixon's head speech writer, who was thought of as a moderating influence on policy questions, tactics, and strategy, wrote that "Nixon was in a ferocious mood over the Pentagon Papers leak" and was "serious—deadly serious" about containing the leak and punishing the leaker.[12]

There is much evidence to support a claim that an important shift in White House attitudes occurred at the time. It comes, for the most part, from autobiographies and reflections of White House insiders. Charles Colson, Nixon's close political adviser, wrote in his autobiography that the Nixon presidency passed a "crossroads of sorts" during the Pentagon Papers episode.[13] Colson reaffirmed this view at a conference years later: as a result of the Pentagon Papers episode "the ground rules [within the White House] began to change." Egil "Bud" Krogh, a lawyer who worked for John Ehrlichman, reached a similar conclusion. He thought that the Pentagon Papers was "probably the seminal event" that caused the downfall of the administration.[14] Haldeman was of a similar mind: Nixon "lost" his head during these days.[15] Herb Klein agreed: "The prior-restraint action united friends and foes of the administration and the President in one common cause to protect press rights and fight administration efforts. It widened the press–government gap. . . . The process undermined the President at every step of the way. Anger influenced judgments which should have been made unemotionally."[16] William Safire, one of Nixon's speech writers, concurred: "The Pentagon Papers case led him [Nixon] into an overreaction that led to his most fundamental mistakes." Safire argued: "For the second time, a hatred of the press—a need to stop the leaks and to teach the leakers a lesson—caused Nixon to go over the brink, to lose all sense of balance, to defend his privacy at the expense of everyone else's right to privacy, and to create the climate that led to Watergate."[17]

Although the shifts generated by the Pentagon Papers case were not perceived at the time by those within the White House, the shifts resulted in immediate decisions and actions that substantially contributed to Nixon's downfall. Nixon wanted quick aggressive action taken against those responsible for leaking the Pentagon Papers. He was determined that the government prosecute Ellsberg, whom he believed "had acted as part of a conspiracy" and who "was successfully using the press, television talk shows, and antiwar rallies to promote the concept of unlawful dissent." Although Nixon wanted the FBI to investigate the matter vigorously, he was told that J. Edgar Hoover "was dragging his feet and treating the case on merely a medium-priority basis." Nixon concluded, as he wrote in his autobiography, that Hoover

> had assigned no special task forces and no extra manpower to it. Hoover evidently felt that the media would automatically make Ellsberg look like a martyr, and the FBI like the "heavy," if it pushed the case vigorously. Mitchell had been told that Hoover was sensitive about his personal friendship with Ellsberg's father-in-law [Louis Marx, a toy manufacturer, who apparently gave Hoover toys each Christmas so that he could give them away]. Finally, other agencies, prin-

> cipally the Defense Department, were conducting simultaneous investigations, and Hoover strongly resisted sharing his territory with anyone.[18]

Nixon's bland words concealed his rage. Nixon had wanted to replace Hoover for some time, but he felt hamstrung because he feared that Hoover could damage him politically by leaking information about him. In July Nixon authorized the establishment of an investigative unit within the White House to get around Hoover.[19] Nixon told Ehrlichman: "'If we can't get anyone in this damn government to do something about the problem that may be the most serious one we have, then, by God, we'll do it ourselves. I want you to set up a little group right here in the White House. Have them get off their tails and find out what's going on and figure out how to stop it.'"[20]

Nixon wanted the unit to investigate Ellsberg, to find out "everything" it could about his "background, his motives, and his co-conspirators, if they existed." Nixon also wanted the unit to dig up information that could be used as "ammunition" against Democrats who had been "architects of our Vietnam involvement [and who were trying] to make me pay for the war politically." Nixon wanted "a good political operative who could sift through the Pentagon Papers as well as State and Defense Department files and get us all the facts on the Bay of Pigs, the Diem assassination, and Johnson's 1968 bombing halt. We were heading into an election year, in which the Vietnam War was almost certainly going to be the biggest issue. I wanted ammunition against the antiwar critics, many of whom were the same men who, under Kennedy and Johnson, had led us into the Vietnam morass in the first place."[21]

On July 17, 1971, Nixon installed Egil Krogh, a young lawyer working for Ehrlichman on domestic matters, to direct the unit. Krogh was joined by David Young, another young lawyer and Kissinger aide, Howard Hunt, a former CIA agent, and G. Gordon Liddy, a former FBI agent. Within a few weeks of getting organized Young hung a sign on the front door of Room 16 in the basement of the Executive Office Building which housed the Special Investigations Unit. The sign read "Plumbers Unit," a name that became popular once the unit and its activities became public knowledge.[22]

Six days later the *New York Times* reported on the United States's formal position at the SALT talks in Helsinki, and Nixon's fury was once again ignited by an unwanted leak. Nixon met with Krogh and "tried to motivate" him in the "strongest terms." Nixon told him: "We're not going to allow it. We just aren't going to allow it."[23] Krogh left the meeting "shaken" and as Liddy recounted: "The President . . . was absolutely furious, as was Henry Kissinger, about the 'deliberate' leaks. Krogh and Young were to orchestrate a government-wide search to find the leakers and root them out. It had the 'absolutely highest priority.' Daniel Ellsberg, who had been made a hero by the press, was now the symbolic personification of all the leakers. He had been indicted on 28 June, and it was mandatory that the prosecution succeed. Krogh, Young, and I were to supervise and coordinate all this for the White House. I had my marching orders."[24]

Before the summer had passed Ehrlichman had approved a plan to break into Dr. Fielding's office. The purpose of the burglary, as Nixon has related it, was to "get information from his files on his motivation, his further intentions, and any possible co-conspirators."[25] Ehrlichman has maintained that Nixon approved of the break-in; Nixon concedes that he may have approved of it but that he does not remember.[26] In September Hunt and Liddy participated in the break-in, located Ellsberg's file, but found no information to help the prosecutors or the public relations campaign.[27]

▪ ▪ ▪ ▪ ▪

Other incidents also revealed the powerful impact of the Pentagon Papers affair on the Nixon administration. For example, it was only after the Supreme Court denied the government an injunction that the idea of firebombing the Brookings Institution was discussed within the White House. Nixon had received a report that some classified documents pertaining to the Nixon years were in the Brookings safe. Nixon was beside himself: "In the midst of a war and with our secrets being spilled through printing presses all over the world, top secret government reports were out of reach in the hands of a private think tank largely staffed with antiwar Democrats. It seemed absurd. I could not accept that we had lost so much control over the workings of the government we had been elected to run—I saw absolutely no reason for that report to be at Brookings, and I said I wanted it back right now—even if it meant having to get it surreptitiously."[28] If Nixon wanted action, Colson responded. He brought Liddy into the planning, and Liddy hatched a plan:

> Daniel Ellsberg had been associated in the past with Morton Halperin and the Brookings Institution and, according to Colson as relayed by Hunt, either or both of them were believed to be using Brookings for storage of substantial additional amounts of classified documents at least as sensitive, if not more so, than the Pentagon Papers. Further, the Brookings security vault might have evidence shedding light on the identity of any of Ellsberg's criminal associates in

> the purloining of Top Secret Defense files; whether Paul Warnke and Leslie Gelb were among them; and whoever delivered the classified documents to the Soviet Embassy. Could we get into the vault, say, by using a fire as a diversion, and retrieve the material? . . .
>
> We devised a plan that entailed buying a used but late-model fire engine of the kind used by the District of Columbia fire department and marking it appropriately; uniforms for a squad of Cubans and their training so their performance would be believable. Thereafter, Brookings would be firebombed by use of a delay mechanism timed to go off at night so as not to endanger lives needlessly. The Cubans in the authentic-looking fire engine would "respond" minutes after the timer went off, enter, get anybody in there out, hit the vault, and get themselves out in the confusion of other fire apparatus arriving, calmly loading "rescued" material into a van. The bogus engine would be abandoned at the scene. The taking of the material from the vault would be discovered and the fire engine traced to a cut-out buyer. There would be a lot of who-struck-John in the liberal press, but because nothing could be proved the matter would lapse into the unsolved-mystery category.[29]

The plan was not approved, although it is unclear who blocked it.[30] Nevertheless, the idea that such a plan was even conceived, discussed, and evaluated within the White House suggests that Nixon and his advisers had, to use Mary McCarthy's apt phrase, gone "around the bend."[31]

It was also only after the Pentagon Papers case that Nixon told Haldeman that he was "going to be my Lord High Executioner from now on," and he ordered Haldeman "to confront personally every single cabinet officer and agency head, brutally chew them out and threaten them with extinction if they didn't stop all leaks in the future."[32]

▪ ▪ ▪ ▪ ▪

The establishment of the Plumbers Unit and the break-in at Dr. Fielding's office put the administration on the road to Watergate. Nine months after the Fielding break-in, Liddy and Hunt participated in the Watergate break-in of the Democratic National Committee and were ultimately convicted for their conduct.[33]

In addition to creating a set of attitudes that made the Watergate burglary conceivable and possible the illegal burglary of Dr. Fielding's office ultimately created circumstances that persuaded Nixon to participate in the cover-up of the Watergate break-in, which in turn contributed to his final disgrace. Once law enforcement officials began to investigate the Watergate burglary, it immediately became clear to Nixon and his top aides that they had to keep the Plumbers Unit burglary of Fielding's office secret or risk a far-flung investigation of preelection activities that might potentially destroy Nixon's capacity to govern. Nixon and Haldeman "made a desperate gamble to curtail" the FBI investigation by enlisting the CIA and L. Patrick Gray, acting director of the FBI.[34]

Ultimately, the Plumbers Unit and the break-in of Dr. Fielding's office helped form the basis for two of the three impeachment articles adopted against President Nixon by the House Judiciary Committee in July 1974. They supported the articles that accused Nixon of abusing his powers as president and that charged him with obstruction of justice. Thus, John Ehrlichman's judgment that the Fielding break-in was the "seminal Watergate episode" seems beyond reproach.[35]

The Pentagon Papers affair was a watershed experience for the Nixon administration. It helped transform the administration by creating an atmosphere that made possible the exaggeration of tendencies and habits of mind that had existed in the administration but had remained more or less within acceptable boundaries. What the Pentagon Papers affair did was to inflate these characteristics, which in turn made possible decisions and actions by Nixon and his top advisers that led to Watergate and Nixon's resignation on August 8, 1974.

CHAPTER TWENTY-FIVE

The Supreme Court's Decision and Democracy

The meaning of the Supreme Court's decision in the Pentagon Papers case was debated during the summer and fall of 1971. Because the outcome permitted prior restraints, at least in theory, it was criticized as giving the government a potent weapon to use to censor the press. Because the Court had denied the government the injunction it sought, it was attacked as setting the stage for future improper disclosures that might seriously harm the national security. Still others praised the middle course the Court followed in the case—a course that ultimately gave the Court substantial authority to decide what information could be made public—but pointed to the Court's failure to define in detailed and concrete terms the circumstances under which the government could obtain an injunction as a considerable weakness.

In many respects the disagreements among those involved in the litigation over the significance of the Court's decision was a microcosm of this debate. The day after the Court announced its judgment, a *Times* editorial praised the decision as "historic" and "a ringing victory for freedom under law." "The nation's highest tribunal," the editorial proclaimed, "strongly reaffirmed the guarantee of the people's right to know."[1] In contrast the *Washington Post*'s editorial was far more cautious and brooding: "there is not all that much comfort, let alone clear cut law, to be found in yesterday's outcome." Moreover, the *Post* continued: "what the court majority seems to be saying . . . is that the government failed to make its point—not that a point was not necessarily there to be made."[2]

Ben Bradlee, the *Post*'s executive editor, was unimpressed by the outcome. This was not a "resounding victory"; Justice White "was just begging them [the government] to prosecute us for treason." Bradlee warned that we "mustn't kid ourselves about how much of a landmark decision, what broad guidelines, what new law the Justices made. Their ruling was very narrow."[3] Bradlee's counterpart at the *Times*, Abe Rosenthal, had a different perspective on the decision. "I think we won and we lost. We won the key decision in court. The negative . . . was a combination of two things: the Government's willingness to go in and get an injunction . . . plus the various courts' willingness to hear cases of injunction and to grant a temporary injunction."[4]

The lawyers involved in the case no more agreed with each other than the editors and the editorial pages did. Alexander Bickel approved of the result, because the "conditions in which government will not be allowed to restrain publication are now clearer and perhaps more stringent than they have been." He thought that the "rule of the Pentagon Papers case calls for evidence of immediate harm of the gravest sort (typically loss of life or catastrophic injury to the national interest) flowing directly and ineluctably from publication, before a restraint will be allowed." Bickel characterized this result as a "disorderly situation surely," but he believed that the promised disorder was preferable to the alternatives. "If we order it we would have to sacrifice one of two contending values—privacy or public discourse. . . . If we should let the government censor as well as withhold, that would be too much dangerous power, and too much privacy. If we should allow the government neither to censor nor to withhold, that would provide for too little privacy of decision-making and too much power in the press and in Congress."[5]

William Glendon, who represented the *Washington Post* before the Supreme Court, was more unqualified than Bickel. In his view the government's effort to obtain a prior restraint placed "freedom of the press as we know it in the balance"; if the government had prevailed, the courts would have become "censorship boards." He believed that the "Court stood firm," the cases were "rightly decided," the "barriers were maintained," and a "free press emerged stronger."[6]

Solicitor General Griswold thought the Court should have ordered the lower trial courts to conduct a second hearing in the case. He believed that such an outcome would have given the courts adequate time to assess the complicated issues raised by the cases and the parties an opportunity to narrow their differences, if not resolve them completely. Griswold was concerned that newspapers would misconstrue the Court's decision to mean that they should encourage government employees, who had a "fiduciary responsibility" to keep classified information confidential, to betray that trust and improperly disclose national security information. Griswold hoped that the press would "not feel that they are privileged to print anything which comes to hand."[7]

As one might have expected, given his attitudes throughout the litigation, Robert Mardian had the most extreme reaction. Mardian could not understand how a court could fashion a legal doctrine that permitted newspapers, which had "received stolen [government] property" that was classified, to go so far as to copyright "the god damn thing," and then to publish it.[8]

■ ■ ■ ■ ■

Although the meaning of the Court's decision seemed uncertain in 1971, its significance seems—at least in retrospect—quite clear. The Court properly rejected two legal positions that marked the opposite ends of the spectrum. The idea that the government should be able to enjoin publication of information merely because it was classified would certainly have constituted a radical departure from well-settled expectations of what American law was. More important, such an outcome would have given the government too much control over the public disclosure of information. In the 1990s, as in 1971, the government has near absolute control over what defense and national security information is made public. This is true because the classification system is widely abused to keep confidential information that could be disclosed without injuring the national security. It is also true because the government has almost total discretion in deciding what information, once classified, to declassify. To supplement this enormous power with the ability to censor information merely because it is classified would give the government a dangerous capacity to keep secret information that should be public.

The Court also rejected the idea that the First Amendment barred all prior restraints. It was certainly no surprise the Court did this. Only two Supreme Court justices—Justices Black and Douglas—had ever taken an absolutist view. Although they tried over a span of decades to persuade others on the Court to join them, they never persuaded anyone else to do so. Justice Brennan came the closest, but even he stopped short of embracing the absolutist view.

Moreover, neither the *Times* nor the *Post* had asked the Court to adopt such a legal rule. Instead, they conceded that the First Amendment permitted prior restraints but insisted that such relief was inappropriate, given the facts of the cases. Even the parties who had filed various *amici* briefs with the Supreme Court—the American Civil Liberties Union, the

Emergency Civil Liberties Union, and members of Congress—had not argued in favor of an absolute bar against all prior restraints. Hence, the idea that the outcome in the case was somehow a serious setback for freedom of the press because the Court did not shut the door on all prior restraints was unrealistic.

The Court's unwillingness to adopt an absolute prohibition made sense. The absolutist position rested on two grounds. Justice Black had long asserted that the plain wording of the First Amendment prohibited all judicially imposed prior restraints. But that was incorrect; the First Amendment stated no such thing. The First Amendment stated that "Congress shall make no law abridging . . . freedom of the press." By its terms the amendment restricted only Congress; it said nothing about the courts. It was only by judicial interpretation—an interpretation that Justice Black supported—that the restrictions of the amendment applied to the courts. Thus, whatever strength there was to Justice Black's position was not derived from the plain wording of the First Amendment.

The argument for an absolute prohibition also rested on the assumption that whatever injury the press might cause through publication was outweighed by the injury the government might cause if prior restraints were permitted, even in the most narrow circumstances. Given that both the press and the government may abuse its power, there seems little reason to grant the press absolute immunity from prior restraint if some other approach—the middle course followed by the Court—held out hope of avoiding potentially devastating injury to the nation's security while assuring substantial and critical press freedoms.

Rejecting these two extremes, and holding open the possibility of a prior restraint, the Court stated that the government had a heavy evidentiary burden when it sought such relief. The Court, however, did not explain why the government's evidence did not satisfy this burden. Nonetheless, we can draw some conclusions as to why the government's evidence was not sufficient.

It is not enough for the government merely to present numerous allegations that further disclosures will seriously harm current military, diplomatic, and intelligence interests. Nor do these allegations become sufficient, even during war time, because the government claims that specific and detailed references to classified documents support them. What the government must do is actually prove that the information, if disclosed, will result in immediate, irreparable harm. And in proving this, the government cannot expect the courts to defer to national security officials, even though it insists that judges lack the training, knowledge, and experience to second guess such officials.

The heavy burden is also not satisfied merely because the government makes general allegations that disclosures will injure diplomatic relations. Nor does this proof become legally sufficient because the government loosely relates it to vaguely explained efforts to advance an important objective such as ending a war or improving the conditions of prisoners of war.

Nor can the government expect to prevail on important but narrower legal issues because it is unable to define precisely what documents have been improperly disclosed to the press. Thus, citing its inability to define the parameters of the leak, the government unsuccessfully requested additional time to prepare its evidence for trial, as well as an order forcing the newspapers to permit government officials to review their documents.

Although the Court's decision strongly affirmed the presses' freedom, many in the press feared that the government would frequently invoke the prior restraint weapon against the press. This fear was further strengthened because the Court did not spell out guidelines for lower courts to follow in deciding whether to grant a temporary injunction pending the completion of an evidentiary hearing.

During the years immediately following the Court's decision it appeared to many in the press that their fears were being realized. In 1972 the government prevailed in an action to enjoin a former CIA agent from publishing classified information that had not been placed in the public domain. In this case a federal appeals court upheld the injunction because the former agent had signed a "secrecy agreement promising not to divulge in any way any classified information" unless the CIA director authorized the disclosure in writing.[9] In 1979 the government obtained a temporary injunction barring the *Progressive* magazine from publishing technical material on hydrogen bomb design in an article entitled "The H-Bomb Secret: How We Got It, Why We're Telling It." The government did this, even though it conceded that some of the information in dispute was in the public domain. But the government insisted that the article presented an immediate, direct, and irreparable harm to the interests of the United States because the article's synthesis of the information gave it a new and different character than it otherwise had. The government also submitted affidavits from cabinet members asserting that publication would increase the risk of thermonuclear proliferation. Before the dispute could be conclusively litigated, similar information pertaining to nuclear weapons was independently published, which prompted the government to abandon the proceedings.[10]

In yet a third case the Supreme Court granted the government a constructive trust under which all the profits from a former CIA agent's unauthorized book went into the public treasury. The basis of this unusual form of relief was the secrecy agreement the agent had signed as condition of employment. Although this remedy was not a prior restraint, it was thought to reflect a new willingness by the judiciary to use its power to protect national security even at the expense of free speech values.[11]

Finally, the case of *Haig v. Agee* also supported the view that the courts were receptive to the government's new aggressiveness to clamp down on speech that implicated security. In this case the Court sustained the secretary of state's revocation of a former CIA agent's passport on the ground that his disclosures of sensitive information threatened national security. In reaching this result the Court stated that it was unnecessary to balance Agee's free speech rights against the government's security claims because revoking Agee's right to travel abroad restricted only his action, not his speech.[12]

But as it turned out, those early indications that the press would pay the price of its Pentagon Papers victory were misleading. Since the early 1980s the government has not tried to restrain the press from publishing information that allegedly threatened the national security.[13]

Several reasons explain the government's failure to utilize prior restraints. The government seldom knows, prior to publication, that the press will publish classified information. Even if government officials do know, they might well lack the time to assess the impact of the disclosures; or they might disagree over whether a prior restraint was warranted; or they might conclude that an effort to secure a prior restraint would draw more attention to the sensitive information than if the government pretended to ignore it. In addition prior restraints involve complicated political risks, because censoring the press arouses the public's suspicion that the government is merely trying to hide embarrassing information.

▪ ▪ ▪ ▪ ▪

The Court's decision in the case was certainly not compelled by the wording of the First Amendment. Nor did prior judicial decisions require it. Indeed, as already noted, the Court could have announced a standard for granting injunctions that was less protective of press freedoms without having overruled one prior decision.

If the significance of the Pentagon Papers decision is to be fully appreciated, it must be recognized that the Court's decision put the nation's security at risk, at least to some degree. The government had failed to offer evidence that was as detailed, as specific, and as compelling as the Court required. But that did not mean that adequate evidence might not have been presented; it did not mean that subsequent publications might not reveal injurious information; it only meant that the government had failed to prove that the disputed documents contained information that would gravely and immediately injure the national security. Thus, the Court's decision entailed some degree of risk that further disclosures might inadvertently harm the nation's security.

In reaching this result the Court in effect weighed different risks inherent in one legal standard or another. By following the course it did the Court decided that the risks of favoring press freedoms were significantly less than those involved in making injunctive relief more readily available to the government. Or, to put the matter slightly differently, the Court decided to risk the dangers inherent in a freer press because the alternative resolution—enhancing government power to censor the press—was even more threatening to a stable and vital democracy.

This was a courageous decision supportive of the public's right to be informed about important public affairs. Indeed, the courage and significance of the decision can be appreciated only if one recognizes that the decision was rendered when the nation was at war, in the face of government demands that the Court defer to national security officials and in a context in which there was no guarantee that additional disclosures would in fact be harmless.

▪ ▪ ▪ ▪ ▪

The legal significance of the Court's decision in the Pentagon Papers case would be difficult to exaggerate, but its meaning extends well beyond the walls demarcating the legal world. The Court's weighing of freedom and security in shaping the law of prior restraint reflected what a democratic society does daily. In innumerable contexts and with varying degrees of risk a democratic society regularly balances freedom against security, just as the Court did in the Pentagon Papers case. This is especially true in the United States, where the government broadly defines the national security interests and uses the classification system to keep classified an enormous amount of information in the name of security. In this context there is often a temptation to curtail freedom because of a fear that it threatens some crucial element of security. But such a reaction is frequently shortsighted and ultimately corrosive of the underlying conditions required for a meaningful democracy. Indeed, a vital democracy must necessarily embody within itself freedom that may give rise to dangers that threaten the very premises of the political order.

The Court's decision in the Pentagon Papers is a guidepost for any democratic society to follow as it daily resolves clashes among competing claims that implicate freedom and security. Distilled, the decision represents the judgment that democracy must tolerate risks—even potentially serious risks—inherent in freedom because freedom also strengthens a democracy's fundamental security. District judge Murray Gurfein got to the heart of the matter in his decision—the first judicial decision in the Pentagon Papers cases—dissolving the injunction in the *Times* case: "The Security of the Nation is not at the ramparts alone. Security also lies in the value of free institutions."[14]

The challenge presented by a democratic order to society—as it is to courts in legal disputes—is to scrutinize closely and to treat with skepticism all claims for security that would delimit the fundamental freedoms and free institutions essential to a democratic order. That is what the Supreme Court did in the Pentagon Papers case, and by so doing it made an inestimable contribution to a free press and American democracy.

Notes

ABBREVIATIONS

NYT	*New York Times*
NPMP	Nixon Presidential Materials Project
PP case	*New York Times Company v. United States*, 403 U.S. 713 (1971)
WP	*Washington Post*

INTRODUCTION: A RECONSIDERATION

1. Salisbury (1980), 12.

2. Neil Sheehan, "Vietnam Archive: Pentagon Study Traces Three Decades of Growing U.S. Involvement," *NYT*, June 13, 1971, 1.

3. Neil Sheehan, "Vietnam Archive: A Consensus to Bomb Developed before '64 Election, Study Says," *NYT*, June 14, 1971, 1.

4. NPMP, Haldeman Notes, Box 43, June 13, 1975.

5. Fred Graham, "Judge, at Request of U.S., Halts Times Vietnam Series Four Days Pending Hearing on Injunction," *NYT*, June 16, 1971, 1.

6. Fred Graham, "The Times Series Still Held up Pending Court Ruling Today; Washington Post Restrained," *NYT*, June 19, 1971, 10. Unpublished Transcript of Hearing before United States District Judge Murray I. Gurfein, Southern District of New York, in the action of *The United States of America v. The New York Times Company et al.*, 71 Civ. 2552, June 18, 1971, 19.

7. *United States v. New York Times Company et al.*, 328 F. Supp. 324, 330, 331 (S.D.N.Y. 1971), hereafter *U.S. v. NYT*, 328 F. Supp.

8. PP case, 714.

9. Griswold (1992), 310; See also Erwin N. Griswold, "No Harm Was Done," *NYT*, June 30, 1991, sec. 4, 15, in which Griswold wrote: "In hindsight, it is clear to me that no harm was done by publication of the Pentagon Papers. Indeed, with

minor exceptions, the newspapers did not print at the time any items about which the Government was concerned."

10. Sidney Blumenthal, "Letter from Washington: The Education of a President," *New Yorker*, Jan. 24, 1994, 32.

11. In his study of Watergate Stanley I. Kutler uses former Attorney General John Mitchell's phrase "White House horrors" to refer to what Kutler terms "the Nixon Administration's dubious tactics" (1990, xiv).

12. U.S. Department of Defense (1980). The title of this version indicates the study lasted until 1967, but in fact the study continued into 1968.

13. "The Vietnam Documents," *NYT*, June 16, 1971, 44.

14. I state that Daniel Ellsberg made the classified documents "available" to the *Times*. My use of the word "available" is deliberate. Chapters 2 and 3 detail Ellsberg's efforts to make the Pentagon Papers public and his relationship with Neil Sheehan, the *Times* reporter who broke the story of the classified study.

15. See, generally, Sheehan (1988); Wicker (1991); Ungar (1989); Hersh (1983); Salisbury (1980); Schrag (1974).

16. Brief for the United States (Secret Portion) in *New York Times Company v. United States* (Oct. Term, 1970, No. 1873) and *United States v. The Washington Post Company* (Oct. Term, 1970, No. 1885), in the United States Supreme Court, 4, 5.

17. See, generally, Wicker (1991); Kutler (1990); Salisbury (1980); Wise (1978); Lukas (1976); Ungar (1989).

1. McNAMARA'S STUDY

1. "President Lauds McNamara and Gives Him Medal," *NYT*, Feb. 29, 1968, 3.

2. Ibid.

3. Shapely (1993), 492, 497. It was not until McNamara wrote a memoir, *In Retrospect: The Tragedy and Lessons of Vietnam*, published in 1995, that he confessed that the policies of the Kennedy and Johnson administrations were "wrong, terribly wrong" (McNamara and VanDeMark [1995], xvi). "I truly believe," he continued, "that we made an error not of values and intentions but of judgement and capabilities" (xvi). McNamara also stated that he did not publicly criticize the war policies of the Johnson administration when he resigned because he believed that such conduct "would have been a violation of my responsibility to the president and my oath to uphold the Constitution" (314). McNamara further wrote that, "despite my deep differences" with Johnson, "I was loyal to the presidency and to him" (314).

4. Rusk interview; McNamara interview; NPMP, Haldeman Notes, Box 43, June 18, 1971; Hersh (1983), 388.

5. Shapley (1993), 85. In his memoir, *In Retrospect*, McNamara described his first meeting with Sargent Shriver, who offered him a cabinet position in the Kennedy administration:

> At four sharp, Sarge Shriver entered my office. He began the conversation by saying, "The president-elect has instructed me to offer you the position of secretary of the treasury."
>
> "You're out of your mind," I said. "I'm not qualified for that."

> "If you hold to that position," said Sarge, "I am authorized to say Jack Kennedy wishes you to serve as secretary of defense."
>
> "This is absurd!" I said. "I'm not qualified." (14)

6. Shapley (1993), 138; Trewhitt (1971), 197.
7. Trewhitt (1971), 197; Shapley, (1993), 299, 135–61.
8. Trewhitt (1971), 201; Karnow (1984), 342; McNamara and VanDeMark (1995), 116.
9. Karnow (1984), 395–426; Shapley (1993), 319–48; Trewhitt (1971), 215–21; McNamara and VanDeMark (1995), 170–71.
10. Karnow (1984), 498–502; Trewhitt (1971), 232–36.
11. Trewhitt (1971), 236–45; Karnow (1984), 502–12.
12. Trewhitt (1971), 239; Karnow (1984), 499–501; McNamara and VanDeMark (1995), 264–65.
13. Trewhitt (1971), 243–44; Karnow (1984), 507–14.
14. McNamara interview; Salisbury (1980), 57–59; McNamara and VanDeMark (1995), 256.
15. Salisbury (1980), 59.
16. Trewhitt (1971), 237; Halberstam (1972), 633; Karnow (1984), 20. In his memoir, *In Retrospect*, McNamara wrote of his strain in 1967: "The accumulating stresses and tensions took their toll on those of us who had to make the decisions, and I was not exempt. Some nights in 1967 I had to take a pill in order to sleep" (McNamara and VanDeMark [1995], 260). McNamara also wrote that he knew that President Johnson had told his aides he was worried "I might commit suicide, as had Truman's first defense secretary, James V. Forrestal. It has since become a common assumption that I was near emotional and physical collapse. I was not. I was indeed feeling stress" (313).
17. Halperin interview.
18. McNamara interview; Halperin interview; Ungar (1989), 23, 38.
19. Hersh (1983), 321.
20. McNamara interview; McNamara and VanDeMark (1995), 280.
21. *The Pentagon Papers: The Defense Department History of United States Decisionmaking on Vietnam* (1971), 1:xv–xvi. (Hereafter, Gravel edition.)
22. Halperin interview.
23. Warnke interview; Halperin interview; Gelb interview.
24. "The Secret History of Vietnam," *Newsweek*, June 28, 1971, 22. The *New York Times* reported that the views ascribed to the former president "were actually expressed by Mr. Johnson in a telephone interview" with a *Newsweek* reporter (David Rosenbaum, "Review of Report Proposal by U.S.," *NYT*, June 23, 1971, 23).
25. "Secret History of Vietnam," 22.
26. "The Metamorphosis of Robert McNamara," *Business Week*, July 17, 1971, 16.
27. Schoenbaum (1988), 466.
28. Rusk interview.
29. Rusk and Rusk (1990), 576; Rusk interview.
30. McNamara interview.
31. Rusk interview.
32. Halberstam (1972), 632.

33. Tom Braden, "An Odd Fact about the Viet 'Record,'" *WP*, June 22, 1971, A19.

34. McNamara interview. In his memoir, *In Retrospect*, McNamara wrote: "Wild rumors circulated about why I had started the project. One report even alleged I had done so at Robert Kennedy's behest, to undermine LBJ and help Bobby's 1968 presidential campaign. That was nonsense" (McNamara and VanDeMark [1995], 282).

35. Katzenbach interview.

36. McNamara interview.

37. Karnow (1984), 20, 498; Trewhitt (1971), 221.

38. Katzenbach interview.

39. Halperin interview; Charlton and Moncrieff (1989), 169.

40. Halperin interview.

41. McNamara interview.

42. Gelb interview.

43. McNamara interview.

44. Halperin interview.

45. Gelb interview.

46. Gelb (1972), 27–28.

47. Ibid.

48. Ullman, "The Pentagon's History as 'History,'" *Foreign Policy*, no. 4 (Fall 1971), 151.

49. Katzenbach interview.

50. Gravel edition, 1:xv–xvi.

51. Leslie Gelb, "Today's Lessons from the Pentagon Papers," *Life*, Sept. 17, 1971, 34.

52. Ungar (1989), 28.

53. Gravel edition, 1:xv–xvi.

54. *The New York Times Edition of the Pentagon Papers* (1971), x. (Hereafter, NYT edition.)

55. Herring, ed. (1985), x.

56. Gravel edition, 1:xv–xvi.

57. Halperin and Hoffman (1977), 6.

58. Halperin interview. Halperin's claim that the study's existence was supposed to be a secret is not shared by Warnke and Gelb. "I don't think the fact that the study was going on was a secret," Warnke has claimed (Warnke interview).

Gelb, who was the person who contacted individuals in different parts of the government, including the White House and the National Security Agency, has also asserted that the project's existence was known to "lots of people in the White House. . . . Lots!" Gelb has conceded that he does "not know whether the president was informed. But in short order, everyone else knew" (Gelb interview).

There is merit to each of these views. Certainly Halperin is correct in that an effort was made to give the task force a low profile. There was no public announcement of the project. McNamara did not speak to Johnson or Rostow about the project, and although Rostow may have learned of the project while it was being done, at least Rusk believed that Johnson first learned of the study when the *New York Times* began its series. McNamara did speak to Rusk about the project, but he characterized it as one involving the collection of documents and so minimized its scope that Rusk felt betrayed when he eventually became aware of the study's dimensions only after the *Times* began its publication. It is also likely that McNamara forbade the project's staff from trying to secure access to White House files since Gelb's letter of transmittal stated: "We had no access to White House files." And although Gelb did eventually gain access to White House materials, Gelb has written that it was only because several members of the White House staff provided such material, thus suggesting that the project's access to White House documents was dependent upon personal relationships and confidential disclosures.

But Gelb and Warnke were also correct that efforts to give the project a low profile were at odds with efforts to collect documents at the State Department, the CIA, and the White House. Many people were in fact informed about the project; as Gelb has said, "lots" knew of the project. Furthermore, as Warnke has remembered, when the project was completed, Gelb gave a large party marking its completion (Warnke interview).

There may be less conflict among these views than it appears. McNamara surely had his reasons for indicating to McNaughton and his aides that the task force should keep a low profile. By the time McNamara actually authorized the study his disagreements with the administration's policies were known both within and outside the administration. As a result there was a basis for McNamara to worry that Johnson and other principals within the administration with whom he had labored for years in planning the war and overseeing its execution might be suspicious about why he wanted the study done. So out of conflict between his decision to have the project done and his concern that his administration's colleagues would not countenance it, McNamara refrained from disclosing the project to Johnson and Rostow and downplayed it to Rusk.

Halperin as well as Gelb certainly seem to have worried once the project was underway that Johnson or Rostow might terminate it if they learned of it. At the same time they could not keep the project a complete secret, since they needed staff and documents. Hence, they had to inform some people of the project, as Gelb has maintained, but they were probably careful about who was informed out of fear that the study would be "shut down," as Halperin has recalled.

The staff's fear that the study would be terminated and destroyed must have been intensified when Johnson nominated Clark Clifford to replace McNamara as secretary of defense. Clifford was Johnson's friend and confidant—a major reason Johnson had appointed him—and it would only have been natural for the staff to regard him with suspicion. But Clifford did not terminate the project. When asked years later why he did not shut down the study that eventually caused his friend, the president, so much anguish, Clifford answered that it had never occurred to him to take such a step (Clark interview). This may be because Clifford was not told about the ongoing study (Clifford cannot recall knowing about it, although Warnke has stated that he told Clifford [Warnke interview]), or if he was informed of it, the study's scope was so minimized that Clifford considered it inconsequential, thus permitting it to go forward out of courtesy to McNamara.

59. Gravel edition, 1:xv–xvi.
60. Ibid.
61. Ibid.
62. Ibid.
63. Herring, ed. (1985), x.
64. Gravel edition, 1:xv.
65. Herring, ed. (1985), xxv.

66. Ibid.
67. Ungar (1989), 32.
68. Herring, ed. (1985), xxii.
69. George McT. Kahin, "The Pentagon Papers: A Critical Evaluation," *American Political Science Review* 69 (1975), 675. McNamara was personally pleased with the outcome of the study: "Overall the work was superb, and it accomplished my objective: almost every scholarly work on Vietnam since then has drawn, to varying degrees, on it" (McNamara and VanDeMark [1995], 281).
70. Halperin and Hoffman (1977), 7; Gelb interview; Halperin interview.
71. Exec. Order 10501, 10 Oct. 1953, 18 Fed. Reg. 220 7049 (a).
72. Halperin interview. The testimony before Judge Gurfein in the government's suit against the *New York Times* also established that this was policy at the time. Unpublished Transcript of Hearing before United States District Judge Murray I. Gurfein, Southern District of New York, in the action of *The United States of America v. The New York Times Company et al.*, 71 Civ. 2552, June 18, 1971, 67.
73. Halperin and Hoffman (1977), 10; Ungar (1989), 31.
74. Schrag (1974), 37.
75. Gelb interview.
76. Ullman interview.
77. Halperin interview; Gelb interview.

2. DANIEL ELLSBERG

1. Sheehan (1988), 12; Daniel Ellsberg, "Ellsberg Talks," interview by J. Robert Moskin, *Look*, Oct. 5, 1971, 34; Ungar (1989), 43–44; Schrag (1974), 41–42.
2. Sheehan (1988), 13.
3. Sheehan (1988), 591.
4. Ibid., 13.
5. Schrag (1974), 25.
6. Hersh (1983), 53 n.
7. Salisbury (1980), 54.
8. Sheehan (1988), 13.
9. Ibid., 592.
10. Ellsberg interview.
11. Sheehan (1988), 592.
12. Ibid.; Ungar (1989), 46.
13. Hersh (1983), 30 n.
14. Charlton and Moncrieff (1989), 173–74; Ellsberg interview.
15. Ungar (1989), 47.
16. Sheehan (1988), 13, 547, 592–93; Hersh (1983), 15 n; Ellsberg, "Ellsberg Talks," 32; Ellsberg interview.
17. Salisbury (1980), 56.
18. Ellsberg, "Ellsberg Talks," 34.
19. Hersh (1983), 15 n, 46.
20. Ungar (1989), 48.
21. Schrag (1974), 33.
22. Ellsberg, "Ellsberg Talks," 34.
23. Sheehan (1988), 13; Ellsberg interview.

24. Schrag (1974), 32; Ellsberg, "Ellsberg Talks," 33.
25. Ellsberg, "Ellsberg Talks," 33; Schrag (1974), 32–34; Ellsberg, "Ellsberg Talks," 34.
26. Ellsberg interview; Ellsberg, "Ellsberg Talks," 34.
27. Ellsberg interview; Salisbury (1980), 61.
28. Ellsberg interview.
29. Ungar (1989), 29.
30. Daniel Ellsberg, "Janaki: Princeton, April 1968," typescript (on file in author's offices at Benjamin N. Cardozo Law School, Yeshiva University, New York), 1, 3, 4.
31. Ibid., 4, 5.
32. Ibid., 1.
33. Schrag (1974), 42–43.
34. Hersh (1983), 49; Gibson (1986), 170.
35. Hersh (1983), 49–50; Ungar (1989), 56.
36. Ellsberg interview; Halperin interview; Gelb interview.
37. Ellsberg, "Ellsberg Talks," 34, 39.
38. Hersh (1983), 325.
39. Daniel Ellsberg, "Randy Kehler: Haverford, August 1969," typescript, 1.
40. Ellsberg, "Ellsberg Talks," 39.
41. Ellsberg, "Randy Kehler," 11, 12.
42. Ibid., 15.
43. Ellsberg, "Ellsberg Talks," 39.
44. Hersh (1983), 326; Schrag (1974), 45.
45. Schrag (1974), 45; Ungar (1989), 66–67; Ellsberg interview.
46. Ellsberg interview.
47. Ellsberg, "Ellsberg Talks," 39; Ungar (1989), 81.
48. Hersh (1983), 326.
49. Ungar (1989), 68.
50. Ibid., 70.
51. Ellsberg interview; Ungar (1989), 73.
52. Schrag (1974), 48.
53. Ungar (1989), 68, 72.
54. Ibid., 76; Salisbury (1980), 97, 88 n.
55. Hersh (1983), 327.
56. Peter Schrag suggested that the circumstances surrounding Ellsberg's departure from RAND were different from what Ellsberg has indicated. Schrag reported that Ellsberg was "forced out" of RAND "because he couldn't complete his projects" (Schrag [1974], 50).
57. Salisbury (1980), 74–75; Hersh (1983), 327.
58. Hersh (1983), 327; Salisbury (1980), 75.
59. Hersh (1983), 327; Salisbury (1980), 75.
60. Salisbury (1980), 75; Schrag (1974), 39.
61. Hersh (1983), 325–29; Ungar (1989), 77–80.
62. Ungar (1989), 81–82.
63. Hersh (1983), 330–31.
64. Salisbury (1980), 79.
65. Halberstam (1979), 566–67.
66. Ellsberg interview.

67. Sheehan (1970), 19.
68. Salisbury (1980), 87.
69. Ibid.; see Neil Sheehan, "Should We Have War Crime Trials?" *NYT Book Review*, 28 March 1971.
70. Salisbury (1980), 87.
71. Ibid.
72. Ibid., 85.
73. Ellsberg interview.
74. Ibid.

3. THE *NEW YORK TIMES* PUBLISHES

1. "The Vietnam Documents," *NYT*, June 16, 1971, 44.
2. Salisbury (1980), 80–93; Halberstam (1979), 565.
3. Salisbury (1980), 80.
4. Wicker (1978), 8.
5. Salisbury (1980), 81.
6. Ibid.
7. Halberstam (1979), 205.
8. Wicker (1978), 90.
9. Salisbury (1980), 82.
10. Ibid., 96.
11. Ibid., n. Ellsberg had given portions of the study to Raskin and Barnet (see chap. 2) but demanded that they return the classified documents to him, which they did. But Ellsberg suspected they had made a photocopy before doing so, and it is likely that Raskin and Barnet used this set to photocopy the papers they gave Sheehan (ibid., 88 n.).
12. Ibid., 96.
13. James Goodale, *Communications Policy and Law: The Pentagon Papers 1–2* (available from Benjamin N. Cardozo Law School, Yeshiva University, New York, photocopy), 1; Salisbury (1980), 94–96.
14. Section 794(a) reads:

> Whoever, with intent, or reason to believe that it is to be used to the injury of the United States or to the advantage of a foreign nation, communicates, delivers, or transmits, or attempts to communicate, deliver, or transmit, to any foreign government, or to any faction or party or military or naval force within a foreign country, whether recognized or unrecognized by the United States, or to any representative, officer, agent, employee, subject, or citizen thereof, either directly or indirectly, any document, writing, code book, signal book, sketch, photograph, photographic negative, blueprint, plan, map, model, note, instrument, appliance, or information relating to the national defense, shall be punished by death or by imprisonment for any term of years or for life.
>
> [18 U.S.C. 794.]

15. Goodale, *Communications Policy and Law*, 11.
16. Section 793(e) reads:

> Whoever having unauthorized possession of, access to, or control over any document, writing, code book, signal book, sketch, photograph, photographic negative, blueprint, plan, map, model, instrument, appliance, or note relating to national defense, or information relating to the national defense which information the possessor has reason to believe could be used to the injury of the United States or to the advantage of any foreign nation, willfully communicates, delivers, transmits or causes to be communicated, delivered, or transmitted the same to any person not entitled to receive it, or willfully retains

the same and fails to deliver it to the officer or the employee of the United States entitled to receive it.

17. Goodale, *Communications Policy and Law*, 11.

18. Salisbury (1980), 96–98; Ungar (1989), 83–84; Griswold (1992), 310 n. 37.

19. Salisbury (1980), 97.

20. Ibid., 35–36.

21. Neil Sheehan declined my several requests for an interview.

22. Although Ellsberg may have indicated during one of his discussions with Sheehan that the *Times* would have to agree to publish a substantial portion of the classified history if he were to make the papers available to Sheehan, it is unlikely that Sheehan communicated Ellsberg's condition to Frankel or any other senior *Times* officials. That was not so much because of the substance of Ellsberg's condition but because of the fact that Ellsberg imposed a condition at all. Sheehan thought the top secret history of exceptional significance. If he was willing to deceive Ellsberg to get his hands on it, there is little reason to believe he would have complicated his editors' consideration of the material by passing on Ellsberg's wish that a substantial portion of the study be published (Ellsberg interview; Salisbury [1980], 167).

23. Ungar (1989), 90–91; Salisbury (1980), 118–19.

24. Rosenthal interview.

25. Ibid.

26. Ungar (1989), 93–95.

27. Salisbury (1980), 118; 120–21.

28. Ibid., 122.

29. Goodale, *Communications Policy and Law*, 43; Salisbury (1980), 123.

30. Goodale interview.

31. Talese (1981), 383.

32. Halberstam (1979), 445.

33. Salisbury (1980), 175.

34. Talese (1981), 384.

35. Salisbury (1980), 174.

36. Halberstam (1979), 565.

37. Ungar (1989), 93.

38. Ibid.; Goodale interview.

39. Salisbury (1980), 125; 125–27.

40. Salisbury and Goodale disagree on the date of this meeting. Salisbury stated that this meeting occurred on April 29, 1971. Goodale's unpublished materials state that it occurred on April 22, 1971 (Salisbury [1980], 136–37; Goodale, *Communications Policy and Law*, 33).

41. Salisbury (1980), 136–37; Goodale interview; Rosenthal interview; Sulzberger interview.

42. Goodale interview; Ungar (1989), 98–99; Salisbury (1980), 123, 184–88.

43. Sulzberger interview.

44. Ungar (1989), 93; Salisbury (1980), 185.

45. Rosenthal interview.

46. Ungar (1989), 93–94.

47. Wolfgang Saxon, "Harding Bancroft, 81, Executive at the *Times* and *Diplomat*, Dies," *NYT*, Feb. 7, 1992, A19.

48. Halberstam (1979), 570.

49. Goodale interview.

50. Rosenthal interview; Sulzberger interview.

51. At the time Goodale believed that Rosenthal and the other news officials did not fully appreciate the force of his position, and he felt frustrated by his inability to get his colleagues to take seriously his suggestion that all the material be presented in one day. Tom Wicker's attitude may have been typical. It was that he "was absolutely convinced that the Government would not move as it did and seek prior restraint" (*Columbia Journalism Review* [Sept./Oct. 1971], 28).

52. Rosenthal interview; Salisbury (1980), 203–5.

53. Ungar (1989), 100; Salisbury (1980), 188; Goodale, *Communications Policy and Law*, 46. Goodale favored the publication of the documents, because he considered them "essential to conveying the flavor accurately."

54. Salisbury (1980), 171–73.

55. Ibid., 173.

56. Ibid., 172.

57. Ungar (1989), 96.

58. Ellsberg has claimed that, during their conversations in March and April, he and Sheehan worked out an implicit understanding that permitted Ellsberg to give Sheehan permission to photocopy the papers without having to say so in so many words. The arrangement called for Sheehan to ask Ellsberg to allow him to read the classified material in a Manhattan apartment in which Ellsberg had a copy stored. If Ellsberg gave Sheehan permission, it meant he was giving Sheehan permission to photocopy the material and to give it to the *Times* for publication.

Sometime during these weeks, Ellsberg has stated, Sheehan asked him for permission to read the material in New York, and he agreed. It is not known whether Sheehan actually went to the apartment or not. Since he already had the material, he obviously did not need to go to the designated place.

Sheehan never told Ellsberg that he had made a copy of the classified material he had seen in Cambridge and never told Ellsberg during this period prior to publication that the *Times* was preparing the material for publication. On Saturday evening, June 12, 1971, just a few hours before the Sunday *Times* carrying the first installment of the Pentagon Papers was available for sale in New York, a *Times* editor, Anthony Austin, who had written a book on the Tonkin Gulf affair, telephoned Ellsberg. Austin had consulted Ellsberg on his book, and when he learned that the *Times* was about to publish the Pentagon Papers, he feared his book was about to be scooped. He called Ellsberg looking for reassurance. When Austin told Ellsberg of the impending publication—which was only a few hours off—Ellsberg learned for the first time that the classified material that he had worked so long to make public was about to be published (Ellsberg interview; Salisbury [1980], 23–24).

59. Rosenthal interview.

60. Salisbury (1980), 183.

61. Ibid.

62. Ibid., 185, 184, 185.

63. Sulzberger interview.

64. Ungar (1989), 103; Salisbury (1980), 185.

65. Salisbury (1980), 205; Ungar (1989), 105.

66. Ibid., 202.

67. Ibid., 203.
68. Ibid., 204.
69. Ibid., 204, 205.
70. Ibid., 205.
71. Ibid., 3–7.
72. Shapley (1993), 488. In his memoir, *In Retrospect*, McNamara wrote that he reviewed the *Times*'s draft statement concerning why the *Times* was declining the government's request to discontinue the series on Monday, June 14, during a dinner that he and his wife had with Reston and his wife (McNamara and VanDeMark [1995], 281).

4. NIXON'S TURNABOUT

1. Safire (1975), 341–65.
2. NPMP, Haldeman Notes, Box 43, June 13, 1971.
3. Ibid.
4. Gelb interview.
5. Ibid.
6. Ibid.
7. Warnke interview.
8. Shapley (1993), 488.
9. Clark interview; McNamara interview.
10. Salisbury (1980), 10.
11. Ibid, 10 n.
12. Ibid., 207–8; Ambrose (1989), 445.
13. "U.S. Weighed Moves to Halt the *Times* Series within Hours of First Publication," *NYT*, June 19, 1971, 11.
14. Ibid.; Salisbury (1980), 210.
15. Laird interview.
16. *NYT*, June 19, 1971, 11.
17. Salisbury (1980), 223; Jules Witcover, "Two Weeks That Shook the Press," *Columbia Journalism Review* 10, no. 3 (Sept./Oct. 1971): 10.
18. Salisbury (1980), 210–11.
19. Ibid., 211.
20. Ibid., 210.
21. Hersh (1983), 321 n.
22. Ibid.; see also Kraslow and Loory (1968), 221–24.
23. Herring, ed. (1985), x; Hersh (1983), 329.
24. Kissinger (1979), 730; Hersh (1983), 386.
25. "The Secret History of Vietnam," *Newsweek*, June 28, 1971, 12.
26. Salisbury cited three reports about the Pentagon Papers: an editorial in the *Washington Post* by Ward Just; a *New York Times Magazine* article by Henry Brandon published on November 9, 1969; a *Parade* magazine article dated October 25, 1970 (Salisbury [1980], 88). A fourth report by Thomas Oliphant appeared on the front page of the *Boston Globe* on March 7, 1971.
27. NPMP, Haldeman Notes, Box 43, June 13, 1971.
28. Mitchell interview.
29. Rehnquist interview.
30. Mardian interview.

31. NPMP, Nixon's Daily Diary, Box FC-26, June 13, 1971.
32. Kissinger (1979), 730.
33. Haldeman and DiMona (1978), 110.
34. Ehrlichman (1982), 301–2.
35. Colson (1976), 57–58.
36. Kissinger (1979), 729, 729–30, 730.
37. Haldeman and DiMona (1978), 110.
38. Hersh (1983), 385.
39. Ibid.
40. Ibid., 91, 319–21, 325.
41. NPMP, Haldeman Notes, Box 43, June 14, 1971.
42. Ibid.
43. Ibid.
44. Safire (1975), 353.
45. Spear (1986), 113.
46. Ambrose (1983), 326.
47. NPMP, Haldeman Notes, Box 43, June 14, 1971.
48. Ibid., Box 230, June 15, 1971.
49. Ibid.

5. THE JUSTICE DEPARTMENT'S RECOMMENDATION

1. On Wednesday, June 16, 1971, Dean gave Ehrlichman a two-page memorandum that summarized some statutes pursuant to which a criminal prosecution might be brought. This was one day after the government had persuaded United States district judge Murray I. Gurfein to restrain the *Times* from further publication pending a hearing, which he scheduled for Friday, June 18, 1971 (NPMP, Dean Correspondence, Box 2, June 16, 1971).
2. Mardian interview; Mitchell interview.
3. Harris (1970), 195.
4. Mardian interview.
5. Mitchell interview.
6. Mardian interview.
7. Mitchell interview.
8. Mardian interview; Rehnquist interview.
9. Kleindienst (1985), 122.
10. Rehnquist interview.
11. Ibid.
12. *Near v. Minnesota*, 283 U.S. 697 (1931).
13. Ibid.
14. Rehnquist interview.
15. Ambrose (1989), 470–71.
16. Dean (1976), 50–51; Lukas (1973), 512.
17. Kleindienst (1985), 122.
18. Ehrlichman (1982), 136.
19. Max Frankel, "Mitchell Seeks to Halt Series on Vietnam but *Times* Refuses," *NYT*, June 15, 1971, 18.
20. Mardian interview.
21. Mitchell interview.

22. Mardian interview.
23. Klein (1980), 344.
24. Mardian interview.
25. Friedheim interview.
26. Mitchell interview.
27. Laird interview.
28. Mardian interview.
29. Salisbury (1980), 223.
30. Frankel, "Mitchell Seeks to Halt Series on Vietnam," 18.
31. Mardian interview; Mitchell interview.
32. Mardian interview.
33. Ibid.; Griswold interview.
34. Mardian interview; Griswold interview.
35. Herring, ed. (1985), x.
36. Mardian interview.
37. Marilyn Berger, "Warnke Opposes Publication of Report on Diplomacy," *WP*, June 24, 1971, A13.
38. Hedrick Smith, "Vast Review of War Took a Year," *NYT*, June 13, 1971, p. 1.
39. Herring, ed. (1985), xxii.
40. Mardian interview; Mitchell interview.
41. Mardian interview.
42. Laird interview.
43. Mardian interview.
44. Ibid.
45. Ibid.
46. Mitchell interview.
47. Klein (1980), 344.
48. Mitchell interview.
49. Harris (1970), 102, 105.
50. Safire (1975), 264.
51. Harris (1970), 102.
52. Ibid., 105–6.
53. Safire (1975), 264–65; 265; 266; 263; 265; 263.
54. Mitchell interview.
55. Mardian interview.
56. Nixon (1978), 508–11.
57. Ambrose (1989), 271.
58. NPMP, Nixon's Daily Diary, Box FC-26, June 14, 1971.
59. Kissinger (1979), 730.
60. NPMP, Nixon's Daily Diary, Box FC-26, June 14, 1971.
61. Ungar (1989), 120.
62. Mardian interview; Salisbury (1980), 241.
63. Mitchell interview.
64. Ibid.
65. Brownell interview.
66. Wise (1973), 17.
67. Powledge (1971), 15.
68. Ungar (1989), 114.

69. Safire (1975), 342.
70. Ambrose (1987), 671.
71. Safire (1975), 265.

6. THE *TIMES* IS RESTRAINED

1. Max Frankel, "Mitchell Seeks to Halt Series on Vietnam but *Times* Refuses," *NYT*, June 15, 1971, 1; Salisbury (1980), 238–39; Mardian interview.
2. Mardian interview; Salisbury (1980), 241; *NYT*, June 15, 1971, 1.
3. Goodale interview; Rosenthal interview; Salisbury (1980), 239–44.
4. Salisbury (1980), 243.
5. Ibid., 244.
6. Ibid., 244, 246; Mardian interview.
7. Frankel, "Mitchell Seeks to Halt Series on Vietnam," 1. The complete telegram sent by the *Times* to Attorney General Mitchell stated:

> We have received the telegram from the Attorney General asking The Times to cease further publication of the Pentagon's Vietnam Study. The Times must respectfully decline the request of the Attorney General, believing that it is in the interest of the people of this country to be informed of the material contained in this series of articles. We have also been informed of the Attorney General's intention to seek an injunction against further publication. We believe that it is properly a matter for the courts to decide. The Times will oppose any request for an injunction for the same reason that led us to publish the articles in the first place. We will of course abide by the final decision of the court. (quoted in Salisbury [1980], 245–46)

8. Goodale interview; Brownell interview. Brownell's decision that Lord, Day, and Lord would not represent the *Times* left a bitterness among some at the *Times* that has endured over twenty years. For example, in a recent column, A. M. Rosenthal wrote that Lord, Day, and Lord "made its point by walking out on us. But we also had lawyers who understood the First Amendment and the purpose of newspapers—led by the *Times*'s own chief counsel, James Goodale" ("The Pentagon Papers," *NYT*, June 11, 1991, 23).
9. Mitchell interview.
10. Goodale interview; Abrams interview; Salisbury (1980), 237–38.
During the lunch the conversation got around to whether the government would sue the *Times*. Bickel and Abrams told Goodale, with what Abrams later recalled as "the freedom of lawyers without clients," that the administration would not sue the newspaper for a prior restraint and, if it did, the Times would prevail (Abrams interview).
11. "Alexander M. Bickel Dies; Constitutional Law Expert," *NYT*, Nov. 8, 1974, 42.
12. *New York Times v. Sullivan,* 376 U.S. 254 (1964); Lewis (1991), 128; Salisbury (1980), 246.
13. Abrams interview; Goodale interview.
14. Abrams interview.
15. Hess interview; Seymour interview.
16. Hess interview. These five documents, as well as other legal documents in the *New York Times* case that were public in 1971, were compiled by James Goodale (Goodale, comp. [1971], 1–22).
17. Hess interview.

18. Abrams interview.

19. In part, the First Amendment to the U.S. Constitution states: "Congress shall make no law . . . abridging the freedom of speech, or of the press."

20. Abrams interview.

21. Ibid.

22. *NYT*, June 20, 1971, 26.

23. Assistant Attorney General Mardian had not arranged for the Pentagon Papers to be shipped to New York, so neither Hess nor Gurfein was able to examine the classified study.

24. Hess cited 18 U.S.C. § 793(d). Mardian seems to have had two considerations when he defined the government's legal strategy. First, he wanted to sidestep a potentially important legal question—namely, whether the executive branch of the federal government was authorized to seek a prior restraint against the *Times* absent a statute authorizing such action. This question involved several subsidiary ones: the scope of Congress's authority to control the executive branch's initiation of lawsuits; the power of the judiciary to grant relief absent specific congressional authorization; and the power of the executive branch to act unilaterally in limited circumstances so as to protect the national security. No Supreme Court decision conclusively answered these questions, and a handful of lower court decisions had disagreed in deciding related but different issues. Mardian hoped he could avoid this problem by claiming that the *Times* publications violated the espionage laws, which in turn authorized the government to sue the *Times* for an injunction.

But Mardian's selection of Section 793(d) as the provision of the espionage laws that supported the administration's civil action against the *Times* only aggravated the legal problems he tried to resolve. Section 793(d) made it a crime for a person who "lawfully" possessed, or had access to, or had control over, or was entrusted with information related to the national defense to pass it on to someone "not entitled to receive it." The statute was obviously aimed at spying—making it a crime for a person within the government to pass defense information to an enemy. But what did Section 793(d) have to do with the *Times* publication of the Pentagon Papers? The *Times* was not authorized to possess the disputed documents; the administration made that point unequivocally. Thus, there was no basis in the wording of the provisions for the administration to claim that the *Times* had violated it. In addition, the provision did not explicitly authorize the injunction action against the *Times*. Thus, Hess's reference to Section 793(d) raised more questions than it answered and, instead of deflecting attention from a problematic legal question, it only focused attention on it.

25. No transcript of the proceedings has survived, and there is even a question as to whether a transcript was in fact made of arguments. This description of Hess's legal arguments before Gurfein is drawn from Fred P. Graham, "Judge, At Request of U.S., Halts Times Vietnam Series Four Days Pending Hearing On Injunction" (*NYT*, June 16, 1971, 18), and the legal papers submitted by the government in support of a temporary restraining order (Goodale, comp. [1971], 1–22).

26. Hess interview.

27. Fred P. Graham, "Judge, at Request of U.S., Halts *Times* Vietnam Series Four Days Pending Hearing on Injunction," *NYT*, June 16, 1971, 18.

28. Abrams interview.

29. Goodale interview.

30. Graham, "Judge, at Request of U.S., Halts *Times* Vietnam Series," 18.

31. Hess interview. If Judge Gurfein had required such an evidentiary showing, it would have taken the administration several hours before it could have offered such documents for Gurfein's appraisal since Mardian had not arranged for the classified material to be shipped to New York.

32. Abrams interview.

33. Ibid.

34. *NYT*, June 16, 1971, 1.

7. ON THE EVE OF THE *TIMES* TRIAL

1. Dorsen interview; Wulf interview.

2. Melvin L. Wulf, "What's Fit to Print: Tragedy of 'The Times,'" *Civil Liberties* 280 (Sept. 1971): 1.

3. Dorsen interview.

4. Wulf, "What's Fit to Print," 11.

5. Bickel (1986), 111–98.

6. A case raising the scope of a reporter's right to keep sources confidential was slated to be argued before the Supreme Court in the fall of 1971. The case involved the government's effort to get a *Times* reporter, Earl Caldwell, to identify his news sources within the Black Panthers. Indeed, it was this very case for which Bickel was writing an *amicus* brief and which provided the occasion for the University Club lunch on Monday of that week.

7. Seymour (1975), 199.

8. Barkan interview.

9. Ibid.

10. Unpublished Transcript of Hearing before United States District Judge Murray I. Gurfein, Southern District of New York, in the action of the *United States of America v. The New York Times Company et al.*, 71 Civ. 2662, June 17, 1971, 2–3. (Hereafter cited as Transcript, Hearing before Judge Gurfein, June 17, 1971.)

11. Ibid., 3.

12. Brief for Edward J. Ennis in the action of *Edward J. Ennis et al., Defendants-Intervenors v. United States of America v. The New York Times Company et al.*, 71 Civ. 2662, filed in the United States District Court, Southern District of New York, 3. Transcript, Hearing before Judge Gurfein, June 17, 1971, 3.

13. Ibid., 4, 6.

14. Hess interview.

15. Transcript, Hearing before Judge Gurfein, June 17, 1971, 9, 11, 10.

16. Ibid., 15.

17. Ibid., 18, 20, 26.

18. Ibid., 33.

19. Hess interview. The lawyers apparently did not know that the classification rules required that the entire study have the same classification as that of the most highly classified document in the study. On this point see chap. 1.

20. Hess interview. The list was two and one half pages in length and listed twenty-seven items described as "materials" that related to the "Vietnam Archive commissioned by Secretary of Defense McNamara." The list indicated that the *Times* had just about the entire study except for the four volumes that traced the diplomatic history of the war from 1964 to 1968.

21. Hess had several telephone conversations with Seymour, who was attending a conference for U.S. attorneys in Washington, to persuade him to return to the New York office. But Seymour resisted, telling Hess he was perfectly capable of handling the case. Hess was irritated and eventually told Seymour during one telephone conversation: "Look, this is the most important case probably in this area of the law ever. You're the U.S. attorney and you're not here. Get yourself back." Seymour returned to New York late Thursday afternoon (Hess interview).

22. Seymour (1975), 199–200.

23. Mardian interview.

24. Seymour (1975), 201, 198.

25. Mardian interview; Seymour (1975), 202–3.

26. Mardian interview; Seymour interview; Seymour (1975), 201–3.

8. INSIDE THE WHITE HOUSE, PART 1

1. Nixon (1978), 517, 497–540.

2. NPMP, Haldeman Notes, Box 43, June 15, 1971. Nixon received word that Gurfein had enjoined the *Times* at 4:09 P.M. on Tuesday, June 15, 1971, when Ronald L. Ziegler, his press secretary, interrupted a meeting in the Oval Office to inform Nixon of the development. NPMP, Ehrlichman, Notes of Meetings with President, Box 11, June 15, 1971.

3. NPMP, Haldeman Notes, Box 43, June 15, 1971.

4. Ibid.

5. Ibid., Haldeman Chronos, Box 196, June 15, 1971.

6. NPMP, Haldeman Notes, Box 43, June 15, 1971.

7. Ibid.

8. NPMP, Ehrlichman Notes, Box 11, June 15, 1971.

9. Ibid.

10. NPMP, Haldeman Notes, Box 43, June 16, 1971.

11. Ibid.

12. Ibid.

13. David E. Rosenbaum, "Opponents of War in Congress Decry U.S. Suit on Study," *NYT*, June 17, 1971, 18.

14. Ibid.

15. NPMP, Haldeman Notes, Box 43, June 17, 1971.

16. Ambrose (1989), 406; NPMP, Ehrlichman Notes, Box 11, June 17, 1971.

17. NPMP, Haldeman Notes, Box 43, June 17, 1971.

18. NPMP, Ehrlichman Notes, Box 11, June 17, 1971.

19. Ibid.

20. Haldeman and DiMona (1978), 110–11. Haldeman wrote in his autobiography: "The thought that an alleged weird-o was blatantly challenging the President infuriated him far more than it might, let's say, if Ellsberg had been one of those gray-faced civil servants who, according to Nixon, 'still believed Franklin D. Roosevelt was president'" (111).

21. Haldeman and DiMona (1978), 111. Ehrlichman's reaction to Kissinger's statements about Ellsberg were similar to Haldeman's. Kissinger was "passionate in his denunciation of Daniel Ellsberg. He knew quite a bit about Ellsberg's social proclivities (which Henry deplored) and Ellsberg's conduct in Vietnam" (Ehrlichman [1982], 301).

22. Safire (1975), 74.

23. John W. Finney, "Senate Study Set: Roots of Involvement Sought—Disclosure Worries Rogers," *NYT*, June 16, 1971, 1.

24. Ibid.

25. NPMP, Haldeman Notes, Box 43, June 17–18, 1971.

26. In reply to a question as to whether he believed that the *Times* publication could endanger national security, Sulzberger answered: "I certainly do not. This was not a breach of national security. We gave away no national secrets. We didn't jeopardize any American soldiers or marines overseas. These papers, I think, as our editorial said this morning, are a part of history" ("Sulzberger Terms Documents History," *NYT*, June 17, 1971, 18).

27. NPMP, Haldeman Notes, Box 43, June 18, 1971.

28. Ibid.

29. Nixon (1978), 513.

30. NPMP, Ehrlichman Notes, Box 22, June 17, 1971.

9. THE *WASHINGTON POST* PUBLISHES

1. Ungar (1989), 15.

2. Salisbury (1980), 10.

3. Bradlee interview.

4. Ibid.; Graham interview.

5. Halberstam (1979), 570.

6. Bradlee (1995), 311. In his memoir Bradlee wrote: "Every other paragraph of the *Post* story had to include some form of the words 'according to the *New York Times*,' blood—visible only to us—on every word" (ibid.).

7. Graham interview; Halberstam (1979), 570; Ungar (1989), 130–31.

8. Ungar (1989), 131; Bradlee (1995), 312.

9. This may not have been true because of the possibility that Raskin and Barnet had photocopied the study. See chap. 3, n. 11.

10. Ungar (1989), 131.

11. Salisbury (1980), 292; Ungar (1989), 132.

12. Halberstam (1979), 571; Ungar (1989), 132–33.

13. Ellsberg interview. Much later Sheehan told Ellsberg that publishing the Pentagon Papers was "bigger than both of them," by which he presumably meant that getting the Times to publish the papers was more important than keeping Ellsberg appraised about developments at the newspaper (ibid.).

14. Ungar (1989), 132–33.

15. Klein (1980), 107, 153, 170–74. Agnew sparked "open warfare" between the administration and the press with a November 13, 1969, speech in which he charged that small groups of men—no more than a dozen who lived and worked in Washington, D.C., and New York—control the news. The tension between the administration and the press continued, and throughout the period Agnew stoked the fires with his speeches. Ibid., 153, 169. Safire (1975), 341–65.

16. Ellsberg interview; Ungar (1989), 132–33; Halberstam (1979), 571.

17. Ungar (1989), 134; Halberstam (1979), 571.

18. Ellsberg dropped out of sight Wednesday night. He had heard that the FBI were in Cambridge looking for him because they had questions they wanted him to answer. Rather than be caught before he could make sure that the classified

documents were more fully in the public domain, Ellsberg went underground for twelve days, during which time he coordinated the release of the classified material to several newspapers. Ellsberg interview.

19. Bradlee interview.

20. Ungar (1989), 135.

21. Bradlee interview; Halberstam (1979), 572; Ungar (1989), 138; Bradlee (1995), 313–14.

22. Clark interview; Bradlee interview; Graham interview.

23. Bradlee interview.

24. Clark interview.

25. Ibid.

26. Bradlee interview.

27. Halberstam (1979), 575; Graham interview; Bradlee interview; Ungar (1989), 140.

28. Halberstam (1979), 576.

29. Bradlee interview.

30. Ibid.

31. Ibid.

32. Ibid.

33. Ibid.; Halberstam (1979), 575; Bradlee (1995), 315.

34. Bradlee interview. David Halberstam has a different version of this conversation. He wrote that Williams told Bradlee: "Let me tell you about Nixon, Bradlee. He doesn't have the balls to go after you, Bradlee. He hates you. He probably thinks about going after you more than any man who ever sat in that office. He'd love to go after you, but he doesn't have the balls" ([1979], 575).

The Nixon administration had already sued the *Times*; if it failed to sue the *Post*, then the injunction against the *Times* would be dissolved on the ground that the *Post*'s publication of the same material had made the *Times* injunction moot. Thus, it is highly unlikely that Williams told Bradlee the administration would not sue the *Post* for a prior restraint. See also Bradlee (1995), 316.

35. Bradlee interview.

36. Ungar (1989), 144; Halberstam (1979), 576.

37. Bradlee (1995), 315; Ungar (1989), 145; Halberstam (1979), 576. In the judgment of Sanford Ungar, a *Post* reporter at the time, Roberts's words were influential because of "sheer seniority and a self-confident presence [that] commanded enormous respect at the *Post*" ([1989], 144–45). Halberstam agreed that Roberts was a distinctive influence. Roberts was "the epitome of the establishment reporter; he was the journalistic extension of the national security complex, he judged dangers and enemies on the same scale as the people he covered, and he had almost unconsciously over a career accepted the limitations that his sources had wanted him to accept. He was the kind of reporter high officials judged to be "sound." The fact that he was such a "traditionalist figure" in the eyes of his colleagues, Halberstam has written, gave his words "an extra dimension" that profoundly impressed the others ([1979], 576).

38. Graham interview.

39. Ibid.

40. Ibid.

41. Halberstam (1979), 577.

42. Graham interview.

43. Ibid.
44. Ibid.
45. Ibid.; Bradlee (1995), 316.
46. Ibid.
47. Ibid.
48. Bradlee interview; Halberstam (1979), 578; Ungar (1989), 142.
49. Ungar (1989), 146.
50. Ibid., 146–47.
51. Bradlee interview.
52. Ibid.
53. Ibid.
54. Graham interview.

10. THE FRIDAY HEARING: THE PUBLIC SESSION

1. Unpublished Transcript of Hearing before United States District Judge Murray I. Gurfein, Southern District of New York, in the action of the *United States of America v. The New York Times Company et al.*, 71 Civ. 2662, June 18, 1971, 2. (Hereafter, citations by page number will appear in the text.)

2. Emerson interview.

3. Marilyn Berger, "Warnke Opposes Publication of Report on Diplomacy," *WP*, June 24, 1971, A13.

11. THE FRIDAY HEARING: THE CLOSED SESSION

1. Transcript, Hearing before Judge Gurfein, June 17, 1971, 47.

2. Harrison Salisbury's *Without Fear or Favor: The New York Times and Its Times* (1980) is the only published secondary account that was written with access to the transcript of the closed hearing. Although Salisbury was correct that "the secret session . . . turned Judge Gurfein irrevocably away from the government," his four-page summary of the testimony of the government's four witnesses and his two-page summary of the oral argument are too brief to convey the complexity of the testimony and the way it contributed to the government's defeat before Gurfein.

3. Unpublished Transcript of In Camera Hearing before United States District Judge Murray I. Gurfein, Southern District of New York, in the action of the *United States of America v. New York Times Company et al.*, 71 Civ. 2662, June 18, 1971, 2–3. (Hereafter, citations by page number will appear in the text.)

4. See, for example, Herring, ed. (1985), 629–53.

5. Blouin stated in full: "The targeting I could refer you to IV C 3, pages 17 and 18. On reaction times for airstrikes, volume IV, C 3, page 20. Rules of Engagement, IV, C-3, page 17. Deployment of Ground Forces, page IV c-6, pages 24, 25, and 48, and what I have listed as volume 3, but I forget how that was, and then page 54 I have listed. On contingency plans I recall there is a reference to the SEATO plan, for example, on page V, B 4, book 1, pages 295 and 296." Blouin's references were to the government's original forty-seven volume unpublished version of the Pentagon Papers.

6. In Camera Transcript, Hearing before Judge Gurfein, 18 June 1971, 55. Blouin referred to volume V(B) 451–474 of the original study.

7. For the purpose of discussing the legal arguments, it is easier—certainly less redundant—not to draw a distinction between what was said during the closed hearing and what was argued in the public session, and nothing of significance is sacrificed. Until further notice, subsequent in-text references continue to refer to the *in camera* transcript.

8. Barkan interview.

12. GURFEIN'S DECISION

1. Barkan interview.

2. Ibid.

3. Ibid.

4. *United States v. New York Times Company et al.*, 328 F. Supp. 324, 326, 327 (S.D.N.Y. 1971), hereafter *US v. NYT*, 328 F. Supp.

It is worth noting that the entire Pentagon Papers litigation proceeded on two important assumptions. Because these assumptions were not defined or challenged by any of the parties or by any judicial opinion, I will discuss them here.

It was assumed that the injunction the government sought constituted a prior restraint and that restraints prior to publication should be disfavored in comparison to post-publication sanctions. The practical significance of these two assumptions was that they made it much more difficult for the government to prevail over the newspapers. As the Supreme Court's *per curiam* opinion stated in the Pentagon Papers case: "any system of prior restraints of expression comes to this Court bearing a heavy presumption against its constitutional validity" (403 U.S. 713 [1971]).

Both of these assumptions were at least questionable. Arguments against prior restraints first arose in the sixteenth and seventeenth centuries in response to efforts by secular and religious authorities to limit the flow of information to the public by means of a comprehensive and repressive licensing scheme of printing presses. In England, for example, where the American doctrine of prior restraint had its most immediate roots, printing was prohibited without permission of the Crown, and the prohibitions were enforced by "a stream of royal proclamations, Star Chamber decrees, and Parliamentary enactments" (Thomas Emerson, "The Doctrine of Prior Restraint," *Law and Contemporary Problems* 20 [1955], 648). This system collapsed in 1695, with the expiration of the Licensing Act of 1662, not so much because of any public outcry about the curtailment of free expression but because of the "petty grievances, the exactions, the jobs, the commercial restrictions, the domiciliary visits, which were incidental" to enforcing the licensing laws (Thomas B. Macaulay, *The History of England* [1879], 13, as quoted by Emerson, "Doctrine of Prior Restraint," 651). The First Amendment to the U.S. Constitution was drafted, debated, and adopted against this background, and, as Professor Emerson has concluded, "there can be little doubt that the First Amendment was designed to foreclose in America the establishment of any system of prior restraint on the pattern of English censorship system" (652).

The Supreme Court gave the First Amendment "scant attention" until World War I, when it reviewed several prosecutions brought under the espionage act (Emerson, "Doctrine of Prior Restraint," 652). It did not invoke the doctrine of prior restraint until *Near v. Minnesota,* when it invalidated a Minnesota statute that permitted the state to obtain a judicial order that enjoined "perpetually" any person "engaged in the business" of regularly publishing or circulating an "obscene, lewd and lascivious" or a "malicious, scandalous and defamatory newspaper or periodical." In a dissent on behalf of four justices, Justice Butler contested Chief Justice Hughes's characterization of the Minnesota statute as a prior restraint. He claimed that the Minnesota statute "does not operate as a *previous* restraint on publication within the proper meaning of that phrase." "It is fanciful to suggest," he wrote, a "similarity between the granting or enforcement of the decree authorized by this statute to prevent *further* publication of malicious, scandalous and defamatory articles and the *previous restraint* upon the press by licenses as referred to by Blackstone and described in the history of the times to which he alludes." Butler claimed that the doctrine of prior restraints should be limited to restrictions such as the denial of a license by executive branch officials, since those were the kinds of restraints that gave rise to the doctrine initially (*Near v. Minnesota,* 283 U.S. 697 [1981]).

Professor Emerson, an influential opponent of prior restraints, concluded that there was "much to be said" for Butler's position ("Doctrine of Prior Restraint," 654). When the executive censors it censors without explanation, and it often does so pursuant to vague standards, or no standards at all. If the press believes that the censorship is unjustified, it has the burden of trying to undo the restraint, assuming it has any remedy at all. This is in contrast to when the executive branch requests a court to enjoin publication. In that circumstance a court will hold a hearing, the government has the burden of proving the necessity for such relief, the presiding judge is at least theoretically neutral, and the decision will be based on the evidence introduced at the hearing and in conformity with announced legal standards.

Even though the majority in *Near* concluded that the doctrine of prior restraint applied to judicially granted injunctions, it did not explain why that should be, nor did it define what constituted a prior restraint. Moreover, the Court did not improve on its statements in *Near* during the intervening years. Thus, Professor Emerson was able to write in 1955 that there is "at present, no common understanding as to what constitutes 'prior'" ("Doctrine of Prior Restraint," 655), and Professor Harry Kalven, another noted First Amendment scholar, made a similar observation in 1971: "it is not altogether clear just what a prior restraint is or just what is the matter with it" (H. Kalven, Jr., "Foreword: Even When a Nation Is at War," *Harvard Law Review* 1 [1971], 85). Judge Hans Linde has remarked: "The rule against . . . prior restraint entered modern Supreme Court doctrine under the aegis of history rather than logic or policy" ("Courts and Censorship," *Minnesota Law Review* 66 [1981], 171, 185).

As for the Court's second assumption, prior restraints were disfavored because they were imposed by executive branch officials, who usually possessed unreviewable authority in deciding what to censor or whom to license. But once the Court in *Near* defined prior restraint to include prepublication restraints imposed by the judiciary, the reasons that had historically supported disfavoring prior restraints were no longer so persuasive. The result was that the scholarly debate over why prior restraints should be disfavored in comparison to post-publication sanctions was enlivened. Scholars made numerous specific claims, but two camps emerged—those who claimed that prior restraints should be disfavored and those who did not. Although there was broad agreement that a legal presumption against prior restraints permitted more information to reach the public domain than would otherwise happen, the two camps disagreed over the wisdom or utility of this result.

Those who favored a presumption against prior restraints believed the benefits of disclosure outweighed the risks inherent in such a legal regime, while those opposing a legal presumption disagreed.

In the Pentagon Papers case all nine justices of the Supreme Court characterized the government's request for an injunction as a prior restraint and assumed that prior restraints were disfavored in comparison to post-publication sanctions.

5. *US v. NYT*, 328 F. Supp., 327.

6. Ibid., 328–29.

7. Ibid., 330.

8. Ibid., 330–31.

9. Ibid., 331.

10. Ibid., 331. Prior case law construing the First Amendment was voluminous. Yet there was very little case law concerning prior restraints. The law of prior restraints had been applied to invalidating procedurally faulty schemes of government censorship of books and films and to strike down discriminatory taxes and the press. See, for example, *Bantam Books, Inc. v. Sullivan*, 372 U.S. 58 (1963); *Freedman v. Maryland*, 380 U.S. 51 (1965); and *Grosjean v. American Press Co.* 297 U.S. 233 (1936). Only a few weeks before the Court's decision in the Pentagon Papers case the Court utilized the prior restraint doctrine to invalidate restraints intended to protect homeowner's privacy (*Organization for a Better Austin v. Keefe*, 402 U.S. 415 [1971]). Nonetheless, there was no case in which the federal government sought a prior restraint to protect the national security.

As a reflection of this overall condition the briefs submitted by the parties to Judge Gurfein—as would be true with all the briefs and all the judicial opinions in the entire Pentagon Papers litigation—discussed *Near v. Minnesota* as the main (and, in most situations, the only) relevant prior decision.

11. Hess interview; Seymour interview; Abrams interview.

12. *United States v. New York Times Company et al.* (2nd Cir. 1971), Judge Irving R. Kaufman's order, printed in *NYT*, June 20, 1971, 26.

13. Ibid.

13. THE *POST* IS RESTRAINED

1. Mardian interview.

2. Bradlee (1995), 318.

3. Bradlee interview; Rehnquist interview.

4. Graham interview.

5. Bradlee interview.

6. Mardian interview.

7. I do not have the two affidavits, but, given what Gesell eventually said about the government's evidentiary showing when he denied the request for a temporary restraining order, they were without question conclusionary in nature and brief. They were probably modeled after the ones signed by Buzhardt and Mardian and submitted in the *Times* case on Tuesday.

8. Unpublished Transcript of Hearing before United States District Judge Gerhard A. Gesell, D.C. District Court, in the action of *United States v. Washington Post Company et al.*, 71 Civ. 1235, June 18, 1971, 17. (Hereafter, citations by page number will appear in the text.)

9. Unpublished Memorandum by U.S. District Judge Gesell, *United States v. The Washington Post Company et al.*, 71 Civ. 1235, filed June 18, 1971, United States District Court for the District of Columbia.

10. Ibid.

11. Bradlee interview.

12. Sanford J. Ungar, "U.S. Court Bars Future Vietnam Articles in *Post*," *WP*, June 19, 1971, A12.

13. Bradlee interview.

14. *United States v. The Washington Post*, 446 F. 2d 1322 (D.C. Cir. Ct. 1971).

15. Ibid., 1323–25.

16. Ibid.

17. Ibid., 1325–27.

14. ON THE EVE OF THE *POST*'S TRIAL

1. Unpublished Transcript of Hearing before United States District Judge Gerhard A. Gesell, D.C. District, in the action of *The United States v. The Washington Post Company et al.*, 71 Civ. 1235, June 21, 1971, 3–5.

2. Ibid.

3. Affidavit of Dennis J. Doolin, June 20, 1971, filed in the action of *United States v. The Washington Post Company et al.*

4. Affidavit of Melvin Zais, June 21, 1971, filed in the action of *United States v. The Washington Post Company et al.*

5. Affidavit of William B. Macomber, June 20, 1971, filed in the action of *United States v. The Washington Post Company et al.*

6. "*Post*'s Brief against Barring Series," *WP*, June 22, 1971, A10.

7. Ibid.

8. Ibid.

9. Bradlee was referring, of course, to *Washington Plans an Aggressive War*, by Marcus Raskin, Ralph Stavins, and Richard J. Barnet.

10. Affidavit of Benjamin C. Bradlee, June 20, 1971, 1–2.

11. Affidavit of Chalmers M. Roberts, June 20, 1971, 2.

15. GESELL'S DECISION

1. Unpublished Transcript of Hearing before United States District Judge Gerhard A. Gesell, D.C. District, in the action of *United States v. Washington Post Company et al.*, 71 Civ. 1235, June 21, 1971, 3–7. (Hereafter, citations to this transcript by page number will appear in the text.)

2. Unpublished Transcript of the In Camera Hearing before United States District Judge Gerhard A. Gesell, D.C. District, in the action of *United States v. Washington Post Company et al.*, 71 Civ. 1235, June 21, 1971, 100. (Hereafter, citations by page number, preceded by "In Camera," will appear in the text.)

3. It is possible that Gesell may have considered the exact wording of the affidavit legally insufficient when compared to his idea of the government's legal burden—evidence of a grave and immediate threat—but there could be no question that Zais's statements concerned current and not past troop movements. Or perhaps Gesell thought that Zais's allegation could be ignored since he did not testify.

But that thinking would have been contrary to the agreement among Gesell and the lawyers for both sides that the affidavits submitted by the government witnesses were to be considered the equivalent of testimony. Or Gesell may have studied the references Zais offered in his affidavit and concluded that they did not support the charge that further disclosures would affect current troop movements. But if Gesell had done that he might have said so. In addition, he did not have time to read the citations, since the Pentagon Papers were not delivered to the courthouse until well after the proceedings had begun that day.

16. THE SECOND CIRCUIT

1. Seymour interview; Hess interview.
2. Seymour interview.
3. Ibid.; Hess interview.
4. Seymour interview; Hess interview.
5. Brief for Appellant United States of America in *United States of America v. New York Times Company et al.*, 71–1617, filed in the United States Court of Appeals for the Second Circuit, 5.
6. Ibid., 14–17.
7. Ibid., 32.
8. Ibid., 30.
9. Ibid., 30, 31, 31a, 32. Special Appendix Relating to In Camera Proceedings and Sealed Exhibits Submitted by Appellant United States in *United States v. New York Times Company et al.*, 71–1617, filed in the United States Court of Appeals for the Second Circuit.
10. Brief submitted by the *New York Times* in *United States v. New York Times Company et al.*, 71–1617, filed in the United States Court of Appeals for the Second Circuit, 35.
11. Ibid., 42.
12. 18 U.S.C. 793(e).
13. Perhaps of even more importance, Section 793(e) did not seem to apply to newspaper publications. The statute made it a crime for a person who "willfully communicates, delivers, transmits or causes to be communicated, delivered, or transmitted, or attempts to communicate, deliver, transmit or cause to be communicated, delivered, transmitted" information relating to the national defense. Assuming that the classified information that the *Times* published related to national defense, as that phrase was used in the statute, it was hardly a straightforward question whether the statute covered newspaper publications and whether a nationally renowned newspaper published information with the requisite willfulness that the statute required.

The *Times* asserted that Section 793(e) made it a crime for a person to communicate, deliver, or transmit defense secrets to an individual not authorized to receive such information and to do so with the intent of injuring the United States. It maintained that it published material and that the statute intentionally did not use the word "publish" so there would be no mistake that the statute did not apply to newspapers. It also maintained that the legislative history made it clear that Congress did not intend to criminalize newspaper publications.

14. Confidential Memorandum of Defendant *New York Times* Company Re In Camera Testimony, submitted by the *New York Times* in *United States v. New*

York Times Company et al., 71–1617, filed in the United States Court of Appeals for the Second Circuit.

15. Transcript of Hearing before the United States Court of Appeals for the Second Circuit, in *United States v. New York Times Company et al.,* 71–1617, June 21, 1971. (Hereafter, citations by page number will appear in the text.)

16. Unpublished Transcript of the Hearing before United States Court of Appeals, *en banc,* in *United States v. New York Times Company et al.,* 71–1617, June 22, 1971, 4, 8. (Hereafter, citations by page numbers preceded by "June 22" will appear in the text.)

17. Upon the completion of Bickel's argument the Circuit Court heard from Norman Dorsen, who represented the ACLU, which appeared as *amicus curiae.* Dorsen's brief remarks were sizzling and effective. Dorsen emphasized that the deep flaw of a prior restraint was that it suppressed speech "by a stroke of the pen," which, he pointed out, was exactly what happened when Judge Gurfein granted the temporary restraining order in this case (ibid., 74). According to Dorsen, Gurfein's restraining order, which by then had been in place for eight days, itself constituted "a severe defeat for the First Amendment" (77). Dorsen also maintained that even if the *Times* prevailed, the victory might itself present a serious threat to a free press unless the court explicitly narrowed the availability of prior restraints to the disclosure of information that was directly relevant to "future military operations" and that was irrelevant to the public discussion of the important public issues (76). Once the case was finally decided, Judge Oakes of the court of appeals told Dorsen that his remarks persuaded him to vote to affirm Judge Gurfein's decision (Dorsen interview).

18. Unpublished Transcript of the In Camera Hearing before the Court of Appeals for the Second Circuit, in *United States v. New York Times Company et al.,* 71–1617, June 22, 1971. (Hereafter, citations by page numbers preceded by "In Camera" will appear in the text.)

19. *United States v. New York Times Company et al.,* 444 F. 2d 544 (2nd Cir. 1971).

20. Ibid.

17. THE D.C. CIRCUIT

1. "U.S. Brief Appealing Judge Gesell's Rejection of Injunction," *WP*, June 23, 1971, A15.

2. "*Post*'s Brief against Enjoining Series on Vietnam," *WP*, June 23, 1971, A14.

3. Griswold interview.

4. Griswold (1992), 301.

5. Mitchell interview.

6. Ibid.

7. No transcript of the hearing is available. Whether that is because none was kept or because it is misplaced, which is more likely, is uncertain. Hence, the account of the hearing is based on contemporary reports published in the *New York Times* and the *Washington Post.* See Fred P. Graham, "*Times* Case Heard, Restraint Extended; U.S. Action Halts a *Boston Globe* Series," *NYT*, June 23, 1971, 1; James M. Naughton, "Washington Appeals Court Continues Ban on the *Post*'s Series on Vietnam," *NYT*, June 23, 1971, 23; "Courts Continue *Post, Times* Ban;

Globe Restrained," *WP*, June 23, 1971, 1 (includes two articles: Sanford J. Ungar, "The *Post*"; George Lardner, Jr., "The *Times*"). See also Ungar (1989), 201–3.

8. Ungar (1989), 203.

9. Sanford J. Ungar, "*Post* Upheld by Appeals Court: Publication Extended Two Days," *WP*, June 24, 1971, 1; Carroll Kilpatrick and Richard L. Lyons, "Nixon Gives Hill Access to Studies," *WP*, June 24, 1971, 1.

10. Ungar (1989), 204; Bradlee (1995), 320.

11. *United States v. Washington Post Company et al.*, 446 F. 2d 1327 (D.C. Cir. 1971).

12. "Chicago and Boston Papers Publish Accounts of Study," *NYT*, June 23, 1971, 1.

13. Sanford J. Ungar, "U.S. Appeals *Post* Case to High Court," *WP*, June 25, 1971, 1; Ungar (1989), 210–11.

14. *United States v. Washington Post Company et al.*, 446 F. 2d 1327, 1331 (D.C. Cir. 1971).

15. Transcript, Conference on the Pentagon Papers, Kennedy School of Government, Harvard University, April 2 1991, 109.

18. INSIDE THE WHITE HOUSE, PART 2

1. Ellsberg's frustration caused by Gurfein's injunction of the *Times* became complicated by Wednesday afternoon, June 16, as he became increasingly afraid that the FBI might catch up with him. Although the *Times* did not reveal its source for the documents when it published its first installment, Ellsberg's instincts were reliable. In the minds of people who knew of the Pentagon Papers, the number of individuals who might have conceivably leaked the documents to the press were not many, and of those who might have Ellsberg was considered most likely. Moreover, Ellsberg had let it be known to many people during the preceding eighteen months that he had some important, classified documents pertaining to the war that he was trying to make public. The FBI had learned from Ellsberg's former wife that he had photocopied the Pentagon Papers over a year before.

On Wednesday, June 16, Ellsberg gave a three-hour interview with *Newsweek*. *Newsweek* asked for the interview because Ellsberg had emerged among the reporters investigating the leak as the most likely suspect. During the same afternoon Ellsberg was telephoned by the television networks for interviews, as well as by Sidney Zion, a former *Times* reporter.

These telephone calls convinced Ellsberg that he was on the verge of being charged and arrested. Once the *Newsweek* interview was completed, he and his wife, Patricia, went into hiding. He did not emerge until Monday, June 28, when, in the company of his lawyers, he surrendered himself to federal law enforcement officials.

While he was in hiding Ellsberg managed to make part of the Pentagon Papers available to the *Washington Post*. After the D.C. Circuit enjoined the *Post* Ellsberg took steps to make the classified documents available to other newspapers. Ellsberg will not disclose how he actually distributed the documents to other newspapers and who aided him in the distribution.

These disclosures began with the *Boston Globe* publishing excerpts from the Pentagon Papers on Monday morning, June 21. Later that day the *Chicago Sun-Times* published excerpts. The next day, Tuesday, June 22, the *Los Angeles Times* and eleven newspapers in the Knight chain published articles based on excerpts from the classified history. On Friday, June 25, the *Chicago Sun-Times* published another article that it claimed was based on the Pentagon Papers, and the *St. Louis Post-Dispatch* published an article based on the classified documents. On Monday, June 28, the *Christian Science Monitor* published an article based on the secret history. Two days later, the day that the Supreme Court made its decision public, the *Christian Science Monitor* and *Newsday* each published articles based on the disputed documents.

Of all of these newspapers, the administration sued only the *Boston Globe* and the *St. Louis Post-Dispatch*, and in both cases it obtained an injunction barring further publication. Attorney General John Mitchell and Assistant Attorney General Mardian have each claimed that the administration sued just these two newspapers because they were the only ones that published material not already in the public domain and considered by defense officials injurious to the national security. These two Justice Department officials also claimed that there was a risk that these newspapers might publish additional excerpts from the Pentagon Papers.

Sanford J. Ungar has suggested that Mitchell's and Mardian's explanation is unpersuasive because essentially all the newspapers published "secret material of the same basic nature." Instead, Ungar has claimed that the Nixon administration sued the four newspapers (*Times, Post, Globe*, and *Post-Dispatch*) that were "strong opponents of the Nixon administration" (Ungar [1989], 191–92).

It is unlikely that Ungar's explanation is correct. By the time the *Boston Globe* and the *Chicago Sun-Times* published their articles on Monday the Nixon administration had the *Times* and the *Post* under injunction. The courts that had granted those injunctions would have quickly dissolved them if the administration had permitted another newspaper to publish excerpts that threatened national security on the ground that the administration was permitting a third newspaper to publish material that other newspapers were enjoined from publishing. Because the administration would not have wanted to risk having its lawsuits against the *Times* and the *Post* to be dismissed, it is most unlikely that the administration chose who to sue based on the political persuasion of the editorial page.

There is another reason Ungar's explanation is unpersuasive. If the decision to sue or not to sue was made on the basis of the political persuasion of the newspaper, it is most likely that that decision would have been made by Nixon and his top White House aides. But the documents—Haldeman and Ehrlichman's notes of meetings with the president and memoranda prepared by numerous White House officials—contain not the slightest bit of evidence that Nixon or his top aides ever discussed whether a lawsuit should or should not be brought against a particular newspaper. These same documents unequivocally indicate that the litigation over the disputed Pentagon documents and the broader political fallout stemming from the disclosures as well as the lawsuits were constant topics of discussion within the White House. But they contain no indication of any discussion over the decision to sue the *Boston Globe* or the *St. Louis Post-Dispatch*, or the *Washington Post*, for that matter. This suggests that the decisions to sue the *Globe* and the *Post-Dispatch* was made by Justice Department officials. That probably means the decisions were made by Mardian and cleared with Mitchell. It also means that the decision whether to sue a particular newspaper or not was made mainly on the basis of preserving the administration's claim for injunctive relief.

2. NPMP, Haldeman Notes, Box 43, June 14–26, 1971.
3. Ibid.
4. Ibid.
5. Ehrlichman (1982), 302; Haldeman and DiMona (1978), 110.
6. NPMP, Haldeman Notes, Box 130, Memorandum by Colson to H. R. Haldeman, June 25, 1971.
7. Ibid.
8. Ibid.
9. Haldeman's notes of meetings with Nixon during these days in June (14–26) included innumerable references to the Hiss case.

19. THE SUPREME COURT TAKES THE CASE

1. Goodale, comp. (1971), 987–1007.
2. Ibid., 13–14.
3. Ibid., 1001.
4. Goodale, comp. (1971), 1045.
5. Sanford J. Ungar, "U.S. Appeals *Post* Case to High Bench," *WP*, June 25, 1971, 1.
6. Ibid.; "Government Plea to Supreme Court," *WP*, June 26, 1971, A11.
7. Griswold (1992), 303.
8. Fred P. Graham, "*Times* Asks Supreme Court to End Restraints on Its Vietnam Series; U.S. Loses in Move to Curb *Post*: Action Today Seen," *NYT*, June 25, 1971, 1.
9. Woodward and Armstrong (1979), 141–42.
10. Griswold (1992), 303.
11. Abrams interview.
12. Goodale, comp. (1971), 1050–51.
13. Fred P. Graham, "Supreme Court Agrees to Rule on Printing of Vietnam Series; Arguments to Be Heard Today," *NYT*, June 26, 1971, 1.
14. Ungar (1989), 214. In his recent memoir Ben Bradlee recounts an incident that sheds considerable light on how complex the equation can be in an editor's mind in deciding on what weight to give to the public's right to know. It also offers a dramatic example of just how tense and difficult the days were for the individuals involved while the litigation was pending.

Very late Wednesday night, after the D.C. Circuit had ruled for the *Post*, Bradlee dispatched two reporters, Spencer Rich and Martin Weil, to Chief Justice Warren Burger's home, expecting the government to apply to him for an order barring the *Post* from publishing. Rich and Weil rang the Chief Justice's doorbell about midnight, and what happened after that is described in a memorandum that Weil wrote:

> After about a minute or two, the Chief Justice opened the door. He was wearing a bath robe. He was carrying a gun. The gun was in his right hand, muzzle pointed down. It was a long-barreled steel weapon. The Chief Justice did not seem glad to see us. Spencer explained why we were there. There was a considerable amount of misdirected conversation. It seemed for a bit that the people were talking past each other. Spencer, who held up his credentials, was explaining why we were there, but the judge seemed to be saying that we shouldn't have come. Finally, after a little more talk, everybody seemed to understand everybody. The Chief Justice said it would be all right for us to wait for any possible

> Justice Department emissaries, but we could wait down the street. He held his gun in his hand throughout a two or three minute talk. Sometimes it was not visible, held behind the door post. He never pointed it at us. He closed the door. We went down the street and waited for about three hours. Then we went home.

Bradlee wrote that he was at home when someone at the newspaper called him to ask whether the report of the incident should run on page 1 or inside. Bradlee exploded: "What story? . . . Just because the Chief Justice of the United States comes to the door of his home in the dead of night in his jammies, waving a gun at two *Washington Post* reporters in the middle of a vital legal case involving the *Washington Post*, you guys think that's a story?"

Bradlee killed the report, and in his memoirs he apologized for his decision: "All I could think of was how much Chief Justice Burger disliked the press in general, and the *Post* in particular, how ridiculous the alleged story would make him look (I could visualize the Herblock cartoon with clarity), and how much I wanted to avoid pissing him off a few days before he took our fate in his hands" (Bradlee [1995], 321–22).

15. Ungar (1989), 214–15.

16. Brennan interview.

20. THE BRIEFS

1. Griswold (1992), 303; Griswold interview.

2. Griswold (1992), 304.

3. Ibid.

4. Brief for the United States (Secret Portion) filed in *New York Times Company v. United States* (Oct. Term, 1970, No. 1873), and *United States v. The Washington Post Company* (Oct. Term, 1970, No. 1885), in the U.S. Supreme Court. (Hereafter, citations by page number will appear in the text.)

5. The most conveniently available version of the four diplomatic volumes is Herring, ed. (1985).

6. Griswold began with this point because he considered it of the utmost importance. As he wrote in his autobiography, "I particularly relied" on the "negotiating track" volumes and "devoted a full page to these materials in my closed or secret brief," in addition to laying "particular emphasis on this material" in his oral argument" ([1992], 304).

It was peculiar that Griswold placed so much emphasis on the diplomatic volumes, because both the *Times* and the *Post* had represented that they did not have them. But Griswold has stated he did not know this during the litigation and that he learned it for the first time from Daniel Ellsberg in April 1991 (ibid., 310, n. 37). Although there is no reason to question any of Griswold's claims, it is strange that no government official who worked on the two cases told him what the record revealed.

7. To support these claims, the sealed brief referred to Volume V(B)(4)(a), 249–257 and 259–311; and Volume IV(A)(1), A26–A31. Pages 249–257 of Volume V(B)(4)(a) and pages A26–A31 of Volume IV(A)(1) remain excised and thus are not publicly available.

8. To support this claim, the sealed brief referred to Volume IV(C)(6)(b), 129. This information remains excised and thus is not publicly available.

9. To support this claim, the sealed brief referred to Volume IV(C)(6)(b), 157. This information remains excised and thus is not publicly available.

10. To support this claim, the sealed brief referred to Volume IV(C)(6)(b), 168. This information remains excised and thus is not publicly available.

11. To support this claim, the sealed brief referred to Volume IV(C)(7)(b), 161–63. This telegram remains excised and thus is not publicly available.

12. To support this claim, the sealed brief referred to Volume IV(C)(9)(b), 52. A relatively small passage on page 52 remains excised and thus is not publicly available.

13. E.g., Griswold (1992), 305.

14. Stone interview.

15. Brief for the United States (Public Brief) filed in *New York Times Company v. United States* (Oct. Term, 1970, No. 1873), and *United States v. The Washington Post Company* (Oct. Term, 1970, No. 1885), in the Supreme Court, 1–2, 6, 7. (Hereafter, citations by page number will appear in the text.) This brief is reprinted in Goodale, comp. (1971), 1161–82.

16. Brief for the *Washington Post* Company (Secret) filed in *United States v. The Washington Post Company* (Oct. Term, 1970, No. 1885), in the Supreme Court, 1, 11. (Hereafter, citations by page number will appear in the text.)

17. Brief for the New York Times (Public Brief) filed in *New York Times v. United States* (Oct. Term, 1970, No. 1873), in the Supreme Court, 31. (Hereafter, citations by page number will appear in the text.) This brief is reprinted in Goodale, comp. (1971), 1080–160.

21. THE ARGUMENT

1. Griswold interview; Abrams interview.

2. Brennan interview.

3. Transcript of the Oral Argument in the Supreme Court in the *New York Times v. United States* (Oct. Term, 1970, No. 1873), and *United States v. The Washington Post Company* (Oct. Term 1970, No. 1885), reprinted in the *NYT*, June 27, 1971, 24–26. (Hereafter Transcript, Supreme Court Oral Argument.)

4. Handwritten notes of Justice William O. Douglas from the "conference" on cases 1873 and 1885 (June 26, 1971, Justice William O. Douglas Papers, Box 1519, Manuscripts Division, Library of Congress). (Hereafter Douglas Notes.)

5. Transcript, Supreme Court Oral Argument, reprinted in *NYT*, June 27, 1971, 24. Because subsequent quotations from Griswold's portion of the oral argument come from the *New York Times* reprint, additional references will not be given.

6. Transcript, Supreme Court Oral Argument, reprinted in *NYT*, June 27, 1971, 24–26. Because quotations from Bickel's portion of the oral argument are from the *New York Times* reprint, references will not be given.

7. Burger's point was not beyond appreciation and was more understandable than even he knew when he made it. The government could not be faulted for failing to prevent Sunday's publication because the *Times* had kept its project a secret. The government might be faulted for not acting on Sunday to stop Monday's edition, for Monday's *Times* went to press early Sunday evening, which gave the government Sunday to prepare the necessary legal papers. But as we have seen,

Nixon had decided that no matter how harmful the publication would be to what he characterized as the "war effort," the administration should do nothing because of the political benefits to the administration generated by the disclosure of the study. Kissinger caused Nixon to change his mind on Sunday afternoon, but even then Nixon's initial idea was that the *Times* should be criminally prosecuted, which did not require immediate action. It was not until Monday that Justice Department officials reviewed the *Times* publication with security officials and decided to recommend that the administration sue the *Times* for a prior restraint. At that point the administration faced several hurdles. The study was prepared during the Johnson administration, and only Dennis Doolin, a deputy assistant secretary of defense, seemed to be familiar with its content. It would take some hours before anyone could assess the *Times* publication and decide what threat, if any, it posed for the nation's security. Furthermore, the assessment was complicated because the study included documents from the State and Defense Departments, the CIA, the National Security Agency, and the White House, which meant that assessing them required interagency cooperation. Nevertheless, the administration did have until early Monday evening to seek a restraining order that would have prevented the Tuesday edition from being published, and one might fairly wonder why the government delayed until Tuesday morning to sue and whether the delay was due to the fact that no one within the government actually sounded an alarm, as Bickel suggested. But that too is not accurate. Alexander Haig, Kissinger's deputy at the National Security Council, spent part of Saturday evening trying to figure out what was in the study and who might have leaked it. On Sunday morning Defense Secretary Melvin Laird telephoned Attorney General Mitchell about the report, asking what he should say if asked that morning on one of the Sunday morning TV talk shows. Fred Buzhardt spent part of Sunday reviewing the study and consulting with Defense officials about it. Mardian, who was not aware of the *Times* series until Monday morning, seems to have been so agitated by it that he could be fairly described as sounding an "alarm" even if the others could be described as merely concerned. Secretary of State Rogers was so angered by the report he advised the Justice Department to bring an action for replevin against the *Times*. In addition, according to Mardian, it was not easy to reach an agreement within the Justice Department to seek a prior restraint, and then White House officials had to be persuaded this was the right course of action to pursue.

8. Transcript, Supreme Court Oral Argument, reprinted in *NYT*, June 27, 1971, 24–26. Because quotations from Glendon's portion of the oral argument are from the *New York Times* reprint, references will not be given.

9. Transcript, Supreme Court Oral Argument, reprinted in *NYT*, June 27, 1971, 24–26. Because all quotations from Griswold's rebuttal are from the *New York Times* reprint, references will not be given.

10. Douglas Notes, June 26, 1971.

11. Ibid.

12. Ibid.

13. Ibid.

14. Ibid.

15. Ibid.

16. Ibid.

17. Ibid.

18. Ibid.

22. THE DECISION

1. The Supreme Court's decision in the Pentagon Papers Case is reported at 403 U.S. 713 (1971). (Hereafter, citations by page number will appear in the text.)

2. Brennan interview.

3. John Marshall Papers, Princeton University Library, Box 440, "First Draft (June 28, 1971)." (Hereafter Harlan Papers.)

4. Harlan Papers, Box 440. Both notes to Justice Brennan were dated June 29, 1971.

5. Ibid.

6. Fred P. Graham, "Supreme Court, 6–3, Upholds Newspapers on Publication of the Pentagon Report; *Times* Resumes Its Series, Halted Fifteen Days," *NYT*, July 1, 1971, 1.

7. Black was quoting Hughes in *DeJonge v. Oregon*, 299 U.S. 353, 365 (1937).

8. Black (1986), 266. The lyrics of the song are set out in Woodward and Armstrong (1979), 147–48. Although Mrs. Black states that the song's name is "I Am a Dirty Rebel," Woodward and Armstrong use the title "I'm a Good Old Rebel."

9. Black (1986), 266.

10. William O. Douglas Papers, Box 1519, Manuscript Division, Library of Congress, draft opinion, June 26, [1971]. (Hereafter Douglas Papers.)

11. See multiple draft opinions, Douglas Papers, Box 1519. Douglas's handwritten draft opinion stated that the president was commander in chief and dominant in foreign affairs. But those mundane assertions were followed by this sentence: "So I assume there is scope for Presidential suppression of some categories of 'news.'" Standing alone, that sentence might have meant that the president had the power to suppress news within the executive branch. But that construction was contradicted by Douglas's next sentence, which stated that lower courts had concluded that disclosure of the disputed documents "would not seriously breach the national security." Douglas would have had no occasion to write that sentence unless he thought the president had power to suppress the publication of some "news." But Douglas insisted that suppression was improper in this case because the threatened disclosures did not amount to a "serious breach of the national security" (ibid.).

After his handwritten draft was typed but before it was printed as "1st Draft" Douglas inserted at the beginning a paragraph that quoted the First Amendment and contained the following two sentences: "What room may be left for Congressional restraint on the press raises a nice and narrow question which we need not answer here. But the First Amendment counsels that any Act of Congress having that purpose be read in an extremely narrow way." Here Douglas explicitly conceded that Congress could pass a law abridging the right of the press to publish material it possessed. This was at odds with his comments during the oral argument and several prior opinions. But the concession was unequivocal, and when joined with his statement that the president could suppress some "news," it was clear that Douglas was accepting a degree of government censorship inconsistent with the absolutist position with which he had long been associated (ibid.).

In editing the first printed draft of his opinion Douglas replaced the sentences that conceded to Congress the power to limit press freedoms with a claim that the

First Amendment left "no room for Congressional restraint on the press." But this prohibition was limited to "Congressional restraint" as opposed to "governmental restraint." At the same time Douglas added a footnote that diluted the protection offered in his text. The footnote stated:

> I have gone over the material that is listed in the *in camera* brief of the United States. Some of it discloses only what sharp reporting by one who knows Vietnam has already done or could easily do on his own. For example, clandestine recruitment by CIA of Vietnamese civil and military officials is notorious, including their starting salaries. The seam of influence of Formosan Chinese in Vietnam is well-known. The conversations between Soviet and United States Ambassadors are assumed to be 'bugged' and any semblance of privacy is non-existent. Messages of intermediaries who went between Washington, D.C., and Hanoi in 1964 and 1965 are ancient history. A 1961 appraisal of SEATO is also ancient history. The implication that the CIA was involved in the removal of Diem was published years ago in a Vietnamese paper. The material in the *in camera* brief of the United States certainly falls far short of the exceptional situation, if any, where the command of the First Amendment (which in terms is absolute) should give way.
>
> The case for bureaucratic embarrassment is strong; the case for carving out an exception to the First Amendment by judicial *fiat* is extremely weak.
>
> Ibid.

In the draft Douglas obviously accepted the idea that the Court could enjoin publication if the government's evidence was weighty enough. But to persuade his reader that the government's evidence was in fact weak Douglas summarized the classified information the government presented in its *in camera* brief.

Douglas's printed third draft moved closer to an absolutist position. His first paragraph retained the statement that the wording of the First Amendment "leaves . . . no room for Congressional restraint on the press." He deleted the sentence that the president had power to suppress the news and claimed that the president lacked power to seek a prior restraint from the courts. As for the footnote Douglas excised the sentences that indicated that the First Amendment permitted prior restraints, thus making his draft opinion consistent. In place of the summary of national security matters cited in the government's sealed brief, he wrote: "I have gone over the material listed in the *in camera* brief of the United States. It is all history, not future events. None of it is more recent than 1968" (ibid.).

Even given these changes, Douglas's opening paragraph still made the limited assertion that the First Amendment prohibited "Congressional" restraints on the press, which left open the possibility of executive or judicial restraints. It was only when Douglas edited his third printed draft that he substituted "governmental" for "Congressional" (ibid.).

12. Ibid.

13. Ibid.

14. Ibid.

15. Brennan interview.

16. Ibid.

17. Brennan interview.

18. Douglas Notes, June 26, 1971.

19. Harlan Papers, Box 440. See drafts 1 and 3, June 29, 1971.

20. Ibid. See drafts 1 and 2, June 29, 1971.

21. Douglas Notes, June 26, 1971.

22. Marshall may have written this passage with only the Pentagon Papers cases in mind. But that seems unlikely. In April the Justice Department had sought an injunction barring the Vietnam Veterans Against the War from establishing a

mock Vietnam encampment on the Mall in front of the U.S. Capitol. The injunction was granted by U.S. district judge George L. Hart, Jr., "an outspoken conservative with impeccable Republican credentials and a well-established dislike for protesters." Hart granted the injunction, but a three-judge panel of the United States Court of Appeals for the D.C. Circuit reversed. The Justice Department made an emergency appeal to Chief Justice Warren Burger in his capacity as circuit justice for the District of Columbia, and he reinstated the injunction, even before Ramsey Clark, the former Johnson administration attorney general who was representing the veterans, had time to submit his opposing papers. At that point Nixon had doubts about police forcing the veterans off the Mall, and the Justice Department failed to enforce the injunction. Judge Hart was enraged. He upbraided the government lawyers and dissolved his injunction (Ungar [1989], 118, 119). The morning the *Washington Post* reported on this incident, Justice Marshall circulated a memorandum to his colleagues on the Court. Part of the news report quoted by Marshall stated: "Hart, scowling and shouting, told Gray and three other government lawyers that 'this court feels that one equal and coordinate branch of the government, the judiciary, has been dangerously and improperly used by another, the executive.'" Marshall then added his own words: "While I will neither scowl nor shout, I find myself in complete agreement with Judge Hart. I suppose this is another anomaly inherent in 'government by injunction'" (Harlan Papers, Box 499, Memorandum to the Conference, April 23, 1971, from Justice Thurgood Marshall).

23. Brennan interview.

23. THE IMPACT OF THE DISCLOSURES

1. Ungar (1989), 251.

2. "Sulzberger Expresses 'Complete Joy' at Ruling," *NYT*, July 1, 1971, 15.

3. Leslie Gelb, "Today's Lessons from the Pentagon Papers," *Life*, Sept. 17, 1971, 34.

4. George McT. Kahin, "The Pentagon Papers: A Critical Evaluation," *American Political Science Review* 69 (1975): 675.

5. Neil Sheehan, "1945 Pleas by Ho Revealed by U.S.," *NYT*, Sept. 22, 1971, 5; Ungar (1989), 293, 302.

6. The Gravel edition was "on the presses" when the government's version went on sale on Sept. 27, 1971 (*NYT*, Sept. 28, 1971, 5). See also *The Pentagon Papers: The Defense Department History of United States Decisionmaking on Vietnam* (1971), 5:314. (Hereafter, Gravel edition.)

7. Gravel Edition, 5:314. On Tuesday evening, June 29, 1971, the night before the Supreme Court's decision, Senator Gravel began doing what Ellsberg had not been able to get other members of Congress to do during the previous year and a half: he began to read the classified documents into the congressional record and to distribute large portions of them to members of the press.

8. "This material does not embody the whole Defense Department study, but only those portions which had come into the Senator's possession at that time" (ibid.).

9. Ungar (1989), 302.

10. Gravel edition, 5:314–15. See also Kahin, "The Pentagon Papers," 695–96.

11. Ungar (1989), 302.

12. Herring, ed. (1985), xiii, xiv, xv.

13. Herring, ed. (1985), xvii–xxii.

14. Erwin N. Griswold, "No Harm Was Done," *NYT*, June 30, 1991, sec. 4, 15.

15. Nixon (1978), 508–15.

16. Kissinger (1991), 729–30.

17. Ellsberg did not give the press the footnotes to the study where some or most of this information was located. Griswold (1992), 310, n. 37.

18. Kissinger (1979), 1012.

19. Halberstam (1972), 633.

20. Gelb, "Today's Lessons from the Pentagon Papers," 34.

21. NPMP, Haldeman Notes, Box 43, June 18, 1971.

22. Shapley (1993), 485, 489–90.

23. Halberstam (1965), 338.

24. Ibid., 333–34.

25. Hoopes (1987), 31–32.

26. Schlesinger (1967), 31–32.

27. Leslie H. Gelb, "Vietnam: Nobody Wrote the Last Act," *WP*, June 20, 1971, B1.

28. Ibid., B1, B4.

29. Ibid.

30. Ibid.

31. Daniel Ellsberg, "The Quagmire Myth and the Stalemate Machine," *Public Policy* (Spring 1971): 218.

32. Max Frankel, *NYT*, July 6, 1971, Murrey Marder, *WP*, July 4, 1971, Charles Bailey, *Congressional Record*, July 20, 1971, S11602, all as quoted by Arthur M. Schlesinger, Jr., "Eyeless in Indochina," *New York Review of Books*, Oct. 21, 1971, 23, nn. 4, 5, 6.

33. Gelb wrote an article, "Vietnam: The System Worked" (*Foreign Policy*, summer 1971), that restated the arguments he set forth in his *Washington Post* article.

34. Schlesinger, "Eyeless in Indochina," 32.

35. Leslie H. Gelb, "On Schlesinger and Ellsberg: A Reply," *New York Review of Books*, Dec. 2, 1971, 31–32.

36. Ibid., 34.

37. Arthur M. Schlesinger, Jr., "The Quagmire Papers (Cont.)," *New York Review of Books*, Dec. 16, 1971, 41.

24. CRIMINAL INVESTIGATIONS AND IMPEACHABLE OFFENSES

1. "Mitchell Will Prosecute Law Violations in Leak," *NYT*, July 2, 1971, 1.

2. Ungar (1989), 283, 279, 287.

3. Rodberg interview; Ungar (1989), 283–84.

4. *Gravel v. United States*, 408 U.S. 606 (1972).

5. Ungar (1989), 291–92.

6. Ibid., 269, 292.

7. Ibid., 288–90.

8. Schrag (1974), 134–36; Ungar (1989), 289–90.
9. Ungar (1989), 8.
10. Ibid., 7–8.
11. Mitchell interview.
12. Price (1977), 366.
13. Colson (1976), 60.
14. Wicker (1991), 640.
15. Haldeman and DiMona (1978), 111.
16. Klein (1980), 350.
17. Safire (1975), 552, 358. Evidence that an important change occurred within the White House during the litigation also comes from journalists and commentators. For example, in *The Mask of State: Watergate Portraits*, Mary McCarthy wrote: "it is worthwhile to examine the circumstances out of which Watergate emerged. The crucial date was probably June 1971. The publication of the Pentagon Papers was a turning point for Nixon. At that moment, maybe at that instant, he went around the bend, from normal politics (however dirty and ruthless) to the politics of irrationality" (1974, 152). In his biography of Nixon, *One of Us: Richard Nixon and the American Dream*, Tom Wicker reached the same conclusion: "Nixon and Kissinger had succeeded in creating around them in the White House a high sense of the 'national security crisis' Kissinger insisted had been caused by publication of the Pentagon Papers. His argument that other nations would mistreat the administration's ability to keep secrets, for example, had convinced Ehrlichman that publication of the papers should be stopped; after the Supreme Court ruling, he was even more concerned about administration credibility in security matters. . . . Colson was persuaded by Kissinger's and Nixon's 'genuine alarm' that 'serious security violations' had occurred, and might occur again" (1991, 644).
18. Nixon (1978), 513.
19. "If the FBI was not going to pursue the case, then we would have to do it ourselves" (Nixon [1978], 513).
20. Haldeman and DiMona (1978), 112.
21. Nixon (1978), 513–14.
22. Nixon (1978), 514; Kutler (1990), 191; Liddy (1980), 145–47.
23. Nixon (1978), 514.
24. Liddy (1980), 146.
25. Nixon (1978), 514.
26. Ehrlichman (1982), 403; Nixon (1978), 514.
27. Liddy (1980), 166–67.
28. Nixon (1978), 512.
29. Liddy (1980), 171–72.
30. Kutler (1990), 111.
31. McCarthy (1974), 152.
32. Haldeman and DiMona (1978), 111.
33. Kutler (1990), 254. As Kutler concluded in his definitive study of Watergate and the Nixon administration: "The Plumbers offered a vital link to Watergate, perhaps even a fatal one" ([1990], 116).
34. Ibid., 189.
35. *Final Report of the Committee on the Judiciary, United States House of Representatives, Impeachment of Richard M. Nixon, President of The United States* (New York: Bantam Books, Inc., 1975).

25. THE SUPREME COURT'S DECISION AND DEMOCRACY

1. *NYT*, July 1, 1971, 46.
2. *WP*, July 1, 1971, A22.
3. "The First Amendment on Trial," *Columbia Journalism Review* 10, no. 3 (Sept./Oct. 1971): 20.
4. Ibid., 18.
5. Bickel (1975), 61, 80.
6. William Glendon, "Fifteen Days in June That Shook the First Amendment: A First-Person Account of the Pentagon Papers Case," *New York State Bar Journal* 65, no. 7 (Nov. 1993): 50.
7. Griswold (1992), 311, 312.
8. Mardian interview.
9. *United States v. Marchetti*, 466 F. 2d 1309 (4th Cir.), *cert. denied,* 409 U.S. 1063 (1972).
10. *United States v. Progressive, Inc.*, 467 F. Supp. 990 (W.D. Wis. 1979). See also G. Gunther, *Constitutional Law*, 12th ed. (1991), 1465–67.
11. *Snepp v. United States*, 444 U.S. 507 (1980).
12. 453 U.S. 280 (1981).
13. Obviously, prior restraints may (and do) arise in contexts not involving national security. One situation worth noting occurs when a criminal defendant seeks to halt publication to ensure his fair and impartial trial. The leading case in this area is *Nebraska Press Association v. Stuart*, 427 U.S. 539 (1970), which involved the brutal slaying of six members of a family in a small Nebraska town. The crime immediately attracted intense national news coverage that included incriminating statements by the accused. In granting an injunction the trial court was concerned about the difficulty of empaneling an impartial jury. Nonetheless, the Supreme Court reversed, finding the trial court's concerns too speculative.

United States v. Noriega is a second example of the use of prior restraints to assure a fair trial. In this case the defendant, Panamanian dictator Manuel Noriega, obtained a temporary restraining order blocking CNN from broadcasting tapes of conversations between Noriega and his lawyers (752 F. Supp. 1032 [S.D. Fla.], *aff'd,* 917 F. 2d 1543 [11th Cir.], *cert. denied,* 498 U.S. 976 [1990]). The Court later concluded that these tapes were made by the Metropolitan Correctional Center in Miami, where Noriega was being held, as part of its usual security procedures. 752 F. Supp. 1045, 1047, 1049 n. 3 (S.D. Fla. 1990).

Noriega successfully argued that the revelation of privileged communications with his defense team and its attendant adverse publicity could have seriously undermined his right to a fair trial. Since CNN was unwilling to disclose the contents of the tapes to Judge William H. Hoeveler or the magistrate he assigned, the TRO was granted as a prophylaxis against any potential harm (752 F. Supp. at 1036, *aff'd,* 917 F. 2d at 1551, *cert. denied,* 498 U.S. at 976). When CNN finally produced the tapes, Judge Hoeveler determined that their contents prejudiced neither Noriega's right to an impartial jury nor his right to effective assistance of counsel, and consequently, he lifted the stay (752 F. Supp. at 1054). However, while the stay was in place, CNN did broadcast the tapes as part of its news coverage, for which it was convicted of criminal contempt (United States v. CNN, 865 F. Supp. 1549 [S.D. Fla. 1994]).

14. *United States v. New York Times Company et al.*, 328 F. Supp. 324, 331 (1971) (S.D.N.Y.).

Selected Bibliography

Ambrose, Stephen E. 1983. *Eisenhower.* Vol. 1: *Soldier, General of the Army, President-Elect, 1890–1952.* New York: Simon and Schuster.

———. 1984. *Eisenhower.* Vol. 2: *The President.* New York: Simon and Schuster.

———. 1987. *Nixon.* Vol. 1: *The Education of a Politician, 1913–1962.* New York: Simon and Schuster.

———. 1989. *Nixon.* Vol. 2: *The Triumph of a Politician, 1962–1972.* New York: Simon and Schuster.

———. 1991. *Nixon.* Vol. 3: *Ruin and Recovery, 1973–1990.* New York: Simon and Schuster.

Ball, George W. 1982. *The Past Has Another Pattern: Memoirs.* New York: W. W. Norton.

Bamford, James. 1983. *The Puzzle Palace: A Report on America's Most Secret Intelligence Organization.* New York: Penguin.

Barendt, Eric. 1987. *Freedom of Speech.* New York: Oxford University Press.

Barnett, Stephen R. 1977. "The Puzzle of Prior Restraint." *Stanford Law Review* 29:539–60.

Bennett, Sherrie L. 1980. "The Broadening of the Pentagon Papers Standard: An Impermissible Misapplication of the National Security Exception to the Prior Restraint Doctrine." *Puget Sound Law Review* 4:123–42.

Berns, Walter. 1976. *The First Amendment and the Future of American Democracy.* New York: Basic.

Bickel, Alexander M. 1970. *The Supreme Court and the Idea of Progress.* New York: Harper and Row.

———. 1986. *The Least Dangerous Branch: The Supreme Court at the Bar of Politics.* New Haven: Yale University Press.

———. 1975. *The Morality of Consent.* New Haven: Yale University Press.

Black, Hugo L. 1968. *A Constitutional Faith.* New York: Alfred A. Knopf.

Black, Hugo L., Jr., and Elizabeth Black. 1986. *Mr. Justice and Mrs. Black: The Memoirs of Hugo L. Black and Elizabeth Black.* New York: Random House.

Blasi, Vincent. 1981. "Toward a Theory of Prior Restraint: The Central Linkage." *Minnesota Law Review* 66:11–93.

Blasi, Vincent, ed. 1983. *The Burger Court: The Counter Revolution That Wasn't.* New Haven: Yale University Press.

Bok, Sissela. 1978. *Lying: Moral Choice in Public and Private Life.* New York: Pantheon.

———. 1982. *Secrets: On the Ethics of Concealment and Revelation.* New York: Pantheon.

Bollinger, Lee C. 1986. *The Tolerant Society: Freedom of Speech and Extremist Speech in America.* New York: Oxford University Press.

———. 1991. *Images of a Free Press.* Chicago: University of Chicago Press.

Bradlee, Ben. 1995. *A Good Life: Newspapering and Other Adventures.* New York: Simon and Schuster.

Brodie, Fawn M. 1981. *Richard Nixon: The Shaping of His Character.* New York: W. W. Norton.

Brogan, Hugh. 1986. *The Pelican History of the United States of America.* New York: Penguin.

Bush, Douglas, ed. 1957. *The Portable Milton.* New York: Viking Press.

Chaffe, Zechariah, Jr. 1964. *Free Speech in the United States.* Cambridge: Harvard University Press.

Charlton, Michael, and Anthony Moncrieff. 1989. *Many Reasons Why: The American Involvement in Vietnam.* New York: Hill and Wang.

Clifford, Clark, and Richard Holbrooke. 1991. *Counsel to the President: A Memoir.* New York: Random House.

Cmiel, Kenneth. 1990. *Democratic Eloquence: The Fight over Popular Speech in Nineteenth-Century America.* Berkeley and Los Angeles: University of California Press.

Cohen, Warren I. 1980. *Dean Rusk.* Totowa, N.J.: Cooper Square Publishers.

Colson, Charles. 1976. *Born Again.* Old Tappen, N.J.: Chosen Books.

Cox, Archibald. 1980. *Freedom of Expression.* Cambridge: Harvard University Press.

Danelski, David J., and Joseph S. Tulchin, eds. 1973. *The Autobiographical Notes of Charles Evans Hughes.* Cambridge: Harvard University Press.

Dean, John W., III. 1976. *Blind Ambition: The White House Years.* New York: Simon and Schuster.

———. 1982. *Lost Honor: The Rest of the Story.* Los Angeles: Stratford Press.

De Tocqueville, Alexis. 1960. *Democracy in America.* Vol. 1. New York: Vintage.

Demac, Donna A. 1990. *Liberty Denied: The Current Rise of Censorship in America.* New Brunswick, N.J.: Rutgers University Press.

Donner, Frank J. 1981. *The Age of Surveillance: The Aims and Methods of America's Political Intelligence System.* New York: Vintage.

Draper, Theodore. 1984. *Present History: On Nuclear War, Detente, and Other Controversies.* New York: Vintage.

Dunne, Gerald T. 1977. *Hugo Black and the Judicial Revolution.* New York: Simon and Schuster.

Edgar, Harold, and Benno C. Schmidt, Jr. 1973. "The Espionage Statutes and Publication of Defense Information." *Columbia Law Review* 73:929–1087.

———. 1986. "*Curtiss-Wright* Comes Home: Executive Power and National

Security Secrecy." *Harvard Civil Rights-Civil Liberties Law Review* 21: 349–408.

Ehrlichman, John D. 1982. *Witness to Power: The Nixon Years*. New York: Simon and Schuster.

Ellsberg, Daniel. 1971a. "Murder in Laos—the Reason Why." *New York Review of Books* 16 (March 11):13–17.

———. 1971b. "The Quagmire Myth and the Stalemate Machine." *Public Policy* 19:217–74.

———. 1972. *Papers on the War*. New York: Simon and Schuster.

Emerson, Thomas I. 1955. "The Doctrine of Prior Restraint." *Law and Contemporary Problems* 20:648–71.

———. 1970. *The System of Freedom of Expression*. New York: Random House.

Evans, Rowland, Jr., and Robert D. Novak. 1971. *Nixon in the White House: The Frustration of Power*. New York: Random House.

Fiss, Owen M. 1972. *Free Speech and the Prior Restraint Doctrine: The Pentagon Papers Case in the Supreme Court and Human Rights.*

Freund, Paul A. 1962. *The Supreme Court of the United States: Its Business, Purposes, and Performance*. New York: World Publishing Co.

Gans, Herbert J. 1980. *Deciding What's News: A Study of CBS Evening News, NBC Nightly News, Newsweek, and Time*. New York: Vintage.

Gelb, Leslie H. 1972. "The Pentagon Papers and the Vantage Point," *Foreign Policy* 6 (Spring):25–41.

Gibson, James William. 1986. *The Perfect War: The War We Couldn't Lose and How We Did*. New York: Vintage.

Goodale, James C., comp. 1971. *The New York Times Company versus United States: A Documentary History*. 2 vols. New York: Arno Press.

Goodwin, Richard N. 1988. *Remembering America: A Voice from the Sixties*. Boston: Little, Brown and Company.

Graber, Mark A. 1991. *Transforming Free Speech: The Ambiguous Legacy of Civil Libertarianism*. Berkeley and Los Angeles: University of California Press.

Griswold, Erwin N. 1992. *Ould Fields, New Corne: The Personal Memoirs of a Twentieth-Century Lawyer*. St. Paul: West.

Hainman, Franklyn S. 1981. *Speech and Law in a Free Society*. Chicago: University of Chicago Press.

Halberstam, David. 1972. *The Best and Brightest*. New York: Random House.

———. 1965. *The Making of a Quagmire*. New York: Ballantine.

———. 1979. *The Powers That Be*. New York: Dell.

Haldeman, H. R. 1994. *The Haldeman Diaries: Inside the Nixon White House*. New York: G. P. Putnam's Sons.

Haldeman, H. R., and Joseph DiMona. 1978. *The Ends of Power*. New York: New York Times Book Company.

Halperin, Morton H., and Daniel Hoffman. 1977. *Freedom versus National Security: Secrecy and Surveillance*. New York: Chelsea House.

Hand, Learned. 1959. *The Spirit of Liberty: Paper and Addresses of Learned Hand*. New York: Vintage.

Harris, Richard. 1970. *Justice: The Crisis of Law, Order, and Freedom in America*. New York: E. P. Dutton.

———. 1971. *Decision*. New York: E. P. Dutton.

Henkin, Louis. 1971. "The Right to Know and the Duty to Withhold: The Case of the Pentagon Papers." *University of Pennsylvania Law Review* 120: 271–80.

Hentoff, Nat. 1980. *The First Freedom: The Tumultuous History of Free Speech in America*. New York: Delcorte.

Herring, George C., ed. 1985. *The Secret Diplomacy of the Vietnam War: The Negotiating Volumes of the Pentagon Papers*. Austin: University of Texas Press.

Hersh, Seymour M. 1983. *The Price of Power: Kissinger in the Nixon White House*. New York: Summit.

———. 1986. *America's Longest War: The United States and Vietnam, 1950–1975*. New York: Alfred A. Knopf.

Hertsgaard, Mark. 1988. *On Bended Knee: The Press and the Reagan Presidency*. New York: Schocken.

Hodgson, Godfrey. 1976. *America in Our Time: From World War II to Nixon: What Happened and Why*. New York: Vintage.

Hoffman, Daniel N. 1981. *Governmental Secrecy and the Founding Fathers: A Study in Constitutional Controls*. Westport, Conn.: Greenwood.

Hoopes, Townsend. 1987. *The Limits of Intervention*. New ed. New York: W. W. Norton.

Hung, Nguyen Tien, and Jerrold L. Schecter. 1986. *The Palace File*. New York: Harper and Row.

Isaacs, Arnold R. 1984. *Without Honor: Defeat in Vietnam and Cambodia*. New York: Vintage.

Isaacson, Walter. 1992. *Kissinger: A Biography*. New York: Simon and Schuster.

Isaacson, Walter, and Evan Thomas. 1986. *The Wise Men: Six Friends and the World They Made*. New York: Simon and Schuster.

Jeffries, John Clavin, Jr. 1993. "Rethinking Prior Restraint." *Yale Law Journal* 92: 409–37.

Kalb, Marvin, and Bernard Kalb. 1975. *Kissinger*. New York: Dell.

Kalven, Harry, Jr. 1971. "The Supreme Court 1970 Term." *Harvard Law Review* 85:3–36.

———. 1988. *A Worthy Tradition: Freedom of Speech in America*. New York: Harper and Row.

Karnow, Stanley. 1984. *Vietnam: A History*. New York: Penguin.

Kattenberg, Paul M. 1982. *The Vietnam Trauma in American Foreign Policy, 1945–75*. New Brunswick, N.J.: Transaction.

Kearns, Doris. 1976. *Lyndon Johnson and the American Dream*. New York: Harper and Row.

Kissinger, Henry. 1979. *White House Years*. New York: Little, Brown and Company.

———. 1982. *Years of Upheaval*. New York: Little, Brown and Company.

Klein, Herbert G. 1980. *Making It Perfectly Clear: An Inside Account of Nixon's Love-Hate Relationship with the Media*. New York: Doubleday.

Kleindienst, Richard G. 1985. *Justice: The Memoirs of Attorney General Richard Kleindienst*. Ottawa: Jameson.

Knoll, Erwin. 1981. "National Security: The Ultimate Threat to the First Amendment." *Minnesota Law Review* 66:161–70.

Kolko, Gabriel. 1985. *Anatomy of a War: Vietnam, the United States, and the Modern Historical Experience*. New York: Pantheon.

Kraslow, David, and Stuart H. Loory. 1968. *The Search for Peace in Vietnam*. New York: Random House.

Kurland, Philip B., ed. 1975. *Free Speech and Association: The Supreme Court and the First Amendment*. Chicago: University of Chicago Press.

Kutler, Stanley I. 1990. *The Wars of Watergate: The Last Crisis of Richard Nixon*. New York: Alfred A. Knopf.

Leonard, Thomas C. 1986. *The Powers of the Press: The Birth of American Political Reporting*. New York: Oxford University Press.

Levy, Leonard W. 1985. *Emergence of a Free Press*. New York: Oxford University Press.

Lewis, Anthony. 1991. *Make No Law: The Sullivan Case and the First Amendment*. New York: Random House.

Lewy, Guenter. 1978. *America in Vietnam*. New York: Oxford University Press.

Liddy, G. Gordon. 1980. *Will: The Autobiography of G. Gordon Liddy*. New York: St. Martin's Press.

Litwack, Thomas R. 1977. "The Doctrine of Prior Restraint." *Harvard Civil Rights-Civil Liberties Law Review* 12:519–58.

Lukas, J. Anthony. 1976. *Nightmare: The Underside of the Nixon Years*. New York: Viking Press.

Magruder, Jeb Stewart. 1974. *An American Life: One Man's Road to Watergate*. New York: Atheneum.

Marchetti, Victor, and John D. Marks. 1974. *The CIA and the Cult of Intelligence*. New York: Alfred A. Knopf.

Mayton, William T. 1981. "Toward a Theory of First Amendment Process: Injunctions of Speech, Subsequent Punishment, and the Costs of the Prior Restraint Doctrine." *Cornell Law Review* 67:245–82.

McCarthy, Mary. 1974. *The Mask of State: Watergate Portraits*. New York: Harcourt Brace Jovanovich.

McNamara, Robert S., and Brian VanDeMark. 1995. *In Retrospect: The Tragedy and Lessons of Vietnam*. New York: Times Books.

Meiklejohn, Alexander. 1948. *Free Speech and Its Relation to Self-Government*. Port Washington, N.Y.: Kennikat Press.

Menges, Constantine C. 1989. *Inside the National Security Council: The True Story of the Making and Unmaking of Reagan's Foreign Policy*. New York: Simon and Schuster.

Miller, John C. 1952. *Crisis in Freedom: The Alien and Sedition Acts*. Boston: Little, Brown and Company.

Mollenhoff, Clark R. 1976. *Game Plan for Disaster: An Ombudsman's Report on the Nixon Years*. New York: W. W. Norton.

Morris, Charles R. 1986. *A Time of Passion: America 1960–1980*. New York: Penguin.

Morris, Roger. 1990. *Richard Milhouse Nixon: The Rise of an American Politician*. New York: Henry Holt.

Murphy, Bruce Allen. 1988. *Fortas: The Rise and Ruin of a Supreme Court Justice*. New York: William Morrow.

Murphy, Paul L. 1981. "Near v. Minnesota in the Context of Historical Developments." *Minnesota Law Review* 66:95–160.

Murphy, William P. 1976. "Prior Restraint Doctrine in the Supreme Court: A Reevaluation." *Notre Dame Law Review* 51:898–918.

The New York Times Edition of the Pentagon Papers. 1971. New York: Bantam.

Nimmer, Melville B. 1974. "National Security Secrets versus Free Speech: The Issues Left Undecided in the Ellsberg Case." *Stanford Law Review* 26:311–33.

Nixon, Richard M. 1978. *The Memoirs of Richard Nixon*. New York: Grosset and Dunlap.

———. 1980. *The Real War*. New York: Warner.

———. 1990. *Six Crises*. New York: Simon and Schuster.

Oakes, James L. 1982. "The Doctrine of Prior Restraint since the Pentagon Papers." *Journal of Law Reform* 15:497–519.

Oudes, Bruce, ed. 1989. *From the President: Richard Nixon's Secret Files*. New York: Harper and Row.

Parmet, Herbert S. 1990. *Richard Nixon and His America*. Boston: Little, Brown and Company.

The Pentagon Papers: The Defense Department History of United States Decision-making on Vietnam. 1971. 5 vols. The Senator Gravel Edition. Boston: Beacon Press.

Podhoretz, Norman. 1983. *Why We Were in Vietnam*. New York: Simon and Schuster.

Powe, Lucas A., Jr. 1988. *American Broadcasting and the First Amendment*. Berkeley and Los Angeles: University of California Press.

Powers, Richard Gid. 1987. *Secrecy and Power: The Life of J. Edgar Hoover*. New York: Free Press.

Powledge, Fred. 1971. *The Engineering of Restraint: The Nixon Administration and the Press: A Report of the American Civil Liberties Union*. Washington, D.C.: Public Affairs Press.

Prados, John. 1986. *Presidents' Secret War: CIA and Pentagon Covert Operations since World War II*. New York: William Morrow.

Price, Raymond K., Jr. 1977. *With Nixon*. New York: Viking Press.

Ranelagh, John. 1987. *The Agency: The Rise and Decline of the CIA*. New York: Simon and Schuster.

Rather, Dan, and Gary Paul Gates. 1974. *The Palace Guards*. New York: Harper and Row.

Redish, Martin H. 1984. "The Proper Role of Prior Restraint Doctrine in First Amendment Theory." *Virginia Law Review* 70:53–100.

Richards, David A. J. 1987. "A Theory of Free Speech." *UCLA Law Review* 34: 1837–1903.

Rubin, Richard Alan. 1972. "Foreign Policy, Secrecy, and the First Amendment: The Pentagon Papers in Retrospect." *Howard Law Review* 17:579–612.

Rudenstine, David. 1991. "The Pentagon Papers Case: Recovering Its Meaning Twenty Years Later." *Cardozo Law Review* 12:1869–1913.

Rusk, Dean, and Richard Rusk. 1990. *As I Saw It*. New York: W. W. Norton.

Safire, William. 1975. *Before the Fall: An Inside View of the Pre-Watergate White House*. New York: Da Capo Press.

Salisbury, Harrison E. 1980. *Without Fear or Favor: The New York Times and Its Times*. New York: New York Times Book Co.

Schauer, Frederick. 1978. "Fear, Risk, and the First Amendment: Unraveling the 'Chilling Effect.'" *Boston University Law Review* 58:685–732.

———. 1982. *Free Speech: A Philosophical Enquiry*. New York: Cambridge University Press.

Schell, Jonathon. 1989. *Observing the Nixon Years: "Notes and Comment" from the New Yorker on the Vietnam War and Watergate Crisis, 1969–1975*. New York: Pantheon.

———. 1976. *The Time of Illusion: An Historical and Reflective Account of the Nixon Era*. New York: Vintage.

Schlesinger, Arthur M., Jr. 1965. *A Thousand Days: John F. Kennedy in the White House*. Boston: Houghton Mifflin.

———. 1967. *The Bitter Heritage: Vietnam and American Democracy, 1941–1966*. Boston: Houghton Mifflin.

———. 1978. *Robert Kennedy and His Times*. Boston: Houghton Mifflin.

———. 1978. *The Imperial Presidency*. Boston: Houghton Mufflin.

Schoenbaum, Thomas J. 1988. *Waging War and Peace: Dean Rusk in the Truman, Kennedy, and Johnson Years*. New York: Simon and Schuster.

Schrag, Peter. 1974. *Test of Loyalty: Daniel Ellsberg and the Rituals of Secret Government*. New York: Simon and Schuster.

Seymour, Whitney North, Jr. 1975. *United States Attorney: An Inside View of "Justice" in America under the Nixon Administration*. New York: William Morrow.

Shapiro, Martin, ed. 1972. *The Pentagon Papers and the Courts: A Study in Foreign Policy-Making and Freedom of the Press*. San Francisco: Chandler Publishing Company.

Shapley, Deborah. 1993. *Promise and Power: The Life and Times of Robert McNamara*. Boston: Little, Brown and Company.

Shawcross, William. 1979. *Sideshow: Kissinger, Nixon, and the Destruction of Cambodia*. New York: Simon and Schuster. 1979

Sheehan, Neil. 1970. "Conversations with Americans." *New York Times Book Review* 5, Dec. 27.

———. 1971. "Should We Have War Crime Trials?" *New York Times Book Review* 1, March 28.

———. 1988. *A Bright Shining Lie: John Paul Vann and America in Vietnam*. New York: Random House.

Shiffrin, Steven H. 1990. *The First Amendment, Democracy, and Romance*. Cambridge: Harvard University Press.

Sims, John Cary. 1993. "Triangulating the Boundaries of the Pentagon Papers." *William and Mary Bill of Rights Journal* 2 (Winter):341–53.

Small, Melvin. 1975. *Johnson, Nixon, and the Doves*. New Brunswick, N.J.: Rutgers University Press.

Snepp, Frank. 1978. *Decent Interval: An Insider's Account of Saigon's Indecent End Told by the CIA's Chief Strategy Analyst in Vietnam*. New York: Vintage.

Spear, Joseph C. 1986. *Presidents and the Press: The Nixon Legacy*. Cambridge: MIT Press.

Stephens, Mitchell. 1989. *A History of News*. New York: Penguin.

Sunstein, Cass R. 1993. *Democracy and the Problem of Free Speech*. New York: Free Press.

Talese, Gay. 1981. *The Kingdom and the Power*. New York: Dell.

Thomas, Evan. 1991. *The Man to See: Edward Bennett Williams: Ultimate Insider; Legendary Trial Lawyer*. New York: Simon and Schuster.

Trewhitt, Henry L. 1971. *McNamara*. New York: Harper and Row.

Turner, Stansfield. 1985. *Secrecy and Democracy: The CIA in Transition*. New York: Harper and Row.

Ungar, Sanford J. 1976. *FBI: An Uncensored Look behind the Walls*. Boston: Little, Brown and Company.

———. 1989. *The Papers and the Papers: An Account of the Legal and Political Battle over the Pentagon Papers*. New York: Columbia University Press.

U.S. Congress. House. 1975. *The Final Report of the Committee on the Judiciary: Impeachment of Richard M. Nixon, President of the United States*. New York: Bantam.

U.S. Department of Defense. 1980. *U.S.–Vietnam Relations, 1945–1967: History of U.S. Decision Making Process on Vietnam Policy*. Washington, D.C.: U.S. Government Printing Office.

Washburn, Patrick S. 1986. *A Question of Sedition: The Federal Government's Investigation of the Black Press during World War II*. New York: Oxford University Press.

Wells, Tom. 1994. *The War Within: America's Battle over Vietnam*. Berkeley and Los Angeles: University of California Press.

White, Edward G. 1982. *A Public Life: Earl Warren*. New York: Oxford University Press.

White, Theodore H. 1969. *The Making of the President 1968*. New York: Atheneum Publishers.

———. 1973. *The Making of the President 1972: A Narrative History of American Politics in Action*. New York: Atheneum Publishers.

———. 1975. *Breach of Faith: The Fall of Richard Nixon*. New York: Atheneum Publishers.

Wicker, Tom. 1978. *On Press*. New York: Viking Press.

———. 1991. *One of Us: Richard Nixon and the American Dream*. New York: Random House.

Wills, Garry. 1970. *Nixon Agonistes: The Crisis of a Self-Made Man*. Boston: Houghton Mifflin Company.

Wise, David. 1973. *The Politics of Lying: Government Deception, Secrecy, and Power*. New York: Random House. 1973

———. 1978. *The American Police State: The Government against the People*. New York: Vintage.

Woodward, Bob, and Scott Armstrong. 1979. *The Brethren: Inside the Supreme Court*. New York: Simon and Schuster.

Woodward, Bob, and Carl Bernstein. 1976. *The Final Days*. New York: Simon and Schuster.

———. 1974. *All the President's Men*. New York: Simon and Schuster.

Zinn, Howard. 1967. *Vietnam: The Logic of Withdrawal*. Boston: Beacon Press.

Interviews

Interviews were in person unless otherwise indicated (*), in which case they were by telephone. All interviews except those done by telephone are recorded on audio tape and are in possession of the author.

Abrams, Floyd. May 4, 1991.
Barkan, Mel P. July 13, 1987; Mar. 7, 1989.
Bradlee, Benjamin. May 22, 1991.
Brennan, William J., Jr. Mar. 11, 1988.
Brownell, Herbert. Sept. 14, 1988.
Clark, Roger. May 23, 1991.
Clifford, Clark. Jan. 3, 1989.
Davis, Evan. July 9, 1991.
Dorsen, Norman. July 16, 1988.
Ellsberg, Daniel. May 9, 1990; May 10, 1990.
Emerson, Thomas I. June 27, 1988.
Friedheim, Jerry W.* Mar. 6, 1989.
Gelb, Leslie. July 26, 1988.
Goodale, James G. May 3, 1991; Feb. 10, 1992.
Graham, Katharine. May 23, 1991.
Griswold, Erwin N. Jan. 22, 1988; Jan. 4, 1989.
Halperin, Morton H. July 13, 1988; Jan. 4, 1989.
Hess, Michael D. Nov. 23, 1987; Mar. 30, 1989.
Huddleson, Edwin E., Jr.* Jan. 22, 1990.
Katzenbach, Nicholas de B. Apr. 20, 1989.
Kehler, Randy.* Feb. 18, 1990.
Laird, Melvin R.* Mar. 6, 1989.

McNamara, Robert S. Jan. 22, 1988; Jan. 4, 1989.
Mardian, Robert C. June 2, 1988.
Minow, Newton.* Jan. 17, 1990.
Mitchell, John. Apr. 6, 1988.
Rehnquist, William H. Jan. 4, 1989.
Rodberg, Leonard. Feb. 8, 1990.
Rogers, William P.* Aug. 9, 1988.
Rosenthal, A. M. June 11, 1991.
Rusk, Dean.* Nov. 18, 1988; Dec. 18, 1988.
Seymour, Whitney North, Jr. June 14, 1988; Apr. 7, 1989.
Sheehan, Susan.* Mar. 1, 1989.
Stone, Richard. Mar. 9, 1990.
Sulzberger, Arthur Ochs. June 19, 1991.
Ullman, Richard H.* Nov. 7, 1988.
Warnke, Paul C. Jan. 3, 1989.
Wulf, Melvin L. June 30, 1988.

Index

Compositor: G&S Typesetters, Inc.
Text: Sabon
Display: Franklin Gothic
Printer: Haddon Craftsmen
Binder: Haddon Craftsmen

CPSIA information can be obtained
at www.ICGtesting.com
Printed in the USA
LVOW10s2349250218
567861LV00001B/22/P